S/NVQ Level 3

Children's Care, Learning and Development

Penny Tassoni • Kath Bulman • Kate Beith

www.heinemann.co.uk

✓ Free online support
✓ Useful weblinks
✓ 24 hour online ordering

01865 888058

Heinemann

Inspiring generations

Heinemann Educational Publishers
Halley Court, Jordan Hill, Oxford OX2 8EJ
Part of Harcourt Education

Heinemann is the registered trademark of
Harcourt Education Limited

Text © Kate Beith, Penny Tassoni and Kath Bulman 2005

First published 2005

09 08 07

10 9 8 7 6

British Library Cataloguing in Publication Data is available
from the British Library on request.

13 digit ISBN 978 0 435449 17 9

Designed by HL Studios, Long Hanborough

Illustrated and typeset by HL Studios, Long Hanborough

Printed in China through Phoenix Offset

Original illustrations © Harcourt Education Limited, 2004

Cover design by Wooden Ark studio

Cover photo: © Corbis

Picture research by Jane Hance and Toria Townsley

Acknowledgements

Every effort has been made to contact copyright holders of material reproduced in
this book. Any omissions will be rectified in subsequent printings if notice is given to
the publishers.

Contents

Acknowledgements   iv

Introduction   v

Mandatory Units

301	Develop and promote positive relationships	8
302	Develop and maintain a healthy, safe and secure environment for children	44
303	Promote children's development	84
304	Reflect on and develop practice	157
305	Protect and promote children's rights	183

Option Units

306	Plan and organise environments for children and families	227
307	Promote the health and physical development of children	264
308	Promote children's well-being and resilience	300
309	Plan and implement frameworks for early education	328
310	Assess children's progress according to frameworks for early education	370
312	Plan and implement positive environments for babies and children under three years	386
337	Create environments that promote positive behaviour	445

Glossary   472

Index   477

Acknowledgements

Penny Tassoni would like to thank those many professionals who have given freely of their time and expertise. In particular, she would like to thank Kate Beith, Meg Marshall, Wendy Lidgate, Shirley Eden, Wendy Bristow and Louise Burnham. Thanks also go to the many students, tutors and practitioners who have given her helpful and vital feedback. She would like to thank Mary James, Julia Bruce, Beth Howard and others in the Heinemann team who have driven this writing project forward. Finally, she would like to thank the Tassoni Team, who continue to support her in her work!

Kath Bulman would like to give thanks and love, as ever, to Joanne and Andrew and her nieces and nephews for inspiration and case studies. She would like to give grateful thanks and love to Ian for keeping her sane during the creative process!

Kate Beith would like to thank Emma, Tom and Sam for their help and support.

Introduction

Welcome to this handbook for **National Vocational Qualifications (NVQ) Level 3 in Children's Care, Learning and Development**. You are probably already committed to working with children so it is hoped that this book will support you in gaining a qualification in the challenging and demanding career of working with children.

About the National Occupational Standards in Children's Care, Learning and Development

The revised NVQ 3 in Children's Care, Learning and Development is made up of nationally set standards that are accredited by the **QCA** (Qualifications and Curriculum Authority). The standards cover the care and development of children from birth to 16 years. To achieve the qualification at level 3, candidates must complete **nine** units: all **five** mandatory units and **four** optional units (two from option group 1 and two from option group 1 or 2).

Mandatory units are as follows:

Mandatory Units

301	Develop and promote positive relationships
302	Develop and maintain a healthy, safe and secure environment for children
303	Promote children's development
304	Reflect on and develop practice
305	Protect and promote children's rights

Optional Units

There are eight units in optional group 1 and thirty-three units in optional group 2. These units reflect the different specialist roles of early years practitioners, enabling candidates to select units that apply to their own role and setting.

Each NVQ unit is organised in the same way:

- The **Introduction** says what the unit is about and who it is for.
- The unit is divided into **elements**, which make your studying more manageable!
- Within each element there are **performance criteria**. These tell you what you have to do at work to achieve the standard. You will mostly be observed carrying out the performance criteria by your assessor.
- The **What you must know and understand** section at the end of each unit is a summary of the knowledge you must have for the unit. Your assessor will use this section to check that you understand your practice relating to the unit.

About this book

This handbook is a comprehensive summary of the knowledge you need to become competent in your NVQ. It covers all the mandatory units in the qualification and seven of the option units, giving you plenty of choice.

The text in this book is closely linked with the section at the end of each unit entitled **What you must know and understand.** The introduction to each unit in the book is referenced to the numbered points in the standards so you can be sure that every point is covered. This will also help you and your assessor when checking off the knowledge points in your portfolio. You will also find a variety of activities in the text that will test your understanding of this knowledge. It is important that you carry out these activities as a way of supporting your portfolio of evidence.

Although this book covers the development of children from birth to 16 years, many of the practical examples focus on children in early years settings (that is, under the age of eight years). However, the general guidance provided is applicable to all children and young people up to the age of 16 years.

Throughout the book, reference is made to the most well-known curriculum frameworks (usually those used in England and Scotland). However, you will need to check out the curriculum framework used in your own place of work.

Features of this book

Throughout this book there are a number of features that are designed to encourage you to reflect upon your own experience and to help you see how theory is put into practice in early years settings. They will also encourage you to research and seek out the views of other practitioners working with different age groups or in different settings.

Check it out and **Active knowledge** – activities that will help you relate the knowledge you gain from this book to the workplace

Key terms – descriptions of important terms

Observation – activities to help you practise your observation skills

Test yourself – activities and questions that will help you check that you understand the text

Did you know? – interesting facts about children's care, learning and development

Case studies – real scenarios that will enable you to explore key issues and broaden your understanding of working in early years settings

Keys to good practice – practical ways of developing and promoting best practice in caring for children. These relate to the performance criteria and will specifically help you to improve your performance at work

Reflect on your practice – provides you with checklists against which to measure your own performance

Unit tests – questions at the end of each unit which help you to test your knowledge as you read through the book

We hope you enjoy using this book and good luck with your course!

Penny Tassoni

Kate Beith

Kath Bulman

Develop and promote positive relationships

Working with children and their families is both fascinating and rewarding. This is because, to a large extent, working successfully in this sector is about human relationships. Children flourish when they are relaxed and can see that the people around them care about and respect them, and also respect each other and work well together. In some ways, creating the emotional backdrop is as important as any curriculum, play opportunity or theory of development. That requires an understanding of how best to promote positive relationships. This unit explores the importance of relationships in successful work with children and their families, which includes the matter of confidentiality in these relationships.

What you must know and understand:

- The importance of good working relationships in the setting (K3C154)
- Relevant legal requirements covering the way you interact with children, confidentiality and the needs of disabled children (K3C155, K3M156, K3D157, K3M158)
- The meaning of anti-discriminatory practice and how to integrate this into your relationships with children and other adults (K3P159)
- How you adapt your behaviour to children of different ages, needs and abilities (K3C160)
- Strategies you can adopt to help children to feel welcome and valued in the setting (K3D161)
- What is meant by 'appropriate' and 'inappropriate' behaviour when interacting with children, the policies and procedures to follow and why these are important (K3D162)
- The importance of encouraging children to make choices for themselves and of involving them in decision-making (K3D163 and K3D164)
- How to negotiate with children according to their age and stage of development (K3C165)
- Strategies you can use to show children that you respect their individuality (K3D166)

- How to balance the needs of individual children with those of the group as a whole (K3D167)
- The importance of clear communication with children (K3C168)
- Why it is important for children to ask questions, offer ideas and suggestions and how you can help them do this (K3C169)
- Why it is important to listen to children and to respond to them in a way that shows you value what they have to say (K3C170 and K3C171)
- The importance of being sensitive to communication difficulties with children and how to adapt the way you communicate to different situations (K3C172)
- How you can help children to understand the value and importance of positive relationships with others (K3C173)
- The importance of children valuing and respecting other people's individuality (K3D174)
- Why it is important for children to understand and respect other people's feelings (K3D175)
- Why it is important to be consistent and fair in dealing with positive and negative behaviour (K3D176)
- Strategies you can use to encourage and reinforce positive behaviour (K3D177 and K3D178)
- Why it is important for children to be able to deal with conflict themselves and what support they may need from you (K3D179)
- Why it is important to encourage and support positive relationships between children and other adults in the setting (K3C180)
- Why positive relationships with other adults are important (K3C181)
- Why it is important to show respect for other adults' individuality and how to do so (K3P182)
- The importance of clear communication with other adults (K3C183)
- The importance of being sensitive to communication difficulties with other adults and how and when it may be necessary to adapt the way you communicate (K3C184 and K3C185)
- Typical situations that may cause conflict with other adults and how to deal with these effectively (K3C186)

The importance of good working relationships in the setting

Everyone benefits from having good relationships with others; humans are, after all, sociable beings. Good relationships with parents, colleagues and children are enormously important in early years settings as they benefit everyone, especially children. This is because good relationships can create a welcoming and secure atmosphere for children. This in turn helps young children to settle in and relax.

Good relationships also benefit the quality of interaction between the setting and parents. Where relationships are good, parents are more likely to be able to share information, make comments and take an interest in what their children have been doing. This in turn benefits the children, as not only does additional information help the early years worker to meet their needs, but also, emotionally, they may find it easier to move from the care of one person to another.

For staff and volunteers, good relationships in the setting mean that they can enjoy their work. Most practitioners who are in strong teams and have good relationships with colleagues and parents comment that this is a major source of their enjoyment of work. Good relationships in teams also mean that during times of stress, tiredness or difficulties, practitioners can share the burden and support each other.

Legal requirements covering the way you interact with children, confidentiality and the needs of disabled children

Understanding the legislation that affects the way in which you relate to and work with children and their families is a useful starting point, as it underpins best practice when working with children. Here the current legislation is outlined, but it is important to keep up to date in this respect as legislation changes. A good example of this is the Data Protection Act, which now covers information that is handwritten as well as information stored on computers.

United Nations Convention on the Rights of the Child (UNCRC)

Work with children increasingly reflects society's understanding that they have rights, whereas at one time adults working with children could say and do virtually what they wanted. Practitioners now recognise that children are special and are entitled to be treated with respect and dignity. Some aspects of the UK's legislation reflect this thinking.

The UNCRC was drawn up in 1989 and gives children and young people under the age of 18 their own special rights. The UK is a signatory, and the Convention was ratified in 1991. There are 54 articles, but the main ones affecting the way in which early years workers relate to children can be seen in the diagram below (the Convention is also considered further in Unit 305). In essence, the rights accorded to children mean that they must be shown respect and that their best interests are paramount. It is also worth noting that children have a right of expression under the Convention. This is a good reminder for all adults to think about the way in which they listen to and acknowledge children's comments and views.

The UNCRC can be used as a powerful tool for disabled children and their families, as all children are covered by its provisions. This means that disabled children have a right to be treated with dignity as well as the right to education.

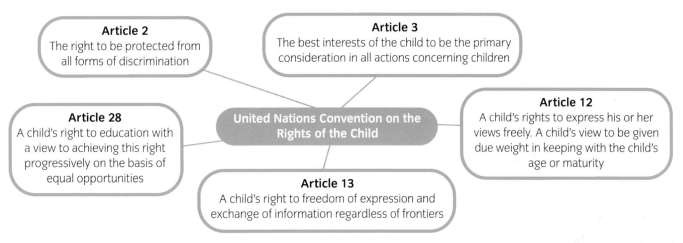

Article 2
The right to be protected from all forms of discrimination

Article 3
The best interests of the child to be the primary consideration in all actions concerning children

Article 28
A child's right to education with a view to achieving this right progressively on the basis of equal opportunities

United Nations Convention on the Rights of the Child

Article 12
A child's rights to express his or her views freely. A child's view to be given due weight in keeping with the child's age or maturity

Article 13
A child's right to freedom of expression and exchange of information regardless of frontiers

● *Some rights affecting relationships with children.*

Human Rights Act 1998

The Human Rights Act strengthens adults' and children's rights. It came into effect in October 1998. It requires courts and tribunals to make judgements based upon the European Convention of Human Rights. The Human Rights Act now means that legislation passed in the UK must reflect its articles. In terms of the way in which we relate to children, it is worth noting that article 8 relates to the right to privacy, article 10 to freedom of expression and article 14 to discrimination.

Legislation and confidentiality

In addition to legislation that governs the way we relate to children and their families, there is also legislation about confidentiality. This essentially gives children and their families the right to privacy.

Data Protection Act 1998

The Data Protection Act is a piece of legislation that is designed to prevent confidential and personal information from being passed on without a person's consent. This Act originally applied only to information that was stored on computers, but it has been updated to include any information that is stored, either on paper or screen. Under the Act, organisations that collect and store information must register with the Data Protection Commission. Anyone processing information must also comply with the eight enforceable principles of practice shown below. In terms of working with children and their families, this means that most information that is collected and held in an early years setting will be confidential. Passing on information to others would be in breach of the Act. This is one reason why consent has to be given by parents before you can contact other professionals such as speech and language therapists.

Check it out

- Is your setting registered with the Data Protection Commission?
- What type of personal information does your setting hold with the permission of parents?

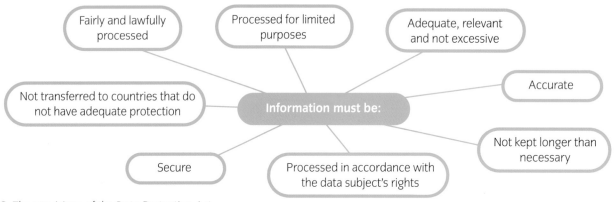

Fairly and lawfully processed

Processed for limited purposes

Adequate, relevant and not excessive

Not transferred to countries that do not have adequate protection

Information must be:

Accurate

Secure

Processed in accordance with the data subject's rights

Not kept longer than necessary

● *The provisions of the Data Protection Act.*

Confidentiality

Confidentiality is essentially about trust and respect. Parents will often give you **confidential information** on the basis that it will be helpful to you when you work with their children. They do so trusting that this information will not be passed on to others, to become the source of gossip or interest. If you breach confidentiality, you will break that trust. When trust between professionals and families breaks down so too does the relationship. This can be catastrophic for the children, who may be removed from the setting or who may detect the rift between their families and the adults who work with them.

Key terms

Confidential information is that which should be shared only with people who have a right to have it, for example your lead practitioner, supervisor or manager.

Maintaining confidentiality

It is a good idea to see *all* information given to you by parents and carers as being confidential, including contact details, medical information and the child's records. Information should be passed on only with parents' consent. This type of information should be accessed only by those people who work directly with the child and only if it is in the child's interest.

When information is of a general nature or you know that it will need to be recorded or passed on, it is a good idea to check with parents that they are happy for this to happen. If, for example, parents let you know that their child has been complaining of a headache, you might simply explain that you will need to let colleagues know. In some situations, such as when a child has a serious medical condition or allergy, it will be important for everyone in the setting to be aware of it. How this information is passed on should still be discussed with parents. A photograph of a child with a nut allergy may, for example, be displayed in the kitchen to help remind staff that that child must not be given nuts, but may be taken down at the end of the afternoon because the kitchen is used by other organisations in the evening.

It is also important to remember to be careful when discussing your work, particularly with children you work with outside the setting. Always think carefully about how easy it would be for anyone to identify a child or family.

Parental consent to the sharing of information

There may be times when particular children need additional support from other professionals. At such times, it is important that parental consent is given. As most parents want the best for their children and are keen for their child to be helped and to have their needs met, this is not usually a problem. The only exception to this might be a child protection issue, where talking to the parent may put the child in significant way of harm. Most professionals are aware of the importance of parental consent and so will understand if a parent's consent has not been given.

Storing information

Under the Data Protection Act, written information about children should be kept securely. (It would, for example, be a breach of confidentiality to update a child's records whilst sitting on a bus.) It may also mean that sensitive information should not leave the office of a setting.

Breaching confidentiality

Effectively, the only time when confidentiality should be breached is when a child's safety is possibly at risk, for example in an emergency or if abuse at home is suspected (in which case the child protection procedures of your setting should be followed – see page 218).

● Filing cabinets that lock and password-protected computer data can be used to keep information about children and their families secure.

✔ Keys to good practice: Confidentiality

✓ Do not gossip about children or their families either inside or outside your workplace.

✓ Never give children's and families' contact details to others without parental consent, unless requested by the police or social services to do so.

✓ Keep written information in a secure place.

✓ If you are unsure about whether you have the authority to pass on information, always check with your supervisor or the parents themselves.

✓ Remember that photographs of children should be taken and displayed only with parental consent.

Case study 1: Contact details are confidential

Erdem's mother wants to invite another mother to a party but cannot find her telephone number. She asks Janice, the nursery assistant, whether she could please just pop into the office and get it for her. Janice can see that this is a genuine request as Erdem's mother does know the other parent's address.

1. *What should the nursery assistant do?*
2. *Explain why it is important that confidentiality is upheld.*
3. *Consider what Janice should say to Erdem's mother.*

The meaning of anti-discriminatory practice

Anti-discriminatory practice is about treating all children and their families fairly. It should underpin your values and shape your work. While it is a legal requirement that no child should be discriminated against, many people would also consider it a moral one too. The term **inclusion** is often used in conjunction with anti-bias practice. An inclusive setting is one where everyone is welcome and where people think about their approach to children and their families to ensure that no one is excluded. This is a wide brief and includes thinking about the way in which you manage children's behaviour, the physical layout of the setting, and also the way in which you communicate with children and their parents. An inclusive setting is keen to encourage parents to become active partners. Staff in inclusive settings think about the barriers that might prevent children and their families from feeling welcome, such as language and culture, and look for ways of overcoming these.

Key terms

Anti-discriminatory practice means taking action to counter discrimination; this will involve identifying and challenging discrimination and being positive in your practice about people's differences.

Inclusion is the process of identifying, understanding and breaking down barriers to participation and belonging.

Embracing anti-discriminatory practice in this way has implications for relationships. Where children and their families are respected and valued, trust can flourish. This is essential if children are to fulfil their potential and also learn how to have **positive relationships** with others.

An inclusive setting is one where everyone is welcome and where people think about their approach to children and their families to ensure that no one is excluded.

Case study 2: Anti-bias practice helps relationships

Meltem has just begun in nursery. Her family are Kurdish refugees. The nursery staff are keen to help Meltem settle in, but quickly realise that there is a language barrier and communication is difficult with Meltem's parents. The nursery staff smile and try hard to make Meltem's parents feel welcome, but know that for a good relationship to develop better communication will be important. The manager contacts the local early years team to ask if there is a refugee support worker or team. After a morning on the telephone, the manager finally tracks down someone who is able to help. When Meltem's parents come into the setting the next day, the manager is there to greet them and is assisted by a translator. The manager has also found out about a local project to help refugees learn English and is able via the translator to pass on the information. She also tells the parents that they are welcome to stay to see the work that the nursery does. A few months later, Meltem's family are settled, but the nursery has benefited too. Meltem's mother has been a keen helper in the group and has done cooking and singing alongside a member of staff.

1. *Why do you think the nursery manager decided to find a translator for Meltem's parents?*
2. *Did the manager's actions help Meltem to settle?*
3. *What were the benefits of getting help with communications?*
4. *What other actions could the nursery manager have taken?*

Key terms

Positive relationships are those that benefit the children and their ability to participate in and benefit from the setting.

Integrating anti-bias practice into relationships

Anti-bias practice can be considered as a way of thinking. In terms of relationships with children and their families, it is about taking an interest in different viewpoints, values and traditions, as well as showing respect.

It also means thinking about how others might feel when they step into the setting, and looking for ways of making early years workers appear approachable. To do this well often means learning to listen and showing empathy with and interest in others. Good practice is to show real interest in children and their families' lives. Greeting children and their families should always be the starting point, and it is important that the greeting is warm and genuine. Body language (see below) is always more powerful than words and is also transparent (a half-hearted smile is easily picked up).

It is also important that you show that you are ready to learn and are interested in what parents want to tell you. This is important because you should be aiming to develop a two-way relationship with them. For example, parents of children who have additional needs are often skilled at being with their children and can share their expertise. Learning from them means that you in turn may also be able to support those children's needs. If the parents feel valued, they may feel that they can turn to you when they are feeling frustrated or tired and in need of help.

Recognising your own values, traditions and beliefs

To be able to take on board others' ideas and thoughts, it is important that you recognise that your own viewpoints are shaped by your culture, upbringing and experiences. The term 'value system' is used to describe the bundle of prejudices that everyone has developed. This does not mean that you are not allowed to have your own thoughts, but you should recognise that they can influence your reactions in negative as well as positive ways. By being aware of your own value system, it is easier to override initial reactions and to understand others' points of view. This is essential, as to listen and to empathise well it is important to be non-judgemental.

Check it out

Look at the following issues and consider the influences on your responses to them:
- How do you feel about abortion?
- Should foetuses be tested for birth defects?
- Should gay men be allowed to adopt children?

Develop relationships with children

The starting point in working effectively with children of all ages is your relationship with them. Children who feel valued and who enjoy being with you will respond better. This means that they are likely to enjoy playing and learning and are far more likely to behave well. The basis of forming a relationship with children is to consider what their needs may be and to adapt the way in which you work to meet these needs.

Adapting your behaviour to work with children of different ages, needs and abilities

While all children need to feel valued, nurtured and acknowledged, the way in which you should go about doing this has to change according to children's needs. Responding to a 14-year-old boy in the same way as you would a three-year-old is obviously not going to work. Not so long ago, some adults working with two children of exactly the same age would have expected them to respond in similar ways, and a child who did not respond as the adult wanted might have been seen as 'shy', 'sullen' or 'difficult'. Today, it is appreciated that it is more appropriate for the adults to change the way in which they work, rather than to condemn the child. This way of approaching children has huge benefits and is inclusive.

Building relationships with babies

While all children will need to establish a sound relationship with early years workers, for babies it is an absolute necessity. Babies need to form an 'attachment' or special bond with an early years worker in order to compensate for the absence of their parents (see attachment theory on page 138). In most day care nurseries or settings that care for babies a 'key worker' system is used. A key worker is responsible for building a constant and responsive relationship with the baby. Constancy is particularly important: while babies are capable of making more than one attachment, they do need to have one particularly strong relationship.

● *A key worker is responsible for building a constant and responsive relationship with the baby.*

Physical contact

One way in you can make a strong relationship with a baby is through physical contact. Simply holding and cuddling a baby can help the child to feel wanted and reassured. While babies do need some time on the floor and to play, it is important that they do not have prolonged periods when they are not handled.

Did you know?

Babies are interested in each other from an early age, but do not have the skills to play actively together. Babies need adults to play with them. Songs, rhymes and repeated actions such as peek-a-boo for older babies are ways in which babies learn about play. While playing with the same adult, babies are also forming a strong relationship.

Body language and responsiveness

Babies quickly tune in to the human face. They recognise the adults they enjoy being with and with whom they have a special relationship. Babies need eye contact and to be responded to quickly. A baby who is crying may need to be picked up and rocked, while a baby who tries to attract your attention with babbling and smiling needs the adult to respond positively.

Using everyday routines

Relationships do not just happen. Babies learn about the people they enjoy being with through everyday events such as nappy changing, feeding and playing. It is therefore good practice for the same person to change the baby's nappy each day and to take on other physical care tasks. During care routines, the baby needs eye contact, cuddles and plenty of response. These are important times for babies and actually have more effect on them than more structured activities such as hand printing.

● *Songs, rhymes and repeated actions such as peek-a-boo for older babies are ways in which babies learn about play.*

Case study 3: Babies need to form an attachment

Leman is a childminder and looks after three children during the week. The youngest, Damien, is four months old. He comes for three mornings a week. Leman has arranged with Damien's mother for him to come on the mornings when she does not have any other children arriving early. This means that she can focus her attention on him.

1. *Why do you think the childminder wants to spend time with Damien on his own?*
2. *What might be the advantages to Damien?*
3. *What kind of activities might be suitable for Leman and Damien to do together?*

Building relationships with children aged one to three years

Like babies, children under the age of three years need to have a strong attachment to one person in the setting. Distress at leaving parents continues until most children are nearly three years old and can be avoided only when the child has a settled relationship with an alternative adult. For a child who starts in a new setting during this period, it is essential that a key worker system is used. To avoid the child becoming distressed, it is good practice that a good relationship is established before the child is left by the parents. This can be achieved by encouraging parents to come into the setting several times before children are left so that children can get to know the person who will be looking after them.

These visits can be quite brief, but the aim is to familiarise the child with both the setting and key worker. It is helpful if parents understand that, during these visits, they need to step back a little so that their child has a chance to play with the key worker and for them to get to know each other. During these visits the key worker needs to find out what the child enjoys doing and to build up a relationship with the child by playing and talking. Once the child has become used to being with the key worker, parents can then start to leave the child and to build up the time away from the child.

Physical contact

This remains important for the young child. Toddlers, for example, clearly signal when they wish to be picked up by raising their arms. Two-year-olds may want to sit on your lap. Physical contact is important to young children and you need to ensure that when children want to have some physical reassurance, they get it. It could even be argued that depriving young children of physical contact when they seek it is tantamount to emotional neglect.

Interestingly, these years are also a time when children can alternate between clinginess and independence. It is not uncommon for a 20-month-old child to want one moment to be carried and the next to be put down on the floor. Respecting such wishes is very important. This is one way in which children instinctively learn that they have rights over their bodies.

Did you know?

Like babies, young children are particularly aware of faces and body language. Words are starting to be understood, but visual information is processed more easily. The way you smile and make eye contact will help children to feel comfortable with you.

Responsiveness

Children of this age also need you to be responsive to them. They may tap you on the back or point out things. It is important that you are able to respond to them, as otherwise they soon learn not to bother trying to make contact.

This is also an age when you need to observe children closely and think about their needs. You may, for example, notice that a two-year-old is heading off towards a sit-and-ride toy on which there is already another child. At this age, most children are not able to understand the need to share; in this example you would have to act quickly and offer an alternative toy.

● Children aged one to three years need the adults caring for them to be responsive.

Play

Most children learn to play cooperatively from around three years of age. Some children are able to play earlier, but all children benefit from playing alongside an interested adult. Enjoying being with an adult is a key part of forming a relationship. It is important when playing with children in this age group to respond to their play ideas rather than to impose your own. It is also worth remembering that they often like some repetition and so you will probably find yourself rolling a ball over to an 18-month-old not just once but six or seven times.

Building relationships with children aged 3 to 6 years

From around three years onwards, children often become more confident about being with people they do not know so well. This can vary according to individual children's experiences, but on the whole children find it easier to separate for brief periods from their parents. Children in this age range are also becoming more aware of other children and gain pleasure from playing with them.

Reassurance and approval

While younger children will often seek physical contact with you, in this age range they will gradually instead look for verbal reassurance and approval. This is linked to their language development. Children who come into the setting and do not speak the language or who have some language delay may still need opportunities for physical reassurance. Reassurance and approval are important as children are beginning to develop an awareness of themselves, and it is important that their self-concept is a positive one. You may give reassurance and approval by smiling, praising a child or simply being alongside children as they try out something new. Interestingly, if you observe children of around three years of age, you may notice that even when they are engaged in play with other children, they look around at odd times just to see where the adults are. They may also be keen to show you what they have been doing or enjoy some friendly interest.

Listening to children

While babies and very young children need you to acknowledge them and physically reassure them, by three years of age they will need you to listen to them. With their growing language skills, children begin to enjoy chatting and expressing their ideas. They may also ask questions and will want a proper response. Children are quick to sense which adults will spend the time listening properly to them.

Being a play and language partner

From around the age of three years, children do enjoy playing with other children. But they also enjoy doing things with adults, especially when they feel that they are part of what is going around. A four-year-old may, for example, enjoy helping to put up a display while a six-year-old will enjoy learning a game of cards with an adult. It can be helpful to work with children as 'partners'. You may, for example, chat to children and respond to their interests and so be a language partner. At other times, you might be a play partner – for example, if they want you to organise a game or take part in their play. Taking time to be with children in this way can strengthen relationships.

● *From around the age of three years, children enjoy doing things with adults, especially when they feel that they are part of what is going on around them.*

Building relationships with children aged 7–11 years

In this next phase of childhood, children need adults to talk, but particularly to listen to them and explore their ideas, feelings and thoughts. Unlike younger children, who will often spontaneously talk to an early years worker, older children may not always make comments and talk at the time, but after reflection may need to talk things through. When you work with older children, it is important therefore to find time to listen to them when they need you. Reassurance and approval remain important for children aged 7–11 years, and it is important that, at times, this is given unconditionally, as children who learn that they are valued only if they are achieving or pleasing an adult can lose confidence.

During these years, it is important that children learn that they can develop their own views and opinions and that you are interested in hearing them.

Building relationships with children aged 11 years and over

Young people still need good relationships with adults. In some ways these relationships are as important as ever. Young people are likely to be undergoing significant changes in their lives as well as physically. They need to be able to turn to adults for advice, reassurance and to be understood. Young people are quick to identify adults who will listen to them and empathise. It is important for adults not to dismiss young people's problems out of hand, however trivial they may seem. When young people feel that they are not being listened to, they often stop communicating at all. This is worrying, as many young people 'warm up' by talking generally before deciding whether or not to talk to an adult about some deeper issues that are affecting them.

You can build good relationships with young people by respecting their views, which may be different to yours, and also by giving them plenty of time and also responsibility.

Check it out

Talk to three children between the ages of 4 and 15 years about adults who they like to be with, besides family members. Ask them why they like being with these people.

Strategies to help children to feel welcome and valued in the setting

Some children will spend a large amount of time with you. This means that you need to create environments and work in ways that make them feel welcome, comfortable and valued.

Greeting

Greetings are socially important. They are a recognition of someone's arrival and so it is essential that you find ways of greeting children in a special way. For young children, you might have a routine so that the greeting also helps them to feel reassured. It may be that children come into the setting and know that you always have a little surprise for them in your hands. This might be a small toy that they can play with or a book that you will read with them.

Helping children to have their own spaces

One way in which you can help children to feel that they belong is by creating spaces that they can have ownership of. At a childminder's, for example, a child might know that there is a

● *How do you welcome children into the setting?*

small fabric bag containing a few toys that are put aside particularly for that child. In a school setting, children might have a named tray or peg to hang their things on. While these are small spaces, they can help children to feel that they belong in some way. You may encourage older children to be responsible for the activities that they do or for the way the environment looks. In an after-school club, for example, some children might paint a mural or be involved in choosing furniture or some aspects of the décor.

Active knowledge

There are many ways in which we can help children to feel wanted and valued. This is an activity that works very well with children when they are new to a setting. The idea is taken from a Danish educator. A child-sized suitcase is filled with objects that show the life and interests of the adult. The adult lets the child open the suitcase and the adult talks about the things the child has taken out and explains why they are important (e.g. a pine cone from the adult's favourite park or a photo of the adult's pet). With the parents' consent, the child is given a small suitcase in which to place a few important objects. This activity helps children to talk about themselves and also helps the adult to learn about things that are important to the child.

Appropriate and inappropriate behaviour when interacting with children

While it is important to establish good relationships with children, it is also important to be aware that these relationships should be friendly but not unprofessional. You are not a member of a child's family and you are not taking the place of the child's parents. Similarly, while you need to find ways of communicating at the child's level, you must not be childish. Interacting with children inappropriately can also be a child protection issue. Your setting should have a code of conduct to help you ensure that interactions remain appropriate.

Physical contact and children

Very young children need physical contact (see above), but for older children the way in which you offer physical contact needs to change. While it is acceptable and even desirable to put a toddler on your lap to share a story, it is not likely to be appropriate to do so with a ten-year-old unless there are exceptional circumstances.

Sharing personal information with children

Children are often interested in what you do and your life outside the setting. Here it is important to strike a balance between friendliness and

Key terms

Appropriate behaviour demonstrates that the child is respected and valued; it is behaviour that is not abusive or derogatory to the child, physically, emotionally or sexually.

inappropriateness. It is not usually **appropriate behaviour** to share in any detail your personal problems (tempting as it might be, especially if you work with older children). This goes back to being a professional: you should be there to work with the children and to care for them, not the other way round.

It is inappropriate to give a child your telephone number or contact details unless parents are involved.

Check it out

Does your workplace have a code of conduct about the way in which adults relate to and interact with children?

Encouraging children to make choices

It can be hard for adults to remember what it is like not have any control in their lives. For some children, having adults always make the day-to-day decisions that affect them can be a major source of frustration. Although adults have a duty of care and a responsibility for children's safety and well-being, it is important that children are given some opportunities to make choices and gain a little control as early as possible. There are several ways of doing this (see also page 26).

Play is a major area in which children can be given some control. Interestingly, many adults, when asked about what play meant to them when they were children, will mention 'freedom'. This is because when children are given opportunities to play in the way they choose, they can take control. You should always look at the structure and routine of your workplace and ensure that there are also plenty of opportunities for children to be free in their play, as well as some directed activities.

As well as in play, you can also encourage children to make choices in everyday activities. Three-year-olds could be given the choice of where they sit at lunchtime, and eight-year-olds might be asked to sort out the equipment they want to play with during the afternoon. Encouraging children to make choices can cut down on behaviours such as tantrums and aggression, and it also helps children to learn to feel confident and take on responsibility.

Check it out

Write a list of the ways in which your setting gives children opportunities to make choices.

Involving children in decision-making

As early on as possible, you should try to involve children in decision-making. This helps build their self-esteem and contributes to their emotional well-being. It is also a way of building stronger relationships with them. Ideally, children need adults who work with them to be authoritative but not controlling and authoritarian. Constantly telling children what they can and cannot do without explanation or negotiation (see below) is likely

● *Free play with a variety of toys, allowing children to choose.*

to cause a range of difficulties. With older children you might find that it causes confrontation or results in them looking for ways of rebelling. An authoritarian style may make some younger children nervous.

Encouraging children in decision-making does not mean giving them overall control. It simply means that you look for ways of involving them. This can begin very early on, with mobile babies being given choices of toys and materials as well as the freedom to explore them. With toddlers, decision-making can be about asking which way they might like to walk around a park, or whether they would like to feed the ducks first or go to the swings. Involving children in decision-making becomes increasingly important with older children. They should be given opportunities for input regarding what they would like to do as well as ways in which they might keep themselves safe, for example.

Negotiating with children

Negotiation is a life skill. Children learn it by being given the opportunity to practise it. If you encourage them to make choices and become involved in decision-making, it is also important that you use a negotiating style with them. This is not about being weak, but about children learning that you do want to listen to their viewpoints and, where possible, accommodate them.

Negotiation grows out of helping the youngest children to be involved in making choices and learning that their voices and thoughts are important. For most children, negotiation is linked to their level of cognitive and language skills. A two-year-old may want a particular toy, and no end of explaining will help him or her realise that it is not available; with an older child this should be less of a problem.

How about five hours without waking up, in return for two lullabies?

Negotiating becomes increasingly important with older children. Limits on behaviour, activities and equipment are best negotiated, as this helps children to take responsibility and also prevents them from feeling excluded and powerless. When encouraging children to become involved in negotiating and decision-making,

● *Children learn negotiation through practising it.*

it is important that they know what the boundaries or constraints are. It is unfair to give them the impression that they might be able to do or change something if in fact this is not possible.

Case study 4: The limits to choice

The after-school club wants the children to organise their own end-of-year party. The children are very excited and immediately begin to think of things they can do. Later on the children talk about their plans, but it soon becomes apparent that their ideas are a little too ambitious for the layout and also the funds of the club. The adults have to tell the children this. Five of the teenagers become very angry and say that it has all been a waste of time. They tell everyone that they do not want a party now.

1. *Why was this an ideal opportunity for children to be involved?*
2. *Explain the reasons for the behaviour of the older children.*
3. *Explain how this situation could have been avoided.*

Respecting children's individuality

Recognising children's **individuality** is the basis of anti-bias practice. Children have different strengths, talents and interests. They also respond in different ways. It is important that you value this individuality in children. This is easier to do in settings that have an ethos that encourages children to talk, make choices and be involved in decision-making. With young children you might acknowledge that they have particular interests and build upon these by, for example, saying 'I know that yesterday you enjoyed playing with the bucket outside and so today I have brought a scoop for you to try out'. You might encourage older children to talk about what they enjoy doing and also what they find difficult. Talking is a powerful tool with older children, especially when adults are able to avoid imposing their own thoughts and ideas. For older children, who are likely to be exploring their identity through clothes, hairstyles and even attitudes, it is especially important that they can talk freely.

Key terms

Individuality means someone being different from others, for example because of their appearance, attitudes or behaviour.

Keys to good practice: Respecting individuality

✓ Provide activities that encourage self-expression (e.g. painting, drawing, modelling, drama and dance).

✓ Provide open-ended activities that children can put their own 'stamp' on (e.g. cooking, making models).

✓ Avoid comments that single children out as being different, such as 'The rest of the children don't mind doing it'.

✓ Acknowledge children's particular strengths and talents.

✓ Show interest in things that the children enjoy doing.

Balancing individual needs with group needs

Where settings are well resourced and have good staff ratios, it is easier to balance individual needs with group needs. It is also easier where a climate of responsibility, choice and freedom has been created. Where routines are rigid and children are not used to taking responsibility or having choice, it can be very hard. This is why it is important to adopt a style of working with children that is not restrictive and that looks for ways of promoting individual children's needs and interests.

There will of course be times when individual children's wishes and needs cannot be met because of what is required for the rest of the group. When this occurs, it is important to explain the reasons to children. It is also important that the reasons are genuine, such as safety or respect for others. Thus, for example, children may have to sit down and wear a seatbelt on a coach for safety reasons or they may have to be quiet in a cinema to avoid spoiling other people's enjoyment.

With older children it is often useful to talk through beforehand the way in which their own freedom and needs might have to come second; for example, when organising an outing, young people might be asked to talk through how the outing can be arranged so that it works for everyone.

Case study 5: Routines can compromise individual needs

Staff at Busy Bees pre-school have noticed that a few children become quite difficult when it is time for them to go outdoors to play. One or two children take a long time putting on their coats or do not come over when they are called. At the end of the outdoor playtime, they find that there are also four or five children who are slow and run away rather than line up. This has led them to think about implementing changes. They are wondering whether it would be better to have a more flexible approach to going outside and allowing children to go in and out when they are ready. They are also wondering about whether it might be an idea for children sometimes to choose the activities and toys that are put out.

1. *Explain why some children are not cooperating with the adults.*
2. *What will be the benefits of taking a more flexible approach to outdoor playtime?*
3. *Why is it important that settings reflect on their practice?*

Communicating with children

Helping children to feel part of the setting, giving them opportunities to make choices and negotiating with them require good communication skills. It is important that you can talk, listen and also use body language and facial expression in a way that is clear.

Communicating clearly with children

It is important that you are able to communicate clearly with children of all ages. Being clear when communicating with children helps them to understand what is expected of them and also helps them learn how to be good communicators. Sometimes adults say one thing but mean another (e.g. 'When you are ready, come over here', meaning 'Can you come over here now?'). Young children are particularly disadvantaged, as they may not have the experience or cognitive development to sort out unclear or mixed messages. Those who have a language delay or who are not fluent in the language that is being spoken may have similar difficulties.

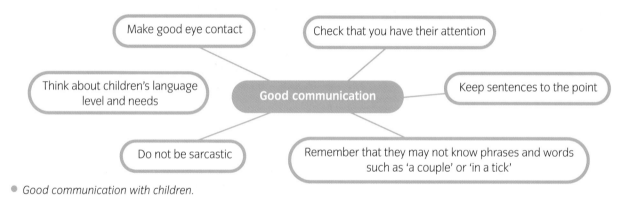

Make good eye contact

Check that you have their attention

Think about children's language level and needs

Good communication

Keep sentences to the point

Do not be sarcastic

Remember that they may not know phrases and words such as 'a couple' or 'in a tick'

● *Good communication with children.*

Encouraging children to ask questions, offer ideas and make suggestions

Communication is not a one-way process. If you are looking to build good relationships with children, it is important that you encourage them to interact with you. This should happen in a relaxed and natural way rather than at 'set' times. You may, for example, ask them if they would like to help put up a display or help choose activities to put out for later. Rather than telling children what to do, you might ask them what they think, and acknowledge – and wherever possible act upon – their advice and ideas. If you encourage children to make suggestions, it is important that you do not continually disregard them, otherwise they will learn that there is no point in saying anything. Where their ideas or suggestions cannot be used, acknowledge them and then explain to them why you might not be able to follow them up.

Check it out

Think about the routine of your setting and the types of activities that are provided. What opportunities are there for adults and children to 'work' together?

Listening and responding to children

If you ask children about adults who they like to be with, time and time again they will tell you that they like someone they can talk to. Teenagers especially need to be listened to, and when they feel that this is not happening they often come out with expressions such as 'They don't understand me!' Listening is therefore an integral part of working effectively with children of all ages. It needs to begin when children are babies. Babies need to see responses to their early vocalisations. Adults working with babies may smile, pick up a baby and then reply by expanding the vocalisation. Later, as children become more fluent speakers, they need to learn the skills of listening. Contrary to popular belief, this is not learnt by getting children to keep still and be quiet. Listening is actually an active skill and children need to learn how to respond appropriately. They can do this if adults are actively listening to them.

Active listening

Active listening is more than just hearing: it involves thinking about what the other person (in this case the child) is trying to convey. Active listening also means giving children your whole attention. This can be hard in busy settings, but needs to be prioritised. In most settings, opportunities for active listening are linked to layout and routines. Preparing the fruit for snack-time and wiping tables are examples of tasks that can be done with a child chatting alongside. The key is to make sure that children feel relaxed and that they know that you are not in a rush or likely to be distracted.

● *Chores can offer a surprisingly good opportunity for active listening and the practise of good communication skills.*

For older children, you may need to make yourself available in discreet ways. By asking if anyone wants to help out in the kitchen, for example, you might enable a young person who really needs to talk to feel they have a way in.

Some children and young people take a while before they really get down to the business of talking. This is one reason why it is important to create situations where you are not rushed. A child may simply begin by wanting to just 'be' with you and then gradually begin to want to talk. Some children also need visual props and cues to help them. This is particularly important for younger children, as well as children for whom the language of the setting is not their home language. A visual cue such as a photograph or an object can help them to think about what they want to say.

Recasting and expanding language

While older children are often quite fluent in their language, younger children may need you to acknowledge their communications by having you recast what they have said to you and also by having you expand their statements. A toddler might say 'Cat gone now' as he or she sees one in the garden disappear. An adult can show the child that he or she has been listening by responding with 'Yes, that cat has gone away now. Do you think it lives near here?'

Expanding babies' early communications is particularly important, as it helps them to feel that they are an active partner.

Keys to good practice: Communicating with children

Do

✓ show positive facial expressions

✓ recast young children's language

✓ expand children's statements

✓ make sure that you are on the same eye level

✓ be interested and ask questions

✓ look for opportunities for sustained conversation.

Don't

✓ interrupt children

✓ dismiss or laugh at ideas

✓ change the subject

✓ allow other children to interrupt

✓ interrogate children

✓ make children feel rushed or hurried.

The importance of adapting communication to meet the individual needs of children

You must think about the communication needs of the children you work with and then adapt your approaches accordingly. A child who stammers, for example, will need opportunities to talk calmly in unhurried situations, away from other children who may interrupt. A child whose home language is not that of the setting may need you to simplify sentences or to use visual cues. In some cases, children (especially younger ones) may simply need a little more time in order to respond.

If you experience particular difficulties with a child, it is a good idea to talk to the parents, as they are likely to know what works best for their child. In addition, it is often worth contacting speech and language teams, as they can suggest special strategies. For some children, a visual approach may be needed to supplement the spoken word. 'Makaton', for example, is used alongside the spoken word to help children understand meanings, while other children may benefit from a pictorial system that allows them to show what they want using photographs or symbols. A child with some hearing loss may benefit from communicating in areas that are well lit and away from distracting background noises.

Helping children to understand the value and importance of positive relationships

As well as building a good relationship with children yourself, you must also look for ways of helping children to build relationships with each other. Children need to learn that other people may have different viewpoints, ideas and preferences, and to understand and value other people's feelings. This is a gradual process. It is made easier if children are feeling emotionally secure, which is why the starting point is always to ensure that children have good relationships with the adults who are with them.

Encouraging children to think of others

Very young children will find it difficult to think about others. Their needs are often immediate and their cognitive development is such that they can find it hard to imagine what others might be feeling and thinking. It is usually not until children are three years old that they start to become good communicators, and many children need another couple of years. This means that you have to find small but practical ways in which to help them to acknowledge others' needs. A good starting point for the youngest children is to arrange for them to have opportunities to give things to other children (e.g. passing around a plate of fruit or pouring a drink for a partner). Doing practical things in this way for other children is non-threatening. It also helps children to learn about the 'exchange' nature of communication.

Helping children to talk to, listen to and find out about others

As children become more skilled at using language, so you can plan activities that will encourage them to listen to and find out more about each other. Five-year-olds might find partners and learn about their favourite foods, television programmes or even whether they have a teddy at the end of the bed. Encouraging children to talk to and listen to each other in this way often works better than 'news time' or formal circle time, when children tend to focus on talking to the adult rather than each other.

Activities that encourage negotiation

Children and young people will learn to listen to others, respect different views and build relationships if they are presented with a challenge or open-ended activity. A small group might like to organise a party, choose and order toys and equipment or put on a play or show. These types of opportunity can help them learn to work together, and they often enjoy the challenge and responsibility. With five- or six-year-olds you might need to work alongside them and encourage them to work as pairs or in very small groups. As children become more skilled at talking to and listening to each other, they can work in larger groups.

Encouraging children's relationships

When you see young children cooperating well together, it is important to acknowledge it. This can be done in quite small ways, such as saying to a couple of children who have been playing well together, 'Are you both enjoying yourselves? You are playing well together!' Learning to be friends with other children is a gradual process and so, in the first few years, it is normal to see the odd squabble or tussle.

From the age of four or five years, most children have developed some social skills that allow them to cooperate with other children. This is dependent, though, on their sense of worth and the way in which they have been treated. Children who feel good about themselves find it easier to accept and enjoy being with others.

● *Encouraging children to feel that they all belong and creating a 'team' feeling among them can often prevent children looking for differences between them.*

With older children, it is important to create an emotional climate that is not competitive but constructive, as children naturally begin to compare themselves with others. At this stage children may begin to resent others or feel threatened by them. Encouraging children to feel that they all belong and creating a 'team' feeling among them can often prevent children looking for differences between them.

Learning about others' feelings

For children to consider others' feelings and respect them, they need to be in touch with their own. The starting point for this work is acknowledging children's own feelings and helping them to talk about them. You might with three-year-olds begin to 'label' emotions and to link them to the behaviour they are showing (e.g. 'You are feeling angry because you thought it was your turn'). It is also important to explain other children's reactions, even to children of an early age (e.g. 'He doesn't want to play with you now because he is feeling tired'). This is a gradual process but an important one. Once children are more aware of how they are feeling, they can then begin to think about others.

You may start to see acts of spontaneous sympathy quite early on and these need to be acknowledged. A three-year-old might put an arm around a child who is crying, while a six-year-old might offer to give up a turn for a younger child.

 Case study 6: Helping children to feel part of a team

Kirsten runs an after-school club. Joseph, Mark and Rafik are eight years old and are all keen football players. Rafik has been chosen to play for the school team, but this has caused tensions with the others. At the after-school club, Joseph and Mark will not often let Rafik play with them and, when they do, they will not pass the ball to him. They have also begun to call him names. Kirsten has noticed the way in which the children's relationship has deteriorated and is also worried by the name calling. She has already spoken to the children about this, but feels that she needs to look at ways to help them pull together. She talks to the children about whether they would like to organise a football skills tournament with other after-school clubs in the area. Immediately, the atmosphere between the boys changes. They start talking and planning. They all seem much happier and Kirsten later talks to them about the whole incident.

1. *Why do you think the boys' behaviour deteriorated when Rafik was chosen for the team?*
2. *How do you think the other boys were feeling?*
3. *Explain why Kirsten's strategy might help the children.*
4. *Why was it important that Kirsten talked to the boys about their feelings?*
5. *In general, why is it important for adults to be aware of children's feelings?*

Communication and children's behaviour

The importance of being consistent and fair

The way in which you deal with children's behaviour will have a significant effect on your relationship with them. It may also influence their future behaviour. This is why it is important to consider the way you deal with behaviour in terms of developing and promoting relationships.

Children look to adults for help. They need to feel that, while sometimes their feelings may get out of control, the adults who are with them are able to remain calm. They also need adults to be consistent and fair so that they are gradually able to understand the boundaries that are set. When adults are inconsistent, children find it hard to learn what the expectations are of the setting. It is a little like playing a game when the rules keep changing with the moods of the other players.

With young children it is important to be clear about what they can and cannot do; with older children you need to explain and also negotiate the parameters. In terms of behaviour, it is a good idea to help children see the need for restrictions on their behaviour in terms of respecting others and valuing their feelings (e.g. 'You will have to wait for a moment longer because Leman was here first').

Acknowledging children's positive behaviour

One of the most effective strategies for promoting positive behaviour is acknowledgement. This means looking out for times when children are showing respect for others, controlling their impulses and staying within the boundaries. For young children, acknowledgement might take the form of praise while older children may be helped with a comment that will help them to become aware of what they are doing (e.g. 'Waiting for your turn was a good idea – it meant that no one got hurt'). Praise takes the form of adult approval (e.g. 'Well done!') while a comment can help the children to reflect on what they are doing. Acknowledgement of whatever form should help the child to understand the specific behaviours you are commenting on. Vague comments such as 'Good girl!' would not actually help the child to know which behaviour is being valued. In contrast, a comment such as 'Well done! I saw that you thought about Jack and passed him some dough' is better because it helps the child to focus on the positive behaviour.

Did you know?

Observational learning or modelling (see page 133) has a powerful effect on children. This means that even when children have irritated you, you need to remain calm and focused. Children need to see the adults around them behaving well.

Dealing with negative behaviour

Unit 303 looks at various strategies to deal with negative behaviour. In terms of children's relationships and self-concept, it is important that you are able to separate the behaviour from the child. When a child does something that is inappropriate, you must take great care over your comments. The child must not learn that 'he' or 'she' is the problem as opposed to the behaviour. This is why terms such as 'naughty' or 'bad' are considered to be unhelpful and even damaging.

When talking to children about their behaviour, it is a good idea to talk about what you are expecting of them. Sometimes too much time is spent telling children about what they should not be doing, and this does not help the child to focus on what behaviour is wanted. 'Don't run!' is an example of this, as it does not tell children what they should be doing. It is also useful to think about the causes of any inappropriate behaviour. Sometimes children are simply unhappy, jealous or bored. Tackling the underlying issues is far more effective in the longer term.

 Keys to good practice: Communication and behaviour

✓ Remember to focus on positive aspects of children's behaviour.

✓ Look out for and acknowledge examples of positive behaviour (e.g. 'Well done! You remembered to tidy away').

✓ Provide plenty of adult attention so that children do not need to gain attention by showing negative behaviours.

✓ Look out for children who are bored, frustrated or unsure of what to do.

✓ Think about the issues behind children's behaviour, for example whether children are bored or needing more adult attention.

✓ Make sure children get clear messages about the behaviour they need to show (e.g. 'Please walk').

✓ Explain to children the reasons behind the boundaries that have been set (e.g. 'The kitchen is not a safe place').

✓ Make sure that older children are involved in boundary setting. Talk through the potential problems of any situation and negotiate how the problems will be avoided.

Helping children to deal with conflict themselves

Life is rarely free of conflict. People have different views and occasionally may outwardly disagree with other people's plans, thoughts or ideas. Learning to resolve conflict, negotiate and also respect others' views is therefore a good life skill for children to learn. In order for them to do so, it is important that adults sometimes allow children to argue and squabble, provided that children are able to do so without resorting to aggression or deliberately hurting feelings. Children who learn how to resolve and deal with conflict can become more confident and are less likely to become passive or victims.

● *For early years workers, knowing at what point to intervene is a key skill.*

Times when adults might intervene

Knowing when to intervene is a skill. Ideally, it is worth observing children carefully before you intervene, in case the children can negotiate or come to some arrangement themselves. Immediate intervention is needed, however, if children begin to use aggression as a solution or look for ways of emotionally harming another child, such as name calling.

● *Why might it be helpful to involve all the children in this conversation?*

The ways in which you might intervene will depend on the level of understanding of the children. A toddler who is snatching a toy from another child does not have the understanding of the upset caused and so distraction is the best technique. Name calling by older children should lead an adult to spend time talking to them about why this is inappropriate behaviour; with young people, it can be helpful to involve the person who is the target of the inappropriate behaviour. The aim is to give children and young people responsibility as well as having the opportunity to explain how they are feeling. It can also be helpful when you intervene to encourage children to come up with their own solutions rather than imposing your own.

Case study 7: Helping children to resolve conflict

A group of children are playing outdoors. One of them has the idea of making a wigwam out of branches. They start to argue about where the wigwam should go. The girl whose idea it was says that she should decide. One boy says that he has a better idea. The practitioner watches and listens from a distance. He decides not to intervene for a few moments, to see whether the children can resolve the matter for themselves. Shortly afterwards, another child suggests that they should have two wigwams, each in different places so that they can visit each other. The other children all agree.

1. *Explain why it was important to observe the children carefully.*
2. *Why is it important to let children learn to resolve conflict for themselves?*
3. *What did the children gain by resolving the conflict?*

Why it is important to encourage and support positive relationships between children and other adults in the setting

In addition to you developing a relationship with children in the setting, it is also important to support their relationships with other adults. One of the key ways in which you might do this is by being a good role model for children. Children notice the way you behave towards others and so often take their cue from you. This means that you need to show your colleagues warmth as well as respect. For younger children who may need to be cared for by your colleagues in your absence, it is essential that they have developed a relationship with them. You could begin this process by involving the other adult, perhaps by going with the child to show something to a colleague or asking the colleague over to see something that the child is doing.

As well as taking steps to help children to get to know other adults, you must also be aware that your own comments about children can have an effect. An adult who talks negatively about a child might influence another adult's view of him or her. This effect is sometimes called 'labelling'. This means that you must be positive in your view and comments about children and their families.

Reflect on your own practice

As you have seen, good relationships and communication with children are an essential part of your role. Have a look at the questions below to assess if you match up to the levels of care needed. The statements all refer to the performance criteria for CCLD 301.1, 301.2 and 301.3.

Performance criteria statement	Always	Sometimes	Never
Do I interact with children in a way that helps them feel welcome and valued in the setting?			
Do I adapt my behaviour and communication to the age, needs and abilities of individual children?			
Do I listen to children and respond to them in a way that shows that I value what they say and feel?			
Do I apply inclusive and anti-discriminatory practice?			
Do I give attention to individual children in a way that is fair to them and to the group as a whole?			
Do I encourage children to ask questions, offer ideas and make suggestions?			
Do I respect confidential information about children, as long as this does not affect their welfare?			
Do I ask questions, clarify and confirm points?			
Do I support children in developing agreements about ways of behaving in the setting?			
Do I support children in understanding other people's feelings?			
Do I encourage children to sort out conflict for themselves?			

Communicating with adults

Positive relationships with other adults

As a professional, you are likely to come into contact with a range of adults. Children always benefit when the adults around them are able to collaborate. Parents, for example, are more likely to support you and share information if you have developed a strong relationship with them. In the same way, children are more likely to get prompt support from professionals outside the setting if you have built a good working relationship with them. Children are also sensitive to the way in which you work with your colleagues. They will notice the atmosphere and model their own behaviour on the way in which you treat each other.

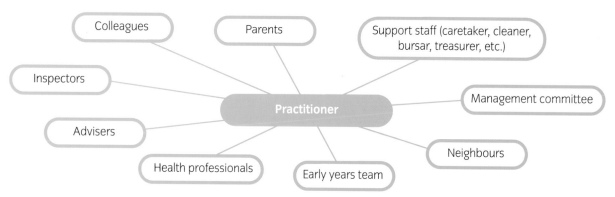

● *The adults with whom you may have contact as a child care practitioner.*

Respect for other adults and clear communication with them

Most practitioners will readily accept that all children are unique and different, but sometimes they expect all adults to have the same views and outlook as themselves. This is hardly the case, and you need to be ready to respect adults who have a different opinion or have a very different lifestyle. When you are able to do this, everyone benefits. Parents may feel able to talk to you more freely, while you may learn from colleagues who see things from a different perspective. This is part of anti-bias practice.

Respecting other adults also means finding out more. The key to this is a clear communication style. It is a common courtesy, for example, to find out how someone wishes to be addressed (e.g. Mrs or Ms O'Malley or Siobhan). It is also a good idea to avoid jumping to conclusions or making assumptions. Parents who do not want their child to join in a nativity play may not necessarily have problems with the same child making an Easter bonnet. Checking on others' views is therefore essential. It would be only proper to check, for example, whether a colleague is happy to cover for you, rather than assuming it.

Using 'I' statements

One of the clearest ways of communicating with others is to use 'I' statements. This means stating what you think, know or believe in such a way that you own the statement. 'I am happy to take the group on Monday' is fairly clear to others, while 'If you want, the group could come to me' is not as clear or as positive.

Keys to good practice: Clear communication with adults

✓ Listen to others.

✓ Do not make assumptions or jump to conclusions.

✓ Always ask others to clarify their comments if you are unsure of their meaning.

✓ Use expressions that invite others to put forward their views (e.g. 'I was thinking about doing this, but I wondered what your thoughts were').

✓ Use 'I' statements.

✓ Avoid seeing others' viewpoints as competition or as undermining you.

The importance of being sensitive to communication difficulties with other adults

The way in which you communicate with people should not be static. It is important that you adjust your style to meet the needs of both the situation and the person with whom you need to communicate. This may mean using pictures, photographs or, if necessary, looking for another adult who might be able to translate for you.

Be aware that differences in communication styles can sometimes lead to misunderstandings. People using a language that is not their native language may not always understand the effect that their words are having. They may come across as being abrupt or passive.

It is also important to be aware that not everyone is comfortable with the written word. Some adults may have difficulty with reading or writing. In the same way, using the telephone may not always be the best method of communicating. Some people need face-to-face contact in order to understand exactly what someone is saying.

Being sensitive to potential difficulties in communicating is essential. This means not making assumptions about the best methods of communicating in any given situation.

Case study 8: Communicating well with parents

Lutfi and Aysel have moved from Turkey. They are concerned that their child, Bekir, is not settling in at nursery. Aysel cannot speak much English and is struggling to make herself understood when she drops Bekir off in the morning. Bekir's key worker and Aysel do a lot of smiling, but Bekir's key worker realises that Aysel is also trying to tell her something. Bekir's key worker has met Lutfi and knows that he can speak English fairly fluently.

1. *Explain why it is important that the key worker finds a way of communicating with Bekir's family.*
2. *Suggest practical strategies that might help the key worker and the family to communicate.*
3. *Why is it important for staff to help Aysel to feel welcome in the setting?*

Situations that may cause conflict with adults and how to deal with these

When you are involved in a conflict (or are worried about the potential for one) it is worth reflecting on why it has arisen (or may arise). Where there is conflict it is important to avoid personalising it (e.g. in the comments that are made) or gossiping about it, which can lead to it becoming more heated and intense. You can often take the heat out of conflicts by acknowledging another's point of view: 'I can see what you mean, but I can't agree with you there'. Sometimes it is necessary simply to agree to differ.

Poor communication

Some conflicts are merely the result of miscommunication. A person may take a comment the wrong way, not understand the context or may not have had the message properly passed on. Poor communication can be dealt with by writing things down or by simply checking again with someone. If someone comes to see you, it is always worth beginning by listening to them and what they feel their problem is. Acknowledging and showing that you are listening often prevents initial misunderstandings from deepening.

In the same way, you can sometimes find that there is conflict because people have not explained their role. This can lead to false expectations: for example, early years advisers may be politely but not warmly spoken to because a staff member thinks that they are inspectors. One way in which you can prevent this from happening is to explain your role and its scope to new people that you meet and, if you are unsure, to ask others about theirs.

Active knowledge

With a partner, role-play the situation where a parent has come into the setting and is angry. Her son has said that some trip money has to be in today. In reality, the teacher simply made a comment in passing to remind the children. One of you should play the parent and the other the teacher.

- Try to use 'I' statements.
- Try to listen to the other viewpoint before you speak.
- What did you learn from the activity?

Lack of confidence

Some conflicts are the result of people not feeling confident in a situation. They may worry that someone might do a better job or know more than them. This can result in them 'lashing out' or being obstructive. Dealing with this is hard, but it is important to look for ways in which you can acknowledge the other person's skills and expertise. If you feel angry or irritated by someone else, it is also worth reflecting on exactly why it is you feel that way.

Case study 9: Good relations with other adults

Frances is fed up. A new member of staff wants to put on a show for the parents. She tells the new member of staff that the idea is stupid and that this kind of thing has already been done before.

1. *Why might Frances feel like that?*
2. *What is the basis of her criticism of the idea of a show for parents?*

External pressures

Sometimes conflicts occur because a person is coping with other, unrelated pressures. You may not know about these and the danger is that you might assume that the negativity is personally aimed at you. Observing other people as they talk to you can sometimes give you an indication of whether there are other factors at work. Simply being sympathetic and a good listener can sometimes take the heat out of a conflict and also help the other person to calm down.

Active knowledge

Ask your supervisor if you can tape yourself talking to a child or small group of children. Think of an activity or task that will provide a relaxed atmosphere in which they can talk. Aim to facilitate conversation with children rather than to teach or direct. Play back the tape recording and consider the balance of communication. Did the children contribute more than you? Write an evaluation of this activity and your role in it.

As you have seen, communicating well with adults as well as children is an essential part of your role. Have a look at the statements below to assess whether you match up to the levels of care needed. The statements all refer to the performance criteria for CCLD 301.4.

Performance criteria statement	Always	Sometimes	Never
Do I communicate with other adults politely?			
Do I respect other adults' individuality, needs and preferences?			
Do I actively listen to other adults, asking questions and clarifying and confirming key points?			
Do I handle any disagreements with other adults in a way that will maintain a positive relationship?			

End-of-unit knowledge check

1. Why is it important to for children to be involved in decision making?
2. Explain why sometimes children need to be allowed to resolve their conflicts.
3. Give an example of when an adult might need to intervene in a conflict between children.
4. Why is it important that babies have a key worker?
5. What is the Data Protection Act?
6. Why is it important to understand when information is confidential?
7. Why is it important to have good relationships with other adults?
8. Explain why it is important to acknowledge children's positive behaviour.
9. List three other types of worker with whom a practitioner may have a professional relationship.
10. Give three tips that might help adults to communicate effectively with children.

Develop and maintain a healthy, safe and secure environment for children

An essential part of your role is to provide an environment for all children that promotes their health, safety and protection. In your work in settings with children you will have responsibility for maintaining a safe environment, contributing to the safety and protection of children and ensuring that risks and hazards are dealt with and reported promptly according to procedures. You need to know how to keep children safe during day-to day work activities including outings. When accidents, emergencies or illnesses occur you need to know how to respond according to the policies and procedures of the setting. This is important for all the children and young people you work with; however, it is even more so that you have regard to the safety of disabled children and young people and those with special educational needs.

What you must know and understand:

- Statutory and regulatory arrangements covering health and safety for the children, colleagues and visitors in your setting or service (K3H246)
- Regulations covering manual handling and risks associated with lifting and carrying children (K3P189)
- The basic stages of child development and the implications these have for health, safety and security arrangements (K3H190)
- Safety checking of the children's indoor and outdoor environment before and during activities (K3H191)
- Security arrangements, including for children's arrival at and departure from the setting, and for outings (K3H192)
- Regulations and procedures for the storage and administration of medicines (K3H193)
- Principles and models of risk assessment that are applied in your setting to cover the environment for children and colleagues indoors, outdoors and on outings (K3H194)
- Why it is important to allow children to assess and manage risk according to their stage of development and how this can be done (K3D195)
- How to record accidents and incidents (K3H196)

- The appropriate contents of a first aid kit (K3H197)
- The correct responses (including paediatric first aid for children under eight years) to situations involving accidents and injuries taking into account the age of the children and the procedures of the setting (K3S198)
- Signs and symptoms of common childhood illness and allergies and appropriate responses according to established procedures (K3H199)
- Good hygiene practice, including principles of cross-infection, waste disposal and food-handling and issues concerning HIV and AIDS virus and hepatitis (K3H200)
- Emergency procedures in your setting covering fire, missing children, evacuation (K3H201)

A healthy, safe and secure environment

The legal and regulatory requirements covering health and safety

As an early years worker you have a primary responsibility for the safety of the children in your care – parents trust you to look after their children. There are a number of legal and regulatory requirements that help to protect children and adults in any setting. The basic principles that apply to protecting people are shared in all such legislation. There are differences in the exact application in each of the countries in the United Kingdom. It is important that you familiarise yourself with the framework in your own country. You should certainly note the following:

- the basic Health and Safety at Work Acts, which lay down the basis of health and safety laws (there are also a number of additional laws that may affect your setting – your country's Health and Safety Executive will supply you with up-to-date information)
- product marking
- the control of substances that could be hazardous to health (e.g. COSHH Regulations 2002)
- National Standards for child care and education settings.

The National Standards are the responsibility of the relevant education services in each of the UK countries. These are the Department for Education and Skills (DfES) in England, the Scottish Executive Education Department (SEED), the Department for Training and Education (DfTE) in Wales, and the Departments of Education (DE) and of Employment and Learning (DEL) in Northern Ireland. The Standards are monitored by inspectorates in each of the countries: Ofsted in England, HMIe in Scotland, ESTYN in Wales and the ETI in Northern Ireland. Once again it is your responsibility to make sure that you are aware of the standards in your country.

Health and Safety at Work Act 1974

All employment settings have responsibility as laid down in the Health and Safety at Work Act 1974 for Great Britain. This Act places overall responsibility for health and safety with the employer but also duties on employees, so everyone in a setting has some responsibility for the health and safety of anyone who is there.

The Act covers the conditions in which places of work must be kept:
- Buildings should be well maintained and designed with the safety of the users in mind.
- The general environment should be clean and safe.
- Equipment must be safely used and stored.
- Working practice must promote the health and safety of children.

All employees should be aware of the written statement of safety policy that is required under the Act. The Act also provides for the protection of employees:
- The workplace should be safe and not pose a risk to employees' health.
- Safe systems of working should be in place.
- Articles and substances should be stored and used safely.
- Adequate welfare facilities should be available.
- Appropriate information, training and supervision should be made for the health and safety of employees.
- Any protective clothing needed should be provided free of charge.
- Certain injuries, diseases and occurrences should be reported to the Health and Safety Executive.
- First aid facilities should be provided.
- A safety representative should be consulted about issues affecting health and safety in the workplace.

Finally, it stipulates the legal duties of employees:
- Employees should take care of their own health and safety and that of others affected by their actions.
- Employees should cooperate with their employer on health and safety.

Did you know?

Accidental injuries are the greatest single threat to life to children aged under 15 years in the UK: about 350 of them die from these causes every year. They are also a major cause of disability and ill-health, with over 100,000 children being admitted to hospital and over 2 million having to visit accident and emergency departments each year. In terms of the number of potentially healthy life-years lost, children's accidents outrank all other causes.

(Source: Child Accident Prevention Trust, 2003)

Observation

Look at your setting's health and safety policy.
- When was it last reviewed, and by whom?
- Where is the policy displayed?
- What is covered by the policy?
- What, if anything, needs adding to the policy?

Product marking

Many items that we use every day have been tested for safety by the British Standards Institution (BSI). An item with a Kitemark means that the BSI has independently tested and confirmed that the product complies with the relevant standard and is safe and reliable. Manufacturers pay for this service and their products are tested and assessed at regular intervals. Products are not legally required to carry a Kitemark, but many everyday appliances such as fridges, electrical plugs and crash helmets have them.

Many products such as toys must meet legal requirements before they can be sold within the European Union and must carry a CE mark. This mark shows that the product meets European rules but it is not a safety or quality mark. Some products carry both a Kitemark and a CE mark.

Observation

- Pick a room in your place of work. How many items can you find that display the Kitemark? Make a note of them.
- Pick five of the items you have listed and in a group discuss why you think they need to conform to British Standards.
- Did you find anything that you thought should have had the Kitemark and did not?

● *Product safety markings.*

COSHH

Legislation called COSHH (Control of Substances Hazardous to Health Regulations 2002) covers substances which can cause ill-health. COSHH lays down a step-by-step approach to the precautions to prevent injury or illness from dangerous substances. Such substances must have particular labels on them, which show the substances are dangerous and need to be kept in special containers and carefully stored.

Ofsted's National Standards

There are 14 National Standards for different kinds of child-care setting in England and Wales, Scotland and Northern Ireland, with different inspectorates responsible for ensuring these are met. For example, in England, Ofsted is responsible for registering nurseries, playgroups, childminders, crèches, after-school clubs and play schemes. Requirements for ratios of staff to children vary – a good rule of thumb is that the younger the children, the more staff are required.

● *The labelling of hazardous substances.*

The 14 National Standards in England (Table 302.1) cover a range of important issues in relation to safe and effective child care, although not all 14 relate directly to health and safety.

Table 302.1 Ofsted's 14 National Standards

Number	Standard
Standard 1. Suitable person	Adults providing day care, looking after children or having unsupervised access to them are suitable to do so.
Standard 2. Organisation	The registered person meets required adult–child ratios, ensures that training and qualifications requirements are met and organises space and resources to meet the children's needs effectively.
Standard 3. Care, learning and play	The registered person meets the individual needs of the children and promotes their welfare. The registered person plans and provides activities and play opportunities to develop children's emotional, physical, social and intellectual capabilities.
Standard 4. Physical environment	The premises are safe, secure and suitable for their purpose. They provide adequate space in an appropriate location, are welcoming to children and offer access to the necessary facilities for a range of activities which promote their development.
Standard 5. Equipment	Furniture, equipment and toys are provided which are appropriate for their purpose and help to create an accessible and stimulating environment. They are of suitable design and condition, are well maintained and conform to safety standards.
Standard 6. Safety	The registered person takes positive steps to promote safety within the setting and on outings, and ensures proper precautions are taken to prevent accidents.
Standard 7. Health	The registered person promotes the good health of children and takes positive steps to prevent the spread of infection and appropriate measures when they are ill.
Standard 8. Food and drink	Children are provided with regular drinks and food in adequate quantities for their needs. Food and drink are properly prepared and nutritious and comply with dietary and religious requirements.
Standard 9. Equal opportunities	The registered person and staff actively promote equality of opportunity and anti-discriminatory practice for all children.
Standard 10. Special needs (including special educational needs and disabilities)	The registered person is aware that some children may have special needs and is proactive in ensuring that appropriate action can be taken when such a child is identified or admitted to the provision. Steps are taken to promote the welfare and development of the child within the setting in partnership with the parents and other relevant parties.
Standard 11. Behaviour	Adults caring for children in the provision are able to manage a wide range of children's behaviour in a way which promotes their welfare and development.
Standard 12. Working in partnership with parents and carers	The registered person and staff work in partnership with parents to meet the needs of the children, both individually and as a group. Information is shared.
Standard 13. Child protection	The registered person complies with local child protection procedures approved by the Area Child Protection Committee and ensures that all adults working and looking after children in the setting are able to put the procedures into practice.
Standard 14. Documentation	Records, policies and procedures which are required for the efficient and safe management of the setting, and to promote the welfare, care and learning of children, are maintained. Records about individual children are shared with the child's parent.

Observation

- Find out about the National Standards that apply to your own country. Which apply particularly to health and safety?
- Make a chart showing how the Standards relating to health and safety are met in your own setting.

Regulations covering manual handling and risks associated with lifting and carrying children

Caring for children and young people naturally involves lifting and carrying of babies and children, as well as equipment. Incorrect lifting techniques can result in serious back injuries as well as the risk of fractures and sprains to limbs. Such injuries account for approximately 25 per cent of all injuries reported each year.

The Manual Handling Operations Regulations 1992 supplement the general duties placed on employers and others by general Health and Safety regulations.

You should always take care to protect yourself when lifting children or equipment by following good practice.

The basic stages of child development and the implications these have for health, safety and security arrangements

The key factor in protecting children in your care from accidents and injury is that you understand the **risks** they are exposed to, especially in relation to their age and stage of development. You should then be able to help to identify risks and **hazards** for situations and certain groups of children. For young children falls may be a particular danger, while at an older age the possibility of a road traffic accident may be a greater concern.

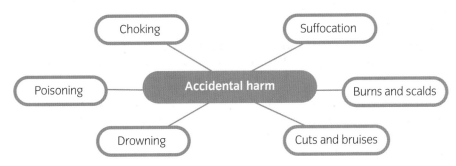

● *The more common types of accidental harm.*

Check it out

Do you think about your lifting technique every time? Observe your colleagues to see if they are following the correct procedure:

- stand in front of the child or object with your feet at shoulder width apart
- always bend your knees, not your back and keep your back straight
- assess the weight of the child or object
- make sure you are firmly holding the child
- test that you can safely lift and is so lift
- avoid twisting or bending as you lift.

Key terms

A *hazard* is something that is likely to cause harm.

A *risk* is the seriousness of a hazard and its likelihood actually to cause harm.

Check it out

Think about the various ways in which children at different stages of development can injure themselves. How could the children you care for be injured in the ways listed here?

As an early years worker you need to know what stage of development the children in your care are at (see Unit 303) and what the associated risks for them are. It is important that other staff are aware of this as well. Very often after an accident you hear parents or carers saying 'But I didn't know he could do that yet…', for example after a child has opened a cupboard to get at dangerous chemicals or fallen after climbing some stairs.

● *The risks children are exposed to relate to their age and stage of development.*

Did you know?

In 2002, over 27,700 babies under six months were injured in accidents.

(Source: Child Accident Prevention Trust 2003)

Case study 1: Dangers for Lily

Lily, aged two and a half years, is tall for her age. She is also extremely curious and has just discovered that she can now reach the door handles at home and feel the pattern on them. She goes to a childminder who lives in an old house with a cellar and a front door that opens on to a busy main road. When she is out and about she does not always like to have her hand held.

1. *Can you think of any dangers that Lily might be in?*
2. *Why do you think these are dangers to Lily?*
3. *What steps should her parents take to protect her?*

Have a look at Table 302.2, which shows the accidents that commonly occur at different ages, why they do so and, most importantly, what you need to think about when supervising children.

Table 302.2. Accidents that commonly occur at different ages

Age/stage	Common accidents	Reasons	Prevention
Birth–crawling (up to about 6 months) Children at this age are very dependent and vulnerable but they can often move more than you think!	Falls from raised surfaces	Even small babies can move by wriggling; the risk of this type of accident increases as a baby grows	Never leave babies unattended on a raised surface or put a bouncing chair on a raised surface

continued on next page

continued from previous page

	Suffocation	Babies cannot push covers or other items away from their faces	Do not use duvets or pillows for babies under one year
	Choking	Young babies cannot deal with a large volume of fluid or hard objects in their mouths. Peanuts can irritate the airways of a young child	Never 'prop feed' Do not give babies solids and then leave them alone Keep small objects away from babies' grasp Watch that older children do not put anything in a baby's mouth Never allow a child under six years to eat peanuts as the oil in them can cause swelling of the bronchial tubes
	Strangulation	Ribbons, jewellery and wool can get caught in a cot or car seat, for example	Never put ribbons or jewellery around a baby's neck. Check clothing is not too tight
	Burns and scalds	Carer with a hot drink when holding baby Not testing bath water Heating feeds in microwave Sun burn	Avoid the risks: no hot drinks near young children, test bath water carefully, no use of microwaves for feeds Keep babies well covered and protected from the sun
	Drowning	Leaving babies alone, even for a few seconds, or with other children, in the bath	Never leave a young baby in water without an adult present
Crawling to walking (about 6–15 months)	Falls (downstairs, raised surface, from highchairs, cots etc.)	As babies start to become mobile they want to explore and have no understanding of danger	Always guard stairs, use five-point harnesses, never leave children on high surfaces
	Suffocation from bedding, plastic bags and choking on food or small objects	Babies at this age can still get trapped in bedding Exploration of plastic bags (seen as toys)	No duvets for children under one year Keep plastic bags out of reach

continued on next page

continued from previous page

Age/stage	Common accidents	Reasons	Prevention
Did you know? In 2002, 38,300 babies under a year old were taken to hospital after a fall, as were 17,000 with burns and scalds. (Source: Child Accident Prevention Trust 2003)		Babies use their mouths to explore; therefore anything new will go in the mouth, but anything larger than a 2p piece may cause choking	Always stay with a baby who is eating or drinking Keep small items out of reach Teach older children not to put anything in a baby's mouth
	Strangulation	Still a risk from clothing Risk with mobile children of unexpected items causing problems (e.g. washing lines, window blind cords, belts) or bedclothes	Never put anything around a child's neck Check clothing Keep blind cords etc. short and out of reach and never next to a cot
	Burns and scalds	With their increased mobility children can now reach things on surfaces – drinks, radiators, ovens – and could pull on kettle flexes or pan handles They are also more difficult to keep in the shade, to protect them from the sun They have no understanding of what 'hot' is and cannot learn from experience at this stage	As for young babies, plus use a coiled flex on kettles, a safety gate to bar access in the kitchen when cooking, etc. Extra care with clothes, sun creams and hats in sun. Keep out of sun between 11 a.m. and 3 p.m. Fit guards and keep all possible sources of burns and scalds out of reach
	Drowning	Curiosity may lead children to peer into water containers They are likely to enjoy water play Being left alone in the bath	Supervise all water play very closely, and empty water containers immediately when finished with Never leave children alone in the bath or with older children
	Cuts and bruises	First mobile movements are often unsteady and poorly coordinated Curiosity may lead children to grab anything that takes their attention, even if it is big and heavy	Move dangerous and/or heavy items that are a risk Position furniture with hard or sharp edges so that there is less chance of injury
	Transport	Failure to secure child in a car seat Falling out of pram/pushchair Baby walkers are associated with range of injuries, especially falls and burns	Always secure in correct car seat, use harnesses in prams, etc. Do not use baby walkers

continued on next page

continued from previous page

Toddlers (about 1–3 years) Children at this age are very inquisitive and full of energy. They have a short attention span and are absorbed in themselves. They are not old enough to understand the concept of danger and do not always learn from experience	Falls (e.g. downstairs, from windows)	New-found climbing skills and increased manual dexterity mean children can get up on to window sills, get upstairs and open catches	Use good safety gates and window locks that cannot be opened by toddlers Teach them to climb stairs but do not allow them to use stairs by themselves Avoid putting furniture underneath windows
	Suffocation and choking	Plastic bags are still a danger Children may still be learning to chew and are still putting things into their mouths	Keep plastic bags out of reach, or preferably destroy As for younger children, it is important to avoid peanuts
	Poisoning	Curiosity and increasing skills mean children can gain access to virtually anything, including medicines (despite child-resistant tops), chemicals and berries	Keep all medicines and chemicals locked away and out of reach Keep chemicals in original containers Do not keep medicines in handbags or by the bed Check gardens for poisonous plants
	Strangulation	Children can get head into but not out of gaps Poor necklines on clothing, cords, etc.	Supervise climbing games Check necklines
	Burns and scalds	Curiosity is still an issue; there is consequent danger with pans and irons, for example. Children may start to imitate adults as well. They will be more able to use matches if they find them Their skin is still fragile and easy to burn (in hot baths, etc.)	As for last stage but with extra vigilance
	Drowning	Increasing mobility, independence and curiosity means children are at danger, especially of garden ponds. Drowning is possible in very small amounts of water	Close supervision around any water Secure fencing of ponds Empty water containers when finished with Stay with toddlers in the bath

Did you know?

In 2002, over 212,000 children aged 1–3 attended hospital after a fall and 22,500 after a suspected poisoning.

(Source: Child Accident Prevention Trust 2003)

continued on next page

continued from previous page

Age/stage	Common accidents	Reasons	Prevention
	Cuts and bruises	Trapped fingers in door jambs Cuts while trying to imitate adults using scissors, knives or razors Running into low glass in doors	Be aware of risk of doors when little fingers are around Keep scissors etc. out of reach Use safety glass or board it up
	Car accidents	Experimenting with car safety seat or buggy harnesses Being left alone in car Running off when out on the street	Use correct seat and harness and discourage messing with fastenings Never leave child alone in a car. Use a harness and reins when out on the road. Start simple road safety training
About 3–5 years At this age children's coordination is improving and they have more understanding of action and consequence. They may well forget safety instructions when tired or distracted. They still enjoy testing their abilities and finding unusual ways to use toys and other objects	Falls (e.g. downstairs from windows, play equipment)	Attraction of playing on the stairs and from windows, using their powerful imaginations to be Superman etc. Testing own skills by climbing higher and so at risk of falling further	Do not allow stairs to be used for playing Fit window locks Tell children about the dangers Choose playgrounds with impact-absorbing surfaces Tell children how to use equipment properly
	Choking and suffocation	Eating on the move Danger from ice cubes or some small sweets Peanuts still a risk	Encourage children to sit still while eating and not to run with sweets in their mouth Do not give peanuts to children under six years
	Poisoning	There is still the risk of confusion between sweets and medicines and berries Children are better able to open locks and resistant caps	Keep medicines etc. locked away Tell children not to eat anything they pick outside without checking with you
	Burns and scalds	Danger from hot foods, liquids, taps, candles Risks from children copying adults Children now understand concept of 'Hot! do not touch' but can easily forget, especially when	Keep dangerous items out of reach, especially matches, candles, etc. Teach children what to do if a fire or smoke alarm goes off Use thermostatic valves on taps

continued on next page

		practising increased manual skills of turning and switching	

	Drowning	Any open water remains a threat, especially as children become more independent. It is safe to leave a child in a bath from about four years, but still have an adult nearby	Close supervision near water. Fence off ponds. Teach a child to swim
	Cuts	Children can now be taught to use scissors and knives safely. There are still risks with sharp objects if they are not used safely or are used in play	Keep sharp objects out of reach. Teach how to sew safely
	Car accidents	Children have little understanding or experience of dealing with traffic. They may have started to ride a bicycle	Never allow a child under 5 on the road alone – on foot or bike. Teach road safety, but be aware of limits of remembering and understanding. Always use a helmet on the bike
5–11 years Older children's risk assessment skills will be improving, but they are still impulsive and may overestimate their abilities. There are more external influences on their behaviour.	Falls, choking, poisoning, burns and scalds, drowning, cuts and bruises, car accidents	Injuries at this age are often due to children being keen to help and copy adults, but misjudging their abilities. Boisterous play can result in accidents. Friends and peers have more influence and a child can be persuaded to 'have a go'	As for last age stages, ensure dangerous items are not easy to reach. Children should now be learning to take some responsibility for their own safety but the extent of this will vary. Being able to repeat a rule does not mean a child understands or will remember to follow it. This improves as the child gets older but outside influence can 'over-rule' this
Over 11 years	Accidents – on foot, bike, skateboard. Poisoning –drugs and alcohol	Increasing independence as children grow into teenagers and spend much more time unsupervised; increased peer pressure to try things out	Teach young people to carry out their own risk assessments of situations: how to recognise hazards and to judge whether they can deal with them (young people need to be able to judge when they cannot handle situations)

Key to good practice: Encouraging children to manage risks for themselves

✓ Let young children take appropriate responsibility for safety decisions in a controlled environment.

✓ Increase levels and risk as children grow and mature.

✓ Support and help parents to encourage their children to manage risk for themselves.

✓ Be aware of timid children who are reluctant to take risks and help them to develop the skills.

Safety checking of the children's indoor and outdoor environment before and during work activities

Every person working with children is responsible for their safety. It is important that the **environment** children are working in is regularly checked, before and during activities. Some of the things to think about are listed below.

Key terms

Environment means all areas, both indoors and outdoors, for which you are responsible.

* Does any of the equipment have broken parts or sharp edges?
* Are large pieces of equipment and toys arranged to allow safe use by all children?
* Are the outside play areas free of broken glass, syringes and other dangerous litter?
* Are the toilet and washing facilities clean and supplied with toilet paper and soap?
* Are all locks, catches and so on that stop children leaving the building alone working?
* Are any dangerous items or substances (e.g. knives or bleach and other chemicals) accessible to children?
* Are procedures for dealing with spillages of urine, faeces, blood and vomit clear and are the facilities available to deal with them?
* Are the procedures for dealing with visitors to the setting clear?
* Do the alarms work and are visitor books and badges in place?
* Are all areas for the preparation of food and drink clean and is suitable equipment present?

Observation

Carry out a safety check in the setting where you work. Compile a checklist of points for safety in your setting and on it show the checks you would carry out to ensure the safety of all the children in your care.

Buildings and maintenance

- Doors opening into entrances and exits from the building must not be capable of being opened by young children.
- Emergency exits must be clear and easy to open from the inside.
- Floors should not have any loose rugs or pieces of carpet.
- Low-level glass should be safety glass or covered with a guard.
- Electrical sockets should be covered.

Cleanliness of the general environment

- There should be a high standard of cleanliness throughout the buildings.
- Spillages should be immediately cleaned.
- Toilet areas should be regularly cleaned and checked.

Food preparation areas

- All staff dealing with food should have a food hygiene certificate.
- All regulations relating to food storage should be in place.

● *The nappy-changing area should be clean and well supplied. Materials and equipment should be safely stored.*

Safe storage and use of equipment

- Cupboards at 'child level' should not contain cleaning items, knives, tools or any other potentially dangerous items.
- Toys with very small parts should be kept well away from children under three years of age.
- Heaters and radiators should be covered and not a risk to children.

Outdoor areas

- Outdoor slides, swings and so on should be safe and have impact-absorbing matting provided.
- Young children should not be able to open gates.
- Sandpits should be kept covered when not in use.

Active knowledge

Note down any changes or improvements that could be implemented in your setting. You could take them to the next staff meeting or discuss them with colleagues.

Keys to good practice: Outdoor play

✓ Always ensure that objects and equipment are regularly checked for wear and tear, such as fraying ropes and rusting joints.

✓ Check that equipment is clean and dry, especially slides, steps, etc.

✓ Ensure that each child has the space to move freely without bumping into other children or objects.

✓ Ensure that the appropriate adult–child ratios are maintained.

✓ Swings and rope ladders should be used by only one child at a time. All other children should be discouraged from playing nearby in case they are hurt by a swing or rope.

✓ The person supervising should be able to see all the children.

✓ Check that outdoor areas are free from harmful waste such as dog faeces (which can cause eye damage to young children), broken equipment or litter.

✓ Ensure that surfaces are soft and safe, to encourage freedom of movement.

Working practices that promote health and safety

- Adults must not leave bags or coats containing medicines within reach of children.
- Adults must not bring hot drinks into the same room as children.
- All stairs should have fixed guards at the top and bottom.
- Children using baby-walkers, bicycles and so on should be supervised at all times and should wear helmets as appropriate.

Active knowledge

- How many accidents have there been in your setting in the last year?
- What caused them?
- How are children in your setting helped to use the outdoor play areas safely?
- Spend some time observing how the children operate outside, paying attention to the numbers on equipment, whether they run or walk, and how many adults are supervising.
- How could the number of accidents be reduced?

Did you know?

In the UK in 1999, over 150,000 children were injured in school or nursery playgrounds. Climbing frames are most commonly involved, followed by swings. Falls accounted for at least 75 per cent of all playground accidents. Collisions with other children and impact with stationary or moving equipment were common causes of injury.

(Source: Child Accident Prevention Trust 2003)

● *What are the safety features of this outdoor play area?*

Case study 2: The outdoor play area

Jane works in a child care setting that also has an after-school club for older children. The older children enjoy ball games in the outdoor play area. This morning she opens the door to take the children out and notices that the outside gate has been left open and there is a dog wandering around the sand pit. There is a broken glass bottle near the climbing frame.

1. *What action should Jane take now?*
2. *What should be done to stop this happening again?*
3. *Design a notice to help remind the supervisors of the after-school club about the health and safety requirements of the setting.*

The suitability of children's games and toys

It is important that all items used by children are suitable for them. This means suitable for the age and stage of development they are at. The product markings discussed above give only an indication of the safety of an item when it is being properly used; the most important factor in ensuring safety is the person using the item or the person responsible for its use – the early years worker.

A child may not be interested in or indeed may be unable to read the instructions on a game or piece of equipment. The responsibility rests with you. You can very easily make following the instructions part of the activity, especially with an older child. This will also help the child to learn about safety requirements and the importance of reading instructions.

● Following instructions can be part of the activity and will help children to learn about safety.

Safety activities

When you are supervising indoor and outdoor activities it is important that equipment is of the highest safety standard. Space must be allowed for children to run, hop, skip, throw, and so on. Space will obviously vary according to availability but no room should be overcrowded. This means that you need to think about the size of groups of children that are using an area.

 Keys to good practice: Using equipment safely

✓ Before children use the equipment, identify and remove any faulty items.

✓ Ensure you can see all the children who are using the equipment.

✓ Ensure that the equipment is used correctly.

✓ Keep moving around so that you can see all activity.

✓ Check that the children do not become overexcited.

✓ Encourage children to rest when tired.

Security arrangements, including for children's arrival at and departure from the setting, and for outings

Parents entrust their children to your care and will expect to see security arrangements in place. As well as appropriate locks and handles on doors and gates, for example, these arrangements will include information about who can collect a child, which means that if a child's grandmother, say, comes to collect the child, and you have not been told, she will be challenged. One obvious way to be sure about parents' wishes for their child is to have the correct details recorded on an easily accessible card. This will usually also have details about the child's diet, favourite toys, any illnesses, allergies and the family doctor, as well as contact numbers and information about who can and cannot collect the child from the setting.

It is essential (as well as polite) that someone responsible always greets children on their arrival, as it allows an exchange of information with parents and children will be more likely to feel they are being passed into the care of people they want to spend time with. The same applies when children leave for the day. Again, you must make sure that the right person collects each child. Do not be afraid to challenge and check if you do not recognise the person collecting the child. In addition to paying attention to the child who is arriving or leaving, make sure that no other children are near the doors – it is very easy for a small child to slip out while parents are perhaps struggling with pushchairs or shopping.

● *The security system....*

Many child care settings have a security system that sounds an alarm whenever anyone comes into the building. Always check you know that other adults coming in are allowed to be there. All visitors should sign in and out, not just as a check on their identity but also in case of fire or accident on the premises.

Outings

Think about what could happen on an outing and then plan accordingly. If you are responsible for security, think about the following.

● Will there be enough adults to supervise the children?
● Have arrangements been made to take a register of the children, name badges, identified groups and adults?
● Are staff experienced in supervising children?
● Have parents been informed of the outing and have they in turn given their written consent?
● Do parents have written information about where and when they will be collecting children after the trip? Is there an back-up if a child is not collected?

All settings have to have policies and procedures for planning and going on a trip, and these will vary with the age of the children. These should include:

- what happens if the trip has to be cancelled and parents cannot be informed in time
- the procedure to follow if a child goes missing
- the procedure for medical and **other emergencies**.

Key terms

Other emergencies are, for example, fires or other threats to the safety of children and colleagues in the environment, missing children.

Active knowledge

- Does the policy for security at your setting cover children arriving and leaving, and outings?
- Imagine various scenarios in which something goes wrong. Does the policy cover them?
- Go around your setting imagining it from the youngest mobile child's eye. Could you get out of the building, or get hold of something that might injure you?

Reflect on your own practice

As you have seen, ensuring the safety of children in your care is an essential part of your role. Have a look at the statements below to assess whether you match up to the levels of care needed. The statements all refer to the performance criteria for elements CCLD 302.1 and 302.2.

Performance criteria statement	Always	Sometimes	Never
Do I have up-to-date and accurate information about the health and safety requirements for my setting?			
Do I routinely check all areas of my setting to identify and record hazards and remove those that can be removed?			
Do I review health and safety procedures and make suggestions for improvements?			
Do I assess the health and safety and security of the setting before, during and at the end of activities?			
Do I make sure that children and adults in the setting follow health and safety requirements?			
Do I always make sure that children are supervised as appropriate to the level of risk, and their age, needs and abilities?			
Do I encourage children to manage risk for themselves and be aware of their own and others' safety?			
Do I contribute to safety on outings?			

Accidents, injuries, illnesses and other emergencies

Regulations and procedures for the storage and administration of medicines

Often, after an absence due to illness or a visit to the doctor, a child may need to take medicine while at nursery or school. Parents must give written consent for their child to have medicine administered by the nursery nurse or teacher. Each setting will have a policy about this and a form for the parents to complete. You should not give medicines to children under any circumstances without this written permission. This includes applying creams and lotions and administering inhalers.

The Control of Substances Hazardous to Health Regulations 1994 (COSHH) require that the medicines are kept in a safe place, preferably a locked cupboard, and are clearly labelled with the child's name. A record must be kept of when the medicine has been given and by whom. Always make sure you know of any particular requirements; for instance, some medicines have to be taken before meals and others afterwards.

Keys to good practice: Creams and lotions

✓ Applying creams and lotions to a child may be necessary if he or she suffers from eczema or other skin conditions.

✓ Ask the parents to show you what to do.

✓ Always apply in privacy, to avoid other children gathering around.

✓ Use plastic gloves or swabs to apply, depending on the instructions (these should be provided along with the lotion or cream).

✓ Remember that creams and lotions are drugs, just as tablets are – written consent is needed.

Active knowledge

What are the requirements in your setting for the administration of medicines? Do you think that the instructions for staff and parents are clear? Produce some materials that would help all staff and parents to understand the requirements.

Principles and models of risk assessment and why it is important to allow children to assess and manage risk

Any activity a child does has some risk attached, even something as simple as painting. If the activity is well planned and organised, with thought given to possible dangers, the risk of accidents or injuries should be minimal. The secret is to balance the risk of an activity against the benefit to and safety of the child. This is known as risk assessment.

It would be very easy to respond to all the risks to which children are exposed by not allowing them to explore or experiment. But just think about how that would affect their development. Children need to explore their environment – it is one of the ways in which they learn – but it needs to be a 'safe' environment where risk is controlled by adults. It is important that children are given the freedom to develop their skills, with adult support but not too much intervention.

Some children need this freedom to explore risk even more than others. For example, a child who has epilepsy may be restricted in play at home because of parental concern that the child may have a fit. In a well controlled setting the child can be encouraged to explore and try out new skills.

Risk assessment in practice

Consider these two common and popular activities: junk modelling and a walk in the local park. What might the potential dangers to the children be from each? Table 302.3 presents a sample risk assessment.

Table 302.3. Examples of risk assessment of two common activities for younger children

Activity	Risks to be assessed
Junk modelling	
Use of scissors	Moving around with scissors, not holding them by the pointed end
Containers and other materials being used	They may have rough or sharp edges that could cause injury
	The materials used may have held food or unsafe substances (e.g. cleaning fluids)
Cleaning up after the activity	Wet surfaces and floors present a risk of slipping
	Scissors etc. left around could be a risk
Outing to the park	
Walk to the park	Traffic dangers
	Child wandering off and getting lost
Use of play equipment	Broken or damaged equipment
	Equipment not suitable for age of child (e.g. very high slide)
Recent rain	Lack of waterproof clothing (wet, cold children)
	Effect on play equipment

A visit or outing has different risk assessment requirements. Staff have a responsibility to ensure that outings are properly planned and carried out. Provided a proper risk assessment is carried out and all reasonably practicable measures are taken to deal with the identified risks, the scope for incidents should be minimised. Your country's department for education will have produced comprehensive guidance for the organisation of visits, to help systems and procedures to be set up that support people leading visits. Ask in your setting to have a look at them, or look at the relevant website for your country (e.g. www.dfes.gov.uk in England). The best way to assess risk for an outing is to make a provisional visit yourself.

Check it out

Identify the potential injuries/illnesses to the children as a result of any of the points highlighted in Table 302.3 and think what you could do to prevent them.

Consider another activity you have recently carried out in your setting and carry out the same process with it.

Case study 3: Risk assessment for an outing

Jason is planning an outing with a colleague to the local woods with some groups of children from his child care setting. He hopes that he can include some nature work, physical skill development and art work with the children. There are two groups he is planning to take, one of six 4-year-olds from the pre-school group and one of eight 7–8-year-olds from the after-school group.

1. *How might Jason carry out a risk assessment?*
2. *List the different safety risks for each of the groups.*
3. *What will Jason need to think about for each group?*
4. *How much freedom should each group be given when they are in the wood?*

How to record accidents and incidents

Case study 4: An incident in outdoor play

You are in charge of a group of six children. During outdoor play Ashok trips and falls heavily on his left leg. You see that his leg is swollen and it looks a strange shape.

1. *What do you do immediately?*
2. *What, if anything, do you do with Ashok's leg?*
3. *What do you do with the other children?*
4. *Whom do you contact first and how?*

How to deal with the immediate situation in an accident is considered below, but this is only part of the procedure for the nursery or school. The next important action is to inform the child's parents or carers. The child will have a record card in the office giving emergency contact numbers.

This may not be the child's parents, because work commitments may make it difficult for a parent to be contacted. The number may be that of the child's grandparents or aunt for example – it should be someone who is usually easy to contact, and who in turn can contact the parents.

The person in charge must get in touch with the emergency contact as soon as possible and inform the relevant person of the incident, and where the child is being taken. Obviously, someone the child knows well should go to the hospital with him or her until the parents or other carers arrive. This will help to reassure the child, and be a point of contact for the parents when they arrive.

Even with a minor accident that does not need hospital treatment, under health and safety law an entry must be made in the accident book. For more serious incidents a full report is needed. After any such event, the person in charge should examine the circumstances to see what could be done to prevent something similar occurring. Preventive measures may be as simple as having more adults supervise the children at outdoor play, or there may be the need to change equipment or to put more safety protection in place, such as more matting under swings.

A review of the policy on accidents may be needed, but at the very least some type of preventive action is likely to be taken.

Did you know?

Fatalities on educational visits are very rare. It was estimated that across England there were 7–10 million pupil visits involving educational/recreational activity in 2003. Each year on average, there are three or four fatalities.

(Source: Health and Safety Executive, http://www.hse. gov.uk/services/education/ schoolvisits.htm)

Potential dangers are seen (e.g. kettle flexes are kept well away from worktop edges, ponds are properly covered or filled in)

Children are not over-protected and are allowed to develop skills to keep themselves safe

Children are never left alone

Accidents are less likely to happen when:

Wherever possible toys and equipment purchased have the Kitemark or safety mark on them to show they are of a good standard

Adults are good role models and set a safe example

- *Types of preventive action.*

The appropriate contents of a first aid kit

All children's settings should have a well equipped first aid kit that is easily to hand in the case of an accident. All staff should know where it is. Always make sure you know where the first aid box is kept, and what is in it.

A good first aid box should have the following items in it:
- a range of plasters in different sizes
- medium and large sterile dressings
- sterile eye pads
- triangular bandages (slings)

Did you know?

Under certain circumstances the accident may need to be reported to the Health and Safety Executive, particularly if the child is seriously injured. Examples of this would include:
- a major injury (e.g. fractured limbs, electric shock, unconsciousness)
- if the child is absent through the injury for more than three days.

More information is available on the HSE website for education settings (http://www.hse.gov.uk/ services/education/index.htm).

- safety pins
- disposable gloves
- crepe bandages
- scissors
- tweezers
- cotton wool
- non-alcoholic cleansing wipes.

A named person should be responsible for checking the kit and replacing missing items, although anyone using an item from the kit has a responsibility to report this.

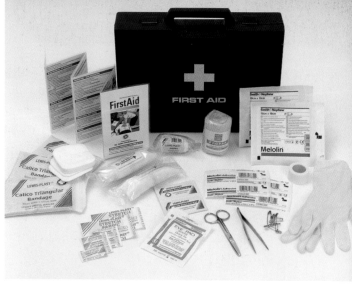

- *A well-equipped first aid kit.*

The correct responses to accidents and injuries, and paediatric first aid

Young children frequently do have accidents. A child who has been injured will be very frightened and upset, as indeed will any other children who are in the area. Your main responsibility is to know what to do in an emergency, and to carry out the required actions calmly and confidently so that you meet one of the prime aims of first aid, which is to preserve life and to prevent the effects of the injury becoming worse than necessary.

The right actions after an accident can save life. For example, people have died unnecessarily as a result of a blocked airway that needed little skill to open. A valid paediatric first aid certificate is a requirement for many child care jobs. Even if this does not presently apply to you, it is worth taking a recognised course, such as those run by St John Ambulance or the Red Cross, as this will give you the confidence to deal with incidents when they happen. These pages will then merely be a reminder to you about what to do.

The most important rule is 'Keep calm'.

Check it out

- Find out where the first aid kit is at work. Is it easy to find?
- Who is responsible for ensuring the kit is full and in a good state?
- Do the contents match the list above? Is anything missing? Are there any extra items, and if so what are they for?
- What is the procedure following an accident to a child in your setting?

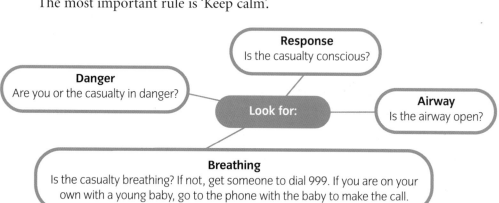

Response
Is the casualty conscious?

Danger
Are you or the casualty in danger?

Look for:

Airway
Is the airway open?

Breathing
Is the casualty breathing? If not, get someone to dial 999. If you are on your own with a young baby, go to the phone with the baby to make the call.

- *Assessing a casualty. Act on your findings and call for help.*

Casualty conscious, breathing present

- Treat any injuries (see below).
- Reassure casualty and keep warm.
- Call for help if needed.

- *Reassurance is especially important for children.*

- *If you are on your own with a young baby, go to the phone with the baby to make the call.*

Casualty unconscious, breathing present

- Treat any life-threatening injuries (e.g. bleeding – see below).
- Place the casualty in the recovery position.
- Call for help.

Recovery position

For babies less than a year old, hold them in your arms, with the head tilted downwards to prevent them from choking on their tongue or inhaling vomit. Keep checking for breathing and call for help. Again, take the baby with you if you need to go into another room or the telephone.

An unconscious child or adult who is breathing but has no other life-threatening conditions should be placed in the recovery position:

- Turn child on to side.
- Lift chin forwards in open-airway position (see below) and adjust hand under the cheek as necessary.
- Check the child cannot roll forwards or backwards.
- Check breathing and pulse continuously.

If you suspect an injury to the back or neck, place your hands on either side of the casualty's face. With your fingertips gently lift the jaw to open the airway. Take care not to tilt the casualty's neck.

● *The recovery position.*

Casualty unconscious and not breathing

Open the airway and call for help if any is available. It may be necessary to give rescue breaths.

Opening the airway

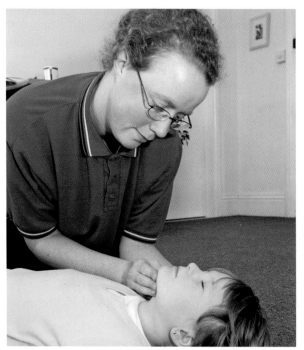

- Open airway by tilting the head backwards, remove any obvious obstructions in the mouth and lift chin upwards and forwards.
- Look, listen and feel for breathing.
- Keep the chin held up and put in the recovery position
- Call for help.

Opening the airway is the single most important first aid action for anyone who is unconscious, adult or child. It is a simple action that can and does save lives.

Rescue breaths

If the child is still unconscious and not breathing but has a pulse (felt for between

● *Opening the airway.*

the windpipe and large neck muscles) you need to start giving rescue breaths to get oxygen circulating around the body. The technique for this is different for different ages of children.

Baby less than one year old

- Make sure the airway is open.
- Seal your lips around the baby's mouth and nose.
- Blow gently into the lungs, looking along the chest as you breathe. Fill your cheeks with air and only use this amount with each breath.
- As the chest rises, stop blowing and allow it to fall.
- Repeat once more, then check for the baby's pulse. If the pulse is still present, continue rescue breaths for one minute then dial 999. If the pulse is absent, start chest compressions.
- Check for circulation after every 20 breaths.
- If the baby or child is small enough, carry him or her to the telephone and call for an ambulance. If you have to leave the child to call for an ambulance, follow the resuscitation sequence again on your return.
- If the baby or child is still unconscious, not breathing but has a pulse, continue to give the rescue breaths until help arrives.
- Check for circulation every 20 breaths.

- Rescue breaths being given to a child aged one to seven years.

Child aged one to seven years

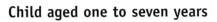

- Make sure the airway is open.
- Pinch the child's nose and seal your lips around the child's mouth.
- Blow gently into the lungs, looking along the chest as you breathe. Take shallow breaths and do not empty your lungs completely.
- As the chest rises, stop blowing and allow it to fall.
- Repeat once more then check for a pulse. If the pulse is still present, continue rescue breaths for one minute, then dial 999. If the pulse is absent, start chest compressions.
- Check for circulation after every 20 breaths.

If breathing starts, place the child in the recovery position.

Child over the age of eight years

- Make sure the airway is open.
- Pinch nose firmly closed.
- Take a deep breath and seal your lips around the casualty's mouth.
- Blow into the mouth until the chest rises.
- Remove your mouth and allow the chest to fall.
- Repeat once more then check for a pulse. If the pulse is absent, start chest compressions.
- Check for a pulse after every 10 breaths.

If breathing starts, place the child in the recovery position.

Casualty unconscious, not breathing and has no circulation

If the child is still unconscious and not breathing and there is no pulse, you need to start giving chest compressions as well as rescue breaths. Again, the technique for this is different for different ages of children and can cause broken ribs, so should be used as a last resort.

Chest compressions

Baby (less than one year old)

- Give chest compressions together with rescue breaths for one minute
- If the baby or child is small enough, carry him or her to the telephone and call for an ambulance. If you have to leave the child to call an ambulance, follow the resuscitation sequence again on your return.
- If the baby or child is still unconscious, not breathing and has no circulation, continue to give chest compressions and rescue breaths until help arrives.
- Place the baby on a firm surface
- Locate a position, one finger's width below the nipple line, in the middle of the chest.
- Using two fingers, press down sharply to a third of the depth of the chest.
- Press five times, at a rate of 100 compressions per minute.
- After five compressions, give one rescue breath.
- Continue resuscitation (five compressions to one rescue breath) without stopping until help arrives.
- Only check for the pulse if the baby's colour improves.
- If the pulse starts, stop the chest compressions but continue rescue breaths if necessary.

If breathing starts, place the child in the recovery position.

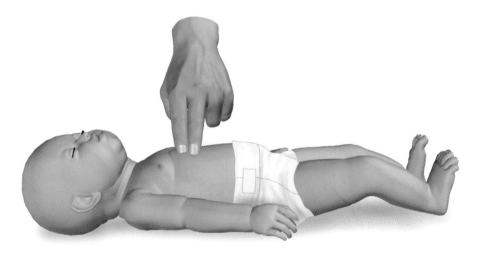

- *Chest compressions being given to a baby.*

Child from one to eight years of age

- Place one hand two fingers' width above the junction of the rib margin and breastbone.
- Use the heel of that hand with arms straight and press down to a third of the depth of the chest.
- Press five times, at a rate of 100 compressions per minute.
- After five compressions, give one rescue breath.
- Continue resuscitation (five compressions to one rescue breath) without stopping until help arrives.
- Only check for a pulse if the child's colour improves.

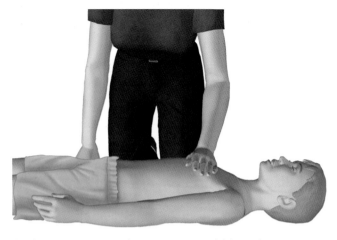

● *Chest compressions being given to a child aged one to eight years.*

If the pulse restarts, stop the chest compressions but continue with rescue breaths if needed. If breathing starts, place the child in the recovery position.

Child or young person over age of eight years

- Place heel of your hand two fingers' width above the junction of the casualty's rib margin and breastbone.
- Place other hand on top and interlock fingers. Keeping your arms straight and your fingers off the chest, press down by 4–5 cm; then release the pressure, keeping your hands in place.
- Repeat the compressions 15 times, aiming at a rate of 100 per minute.
- Give two rescue breaths.
- Continue resuscitation, with 15 compressions to every 2 rescue breaths.
- Check for circulation only if the casualty's colour improves.

If the pulse restarts, stop the chest compressions but continue with the rescue breaths if needed. If breathing starts, place the child in the recovery position.

Bleeding

The first and most important thing is to control the bleeding:
- **Elevate** the wound.
- **Press** on it (over clean material, if at hand).
- Apply a **dressing**.
- If there is a **foreign body** in the wound, leave it and press around the wound to stop the bleeding. Do not try to remove it, as this may make the wound worse.
- Treat for **shock**, reassure and keep warm. Lay the casualty down, lower the head, raise the feet and loosen tight clothing.

In addition, there are some general steps to take:

- **Reassure** the child and encourage him or her to relax.
- **Do not** move the child unnecessarily.
- **Do not** give food or drink.
- Help to keep the child **warm** by covering the child with a blanket or coat.

If the case is serious, or there is doubt, call an ambulance.

Other actions to take in the event of an accident

In the case of an accident, in addition to helping the casualty, you or someone else needs to:

- send for a qualified first aider if you are not qualified yourself
- call for your supervisor
- calm the other children
- inform the child's parents
- record the incident in the accident book.

Table 302.4 shows some other common emergencies that may affect children in your care, and how to deal with them. This is not a substitute for attending a first aid course.

Table 302.4 Some common emergencies

Emergency	Action
Anaphylactic shock (this is a severe reaction to stings, medicines or irritants and is evident as red blotchy skin, swelling of face and neck, and problems with breathing)	Dial 999 for an ambulance immediately. Put into comfortable position or recovery position if unconscious. Monitor airway, breathing and pulse.
Electric shock	Switch off at the power supply or move child from power source with a wooden pole. *Do not* approach until the child is clear of the power supply. Check for breathing and pulse and give cardiopulmonary resuscitation if needed. Call for help.
Burns and scalds	Cool the burn with cold water for at least ten minutes. Remove any clothing that is *not* stuck to the burn. Cover with a sterile or clean dressing or even a clean plastic bag. Call an ambulance or take to hospital for any burn or scald on a young child.
Suspected fractures or sprains	Support the affected limb with a sling if an arm or padding. If the legs are injured, keep child still, pad around leg if possible. Take to hospital or call an ambulance.
Head injury	Control any bleeding by applying pressure with a pad. Lay casualty down. Take or send to hospital. Monitor level of consciousness, vomiting, etc.

continued on next page

continued from previous page

Emergency	Action
Neck or back injury (always suspect this after a fall from swing, slide, tree, etc.)	Do not move or attempt to move. Steady and support neck and head. Dial 999 for an ambulance.
Poisoning (from ingestion of drugs, plants, etc.)	Dial 999 for an ambulance. Try to find out what has been taken and keep the evidence. If the casualty is unconscious, check airway and put in the recovery position.
Bites and stings	If the stinger is in the wound, do not attempt to remove it, and seek medical help (you may force more poison into the child). For other stings or bites keep the child calm and monitor condition for signs of reactions, and take to hospital or call an ambulance. For animal bites, wash the bite area and seek medical help (animal bites carry a high risk of infection).
Effects of extreme heat (very flushed, may be sweating or if advanced skin very dry, rapid pulse)	Get the casualty into the shade, give sips of water, sponge or spray gently with water. Call for immediate help.
Effects of extreme cold (shivering, unreasonable, disorientated, very pale)	In an early years setting cold injury is most likely to be caused by being wet, in which case remove the wet clothing and in all cases wrap in blankets, or add extra clothing layers. Call for immediate help.
Convulsions (often the result of a high temperature in a child)	If the child is hot, help to cool by removing clothing. Protect from injury by clearing surrounding objects, for example. Sponge with tepid water. Place in recovery position. Dial 999 for an ambulance.
Foreign bodies in the eyes	Try to remove carefully with corner of a clean cloth or wash out with water. If this does not work or the foreign body is stuck, cover the eye with a pad and take the casualty to hospital.
Foreign bodies in the nose or ears	Take the child to the local hospital. Do not attempt to remove the foreign body, or ask the child to blow the nose, as this will only send the object in deeper.
Choking in young children (the child may go very quiet and blue around lips, or there may be very noisy breathing and coughing)	Lean an older child forward or put a baby over your knee face downwards, and give five back slaps between shoulders. Remove any obvious obstruction from mouth. Next, give five chest thrusts: stand behind the child, make a fist against lower breast bone, grasp with other hand, and press sharply into chest (for a baby, press two fingertips on lower half of breast bone). Check airway, breathing and circulation (ABC). Dial 999 for an ambulance.

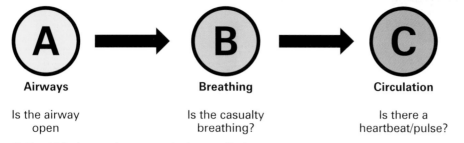

Airways

Is the airway
open

Breathing

Is the casualty
breathing?

Circulation

Is there a
heartbeat/pulse?

● *The ABC of assessing a casualty in a medical emergency.*

Acute medical crises

Occasionally a child may arrive at your setting apparently well and happy and later in the day give cause for serious concern, perhaps even as a result of a life-threatening illness. Obviously, if a child is unwell parents are contacted so that they can take the child home and to the family doctor if needed. But it is nonetheless important to recognise when a child is seriously ill so that rapid action can be taken if needed.

There are many illnesses that give rise to a need for immediate action but the most common is meningitis. There are several strains of meningitis and the immunisation programme offers protection from some of them. However, if you suspect a child may have meningitis do not wait and wonder about immunisation: get medical help immediately.

The common signs and symptoms of meningitis and septicaemia are shown in the diagrams below. In babies and toddlers they are:
- high temperature, fever, possibly with cold hands and feet
- vomiting, or refusing feeds
- high-pitched moaning, whimpering cry
- blank, staring expression
- pale, blotchy complexion
- baby may be floppy, may dislike being handled, be fretful
- difficult to wake or lethargic.

Others can include rapid breathing, diarrhoea, stomach cramps and a rash that does not fade under pressure. In babies, check whether the soft spot (fontanelle) on the top of the head is tense or bulging.

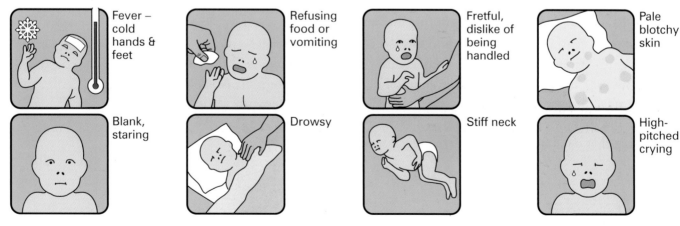

● *The signs of meningitis and meningococcal septicaemia in babies and toddlers. (Source: Meningitis Trust.)*

In older children (and adults) they are:

- high temperature, fever, possibly with cold hands and feet
- vomiting, sometimes diarrhoea
- severe headache
- neck stiffness (unable to touch the chin to the chest)
- joint or muscle pains, sometimes stomach cramps with septicaemia
- dislike of bright lights
- drowsiness
- fits
- confusion or disorientation.

Symptoms may develop slowly, but the person can become ill very quickly. Symptoms do not appear in any order and some may not appear at all.

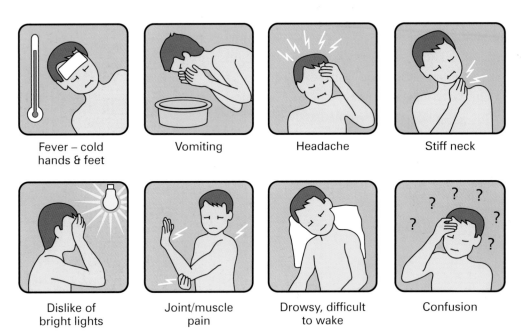

| Fever – cold hands & feet | Vomiting | Headache | Stiff neck |
| Dislike of bright lights | Joint/muscle pain | Drowsy, difficult to wake | Confusion |

- *The signs of meningitis and meningococcal septicaemia in older children (and adults). (Source: Meningitis Trust.)*

Both adults and children may have a rash. One sign of meningococcal septicaemia is a rash that does not fade under pressure (the 'glass test'). The rash is caused by blood leaking into the tissues under the skin. It starts as tiny pinpricks anywhere on the body. It can spread quickly to look like fresh bruises. The rash is more difficult to see on darker skin. Look on the paler areas of the skin and under the eyelids. If someone is ill or obviously getting worse, do not wait for a rash. It may appear late or not at all. A fever with a rash that does not fade under pressure is a medical emergency.

● *The glass test: a rash that does not fade under pressure will still be visible when the side of a clear glass is pressed firmly against the skin.*

Ambulances

When dialling 999, always have ready the details of the accident and injury, the age of the child and of course where the injured child is. In serious incidents involving breathing difficulties or severe bleeding, an ambulance should be summoned as soon as possible – preferably while first aid is being given.

Emergency help for children with chronic medical conditions

Asthma attack or breathing difficulties

If children experience an asthma attack or breathing difficulties while they are in your care, you should make them comfortable (let them sit in the position most comfortable for them) away from other children in a quiet area. Let them use their inhaler if they have one (usually this will be a blue reliever).

Using an inhaler

Most settings have children who require the use of an inhaler for asthma treatment. You should be shown how to support a child who uses an inhaler, and need to be confident that you know how to use the type of inhaler the child is using. Settings will vary in their policies on the storage and use of inhalers. A nurse from the GP's surgery that the child attends may be happy to come and talk to staff if needed.

A child old enough to use an asthma inhaler is old enough to keep it on his or her person, or close at hand. Some settings insist on inhalers being locked away to prevent other children having access to them, although Ventolin, the drug typically used in inhalers, has little or no effect on someone without asthma.

Keys to good practice: A child who has an asthma attack

✓ Stay with the child all the time.

✓ Keep the area around the child clear of other children.

✓ Remain calm and reassuring.

✓ Encourage the child to sit up to increase lung capacity.

✓ Try to find out what triggered the attack (an infection, exercise, stress, emotion, weather, allergens?).

✓ Encourage the child to breathe slowly.

✓ If the attack does not subside, call for medical help.

Active knowledge

Find out about the different types of inhaler used by children at your setting. Your local health clinic should have leaflets describing them. What is your workplace's policy on the storage and use of inhalers?

Epilepsy

Epilepsy has a range of signs and symptoms, ranging from 'absence' attacks to a full-blown fit or convulsion. Many children have some sort of warning that they are about to have a fit, for example by hearing or smelling certain things. A child who is having a fit needs to kept safe from harm and will require reassurance afterwards. The other children present need to be reassured that their friend will be alright. Occasionally a child does not recover immediately from a fit, and starts to have further attacks. If this happens you should ring for an ambulance immediately, as further treatment will be needed at the hospital.

Sickle cell disease

Sickle cell disease is an inherited condition of the red blood cells. People with the condition have 'crises' when the sickle-shaped red blood cells clump together and lodge in organs or joints and cause severe pain. If you have a child in your setting with sickle cell disease, do make sure you know what the routine is in case of a crisis. The parents will tell you and you may well have a supply of the child's pain killers in case of need. Keeping the child warm and reassured, as well as giving the pain killers, is all you can do until the parents and/or medical help arrives.

Diabetes

You should have all the information about how to treat a child with diabetes if he or she has an attack. Diabetes is caused by the failure of the body to produce enough insulin to deal with the sugar and carbohydrates in a normal diet. Diabetic children usually need daily injections of insulin to 'use' the sugars properly. If they have been more active than usual, or are not well, they may have a hypoglycaemic attack. This is caused by a very low blood sugar level, similar to the way you might feel if you have not eaten all day and been very busy. During a 'hypo', the child may look pale and be sweating, feeling faint and disorientated. The child needs sugar – fast! A glass of milk and some biscuits should be enough to restore the balance providing the child is conscious. If not you may have further treatment and instructions from the parents; make sure you know what they are. If in doubt call for an ambulance and get help.

Common childhood illnesses and allergies

You should always make sure that you follow the routines that help to protect children from illness, such as careful hand washing and cleanliness of toilet areas.

Parents may ask for advice about their children when they are ill or appear unwell. Always suggest they take their child to the doctor, as doctors prefer to see a child, even if for a minor illness, rather than miss a serious illness such as meningitis.

When a child is taken ill in your care, the parents or guardians must be informed. You can provide support to a child who is ill while his or her parents are coming by sitting quietly with the child, perhaps reading a story.

Often after an illness a child may need to take medicine while at nursery or school. Most settings have a policy that parents must give written consent for their child to have medicines administered by the nursery nurse or teacher. Early years workers are not allowed to give medicines to children without this written permission under any circumstances.

Table 302.5 summarises the treatment or action needed in many of the common childhood illnesses.

Table 302.5. Common childhood illnesses

Illness	Signs and symptoms needed	Treatment or action	Incubation
Common cold	Sneezing, sore throat, runny nose, headache, temperature, irritability	Rest, fluids Encourage child to blow nose to avoid catarrh	1–3 days

continued on next page

continued from previous page

Illness	Signs and symptoms needed	Treatment or action	Incubation
Gastroenteritis	Vomiting, diarrhoea, dehydration, which in extreme cases can lead to death	Replace fluids using glucose and salt solution such as Rehydrat. Medical help should be summoned	1–36 hours
Tonsillitis	Very sore throat, difficulty in swallowing, fever, headache, aches and pains	Rest, fluids, medical attention as antibiotics may be needed if the cause is bacterial	Varies
Scarlet fever	Fever, loss of appetite, sore throat, pale around mouth, 'strawberry tongue', bright pinpoint rash over face and body	Rest, fluids and observe for complications	2–4 days
Dysentery	Vomiting, diarrhoea with blood and mucus, abdominal pain, fever, headache	Medical attention, rest, fluids. Strict hygiene measures, especially in early years settings	1–7 days
Chickenpox	Fever, very itchy rash, with blister-like appearance	Tepid bath containing bicarbonate of soda and calamine lotion applied to skin to stop itching. Try to stop child scratching to avoid scarring	10–14 days
Measles	High fever, runny nose and eyes; later a cough, white spots in mouth, blotchy rash on body and face	Rest, fluids, tepid sponging. Medical attention to check for complications	7–15 days
Mumps	Pain and swelling of jaw, painful swallowing, fever	Fluids (may need a straw to drink through), warmth to swelling, pain relief	14–21 days
Rubella (German measles)	Slight cold, sore throat, swollen glands behind ears, slight pink rash	Rest, treat symptoms. Avoid contact with pregnant women	14–21 days
Pertussis (whooping cough)	Snuffly cold, spasmodic cough with whoop sound, vomiting	Medical attention. Rest, fluids, feed after a coughing attack	7–21 days

When is a child infectious?

In nearly all illnesses children are at their most infectious before the symptoms appear. Many illnesses have a cold and/or fever as their first signs. It would not be practicable to exclude all children with these symptoms from the setting, nor would it have much effect on the spread of a disease. Different settings have different rules about excluding children with common illnesses, ranging from excluding all children with symptoms, to their exclusion only while they feel unwell.

Keys to good practice: Childhood illnesses

✓ Make sure that you are familiar with the common signs of illness.

✓ Keep up to date with what infectious diseases are around in your area at any time. Make sure you know what to look for and any special precautions.

✓ Make sure that you are up to date with your own immunisations, especially polio, rubella, mumps and meningitis.

Emergency procedures in your setting

As part of the Health and Safety at Work Act 1974 and the associated regulations, your setting – if it employs five or more staff – will have a safety policy. The policy will cover emergency procedures in the event of a fire, accident or other emergency. There are many different types of emergency and it is important to know what the different procedures are especially for fires, security incidents or if a child goes missing.

Evacuation procedures

There are many reasons why a building may need to be evacuated (e.g. in the event of a fire, a gas leak, a bomb scare). All adults need to know what to do. In most settings, one member of staff is responsible for these procedures and will need to make sure that all staff are aware of the evacuation procedures. Practices need to be held regularly and signs and notices must be kept in place. Drills and practices should always be taken seriously so that any difficulties can be reviewed.

In case of fire

- Close doors and windows and try to get the children out of the premises by normal routes.
- Do not leave the children unattended.
- Do not stop to put out the fire (unless it is very small).

Check it out

Find out what the emergency procedure is at your setting.
- How is the alarm raised?
- Who contacts the emergency services?
- Who takes out the registers and checks them?
- What are the safest exit points?
- Where is the assembly point?
- How often is there an emergency practice?
- How are visitors to the setting made aware of evacuation procedures?
- How are children reassured during evacuation practices?
- Are there regulations and notices on view?

Call the fire brigade by telephone as soon as possible as follows: lift the receiver and dial '999'; give the operator your telephone number and ask for 'Fire'; when the brigade replies give the information clearly (e.g. 'Fire at the First Start Nursery, 126 Beach Drive, Blackpool AB2 6PY, situated between the clock tower and the promenade'). Do not replace the receiver until the address has been repeated by the fire operator.

Keys to good practice: Fire practice

✓ Have a fire drill every three months

✓ If there are problems with the procedures repeat the drill or seek advice from a fire officer.

✓ Reassure children during a practice by staying calm and explaining what is happening.

✓ Praise children and thank them for their help in carrying out the evacuation.

✓ Provide an absorbing activity such as reading a story or playing a game to help the children settle down quickly.

Missing children

A child should never go missing from a care or education setting if all procedures are followed. A small child should not be able to open gates or doors, and any adult going through them should follow all precautions to ensure they are properly closed and locked. Strict procedures about the collection of children by parents or carers should be followed. On outings, making sure that the right ratio of adults to children is observed should be a safeguard. However, if a child does go missing alarms should be raised immediately and the setting's procedures followed.

- Make sure all the other children are safe (i.e. with responsible adults).
- Make sure any external exits are secure.
- Inform the person in charge.
- Start a systematic search, based on where the child was last seen, and with whom, and make sure all areas are covered.
- Inform the child's parents.
- Inform the local police.

● *Fire safety is of paramount importance.*

As you have seen, ensuring the safety of children in your care is an essential part of your role. Have a look at the statements below to assess whether you match up to the levels of care needed. The statements all refer to the performance criteria for CCLD 302.3.

Performance criteria statement	Always	Sometimes	Never
Do I make sure that accidents, injuries and signs of illness and other emergencies are promptly identified, recorded and reported?			
Do I follow correct procedures to deal with accidents/injuries and other emergencies?			
Do I make sure that I and others are not put at risk and provide reassurance to those involved?			
Do I make sure that first aid and medication are provided according to the correct procedures?			

End-of-unit knowledge check

1. Name three regulations that cover health and safety in children's settings.
2. How does the risk of injuries from falls change from birth to age 15 years?
3. List six routine daily checks you should make of the indoor and outdoor environments in your setting.
4. Identify two ways in which you can make sure children are secure in your setting.
5. What are the key requirements before you can administer medicines to children in your care?
6. Give three examples of how you might assess the risk of particular activities, taking the children's age into account.
7. Why is it important to record accidents and incidents?
8. List six items from a first aid kit.
9. What should you do in the case of an accident *before* you start to give first aid?
10. What should you do immediately with a cut that is bleeding heavily?
11. In what position would you put an unconscious person?
12. What is the main difference between the chest compressions for a baby and those for an older child?
13. What should you *not* do with a foreign body in a child's nose or ear?
14. List three key signs of meningitis in a child.

Reference

Child Accident Prevention Trust (2003) *Accidents and Child Development.* Child Accident Prevention Trust.

Promote children's development

Working with children is not just about keeping them safe and happy: children need to be with people who can help them develop and fulfil their potential. This is particularly important in children's early years, as the early part of childhood is linked to enormous growth and development of the brain. Stimulating and supporting children are therefore essential. This means that adults working with children need to have a good understanding of how children learn, grow and develop.

What you must know and understand:

- Observing and assessing children (K3M202–208)
- Aspects of children's development (K3D209)
- Patterns of children's development (K3D215, 217–221)
- Areas and theories of child development (K3D210, K3D212, K3D213)
- The principles of promoting and supporting children's development (K3D214, K3D215, K3D216, K3T1111)

Observing and assessing children

Why observing children is important

You can learn a lot about the children you work with simply by stepping back and watching them. This may at first seem to be a waste of time, but if you study the children you are working with, you are more likely to be able to meet their needs. There are many ways in which observations can help you to work more effectively with children. The diagram overleaf shows some of the most common ways.

Ways in which observations can be used

To report to other professionals
There are times when other professionals may need to gain information about how a child behaves or copes in our setting. We may also help other professionals by informing them about a child's progress, for example feeding back to a speech therapist about how a child's language is developing.

To report to parents
Observations can help us report more accurately to parents about their child. We may be able to reassure them as a result of an observation or indicate any areas of difficulty.

To see if children are progressing
Regular assessments of children will help us to see if children are making progress with specific areas of their development.

To check a child's overall development
Carrying out an overall observation of children's development may make us more aware of any areas in which they are not developing as quickly as might be expected. It may also help us to get an overall feel of a child's needs.

To inform planning
Observing children's developmental skills, such as their ability to use scissors, will help us to plan activities that will meet children's needs. This means that we will avoid giving them a task that is too difficult for them to manage. Having an accurate and up-to-date view of a child will also mean that we can plan activities that will encourage areas of development at the child's level.

To learn more about a child's particular needs
Observing individual children can give us the information to help is plan a particular approach to working with them.

To evaluate activities, routines or strategies used with children
We can observe a group of children's reactions and behaviour to evaluate whether our routines, strategies or activities are effective. We may be able to determine from the observation how to make changes to the way we work, plan or handle situations in order to meet the children's needs.

To resolve a particular problem
Observing a child more closely may guide us towards understanding a particular type of behaviour or reaction, for example a child who finds it difficult to play with one other child.

Confidentiality and observations

Most parents are happy for their children to be observed, although they probably will not want other parents or people who have no involvement with their child reading the reports. You therefore need to store observations carefully and make sure that you protect children's identity. This can be done in many ways; for example, some settings always refer to the subject as 'child A', or refer to a child by his or her first name only, while changing names that are unusually spelt or are uncommon. Children's ages are generally given in terms of years and months.

The test of whether you have protected a child's identity will be whether someone else who is familiar with the setting can work out the identity from any details you have recorded.

How to store observations will depend on the setting in which you work. Some settings place observations and assessments of children in their files, whereas in a home setting it is normal to give them to the parent.

Check it out

Find out how records about children are kept in your setting.

Who is able to access them?

Types of assessment

Formative assessment

Many of the observation and assessment methods that you use to record children's **development** will be ongoing. This type of assessment is known as formative. It means that while you may become aware of children's strengths and areas of need and will plan for them, you are still carrying on observing the children.

Key terms

Development means children's gaining of skills and competence.

Summative assessment

From time to time, you may need to collate what you have found out about children. You may, for example, compile a report so that parents can read about their child's progress. Putting together information about the child in this way is known as summative assessment. Summative assessments are often used when information is passed from one professional to another. Educational psychologists may draw up a report based on what they have observed and learnt about a child. Summative assessments are also used in education. Not only might parents receive a report about their child but the teachers may also be involved in filling in a 'profile' or 'baseline' report, as for example in England, where at the end of a child's reception year teachers fill in the Foundation Stage profile.

Planning an observation

It is important that you plan your observation carefully before starting to record. Careful planning is more likely to result in a successful observation.

Before carrying out any type of recording, you must always seek permission from your supervisor or, where appropriate, the parents. Most settings will have their own procedures and policies relating to observing children. It is not uncommon for some settings to ask parents for permission to carry out observations as part of their admissions procedure. Generally, most parents are happy for their children to be observed, provided that they are able to have access to the records.

Checking with the appropriate people beforehand will reduce the chances of other adults in the setting distracting or calling for the child because they do not know that you are carrying out an observation.

Methods of recording

There are several methods of observing and recording children's behaviour and performance. Each has its advantages and disadvantages, and most early years workers find they need to be familiar with several. This allows them to match the recording method to the situation they are observing. Table 303.1 shows some frequently used recording methods. Guidance on how to use each method is given below.

Table 303.1 Common methods of recording observations

Method	Uses
Free description (also known as narrative description and written record)	To record the behaviour of a child over a very short period of time, often less than five minutes. The observer notes down what he or she is seeing, which gives a portrait of a child's activity during this time.
Checklists and tick charts	Mostly used to assess children's stages of development. This is one of the methods used by health visitors during routine check-ups. Specific activities are looked for, either during a structured assessment (i.e. where children are asked to do activities) or by observing children over a period of time.
Time sample	Used to look at children's activity over a predetermined length of time, for example a morning. Children are observed at regular intervals during the recording, say every ten minutes, and the observation is recorded on a prepared sheet.
Event sample	Often used to look closely at one aspect of a child's development or behaviour, such as how frequently the child sucks their thumb, or shows aggression towards other children. Every time a child shows the type of behaviour or activity, it is recorded on a prepared sheet.
Target child	Used to record one child's activity over a long period without any gaps in the recording process. Several codes or signs are used during the observation to allow the observer to maintain the recording. A prepared sheet is used to help the observer.

Open versus closed methods of recording

Some methods of observing children provide more information than others. Methods that give you plenty of information are sometimes referred to as 'open' methods. While they may look the most attractive to use, it is important to note that they are the most subjective. This is because when observers are presented with so much information at once, they have to make conscious and subconscious decisions as to what they notice and record. This means that they 'miss' actions or expressions.

For more objectivity, closed methods are useful. They make the observer's focus clearer. A checklist is an example of a closed method of recording. A checklist on physical development might focus the observer on whether the child uses the left or right hand to hold a pencil; the disadvantage of such a method is that the observer may not notice whether or not the child is smiling at the time.

Matching your recording method to your purpose

With several methods available for use when observing children, it is important to make sure that you choose one that suits your purpose. For example, the free description method is good for examining closely how a

Check it out

How are parents involved in the assessment of children at your setting? Are parents encouraged to contribute and to provide their perspective?

child achieves something, but it will not tell you about a child's general activity over a longer period.

For an observation to be successful, you must carefully consider what you are hoping to achieve. This is normally referred to as the 'aim' of an observation. This is considered in more detail under 'Carrying out an observation' below (page 89).

● *Before conducting an observation you will have to decide whether to be a participant or non-participant observer, and what recording method you are going to use. What decisions were made in the scenario pictured?*

Types of observer

When they know they are being observed, most people find that their performance changes. In some situations being observed means that people try harder, whereas in other situations it makes them nervous and their performance deteriorates. The same is true for children. This means that you must decide, when planning an observation, whether you are going to observe children without their being aware of your presence or of what you are doing, or whether you are going to talk and be part of the recording. The term 'non-participant observer' is used when the observer is unobtrusive and does not interact with the children. The term 'participant observer' is used when the observer interacts with the child.

Advantages of being a non-participant observer

- Children are more likely to show 'natural' behaviour.
- It is easier to record what happens when you are not actively involved.
- The recording is more likely to be objective.
- Most recording methods can be used by a non-participant observer.

Disadvantages of being a non-participant observer

- It can be difficult to find a place where you are unobtrusive while still able to hear what is said.
- You may not see the particular types of activities or behaviour you are interested in.
- It may take a long time to collect all the information about a child's development if they are not asked to do certain activities.

Advantages of being a participant observer

- You can ask children to carry out tasks or activities rather than waiting for them to happen spontaneously – this is useful with a checklist on development.
- You can ask children why they are doing something; for example, if you observe a child working out a simple mathematical problem, you can ask the child what they are doing and why.

Disadvantages of being a participant observer

- Children may feel under pressure because someone is looking at them.
- Children may reply to a question in a different way because they are hoping to please the adult.
- Not all recording methods are compatible with being a participant observer, especially methods where a free description of events is required.
- If an unfamiliar person carries out an observation, the child may feel uncomfortable.

 Keys to good practice: Planning an observation

✓ Make sure that you have permission to carry out an observation.

✓ Make sure that other workers in the setting know who you are hoping to observe and when you plan to do it.

✓ Decide what you need to observe and have a clear aim.

✓ Choose your method and consider whether you will need to be a participant or a non-participant observer.

Carrying out an observation

Free description

The aim of free description is to provide a portrait of what a child is doing. This method is useful if you need to observe a situation closely, such as the difficulty a child has in doing up a coat.

Equipment

- Notepad.
- Pen.

Method

Free descriptions are generally written in the present tense, in the form of a running commentary. The idea is to provide the reader with a detailed description of the activity and the way in which the child carries it out. This means that you should include details of the child's facial expressions, body posture and any speech. In essence, you should try to note down as much as you possibly can about what you are seeing.

Carrying out a free description is an intensive process and this means that most people can record only for short periods.

Some practitioners find it helpful to keep a notepad or something similar with them when they are working with children. Instead of formally spending time on observing children, they simply jot the odd note down together with the time and date when they see something of interest. 'Jack noticed Melissa did not have any dough and gave her some of his'. This idea is useful when time for observing children is limited.

Example of a free description

Ravi is standing up in front of Michaela, who is sitting on a chair. Ravi seems to be looking down at Michaela. She is saying, 'Shall we dress up?' Michaela nods and smiles. Ravi smiles too and they both walk over to the dressing-up corner. Ravi takes a pink dress, grasping it in her right hand, and places it on the floor. She pulls the back of the dress open with both hands. She steps into the dress using her right foot first and pulls up the dress gradually to a standing position, placing her right arm into the dress and then her left. Ravi walks over to the nursery nurse and looks up. She asks, 'Can you do my buttons up?' and turns around.

Checklists and tickcharts

Checklists and tickcharts are quick and easy to use. They are mostly used to record large areas of children's development. They do not usually record how a child achieves a task, simply whether or not he or she is doing it competently.

Equipment

- Prepared sheet – some settings have their own formats, although it is possible to devise your own checklist.
- Pen.

Method

You can fill in a checklist or tickchart by being a participant observer and asking children to do activities and tasks, or you can note down when children are showing the skills during a session. It is important to use a checklist that is appropriate for the ages and stages of the children you are working with. A good checklist will also have space for comments.

The main disadvantage of checklists and tickcharts is that the observer must make a decision as to how competent a child is. This can mean that there is a danger of bias if observers have a strong interest in a child.

Case study 1: Checklist observation

Simon had planned a series of activities to help Sarah, aged four years, learn to count five objects. At the end of the series he thought he should carry out an observation to see if her skills had improved. On one task, Sarah had miscounted the number of objects. Simon was disappointed because he had previously seen Sarah count up to five in other situations. On his checklist he put a tick in the 'Yes' column, indicating that Sarah had mastered counting up to five, as he felt sure she was able to in most situations.

1. *Why did Simon act as he did?*
2. *Why it is sometimes better for staff who are not involved with particular children to carry out assessments?*

Child _____

Child's age_____ Observer_____

Date of observation _____ Time _____

Activity	Yes	No	Comments
Puts together three-piece puzzle			
Snips with scissors			
Paints in circular movements			
Holds crayons with fingers, not fist			
Can thread four large beads			
Turns pages in a book one by one			
Can put on and take off coat			

● *An example of part of a checklist designed to look at a three-year-old's fine manipulative skills.*

Time sample

The aim of a time sample is to observe children at evenly spaced intervals during a session or other predetermined length of time.

Equipment

- Prepared sheet with times when a recording is due to take place.
- Pen.
- Watch or stopwatch.

Method

The spaces between recordings will depend on the duration of the observation. For example, if you wish to observe a child over three hours, you might decide to record activity every 15 minutes, whereas if you were to record a child's activity over one hour, you might decide to observe every 10 minutes.

To carry out the observation, you should look to see what the child is doing and record a 'snapshot' of this, in much the same way as a free description. Recordings should indicate what the child is doing and are often written in the present tense.

The disadvantage of time samples is that a significant behaviour might be shown between recording intervals.

Pre-coded time samples

Time sampling can be structured further, for the recording of specific activities. Such 'pre-coded' time samples can help observers to become more focused and so increase objectivity.

Event sample

An event sample records the frequency of the behaviours or activities of interest. It may provide clues as to why a child is behaving or reacting in certain ways. It may also show that a perceived problem, perhaps a child being aggressive, is not as acute as was thought.

Event samples are normally carried out as non-participant observations, to make sure that an objective account is given.

Equipment

- Prepared sheet.
- Pen.

Method

The sheet you use for recording will vary according to the purpose of the observation. For example, if you wish to record the frequency with which a baby cries over a day, it is important to have a column to show what soothes the baby as well as a column to record how long the crying lasted.

Carrying out the observation is relatively straightforward, although if you wish to record a particular behaviour or activity over a longer period, such as a week, you may need to ask colleagues or parents to fill in parts of the sheet for you when you are unavailable.

Below is an example of a prepared sheet which has been used to look at the interaction of Jo with other children over a day.

Event	Time	Activity of child	Social group	Language used	Comments
1	10.03 am	Playing in the sand	Jo, Jacob, Martha and Curran	'Look a me! Look at this, what I've done'	Jo leaned-over and said this to Jacob
2	10.07 am	Playing with digger in sand tray	Jo, Jacob, Martha	'Brrrmmm, Brrrmm, this is my road, out of the way'	Jo was talking to Martha while pushing her toys out of the way

It is important to design your event sample sheet to capture the information you think will be useful. The event sample below was designed to look at how much food a toddler was eating during a day because of concerns that they were not eating enough. Notice how the columns for recording information have been changed from the previous example.

Event	Time	Food eaten	Quality of food	Setting	Comments
1	8.04 – 8.09 am	Squares of toast, drink of milk	Equivalent to half a slice of toast and half a beaker of milk	High chair, kitchen	Some squares of toast were dropped on the floor. Joachim sipped milk after eating toast and dropped beaker on the floor. Said 'No more, all gone' and raised arms to be taken out of chair.
2	9.45 – 9.47 am	Biscuit	Most of biscuit	Lounge, standing up	Joachim went up to adult and pointed to her biscuit. Adult gave the biscuit
3	10.15 – 10.20 am	Biscuit	half a biscuit	Kitchen, standing up	Joachim pointed to biscuit tin and said "More, more' Adult gave biscuit. Some biscuit eaten, rest dropped on floor.

Target child – a pre-coded observation

This type of observation records the activity of one child during a session or other predetermined length of time. The aim is to focus on one child. To help the observer keep up with tracking the child, a code has to be used to reduce the number of words that need to be written. This type of observation requires practice and familiarity with the coding system. Target child observations are normally non-participant observations.

Equipment

- Prepared sheet.
- Pen.

Method

Many settings have their own methods and codes for carrying out target child observations. If your setting does not have a format, you will need to draw up your own sheet and devise your own codes. It is impossible in this type of observation to provide the detail that can be gained from other observations, such as free description or time samples. This means that the observer must make some choices about what to observe and about what is important during the observation.

Individual child-tracking observation

Name of child Lee   Observer Carrie   Date 24/06/05

Age of child   3 yrs   2 months   No. of adults present 2   No. of adults present 6

Free play/structured play/directed activity

Time	Description of activity	Language	Grouping	Level of involvement
10.00 am	TC scooping sand using left hand repeated movements	TC →	P	4
10.02	TC burying r. hand, scooping with other	→ TC ←	I	4
10.03	TC nods head. Other child copies TC, TC smiles	C → TC	P	3

Key

Grouping	Language		Level of involvement
WG = Whole group	TC → A	Balanced ineraction between adult and child	1 = No activity
SG = Small group	TC → C	Balanced interaction between target child and another child	2 = frequently distracted
P = Pair	A → C	Adult interacts with more than one child	3 = Fairly continuous activity
I = Individual	C → TC	Another child interacts with target child	4 = Absorbed in activity
	→ TC ←	Target child talks to himself/herself	
	TC →	No interaction	

● *Example of the recording of a target child observation.*

Objectivity and accuracy in observations

It can be hard to remain objective when observing. Recording methods such as free description rely on noting down as much as possible, but often so much is happening that some choices have to be made by the observer about what is relevant and important. Two people recording the same activity may produce different observations – for example, one person may decide that a smile is important and record it, while another person may decide otherwise.

In order to gain accurate information, it is a good idea to carry out several observations of a child using different methods. This will allow you to build up a picture of development and should ensure that you are not misled by a single observation. It is also helpful to consider whether some observations should be carried out by colleagues who do not know the child very well, in order to gain an objective view. The single most important thing to remember when recording is to concentrate on what you are seeing, not what you think you know about the child.

Avoiding premature conclusions

All children are different, and while it is useful to be aware of children's progress, interests, strengths and areas of need, it is also essential that you keep an open mind. There is a concern that, in identifying a child's needs, that child will be labelled. Labelling is to be avoided, as adult expectations can affect children's later success (see page 189).

One way in which you can help to avoid labelling children is to remember that children will learn, grow and develop at slightly different rates. Their interests, areas of need and strengths will also change and develop during their childhood. It is therefore important not to base your conclusions on one-off observations. Ideally, you need to look at children over a period of time and when they are engaged in a range of different activities. It is also essential to draw on parents' knowledge.

Involving parents in the assessment of their children

Beyond simply gaining their permission for observations to take place, try to involve parents in the assessment of their children. Children are likely to behave in different ways according to the environment they are in. A child at home may engage in different activities from those at pre-school (e.g. doing jigsaws at home but playing in the sand tray at pre-school as this is not available at home). Parents also see a different side of their children at home. Some children are quite talkative or independent at home but quieter or more demanding elsewhere. Encouraging parents to share their knowledge about their children can help you to gain an all-round picture of children's development. This will help you to avoid drawing inaccurate conclusions from your own observations and assessments.

Parents also need to know what you are seeing when you observe their children. If you have concerns, these need to be talked over with parents. Not only is this good practice, but in England and Wales it is also a requirement of their SEN Codes of Practice.

Case study 2: Parental involvement in assessment

Frankie is four years old. She lives with her parents in a small flat. She has a three-year-old brother and one-year-old twin sisters. Staff at the playgroup have been a little concerned because she is very quiet and spends a lot of time playing alone. She notices the other children, but prefers to sit and play with small-world people, especially in the dolls' house. She does not seem unhappy and looks quite contented. She occasionally enjoys spending time with an adult, especially in the book corner. When Frankie's mum comes in, a member of staff mentions that Frankie seems fairly quiet. Frankie's mum is surprised. She says that at home Frankie spends a lot of her time playing with her brothers and sisters and is actually fairly noisy. She also spends a lot of time in an adventure playground with her older cousins.

1. *Why do you think Frankie plays differently at the playgroup?*
2. *Why is it important to share information with parents?*
3. *Explain the dangers of basing an assessment only on what children do in a particular setting.*

Reflect on your own practice

Have a look at the statements below to assess your formal observation of children. The statements all refer to the performance criteria for CCLD 303.2.

Performance criteria statement	Always	Sometimes	Never
Do I undertake formative and summative assessments?			
Do I make sure that my assessments are based on observational findings and other reliable information?			
Do I use information from colleagues, families, children and other appropriate adults, and avoid hearsay?			
Do I maintain confidentiality in relation to observational records?			

continued on next page

continued from previous page

Do I share my findings with children and family members, as appropriate?

Do I reflect upon my assessments of children's development?

Do I identify implications of my assessments for practice?

Aspects of child development

Influences on how children develop

What makes children so different even when they are the same age? This is an important question and one that has not yet been fully answered. We do know, however, that children's development is shaped both by what they are born with and by the experiences they have. This means that while a child may be born with the potential to be a great artist, this potential is unlikely to be realised unless the child has the chance to paint and draw and is encouraged by adults.

● *What makes children so different, even when they are the same age?*

Influences before and at birth

Children's development actually starts from the moment they are conceived. Genetic information is packaged together from the egg and the sperm. The child's hair, for example, will be decided genetically, as will, to an extent, the child's height (although this will also be affected by the child's later environment and diet). This process at conception is not always perfect. Sometimes genetic information is faulty in some way and will affect the child's health or development.

As well as the genetic information that is put together at the moment of conception, babies' development can be affected during pregnancy. The baby can be harmed if the mother smokes or takes drugs or alcohol at this time. Infections that the mother picks up, such as rubella, can create difficulties for the developing baby.

Children's development can also be influenced by when they are born and what happens during the birth. A few babies are born too early and this can play a part in their later development. This is one reason why premature babies' progress is measured according to the date they were due rather than their actual birth date.

Birth itself can be tricky for a few babies. A baby may not breathe straight away or may be injured during the birth. Lack of oxygen (anoxia) can affect brain function and can result in learning difficulties.

Influences after birth

Once children are born, there are several major factors that can influence their development.

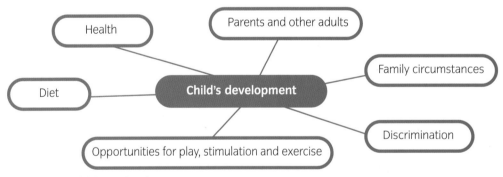

● Key influences on children's development.

Health

Health is determined both by genetic make-up and by factors such as diet, environment and stress. In some cases children are born with a condition that will automatically affect them, such as a blood disorder. Other children may have a predisposition towards certain diseases and do not develop them unless certain circumstances trigger them. A good example of this is asthma, a condition that affects breathing and is currently on the increase.

Children who live in areas where the air quality is poor, who live in damp conditions or whose parents smoke are more likely to develop asthma.

Ill health can affect many aspects of children's development. They may not feel like playing or their condition may restrict what they can do. Children may find it harder to make friends because they miss sessions or cannot physically join in. As a practitioner, you should look for ways to ensure that children with a medical condition miss out on as little as possible.

Education
Some children may miss out on their education because of long stays in hospital or because they are not well enough to attend school. Children may also miss days because of medical appointments.

Friendships
Repeated absence can prevent young children from getting to know each other. Friendship in the early years is linked to 'availability'.

Development

Self-esteem
Children who are repeatedly ill can have low self-esteem and self-confidence. They may not see themselves as autonomous, because, for some aspects of their lives, they may depend heavily on adults (e.g. dressing, feeding or having injections). Self-esteem is now seen as so important that many doctors encourage children to take some control over their medical condition. Diabetic children, for example, are often encouraged to inject themselves.

Taking up opportunities
Depending on the medical condition, some children may not be able to take part in all the activities that are being offered. For example, running outdoors might trigger a child's condition, or a child might not have the energy to join in.

● *How health may affect children's development.*

Parents and other adults

Children's development is influenced by the adults who care for them. Parents in particular are extremely important in children's lives and this is why policies in early years settings are designed to work in partnership with them. Most parents do a very good job at nurturing and providing for their children, but for a number of reasons some parents are not able to cope so well. This can affect the way their children develop. Depression, drug-taking and alcoholism are examples of conditions that might mean that parents cannot fulfil their parenting role easily. While parents may neglect babies and younger children, older children may find themselves taking on a caring role within the family. It is not unknown for children as young as five to dress and feed younger siblings.

Adults other than parents can also have an influence on children's development. This includes other family members, friends and those who work with children. The latter in particular have a great deal of responsibility to ensure that their practice will help children to develop.

Family circumstances

Most families suffer stress from time to time (e.g. as a result of a family member becoming ill or unemployed or because of the need to move house). While some stresses are temporary, others are more permanent, such as coping with a long-term illness or disability. In some cases, a family may separate as one parent leaves, or a lone parent may settle with a new partner. These types of stresses on families can affect children's development, although sometimes the effects prove to be temporary.

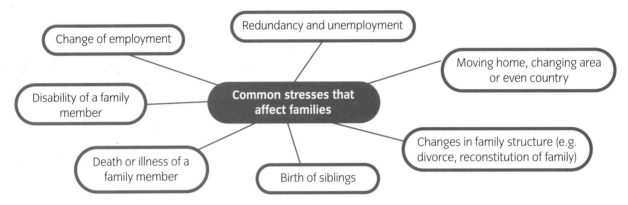

Discrimination

In an ideal world, all children would have the same start in life and be nurtured and cherished in the same way. Sadly, some children and their families face discrimination. The effects of discrimination are difficult to measure, but statistically certain groups of children are likely to fare less well than others. Children may be discriminated against on the grounds of their:

- poverty (considered in Unit 305)
- ethnicity, religion and culture
- disability.

While a family's ethnic origin, culture and religion can be interrelated, they can also be separate reasons for discrimination. A black family who go to church and who live in a Christian area may be discriminated against because of their race rather than their religion. Discrimination may range from direct comments to children made by adults or other children, such as 'Why don't you go back home?', through to more hidden ways of simply making children feel that they do not quite fit in (a child whose family does not celebrate Christmas might be told to wait alone outside while a Nativity rehearsal is taking place). A more insidious form of discrimination is when adults lower their expectations of what they think children can achieve and fail to provide them with the same opportunities for learning and development as other children.

Children may also be discriminated against because they are disabled or have special educational needs. These children may not feel that they are valued and so lose confidence. They may find that other people have low expectations of them and that they are not given the opportunity to acquire new skills or try out new activities, as it is assumed that they will not be able to cope. Families who have children who are disabled or have particular needs may also be in poverty, as parents can find it hard to gain employment that is flexible enough to allow them to care for their children.

Children can find themselves being discriminated against for other reasons, too. Their family's lifestyle might be different to other people's. Children of travellers, for example, face discrimination not only because their education is disrupted but more importantly because teachers, children and other parents find it hard to accept their families. Not feeling valued and being given the message that 'You do not belong' can affect children's attitude to learning and, of course, their self-esteem.

In the same way, families may be discriminated against because of sexual orientation. Two men bringing up a family could find that other parents will not let their children go round for tea. Subtle messages about being accepted do affect children's confidence and subsequent learning.

Did you know?

During the first year of a baby's life, the brain triples in weight.

Opportunities for play, stimulation and exercise

Play is fundamental to children's health, growth, development and overall well-being. Children's brains are stimulated when they play, especially when they have varied and interesting opportunities. Stimulation of the brain is vital for its growth. For most children good play should provide them with both stimulation and exercise. It should also provide them with the opportunity to be in and out of doors. Interestingly, we are beginning to rediscover the importance of encouraging children to have time outside. The outdoor environment gives children better opportunities to use their gross and locomotive skills. It also gives plenty of stimulation, as the outdoor world is inherently sensory.

Children who are deprived of play, stimulation and exercise are likely to have delayed development. In some rare cases, where children have been grossly neglected early on in their childhood, the privation of stimulation has resulted in some more permanent developmental difficulties.

● *It is increasingly being recognised that outdoor play is important to children's development. Think of the variety of sensory stimulation that might be available to the child pictured.*

Diet

Children's growth, behaviour and development can be affected by their diet. A balanced diet will help children to remain healthy as well as to grow. Awareness is growing of the importance of children's diets. This is because the number of children who are overweight has been steadily rising. Children who are overweight may not develop strength in their bodies or high levels of physical skill. They may also be prone to ill health. They may lose confidence and not want to try out new activities as they get older. They may also be teased or discriminated against.

Some children lack sufficient nutrients in their diet. This can affect their concentration and behaviour.

Check it out

Statistics from the British Heart Foundation show that a quarter of children aged two to five years are either overweight or obese.

Observation

Think of one thing that you are good at doing. (It can be anything, from playing darts through to being a good friend.)

- What or who has helped you to be good at this?
- Do you think that you were born with this ability or have you learnt it?

Importance of play

In past times, play was seen as a trivial pursuit that babies and children indulged in. Our understanding of play is now far greater and it is generally recognised as being essential in helping children to grow and develop. This understanding of play is the reason why the Foundation Stage and other early years curricula emphasise the importance of providing play environments and activities that will encourage children to learn through play.

Play and physical development

Play is a great motivator for babies and children. Children enjoy running around, chasing, crawling and climbing as part of their play, and in so doing will be building up muscles, stamina and physical skills. In the same way, children playing with blocks, jigsaws and rolling out dough will be increasing their hand–eye coordination as well as their fine manipulative skills.

Play and cognitive development

Children learn about their immediate environment through play. Babies, for example, often drop objects from their high chairs in a playful way to see what happens. Older children make up games and learn about rules – and making rules – from playing them. Play of all kinds appears to stimulate the brain and expose it to new sensations. This in turn helps children to formulate ideas or schemas about what is happening.

Play and language development

Play often allows children to practise speech and **communication**. A toddler may talk seriously to a teddy or doll, while older children may practise their speech and communication skills on each other, quite often in role play.

Play and social and emotional development

Play is one of the media through which socialisation takes place. Babies gain a sense of security as well as enjoyment through simple games such as peek-a-boo and from being hugged in a playful way. Older children are able to play alongside other children and, from this play, to learn about relationships. Role play helps children to explore feelings and the dynamics of different relationships.

Keys to good practice: Supporting children's play

✓ Make sure that children have sufficient time to enjoy their play.

✓ Avoid constantly intervening and directing children.

✓ Provide materials that are stimulating and attractive.

✓ Make sure that a range of play opportunities is available.

✓ Look out for equipment and materials that are versatile.

✓ Encourage children to make choices and to take responsibility for their play.

✓ Make sure that equipment is appropriate to the children's age and stage of development.

✓ Avoid making assumptions about the way in which children may wish to play.

Patterns of children's development

While all children are unique and special in their own ways, it is helpful for practitioners to have some feel of what children are likely to be able to do at different ages. Children do follow a **pattern of development**. Knowing what you can expect to see at different ages will help you to support children's development and to identify those children who may need additional support, either within your setting or from other professionals.

Expected development can only be a guide

It is extremely important that you understand that the pictures of child development in the following pages are only a guide. There are variations between children of the same age, starting within the first few weeks of life.

While one baby may smile at six weeks, another may take a little longer. Some toddlers are ready for toilet training at 18 months, but many others are not ready until they are three years old. In the broad stages of 'normative child development' outlined below, 'milestones' are used to mark out what an 'average' might be.

As children get older, the variations between children tend to be greater, not only in academic skills such as reading and mathematics but also in terms of emotional maturity. This makes it harder to draw up a 'picture' of development. Also, the way in which the different areas of development are interconnected means that if a child is having difficulty in one area, this is likely to impact significantly on other areas.

Did you know?

Only 3% of babies arrive exactly on time.

Babies at birth

Most babies are born around the 40th week of pregnancy. Babies who are born more than three weeks early are described as premature. Premature babies are likely to need a little more time to reach the same levels of development as a baby who is born at around 40 weeks. Many people think that babies are helpless, but they are born with the ability to do quite a few things: they can recognise their mother's voice and smell; they are able to cry to let everyone know when they need help; they are also actively learning about their new world through their senses, particularly touch, taste and hearing.

What newborn babies need:

- A calm and relaxed environment
- Plenty of cuddles, talk and eye contact
- Gentle handling and bathing
- Opportunities to get to know their primary carers, usually their mothers
- Frequent feeds of milk
- Time to sleep

What you might observe in newborn babies

Reflexes:

Babies are born with many reflexes, which are actions that they perform without thinking. Many reflexes are linked to survival. Examples of reflexes include:

- *Swallowing and sucking reflexes*. These ensure that the baby can feed and swallow milk.
- *Rooting reflex*. The baby will move its head to look for a nipple or teat if its cheek or mouth is touched. This helps the baby to find milk.
- *Grasp reflex*. Babies will automatically put their fingers around an object that has touched the palm of their hand.

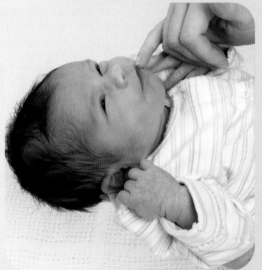
● *Rooting reflex.*

- *Startle reflex*. When babies hear a sudden sound or see a sudden bright light, they will react by moving their arms outwards and clenching their fists.
- *Walking and standing reflex*. When babies are held upright with their feet on a firm surface, they usually make stepping movements.
- *Falling reflex*. This is known as the Moro reflex. Babies will stretch out their arms suddenly and then clasp them inwards in any situations in which they feel that they are falling.

Close contact between mother and baby, especially when feeding:

● *Startle reflex.*

● *Walking and standing reflex.*

Babies and their primary carers, usually their mothers, begin to develop a close bond from very early on. Babies sometimes stare at their mothers, and mothers are very aware of their babies.

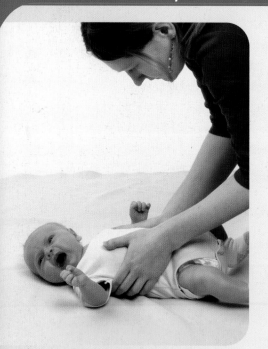

In just one month, babies have changed already. They may appear less curled up and more relaxed. Babies at one month have usually started to settle into a pattern. They sleep quite a lot of the time, but will gradually start to spend longer periods awake. They cry to communicate their needs, and their parents may be starting to understand the different types of cries. Babies are also learning about their parents or carers: they may stop crying when they hear their soothing voices; they also try hard to focus on the face of whoever is holding them (they can focus at a distance of 20–25 cm).

What you might observe in babies at one month

- Babies stop crying because they hear a familiar voice.
- Babies stop crying as they are picked up but start crying when they are put down.
- Babies start to relax at bath time or when their nappies are changed.
- Fleeting smiles when asleep (smiles of contentment begin from five or six weeks).
- Babies coo when contented (from around five or six weeks).

- *Babies stop crying as they are picked up but start crying when they are put down.*

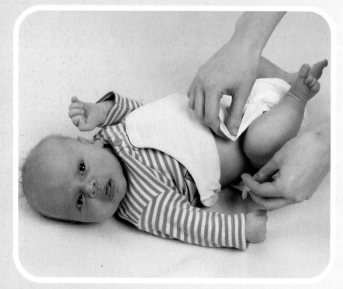

- *Babies start to relax at bath time or when their nappies are changed.*

- *Fleeting smiles when asleep.*

What babies of one month need:

- Plenty of cuddles and physical contact
- Opportunities to sleep
- Frequent feeds of milk, day and night
- Eye contact, smiles and gentle handling
- Opportunities to lie flat and kick without a nappy
- Their head supported when they are picked up or being carried
- Safe physical care, including nappy changing and skin care

Babies at three months

Babies at three months have grown in height and weight. They have grown out of their early clothes and have changed in many ways. Some babies have learnt the difference between day and night and are able to sleep through the night. They are likely to cry less and most parents are getting better at knowing what their cries mean. They are also starting to sleep a little less and are far more alert. They may smile quite often and show that they know the sound of their parents' voices and movements. Babies' bodies are also developing. They are able to lift their head up and look about when they are put on their tummies.

What you might observe in babies at three months

- Babies smile back when they see a smiling face.
- Excitement when it is time to be fed.
- Interest in playing with fingers.
- Enjoyment of bath time.
- Babies lift and turn their heads.
- Babies start to notice mobiles and other objects around them.

● *Babies smile back when they see a smiling face.*

● *Interest in playing with fingers.*

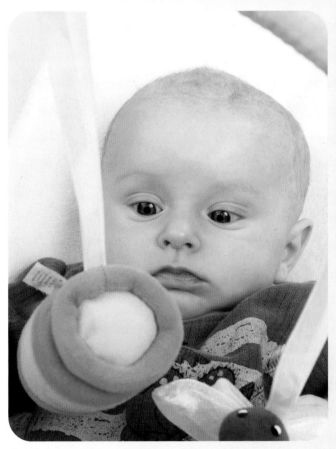

● *Babies start to notice mobiles.*

What babies at three months need:

- Opportunities to be cuddled and to watch others
- Rattles to hold and mobiles to look at
- Their head supported when they are carried
- Regular milk feeds
- Gentle handling
- Safe physical care, including nappy changing and skin care

• *Pushing themselves up with their hands.*

Babies at six months have learnt many skills. They are very alert and turn their heads to see what is happening. They enjoy playing and show it by smiling and squealing with delight. They can now reach out and grab a toy and move it from one hand to another. They are able to focus in on an object and explore it if it seems interesting. Babies also start to show that they understand a little of what is being said to them, and they try to communicate.

They usually enjoy their food and are beginning to try to feed themselves by grabbing a spoon (this can be quite messy). Many babies will also be getting their first teeth, which can be painful for them.

They are also getting stronger. They can sit up with support in a high chair and are able to roll over from their backs to their fronts. They can push themselves up with their hands if they lie on their fronts and can hold this position for a little while. They also sometimes look as if they are parachuting as they lift both their hands and feet up in the air and balance on their fronts. These movements help them to get ready for crawling later on.

Babies at six months have usually settled into a routine and will have periods in the day when they nap and others when they are keen to play and to be held.

What you might observe in babies at six months

• Smiles of delight when they are playing with their primary carers.
• Enjoyment when simple games such as pat-a-cake are repeated.
• Arms lifting up to show a carer that they want to be picked up.
• Curiosity and looking to see what is happening around them.
• Toys and objects being explored in the mouth as well as with fingers.
• Babbling, laughing and squealing.
• Different cries according to whether the baby is tired, bored or hungry.

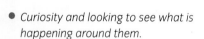

• *Curiosity and looking to see what is happening around them.*

What babies at six months need:

• Plenty of physical contact, talk and eye contact
• Times when they can lie on their stomachs and backs
• Opportunities to play simple games and look at books with adults
• Chances to explore toys and objects
• Time to sleep
• A range of foods that are soft and have been mashed as well as milk
• Good, safe physical care, including nappy changing, bathing and skin care
• A safe environment so that they cannot fall, swallow small objects or hurt themselves

• *Toys and objects being explored in the mouth as well as with fingers.*

Babies at nine months

Babies' physical development is now very noticeable. Many babies will be crawling or finding other ways of being mobile. They are also able to sit up without any support. These new movements mean that babies can explore more. They also spend a lot of time sitting and playing. When they are mobile they can move quite fast, and this is a period in which adults need to think carefully about safety. As well as large movements, babies are also picking up objects, handling them and becoming more skilled at touching things. Objects still get popped into the mouth and so, again, adults need to be very aware of what is around.

Babies' language is also coming along. Babbling has become more tuneful and longer strings of sounds are put together. Babies are also learning what some key words mean. They may start to get excited when they hear words such as 'drink' or 'dinner'. Babies are also starting to show who they enjoy being with. From around eight months, they start to cry when they are left with a stranger and actively try to be with their parents or main carers.

Babies are also likely to have made a cognitive leap in their development. This is sometimes referred to as object permanence. At around eight or nine months most babies will understand that objects and people do not disappear but continue to exist when they are out of sight. This is an important breakthrough and is one explanation why babies at around this time begin to protest when their familiar carer leaves the room. You can test object permanence by playing with a toy with the baby and then hiding it while the baby watches. Younger babies will carry on playing with something else, while babies at around nine months will 'find' the hidden toy.

What babies at nine months need:

- The same carer if they are not being looked after by their parents
- Physical contact and cuddles
- Finger rhymes and songs
- A range of toys such as push-and-pulls, stacking beakers and balls
- Opportunities to play simple games with an adult, including peek-a-boo
- A diet rich in nutrients, including milk feeds
- Opportunities to feed themselves
- Good, safe physical care, including nappy changing, bathing and skin care
- A safe environment so that they cannot fall, swallow small objects or hurt themselves
- Good adult supervision as they play

What you might observe in babies of nine months

- Trying to stay near their parent or carer.
- Protest when a parent or carer leaves the room.
- Tuneful strings of babbling.
- Using fingers to feed.
- Exploring objects using hands and mouth.
- Passing objects from one hand to another.
- Reaching over to pick up an object.
- Crawling or rolling.
- Sitting up without any support.
- Looking for objects that adults 'hide'.

Sitting without support.

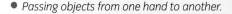

Passing objects from one hand to another.

Crawling or rolling.

The first birthday of a child is for many families a special event and a cause for celebration. This in part dates back to times when not all babies survived their first year. Babies have come a long way and are now mobile and may be on the verge of walking. They may try to stand up by holding onto furniture and some babies are already walking by holding onto things. Good adult supervision is essential. Babies are now able to crawl very quickly and have eyesight that is just as developed as that of adults. This means that if they spot something that they want, they will quickly make a move to get it.

As well as having mobility, babies are also becoming quite skilled at using their hands. Objects are touched, moved and organised. They enjoy putting things into containers and taking them out again or dropping things and looking to see what happens to them. A strong feature of their play is the way in which they enjoy doing something over and over again. They may keep taking their hat off or pulling off their socks.

At one year, babies are able to sit up and feed themselves using their fingers. Most also know what they do and do not like. Food that they enjoy is eaten, while other foods may be thrown on the floor.

● *Repetitive play as they enjoy doing something over and over again.*

Babies also know who are their parents and main carers. They cry when they are left with someone they do not know and smile when they recognise their parents. They are also keen to stay near their parents and carers and will stop playing to see what they are doing.

Babies are able to understand more of what is happening around them. They not only notice what other people are doing but also understand more and more of what is being said. Long strings of babbling are still the way in which babies try to communicate, but hidden in the babbling are the beginnings of first words. These are usually noticed by parents and carers from around 13 months.

What you might observe in babies of one year
- Standing up and holding onto furniture.
- Waving bye-bye.
- Fingers pointing at objects to draw an adult's attention to them.
- Tuneful babbling that sounds like talking.
- Small objects being picked up and handled.
- Repetitive play as they enjoy doing something over and over again.
- Recognising the routines of the day (e.g. becoming excited when they hear the bath water or have a bib put on).
- Able to feed themselves with their fingers.

● *Feed themselves with their fingers.*

What babies at one year need
- Babies at one year need much the same things as at nine months (see the list on page 109).

● *Waving bye-bye.*

Children at 18 months

The word 'toddler' is used for children who have begun to walk. It is a delightful term, as the child does walk with a side-to-side movement. At 18 months children have literally begun to find their feet. They start to move quickly and enjoy the freedom that this gives them. They are also keen to play with adults and are often fascinated by other children. They notice what older brothers and sisters are doing as well as children of their own age.

Around this age toddlers start to want some independence. They have learnt that they are separate from their parents and start to become their own people. They cry and protest if they want something and do not get it. They can be quite persistent and this can be a cause of accidents. A child who wants to hold a cup of tea will, for example, notice where it has been put and may try to climb up to reach it.

Children's language skills are also still developing. Most children will be able to use several words and will understand a lot of what adults are saying. This does not mean, however, that they can understand the need to share, wait and be cooperative. Many parents say that at this age their children start to develop minds of their own.

Toddlers can also be quite restless and change moods quickly. This can be tiring for parents and carers. Toddlers also become distressed when they are left with unfamiliar people, and need a familiar adult if not with their parents or carers.

What children of 18 months need:

- Good adult supervision as they play
- Safety equipment such as reins, harnesses and safety gates
- Physical contact and cuddles
- Finger rhymes and songs
- A range of toys, including toy telephones, sit-and-rides, simple puzzles
- Opportunities to climb and space for physical play such as rolling or kicking a ball
- Opportunities to feed themselves
- Safe physical care, including nappy changing, bathing and skin care
- A safe environment so that they cannot fall, swallow small objects or hurt themselves

What you might observe in children of 18 months

- Walking up and downstairs with adult help.
- Less babbling and more recognisable words.
- Signs of temper and frustration.
- Eagerness for independence (e.g. trying to feed themselves with a spoon).
- Enjoyment of pop-up and posting toys.
- Sitting and pushing off with legs on sit-and-ride toys.
- Determination to try things by themselves.
- Interest in other children.
- Awareness of where their parents are and what they are doing.

● *Walking up and downstairs with adult help.*

● *Signs of temper and frustration.*

● *Enjoyment of pop-up and posting toys.*

By two years old, children are very much showing their individuality. They know what they want to do, touch and hold. They can now move confidently and are enjoying walking and being able to pick up things and play with them. They like to do things for themselves and are keen to do more and get frustrated when they are not able to. This is sometimes because adults realise that what they want is dangerous and at other times because their skill does not match what they want to do. Their frustration can lead to temper tantrums and emotional outbursts. This is often a way of communicating how they are feeling and is why this period is sometimes known as the 'terrible twos'.

While toddlers do get frustrated and angry, they are also emotional in other ways. They smile, laugh and squeal with enjoyment. They notice other children and enjoy being near them, even though they may not actively play together. Favourite games are played over and over again. Children are also starting to enjoy pretend play. They may take an empty cup and pretend to drink from it or give a teddy a hug. Two-year-olds are often starting to chat aloud and to point out objects and name them.

Some two-year-olds are starting to be ready to move out of nappies (although some children are not physically ready until they are three).

Did you know?

Two-year-olds are likely to have a vocabulary of around 200 words.

● *Enjoyment of singing and dancing to music.*

● *Running.*

What you might observe in children of two years

- Enjoyment of singing and dancing to music.
- Pointing to pictures of familiar objects and naming them.
- Anger and frustration if they cannot do what they want to do.
- Delight and happiness when they are enjoying something.
- Keen to show things to adults.
- Playing on sit-and-ride toys.
- Running and climbing.
- Playing with building bricks and doing simple jigsaw puzzles.

What children of two years need:

- Good supervision and safety equipment
- Time to explore and play with safe objects
- Opportunities for physical play, such as slides, swings and balls
- Toys that encourage role play, such as teddies, pushchairs and dressing-up clothes
- Time for cuddles and sharing of books, songs and rhymes
- A good range of toys that build different skills
- Adults who can support and play alongside them
- Adults who can anticipate their needs and potential frustrations

● *Playing on sit-and-ride toys.*

Children at two and a half

Children at two and a half years are still keen to be independent. They may find it hard to wait and to understand why they cannot always have what they see or do want they want. Their language is really starting to develop. Some are putting two words together to express their ideas and others are even starting to use sentences. Good supervision is still needed, as children's developing physical skills combined with their determination can mean that they go to extremes to get hold of an object. Moving chairs to climb up or standing on tables to reach up high is fairly common.

Children are also starting to play more with other children of their own age, although some of their time will be spent simply playing alongside others. Pretend play and play with small-world toys become popular, as do tricycles, slides and climbing frames. They are still keen to have plenty of adult attention and will enjoy snuggling up for a cuddle as well as spending time helping an adult.

Separating from parents remains difficult unless children really know who they will be with. This is often the period in which toilet training starts in earnest, and, if children are ready, they can be out of nappies within a few days.

What you might observe in children aged two and a half years

- Pretend play with farm animals, teddies or in the home corner.
- Playing alongside other children and copying their actions.
- Two-word compounds such as 'daddy-gone' or 'drink-no'.
- Temper tantrums if they are frustrated.
- Pedalling a tricycle or pushing it along with the feet.
- Turning pages in books and pointing out objects.

What children of two and a half years need:

- Balanced diet with sufficient calories for increased energy
- Relaxed approach to toilet training
- Time to choose activities and to play with others
- Opportunities to explore materials such as sand, water and dough
- Familiar carers if children are not with their parents
- Opportunities to develop independent skills such as pouring out drinks
- A range of toys and equipment, including outdoor play, small-world toys, home corner as well as sand, dough and paint
- Adults who play alongside children and play simple games
- Nursery rhymes, songs and sharing books
- Excellent supervision and safety equipment

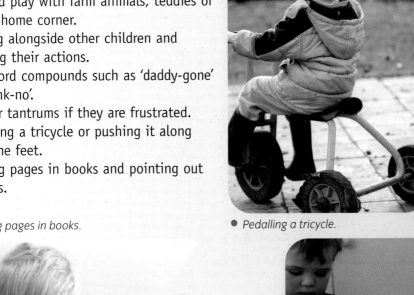

● *Pedalling a tricycle.*

● *Turning pages in books.*

● *Playing alongside other children.*

Most children at three years old are making a huge developmental leap. This is linked to their use of language: suddenly, instead of showing that they are not happy, they can say so, and temper tantrums start to decrease. Children begin to understand more about what is happening and to understand the needs of others. From this point onwards most children are able to play with other children, and sharing of toys and equipment becomes less difficult. Other children start to become important in their lives. In consequence they may look forward to going to pre-school or nursery each day. Children are also happier at being separated from their parents, as they can now understand that their parents will return; they are more able to talk to the staff looking after them.

● *Walking on stairs on alternate feet.*

● *Interest in other children and some cooperative play.*

What you might observe in children aged three years

- Able to use the toilet.
- Enjoy dressing up and playing with small-world toys.
- Keen to help and copy adults.
- Interest in other children and some cooperative play.
- Able to walk up stairs on alternate feet.
- Interested in mark-making, painting and books.
- Enjoyment of sand and water play.
- Speech that is easily understood.

What children of three years need:

- Opportunities to play with other children, under supervision
- Adults who encourage independence, but who also play with and cuddle children
- Opportunities to explore new play materials, objects and equipment
- Time to play repetitively with materials of their own choosing
- A wide range of different play activities and equipment
- Time to play outside as well as inside
- Opportunities to look at books, to draw and to paint
- Adults who act as good role models, as children copy their behaviour
- Praise and acknowledgement from adults
- A safe environment that encourages them to be independent

● *Playing with small-world toys.*

Children at four years

By four years old, most children have made huge steps forward in their development. They will be fairly fluent in their speech and should be easily understandable to adults who do not know them. There will still be the odd grammatical mistake and interesting pronunciation of a word, but by and large they will have mastered the spoken language. Most children's behaviour will be cooperative but this is dependent on their getting plenty of praise and recognition from adults.

Most four-year-olds also enjoy being with other children and will be starting to plan their play and have definite ideas of what they want to do. They are also learning to be independent. They can generally dress and feed themselves and can organise their play if they are given the opportunity. They enjoy being with responsive adults, especially when they are being given responsibility and encouragement.

Singing nursery rhymes.

Most children will be attending some pre-school provision, such as a playgroup, nursery or crèche. This is important for them as they generally enjoy the company of other children and are beginning to develop friendships. They will also be learning – often without realising it, as activities will be planned for them. Depending on where they live, many children during this year will be starting school. For some children, this is a difficult transition, as they have to adapt to being part of a much larger group.

Pretend play that models adult life.

What you might observe in children at four years

- Children are settled into the routine of the setting and are able to separate from their parents easily (if they have been in the setting for a while).
- Cooperative play between children along with the odd squabble and argument.
- Children responding well to adult praise and recognition.
- Children seeking out particular playmates.
- Children asking questions and enjoying talking.
- Speech and pretend play that model adult life.
- Children riding on tricycles, climbing and enjoying simple ball games.
- Drawings that have meaning for the child and are recognisable.
- Skilful use of the hands to do activities such as threading, pouring and using scissors.
- Concentration when an activity has caught their interest.
- Enjoyment of singing and knowledge of some nursery rhymes.

What children of four years need:

- Opportunities to play with other children
- Sensitive adult help and direction when appropriate
- Opportunities to explore new play materials, objects and equipment
- Time to relax and enjoy favourite activities
- A wide range of different play activities and equipment
- Time to play outside as well as inside
- Opportunities to look at books, draw and paint
- Practical activities that help children learn about numbers and their environment
- Adults who act as good role models, as children copy their behaviour
- Time when adults listen and chat to children
- Praise and acknowledgement from adults
- A safe environment that encourages children to be independent

Climbing.

In these years, changes in physical development are much less rapid. Instead, children gain in confidence and coordination. This is true also for other skills, such as their spoken language and ability to socialise. A good example of this is the way that, at around this time, children begin to enjoy hearing and making jokes.

At around five years, most children have begun in formal education. This can be a difficult transition period for some children, especially if they are not interested in learning to read and write. For children who are ready, learning to read and write can prove exciting and they may enjoy the intellectual challenge of a classroom. As well as school, some children will also be doing activities such as swimming, dance or music. The ways in which children play are also starting to change. Children of this age are keen to work out the rules of different situations and enjoy playing games with rules.

Friends are also important to children of this age. Many children will start to have established friendships and preferences. Staying for tea or even overnight is quite common and helps children to learn about other families, although of course children still rely on their parents to meet many of their emotional needs.

● *Enjoyment of jokes.*

● *Ability to kick and control a ball.*

● *Increased fine manipulative movements.*

What you might observe in children aged 5–6 years

- Enjoyment of jokes.
- Beginning to decode some familiar words.
- Keen to understand and use rules.
- Some friendship preferences.
- Ability to kick and control a ball.
- More legible handwriting and increased fine manipulative movements.

What children aged 5–6 years need:

- Adults who encourage independence and are sensitive to children's needs
- Opportunities to listen to stories and to share books
- A balanced diet and sufficient sleep
- Adults who are able to supervise and support play
- Activities outside school
- Boundaries that children can understand

Children at 7–9 years

Children's development in this period is more gradual than before. Children continue to grow in height, but the main changes are in the way they think and reason. This can be seen in the way they play: their games and play become more organised, and they make up as well as follow rules. The way in which children think and reason also shows itself as they start to be able to solve simple problems and enjoy practical situations in which they have to work things out for themselves. Most children are also cooperative and enjoy being given responsibility. They respond well when adults give clear explanations for rules and when their behaviour is acknowledged and praised.

In these years, reading and writing become easier, although there will be variations in the speed at which children become competent and confident in this respect. Children also become more physically skilled. This results in them being able to do things more quickly, confidently and accurately. Doing up a coat, for example, is now an easy task, as is cutting out with scissors or drawing a simple picture. Friendships are becoming increasingly important. Many children will have groups of close friends and some will have 'best friends'. The lack or temporary absence of a friend starts to become an issue. Children may want to attend a club only if they know a friend is also likely to be there.

As most children are at school, life in the classroom and playground is a major influence on them. This is also a period in which children start to compare themselves with others. In some ways this is part of the thinking process, as they carry on working out what they are like. They may notice which children are the fastest runners, best readers or quickest at finishing tasks. This can start to affect their confidence and even enthusiasm.

● *Turn-taking.*

● *Cooperative play.*

● *Reading a book silently to themselves.*

What you might observe in children aged 7–9

- Clear differences in the play activities that interest boys and girls.
- Cooperative play.
- Stable friendships.
- Verbal arguments, persuasion and negotiation.
- Telling jokes and enjoying chatting.
- Play that involves turn-taking.
- Enjoyment of playing and making up games with rules.
- An understanding of rules and consequences.
- Children who tell others the rules and are keen to point out when rules have been broken.
- Skilful, precise and confident hand movements.
- Reading books silently.
- Writing short stories, with less adult help required.
- Painting, drawing and making models independently.
- Enjoyment of stories, imaginative play and small-world play.

What children aged 7–9 years need:

- Opportunities to play with other children
- Toys and equipment that stimulate children's development
- Time to organise own play and games
- Adults who can support but not interfere in children's play
- Praise and acknowledgement that makes children feel special and nurtured
- Support and encouragement during tasks children find difficult
- Chances to be independent (e.g. staying overnight)
- Sensitive adults who can spend time listening to children

● *Detailed and representational pictures, which children enjoy drawing.*

In some ways this period in most children's lives can be summed up as the 'calm before the storm'. Most children are fairly confident and have mastered many skills, and they will often have decided what they are good at. They can now read, write, draw and use some logic. They are often skilled communicators and enjoy having friends. This is a time when many children feel quite settled, although from the age of nine onwards the first signs of impending puberty will show in girls. Breasts are likely to 'bud', and at around 10 or 11 years girls will begin to grow rapidly in height too. Some girls may even start menstruating before the age of 11 years, particularly where their weight to height ratio is high.

What you might observe in children aged 9–11 years

- Detailed and representational pictures, which children enjoy drawing.
- Stories and writing that show imagination as well as being legible and reasonably grammatical.
- Problem solving (e.g. how to play cooperatively, use materials fairly).
- Enthusiasm when given areas of responsibility.
- Greater coordination and speed when carrying out both fine and large movements.
- Stable friendships (usually same sex).
- Awareness of consequences of behaviour and increased thoughtfulness.

● *Greater coordination and speed when carrying out both fine and large movements.*

● *Stable relationships (usually same sex).*

What children aged 9–11 years need:

- Opportunities to try new activities and experiences and to develop new ideas
- Time to be with friends
- Opportunities to develop problem-solving and organisational skills
- Praise and encouragement from adults
- Adults who look for ways of encouraging independence
- A range of toys and equipment that will stimulate children, including books, drawing materials and construction toys
- Opportunities to make dens, hide-outs and engage in physical play
- Information about puberty

Young people at 11–13 years

● *Enjoyment when with their friends.*

This period in children's lives marks the start of their growing independence. While parents remain important, children begin to show signs of wanting to grow up. They may, for example, now ask to walk home or get buses home by themselves. Some children also begin to question rules at home and may try to push the boundaries. Young people's relationships with others of the same age become increasingly important. This can put a lot of pressure on children, as their friends may have very different ideas to their parents. This period also sees other pressures on them. They are likely to be changing to another school for the next stage in their education. Quite often the new school will be larger and the curriculum more formal. They may have a series of teachers during the day, rather than just one or two.

This period also marks physical changes for young people as their bodies begin to prepare for adulthood. Girls' puberty usually begins at around 11 years, while boys may not start until they are 13 or 14 years old. The physical changes can cause embarrassment and anxiety and so create further pressure. Girls who feel that they are developing too quickly or not quickly enough can lose self-esteem.

What you might observe in young people at 11–13 years

- Enjoyment when with their friends.
- Growth and changes to their bodies.
- Growing awareness of the roles of boys and girls.
- More confidence around the home and in familiar situations.
- Arguments with parents as young people start to become independent.
- Times when young people enjoy 'childish' activities (e.g. sitting on a swing, watching cartoons, playing games).
- Anxiety about coping with the pressures of school.

● *Times when young people enjoy 'childish' activities.*

● *Anxiety about coping with the pressure of school.*

What young people at 11–13 years need:

- Opportunities to take control and be given responsibility
- Clear boundaries that they can see the sense of and have helped to negotiate
- Adults who can listen carefully and are sensitive to young people's needs
- Praise and encouragement to support self-esteem
- Support in coping with the transition to new educational settings
- Understanding adults who can listen and help young people to cope with peer pressure and puberty
- Opportunities to relax and also to take exercise
- A balanced diet with sufficient protein and iron for growth
- Time in which to enjoy being a child again, rather than a young person

Young people aged 13–16 years

What young people at 13–16 years need:

- Adults who listen and are non-judgemental
- Adults who are aware of the difficulties that young people may face, such as bullying and peer pressure
- Opportunities to discuss boundaries
- Opportunities to take control and become independent
- Time to relax and enjoy being with friends
- Information about drugs, alcohol and sex and sexuality
- Balanced diet and opportunities to find out about healthy eating
- Opportunities to take exercise
- Information about careers and educational opportunities

In this period, young people move closer to adulthood. Physically, by around the age of 15 or 16, girls will have finished becoming women. For most boys, puberty will start around 14 and is likely to take around three years to complete.

Pressure in school is likely to increase as most young people are preparing for examinations and may be starting to think about their futures. During these years, some young people will begin to 'drop out' of education. They may show avoidance behaviours such as truanting, messing around in classes and bullying.

At around 16 years, young people will need to decide whether to leave education and find a job. Some will have developed skills that are equal to those of adults (e.g. ability to use computers or to draw).

Being with friends is likely to be more important than being with family. Young people who do not have a group of friends are likely to feel that they are missing out and may become anxious. Some may experience bullying if they are not part of a group. This can have a huge effect on their self-esteem and in extreme cases can result in suicide attempts, to draw attention to their unhappiness. For perpetrators, outcomes are not good either, as they may learn that this is a way of gaining respect from others.

This is a time when young people are also trying to explore their own identity. They may have tastes in music, clothes and activities that are different to those of their parents. This may cause clashes as young people try to develop their own personality and space. They may test the boundaries at home and even at school. As the transition to adulthood is not complete, young people will also at times revert to 'child-like' comments, activities and games.

While for some young people this period can be one of anxiety and conflict, for others it can be an enjoyable period as they spend time with friends and are able to dream a little about the future.

What you might observe in a young person aged 13–16 years

- Confidence and enjoyment when with friends.
- Thoughts and ideas that are different to those of their parents.
- Uncertainty about how to talk to unfamiliar adults.
- High level of skills (e.g. using computers).
- Enjoyment of 'child-like' activities.
- The need to experiment with identity and responsibility, e.g. through haircuts, piercings, untidy bedrooms and clothing.
- Examples of behaviour linked to high self-esteem (e.g. wanting to be responsible, caring for others, interested).
- Examples of behaviour linked to low self-esteem (e.g. smoking, misuse of substances, early promiscuity and really untidy bedrooms).

● *Thoughts and ideas that are different to those of their parents.*

● *Confidence and enjoyment when with friends.*

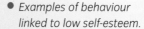

● *Examples of behaviour linked to low self-esteem.*

Identifying and referring children whose development gives cause for concern

Where children's development is not typical of that of most other children of their age, it can be extremely beneficial for those children to be identified early on. This is not about labelling children, but about finding extra support to meet their needs. If you have concerns about a child's development, the first thing to do is to discuss your concerns with the parents. This is considered best practice and is already a requirement of the Special Educational Needs Codes of Practice in England and Wales. Parents may already be aware that their child's development is different from that of most other children or, on the other hand, they may witness their child showing skills that you have not been able to observe. Ideally, if you are working well with parents, talking to them about your concerns will not come as a shock, as previous observations will have already highlighted the difficulties that a child is having. In some cases parents will prefer to refer their child themselves. They can do this by visiting their family doctor or health visitor, who will then organise an appointment with the appropriate specialists. In some parts of the United Kingdom, parents can refer themselves directly to services such as speech and language teams. It is important to understand that unless a child is considered to be at risk from a child protection point of view, referral by an early years worker to services such as educational psychologists can take place only with parental consent.

Observation

You can learn a lot about children when you watch them play. Observe one child from *each* of the following age bands.

- 1–3 years
- 4–8 years
- 9–11 years.

Look for a situation when the child is playing around other children. Try to observe the following:

- hand movements
- coordination
- cooperation and interest in other children
- communication and language skills
- concentration.

Write a report based on your three observations, comparing the development of the three children.

Areas of child development

Check it out

For each of the following services, write down the contact details in your local area:
- speech and language therapy
- physiotherapy
- educational psychologist
- sensory impairment team.

When observing children's development and thinking about children's interests and needs, it can be helpful to focus on particular skills that children are developing. The skills that children learn are often grouped into four key areas:

- physical development
- cognitive development
- communication and language development
- personal, social and emotional development.

By looking at each of these areas, practitioners can learn more about children's development. This section looks at each area and will help you to understand the range of skills that children acquire.

Understanding what each of the areas of development may include

Before looking at the areas of development, it is worth understanding the types of skills that are usually associated with them.

- *Physical development.* This area of development is about learning how to master physical movements. Running, drawing and tying a knot are all examples of movements that most children will gradually learn. Physical development allows children to gain independence.
- *Cognitive development.* This area of development is also known as intellectual development. It is a huge area, as it encompasses the way in which the brain processes information. Being able to remember someone's name or being able to distinguish between two different colours are examples of cognitive skills. Imagination is also a cognitive skill. Cognitive development is strongly linked to communication and language development.
- *Communication and language development.* This area of development is about learning to communicate with other people and understanding their communications. Talking, reading and writing and also use of gestures are all examples of skills that most children learn. Communication and language development are linked to cognitive development because more sophisticated communication involves thinking about what others are trying to convey as well as thinking about what you are trying to express.

- *Personal, social and emotional development.* This area of development is about relationships and also about understanding oneself. Being able to feel sorry for someone, knowing what behaviour is acceptable and also being able to control your emotions are examples of skills that children learn. This area is closely tied to cognitive and language development. Children gradually need to use words or body language to express themselves and so need communication skills. They also need to be able to imagine what other people are thinking and feeling. This is a cognitive skill.

Physical development is considered separately below, and then the other areas are considered under 'Theories of how children develop', as they have proved more controversial.

Development is holistic

Before looking at individual areas of development, it is useful to understand that each is important in its own right. However, the areas of development do not work 'separately'. More than one area of development is involved in many of the skills that children need to develop. A good example of this would be the ability to play hopscotch. This is a game which you might play with other children and which involves being able to jump onto one foot. The spider diagram below shows some of the skills that are involved and how these are linked to different areas of development. The co-dependency means that while you may find it helpful to focus on one area of a child's development, you must always remember that development is holistic and must consider children as 'whole' people.

Personal, social and emotional development
Children must be able to take their turn
They need to find the game pleasurable
They must cope with their feelings if they do not win

Cognitive development
Children need to be able to understand what is happening
They must be able to understand the rules of the game
Children need to be able to count

Playing hopscotch

Communication and language development
Children need to say the numbers aloud
They need to arrange turns
They should be able to chat while waiting for their turn

Physical development
Children need to be able to aim and throw a stone
They need to have the strength in the legs to support their weight
They must be able to balance
They need sufficient coordination to organise the range of movements

- *Skills involved in playing hopscotch and how these link to different areas of development.*

Physical development

The control that people have over their bodies is quite remarkable, and yet most people take it completely for granted. Watch a young baby, though, struggling to pass a rattle from one hand to another and you will soon see how skilled you have become. Physical development, like many other areas of development, is a journey, but interestingly it is a relatively fast one, and by the age of five years most children have a good level of control over their bodies.

Physical development is also linked to growth and maturation

Physical development looks principally at the skills that children acquire, but it is important to understand that there is a link here to growth and maturation. For example, young babies can suck their toes, but this becomes difficult as the body's proportions change. In the same way, some physical development cannot take place until some maturation processes have occurred. In young children, a good example of this is toilet training. This is a skill, but the brain has to be mature enough to be able to send signals to and from the bladder.

Check it out

Look at the following situations:
- reading a book
- playing in the home corner
- playing in the sand tray with other children.

1. Make a list of the skills that are required.

2. Work out which area of development they fit into.

Helps children to become more independent
For example, they can dress themselves, get out toys and equipment, go out and see friends.

Builds children's confidence
When children can do things for themselves, they are more likely to gain in confidence. They can do things how and when they want.

Allows children to express themselves
Physical movements are one way in which babies and young children can express themselves. Babies may signal with their arms that they wish to be lifted up, while toddlers may throw themselves to the ground to express their frustration. In older children, physical skills will enable them to dance, play musical instruments, paint and make models.

Helps children to socialise
As play – especially in children's early years – is quite active, children will benefit if they are physically able to join in. Children may together construct a train track or follow each other on tricycles.

Physical development

Links to cognitive development
In children's early years, a significant amount of learning is practical and requires physical movements. Early physical movements also help to develop the brain.

● *The importance of physical development in children's overall development.*

Different types of physical skills

To gain control over their movements, children need to master different types of movements and skills.

Fine motor skills

This broad term covers small movements that are usually made using the hands.

- *Fine manipulative skills* are movements that require the fingers and thumbs to carry out coordinated small tasks, such as threading beads on to a string. Quite often these movements also require the hands and eyes to work together.
- *Fine motor skills* are movements that involve the wrist and hand, such as unscrewing a lid from a jar.

Gross motor skills

This is another broad term, which covers children's large movements.

- *Gross motor skills* are movements that are made with the whole limb, such as kicking a ball or moving the arm to throw a bean bag.
- *Locomotive skills* are the movements used to be mobile. For babies this may mean rolling, crawling or 'bottom shuffling'. For older children this means walking, running and skipping.

Coordination

In order to achieve many physical skills, a mixture of movements are required in the right order. The maturation of the central nervous system plays a key role in helping children to become coordinated (see below). Children become gradually more coordinated as they practise particular movements and skills and learn to use their hands, feet and eyes together.

- *Hand–eye coordination.* Many activities require hands and eyes to work together. To pour a drink, for example, the brain needs to take information from the eyes and use it to inform the movements that have to be made with the hands.
- *Foot–eye coordination.* Children have to learn to guide their feet. Climbing stairs and kicking a ball require this type of coordination.
- *Balance.* Balance is a complicated skill, although it is one that most people take for granted. The ability to balance develops with age, most children relying on visual input to balance. Balance is required in order for children to carry out any task where weight is shifted from one foot to another (e.g. walking, hopping and climbing).

Check it out

Think of three skills you have used today that required hand–eye coordination.

How the body changes shape as it grows

The diagram overleaf shows how the human body changes shape as it grows. Babies' heads are proportionately quite large, but other parts of the body grow more over time and so the overall shape changes.

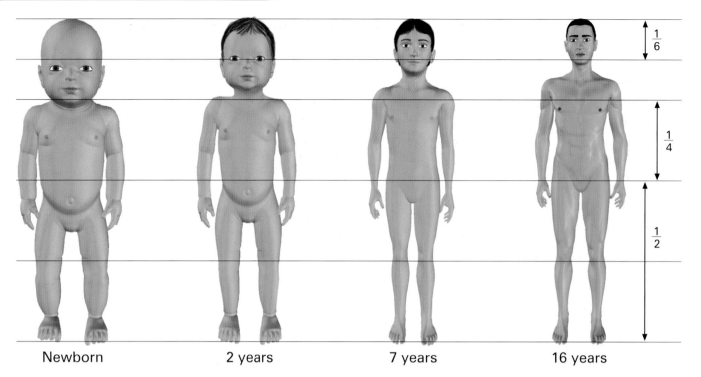

| Newborn | 2 years | 7 years | 16 years |

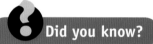

● *The differing shapes of the body during physical development, from birth to 16 years.*

Key principles of physical development

There are three principles of physical development.

1. Development follows a definite sequence

As children grow and develop, a pattern emerges: certain movements have to be in place before others can follow (e.g. children have to be able to walk before they can skip) (see also page 273).

2. Development begins with the control of head movements and proceeds downwards

Babies first gain control of their head and top of the spine before other parts of their bodies. This is thought to be a survival mechanism as it is important for babies to be able to turn their heads to feed.

3. Development begins with uncontrolled gross motor movements before becoming precise and refined

The young baby's arm and leg movements are uncontrolled, but some control is quickly gained, first of the arms and then of the wrists and hands. By six months, most babies are able to take an offered toy reasonably easily. As an adult, you may have had a similar learning experience if you have learnt to use a computer with a mouse. Most people find that at first it is all they can do to keep the mouse visible on the screen before they gradually learn more refined movements, which allow them to position the mouse accurately where they choose.

Did you know?

The three principles of physical development were first suggested by Arnold Gessell, an American paediatrician. He suggested that the maturation of the central nervous system underpinned development, with stimulation not necessarily having a significant role. This led to some paediatricians adopting a 'laissez-faire' attitude towards children with disabilities, which has subsequently been challenged.

The links between the central nervous system and physical development

Children's physical development is underpinned by the central nervous system (principally the brain and the spinal cord). The central nervous system is responsible for collecting, interpreting and sending out information to all parts of the body. Information is constantly collected via the body's senses of taste, touch, smell, sight and sound. This information is then transformed into electrical pulses that are carried by the nerves, up through the spinal cord and into the brain. From the information that is received, the brain then responds and sends out instructions to muscles, glands and organs using the network of nerves again. The whole process is surprisingly quick, which means that the body can take action against possible danger; for example, a person will almost instantly withdraw a hand from something that is very hot.

In babies and young children the central nervous system has to mature. At first babies are reliant on the many survival reflexes that they are born with, but in order to control their movements the central nervous system has to learn how to interpret and control responses. This is a gradual process and is the reason why babies' movements are at first so uncoordinated. The variable rate at which the central nervous system matures is one reason why children may walk, talk and move out of nappies at different paces.

Newborn babies

The first year of life is amazing in terms of physical development. Babies begin with a range of reflexes. The reflexes are actions that happen without the baby thinking about them (see page 105). Over the first few months, some of these reflexes begin to disappear and instead babies learn to control their movements. Muscle tone also increases and the body grows stronger. By the end of their first year, most babies are mobile, able to sit up and can reach out and handle objects easily.

Did you know?

Most babies grow about 30 cm and triple their birth weight in their first year. This rapid rate of growth continues into their second year.

Children at 1–3 years

Children's physical skills continue to develop quickly. Somewhere between 12 and 15 months, most children will start to walk. The pattern of gaining control over larger movements before smaller ones continues. Some movements are made possible because the bones in the body have started to harden or have now formed. These processes do not finish until the end of adolescence and this is one reason why older children become stronger. For example, the wrist of a one-year-old contains only three bones but there are nine bones in the adult's. The brain is also developing and growing. It is responsible for sending and coordinating messages between different parts of the body. Somewhere between 18 months and three years children will become ready for toilet training. This process is mainly linked to how well the brain is able to send the necessary signals. Hand–eye coordination is another skill that is reliant on the signals sent to and from the brain, as is the ability to walk without bumping into objects.

Toilet training

Helping children to move out of nappies is mainly a question of getting the timing right. Beginning too early can leave children worried and confused, as they cannot do what adults around them are expecting. Beginning too early also leaves adults frustrated, as children may have frequent accidents and also refuse to go near the potty. Understanding when children are ready is not simply a matter of age – it is really about physical readiness. A few children are ready at 18 months, but the majority of children will be ready somewhere between two and three years. Fortunately, there are some signs that children are ready.

● *Signs that a child is ready for toilet training.*

Children at 4–7 years

In this period, children's movements become more coordinated and smoother. This is because the brain has developed further and is able to process information more quickly. This can be seen in the way that children are faster at dressing and have fewer accidents resulting from stumbling or bumping into things. As a result of improved coordination, children often gain in confidence.

Children at 8–12 years

Children's physical skills continue to develop and will often depend on their interests (e.g. football or tennis). Children's fine motor skills are also good at this age and so children who enjoy drawing or making things are able to make very precise movements. In terms of boys' and girls' strength, there is little difference. This is because hormone production is very low. This begins to change once the body begins to produce more hormones.

From about 10 years, many girls' bodies will be starting the process of adolescence, which for most girls finishes at around 15 years. For boys this usually starts later at around 12 or 13 years and finishes at around 16 years. Adolescence usually begins with another growth spurt. Interestingly, the different parts of the body do not grow at the same rate. Hands and feet are usually the first to reach adult size, followed by the arms and legs and then the trunk. Bones harden, and muscle strength and hand grip increase.

Children at 13–16 years

By the age of 14 or 15, most girls have completed the process of puberty. Their periods are likely to have started and by 16 are on their way to becoming regular. For boys, the process of puberty has only just begun and for most it will end at about 16 years. At the end of the process, most boys will be stronger than girls because the ratio of fat to muscles is higher in girls than in boys. On average, boys will also be taller. In the teenage years, the brain also carries on developing. Speed, fast reaction times and coordination are the results of this brain development. Overall, in terms of physical development, both boys and girls are near their peaks, if their diet and levels of exercise are good.

Theories of how children develop

There are many theories about how children learn and develop. This area of study is known as developmental psychology, and it covers the areas of cognitive, language and emotional development. It is a fascinating area and it is worth having an overview of some key theories, as they have shaped, and continue to shape, work with children. Constant research and refinement in the field means that practitioners should also try to update their professional knowledge regularly.

Cognitive development

Theories that look at the way children think and learn are extremely important as they can be applied to so many situations in everyday life. This also means that when studying other aspects of child development, such as language, behaviour management or aggression, you will find that the same terms and theories will keep reappearing. Currently, learning theories can be grouped into three bands:
- behaviourist approaches
- constructivist approaches
- information processing.

Did you know?

The study of psychology is relatively new. The word 'psyche' is Greek for the mind or spirit, and psychology looks principally at what happens in the mind. Modern psychology has been influenced both by early philosophers and by biologists.

Behaviourist approaches to learning

The behaviourist approach suggests that learning is influenced by rewards, punishments and environmental factors. The term 'conditioning' is often used by behaviourists. It means that you learn to act in a certain way because past experiences have taught you to do or not to do something. You may know this as 'learning by association' (for example, not touching a flame after once being burnt).

Two types of conditioning are well documented: classical conditioning and operant conditioning.

Classical conditioning

The idea of conditioning was born out of research into dogs' digestive systems. Ivan Pavlov was a physiologist who, while studying dogs, noticed that they always started to salivate before food was put down for them. He came to the conclusion that the dogs were anticipating the food and were salivating because they had learnt to associate the arrival of food with other things, such as footsteps and buckets. To show this more clearly he devised an experiment in which he fed dogs while a bell was sounded. Normally dogs do not salivate when hearing bells, but the dogs began to associate the bell with food and would salivate simply on hearing it.

Pavlov also looked at what would happen if the bell repeatedly rang and no food was offered to the dogs. He found that gradually the conditioned response (dogs salivating) became weaker until finally the dogs did not react to the bell. The term used by behaviourists when this happens is 'extinction'.

Did you know?

Many theories involve 'stages', such as Freud's psychosexual stages of personality and Piaget's stages of cognitive development. For example, in language development children babble before they speak words, so babbling is seen as a stage in itself. Other psychologists feel that development is more gradual and that it is a continuous process. This means staged versus continuous development is another area of debate for psychologists. In your work setting, ask the staff whether they think children's progress fits into stages, or whether they see development as continual.

Case study 4: Classical conditioning linked to irrational fears

Esther was five years old and had always gone to bed without being afraid of the dark. One night she was violently sick when her room was in darkness. Now her parents say that she always cries when she goes into a dark room and that she will not get to sleep unless a light is left on in the room.

1. *Explain why this is an example of classical conditioning.*
2. *Why is it important to recognise children's fears?*
3. *Suggest one way in which Esther might be helped not to be afraid of the dark.*

Operant conditioning

The essence of the operant conditioning theory is that learning is based on the type of consequence or reinforcement that follows an initial behaviour. B. F. Skinner is recognised as being a key figure in developing the behaviourist approach to learning theory and in particular for developing the theory of operant conditioning.

Skinner suggested that most humans and animals learn through exploring the environment and then drawing conclusions based on the consequences of their behaviour. This means that people tend to be active in the learning process – unlike in the theory of classical conditioning.

Skinner divided the consequences of actions into three groups:

- *Positive reinforcers* are likely to make people repeat behaviour when they get something they desire (e.g. they may buy a new food product after having tried and liked a free sample). Skinner suggested that using positive reinforcement was the most effective way of encouraging new learning. Positive reinforcers for children include gaining adults' attention, praise, stickers, sweets and treats.
- *Negative reinforcers* are likely to make people repeat behaviour as well, but the difference is that the behaviour is repeated to stop something happening. Children going down a slide might learn to use their hands to slow them down if they are feeling unhappy about the speed.
- *Punishers* are likely to stop people from repeating behaviour. For example, they may learn to stay away from an electric fence after receiving a shock.

 B. F. Skinner.

 Keys to good practice: 'Conditioning' good behaviour

✓ Operant conditioning is often used to encourage children to show wanted behaviour, although many parents and early years workers will think of it as offering a bribe. The 'bribe', however, can be very small. Children may be given a sticker if they have helped to tidy things away. Moreover, these children will be more likely to help in future as their behaviour has been positively reinforced.

Did you know?

The original concept of 'operant conditioning' was pioneered by E. J. Thorndike, although he did not use the term. Thorndike showed through experiments with cats that the results of behaviour would affect subsequent behaviour. This he called the 'law of effect'. In his experiments, hungry cats were put into a 'puzzle box', which had a lever that allowed the cats to escape. The cats could see from inside the box a piece of fish, which they were able to eat every time they escaped. At first the cats took about five minutes to escape, and did so purely through trial and error. Subsequently they were able to reduce the time that it took them to escape until they managed it in less than five seconds.

Unexpected positive reinforcers

Skinner found during his experiments that it was often hard to predict what would act as a primary reinforcer and that it was sometimes only after the event that this became clear. An example of this is when children sometimes deliberately behave badly in order to attract their carer's attention. If they manage to attract attention, they are more likely to show the behaviour again, although they might be told off. Gaining the carer's attention in this case is the positive reinforcer, even if they are being told off.

Primary and secondary reinforcers

There are some reinforcers that give instant pleasure or satisfaction or meet a need. These are referred to as primary reinforcers. Chocolate is a primary reinforcer because most people find that once they put it into their mouths they enjoy the taste.

Secondary reinforcers are different because they in themselves do not give satisfaction, but symbolise getting primary reinforcement. A good example of secondary reinforcement is money. Coins and notes in themselves are not a reward, but they can be used to buy something that will give primary reinforcement, such as food. (The learning that is used when making the association between money and being able to get something is classical conditioning.)

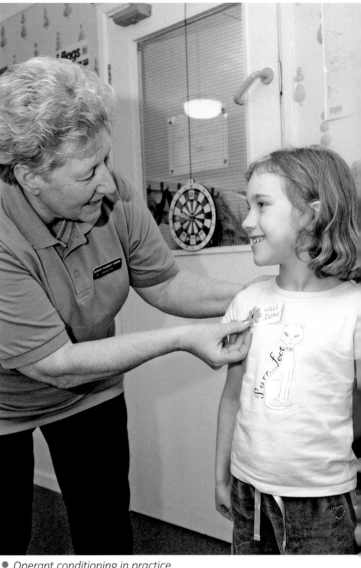

● *Operant conditioning in practice.*

Frequency of reinforcement

Skinner looked at the effect on behaviour of giving positive reinforcements at different intervals. How long would behaviour be shown without a positive reward before extinction takes place? Interestingly, he found that unpredictable reinforcement works better than continual reinforcement. This would seem to work because it teaches learners not to expect a reward or reinforcement every time – hence they keep on showing the behaviour just in case a reinforcement is given.

Children need frequent positive reinforcement as this helps them to learn wanted behaviour. Giving children praise or stickers unexpectedly will help them carry on showing wanted behaviour until such time that it becomes learned and in some ways automatic behaviour.

Did you know?

Young children do not understand the value of money because they have not made the association between money and pleasure. Toddlers, for example, are often more interested in the size, colour and shape of coins. This means that offering money as a reward to young children is not very effective.

Delaying reinforcement

Delaying positive reinforcement, for example saying to children that they can have a sticker at the end of the week, weakens the effect of the reinforcement. Immediate positive reinforcements are the most effective because the behaviour is then more strongly linked to the reinforcement.

Keys to good practice: Reinforcement

✓ Conditioning is a very powerful form of learning. It means that children can be encouraged to show wanted behaviour through positive reinforcement with praise, attention, stickers, etc.

✓ Don't give positive reinforcement for unwanted behaviour (e.g. giving children sweets to stop them whining), as this may further encourage unwanted behaviour.

✓ In some cases it might be better to ignore a child's behaviour if it is not dangerous. Giving children attention may lead to them being positively reinforced and in doing so help children to learn this behaviour.

Social learning theory

Social learning theory is another behaviourist approach. It originated in America in the 1940s. The key figure among social learning theorists is Albert Bandura. Social learning theorists accept the principles of conditioning but suggest that other types of learning are also taking place.

Observational learning

Social learning theorists suggest that people also learn by observing others. This is sometimes referred to as observational learning. It is an interesting theory and many early years workers will have seen children copy each other's or an adult's behaviour. One of the features of observational learning is that it is spontaneous – children will learn naturally learn by imitating rather than being shown or taught. Children may copy some aspects of the behaviour of early years workers and parents that they are unaware of. Observational learning can also occur without any reinforcement, which is a main difference from conditioning.

● *Albert Bandura.*

It is helpful to understand two terms that are used in observational learning:
- *model* – the person whose behaviour is being imitated
- *modelling* – the process by which learning takes place.

Bandura's 'Bobo doll' experiment

Bandura performed a famous experiment (1965) which showed that children can learn behaviour by watching adults; it is often referred to as the Bobo doll experiment. Bandura showed a film to three groups of children. The film showed an adult in a room with a large inflatable 'Bobo' doll. The three groups of children each saw a different variation on the behaviour of the adult:

- Group A saw the adult acting aggressively towards the doll.
- Group B saw the adult being aggressive towards the doll, but at the end of the film the adult was rewarded with sweets and lemonade by another adult.
- Group C saw the adult being aggressive towards the doll, but at the end a second adult appeared and told the adult off.

After the film, each group of children in turn was shown into a playroom that contained a variety of toys, including the Bobo doll. The reactions of the children were recorded. Group C children were the least aggressive towards the doll, but there was little difference between groups A and B. This suggested that they were less influenced by the reward that had been offered to the adult and most influenced by the telling-off.

- Bandura's Bobo doll.

A follow-up to the experiment was to ask the children if they could demonstrate how the doll had been attacked, and they were rewarded for doing so. There was little difference between the three groups of children, which showed that they could all imitate the behaviour they had seen.

Constructivist approaches

Constructivist approaches to how children learn see the child as an active rather than a passive learner. While in the behaviourist model children learn as a result of what they see and what happens to them, the constructivist model suggests that children explore and come to conscious conclusions about their world.

Piaget's theory of cognitive development

Jean Piaget was a zoologist who became interested in children's cognitive development as a result of working on intelligence tests. He noticed that children consistently gave similar 'wrong' answers to some questions and began to consider why this was. Piaget used his own children to make detailed observations and gradually developed a theory that has been very influential.

Check it out

Many early years workers agree that children learn through observational learning. For example, toddlers may try to cross their legs in adult fashion after seeing an adult do the same. Observe a small group of children as they play near an adult. Notice whether any of the children occasionally glance across to see what the adult is doing.

His theory of learning is sometimes referred to as a 'constructivist approach' because he suggested that children constructed or built up their thoughts according to their experiences of the world around them. Piaget used the term 'schema' to refer to a child's conclusions or thoughts. He felt that learning was an ongoing process, with children needing to adapt (hence Piaget's term 'adaption') their original ideas if a new piece of information seemed to contradict their conclusions. For example, a group of toddlers may come to believe that milk is served in blue beakers, because their experience of having milk is linked with it being served in a blue beaker. If one day they are given juice in the blue beaker instead of milk, they will need to reconsider the theory and thus come to the conclusion that milk and other drinks come in blue beakers. Piaget used specific vocabulary to describe the process of children learning in this way:

- *Assimilation.* The child constructs a theory (schema).
- *Equilibrium.* The child's experiences to date seem to fit the schema (everything balances).
- *Disequilibrium.* An experience occurs that casts doubt on the effectiveness of the schema. (Things don't add up any more!)
- *Accommodation.* The child changes the original schema to fit the new piece of experience or information.

- *Jean Piaget.*

Piaget's belief that children develop schemas based on their direct experiences can help us to understand why young children's thinking is sometimes different to ours. Piaget also suggested that, as children develop, so does their thinking. He grouped children's cognitive development into four broad stages. Table 303.2 outlines these four stages.

Table 303.2. Piaget's four broad stages of cognitive development

Stage	Approximate age	Features
Sensori-motor	0–2 years	Development of object permanence Child begins to use symbols (e.g. language)
Pre-operational	2–7 years	Child uses symbols in play and thought Egocentrism Centration Animism Inability to conserve
Concrete operational	7–11 years	Ability to conserve Children begin to solve mental problems using practical supports such as counters and objects
Formal operational	11–15 years	Young people can think about situations that they have not experienced They can juggle with ideas in their minds

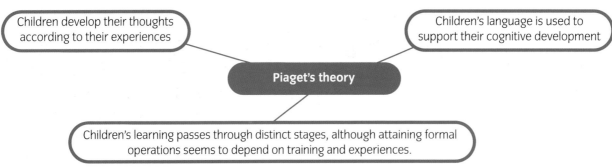

Children develop their thoughts according to their experiences

Children's language is used to support their cognitive development

Piaget's theory

Children's learning passes through distinct stages, although attaining formal operations seems to depend on training and experiences.

● *Main features of Piaget's theory of cognitive development.*

Other constructivist approaches to cognitive development

Although Piaget's work is well known, there are two other approaches which are in some ways similar to Piaget's and have also influenced early years practice: Vygotsky's theory of cognitive development and Bruner's developmental theory.

Vygotsky's theory of cognitive development

Vygotksy believed that children's social environment and experiences are very important. He considered that children were born to be sociable and that by being with their parents and then with their friends they acquired skills and concepts. Vygotsky saw children as 'apprentices', learning and gaining understanding through being with others (a process termed 'scaffolding').

Vygotsky also suggested that maturation was an important element in children's development and that carers needed to extend children's learning so that they could use their emerging skills and concepts. He used the term 'zone of proximal development' to define this idea, although we might think of this as 'potential'.

Vygotsky's work has been influential. He suggested that people working with children need to extend and challenge their thoughts so that their zone of proximal development can emerge. He stressed the importance of social interaction and the need for adults to work alongside children, and he also felt that children could guide and develop each other's potential. It is interesting to note that although Vygotsky saw that direct teaching was important, he also stressed the importance of children being active in their learning.

Did you know?

Vygotksy's work was not published in English until the early 1960s, even though his work was known in Russia in the 1920s and 1930s.

Bruner's developmental theory

Jerome Bruner's work was influenced by Piaget but particularly by Vygotsky's work. Bruner's is not a stage theory as such but he suggests that children gradually acquire cognitive skills, and he refers to these as modes of thinking.

Table 303.3. Bruner's three modes of thinking

Mode	Approximate age	Description and use
Enactive	0–1 years	Through repeating physical movements people of all ages can learn certain types of skill, for example tying our shoelaces or learning to drive a car. This is the first type of cognitive skill that Bruner suggests babies are able to use. This fits in with Piaget's sensori-motor stage, where children repeat movements and learn about their world through their physical movements.
Iconic	1–7 years	An icon is something that is visual, and Bruner suggested that the iconic mode involves people building up a picture of things they have experienced in their minds. They may, for example, be able to shut their eyes and imagine the room they are in. The iconic stage relates to Piaget's pre-operational stage.
Symbolic	7+ years	Like Piaget, Bruner felt that, at around 7 years, children's thinking drastically changed. Bruner linked this change to the child's ability to use symbols but particularly to the use of language. In symbolic mode, thinking can take place without people having direct experience; for example, they may listen to the news on the radio and retain this information, even though they have not directly witnessed the events mentioned.

Bruner believed that cognitive development can be speeded up if it is stimulated. He is well known for the idea of the spiral curriculum. The idea is that children can look at subjects at different times in their lives at different levels of complexity. This means that the topic of 'water' might be introduced to babies simply by allowing them to splash in the bath. As toddlers they may have fun playing in the paddling pool and learning to pour water, but later, as four-year-olds, they may explore volume by pouring water into different-sized containers and so on. Bruner also felt that adults had a very important role in developing children's cognitive skills, by working alongside them and by asking questions, helping children to vocalise their thoughts. This is a similar approach to Vygotsky's scaffolding. As children become more confident and competent, the adult will probe further and encourage children to extend their thinking. Bruner felt that the development of language was the key to children being able to move from iconic mode into symbolic mode.

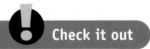

Check it out

Constructivist theories have been very influential on modern thinking about the way in which children play and learn. They are still evolving. Find out about the work of one of the following theorists:
- Chris Athey
- Janet Moyles
- Tina Bruce.

Social, emotional and behavioural development

The way people react to others and the feelings they have about themselves are linked to social and emotional development. It is therefore useful to have an understanding of the theories that relate to children's social and emotional development. These are grouped in temrs of:

- formation of early relationships
- moral development
- personality.

Formation of early relationships

Attachment

The term attachment is widely used by psychologists studying children's early relationships. An attachment can be thought of as a unique emotional tie between a child and another person, usually an adult. Research has repeatedly shown that the quality of these ties or attachments will shape a child's ability to form other relationships later in life. Psychologists have also studied the effects on children when attachments are not made in infancy or when they have been broken (e.g. through separation).

There seems to be a general pattern to the way children develop attachments. Table 303.4 summarises the stages.

Table 303.4. The stages of attachment

Age	Stage	Features
6 weeks to 3 months		Babies begin to be attracted to human faces and voices. First smiles begin at around six weeks.
3 months to 7/8 months	Indiscriminate attachments	Babies are learning to distinguish between faces and show obvious pleasure when they recognise familiar faces. They are happy to be handled by strangers, preferring to be in human company rather than left alone (hence the term indiscriminate attachments).
7/8 months	Specific attachments	At around 7 or 8 months, babies begin to miss key people in their lives and show signs of distress, for example crying when they leave the room. Most babies seem to develop one particularly strong attachment, often to the mother. Babies show a wariness of strangers even when in the presence of their 'key people'. This wariness may quickly develop into fear if the stranger makes some form of direct contact with the baby, for example by touching them.
From 8 months	Multiple attachments	After making specific attachments, babies then go on to form multiple attachments. This is an important part of their socialisation process.

Helping children to make smooth transitions

Moving from home to nursery, school or any new setting can be hard for children of all ages. It is important that you recognise this and find ways of helping them. Table 303.5 makes some suggestions for how to do so.

Table 303.5. Helping to make smooth transitions

Age of child	Good practice
0–3 years	The aim is to make sure that children have made an attachment with a key worker in the new setting before being left there. It is best if children are familiar with the environment as well, so many settings encourage children to make several visits first. It is also important for settings to adapt their routine to the needs of the baby, rather than the other way around.
4–7 years	Children are more able to understand what is happening. If they have had good experiences of being separated, they will adjust more easily. All children will need time to settle down. If possible they should be put with friends or children that they already now. If children go into a setting and do not know any adults or children, extra care is needed. It is good practice to introduce them to children who will be happy to let them join in.
8–12 years	Children may start to express strong feelings about changing setting. It is important that they can see the positive aspects of any change, and so comments such as 'You won't be able to do that when you get there!' are unhelpful. As friendships are important, efforts should be made to keep friends together or to structure activities so that children quickly get to know each other. Some children are naturally outgoing and sociable, but others will find it hard to make new friends.
13–16 years	Young people will find it easier to change settings smoothly when they have had some input and feel in control of the process. It is important for adults not to take over but to listen to young people's thoughts and fears.

Did you know?

A number of studies in America have compared groups of children who have working parents with those who have a parent at home. One of the largest studies suggested that children receiving high-quality day care fare no differently from children whose parents stay at home. In the United Kingdom, the EPPE project has reported that pre-school education for children from three years of age is likely to help children's later learning. The importance of good standards of care and attention has been emphasised by all the research projects.

Case study 3: Settling in

Jodie is two and a half years old. Today is her first session at the pre-school. She visited it yesterday with her mother for the morning and seemed quite happy. The supervisor has told Jodie's mother to give her a quick kiss and then to go. She says that all the children cry at first and after a while they stop. Jodie cries and tries to run after her mother. She is picked up by a member of staff. Jodie pushes her away and runs to the door. The supervisor tells the member of staff to leave her as she will soon quieten down. After half an hour, Jodie appears to cry less, but is withdrawn and not interested in joining the other children. The supervisor tells the staff that she is just sulking. When Jodie's mother returns, Jodie rushes to her. The next day Jodie cries as she approaches the door of the pre-school and refuses to let go of her mother's hand. Jodie's mother says that she had wet the bed for the first time in ages.

1. *What are the signs that Jodie is showing separation anxiety?*
2. *Explain why Jodie showed no signs of distress on the preliminary visit the day before.*
3. *Consider the settling-in procedures of your setting. Do they allow the child to make an attachment to a member of staff before they leave their parents for the first time?*

The development of friendships

As well as children needing to form strong attachments to their carers, they also need to learn how to become cooperative with their peers. Friends become increasingly important as children develop. By the time a young person reaches 12 or 13 years, the chances are that their friends are becoming as important as their family members.

Table 303.6. The development of friendships

Age	What you might observe
0–3 years	In these early years, children's first friends are their parents and main carers. They will learn how to play with them and also how to communicate. Babies and toddlers will notice other children and be fascinated by them. At around two years, they are likely to play alongside each other. From about three years, you will see the beginnings of more cooperative play.
4–7 years	In this period, children really enjoy being with other children. They will show some friendship preferences, but these are mainly based on play interests, especially until the age of about five or six years. It is likely that towards the end of this period children will be playing mainly with others of the same sex.
8–12 years	Children's friendships are becoming more settled and you will see that children now spend time with the same groups of friends. These are often of the same sex, although some play activities will encourage boys and girls to play together. There is some evidence to suggest that boys' friendships are likely to be group based but that girls prefer closer but fewer friendships.
13–16 years	Young people will be starting to want to spend more time with each other than they do with their families. This is in preparation for leaving home and establishing themselves as independent people in the adult world. Young people can find themselves caught between wanting to remain in a friendship group but not wanting to adopt the same values and behaviour.

Moral development

Moral development concerns behaving in a way that others find acceptable (an important social skill), which will vary with the child's age. The development of moral reasoning in children is complex: it involves children's own experiences of being treated fairly, as well as their ability to understand a situation and to empathise with others. At what age are children able to judge right from wrong? One of the most famous approaches to understanding moral development is a cognitive (i.e. stage) model. This cognitive approach was put forward by Jean Piaget and then later built upon by Lawrence Kohlberg.

Piaget's theory of moral development

In line with his view that cognitive development followed a four-stage process (see page 135), Piaget suggested that moral development did the same. He suggested that children's moral development was a three-stage process, as set out in Table 303.7. Piaget also felt that, during the three stages, children gradually move away from the concept of morality and fairness being imposed by others ('heteronomous morality') to a state of understanding that people can be in control of their moral reasoning ('autonomous morality').

Table 303.7. Piaget's stages in the development of moral reasoning

Stage	Age	Development
Pre-moral	0–4 years	Children in this stage learn about right and wrong through their own actions and consider the responses of adults around them.
Moral realism	4–7 years	In this period children's moral development is greatly influenced by the adults in their lives. Their judgements very much depend on what they think the adults' expectations are.
	8–11 years	Children are preoccupied with justice and following rules. They have developed a concept of fairness.
Moral relativism	11+ years	Children understand that treating people in exactly the same way may not result in fairness (e.g. a child who does not understand a piece of homework may need more of a teacher's time than a child who does). The motive for people's actions is also considered by children.

Kohlberg's theory of moral development

Kohlberg built on Piaget's descriptions of moral development. He suggested that, as with other cognitive areas, moral reasoning is linked to stages of development. He suggested that there are three levels of moral development, each of which is subdivided into stages (Table 303.8).

Table 303.8. Kohlberg's levels of moral development

Age	Level	Stage	Explanation
6–13	Pre-conventional	1. Punishment and obedience	Children are not being guided by their own moral reasoning, but are following their parents or carers. They are doing this either to seek reward or to avoid punishment. They find out about what is wrong and right through seeing the consequences of their actions.
		2. Individualism, instrumental purpose and exchange	Children learn that some actions and behaviours are rewarded and they learn to avoid those that might mean punishment. By the end of this stage they are also beginning to enjoy helping people and have learnt the 'If I help you, you might help me' approach.
13–16	Conventional	3. Mutual interpersonal expectations, relationships and interpersonal conformity ('Good boy/nice girl')	Children come to believe that good behaviour pleases other people (e.g. friends, teachers and parents). They are also becoming aware of motive ('He meant to help really').
		4. Social system and conscience ('Law and order')	This is a widening-out stage. Previously, children were wanting to show good and correct behaviour to please people they knew. At this stage they are more aware of society's needs and interests and what is deemed by society to be right or wrong. They are keen to obey regulations and laws.
16–20+	Post-conventional/ principled	5. Social contract	At this stage rules and regulations are seen as useful tools to make sure that there is some protection and fairness in society. People working at this level are prepared to tolerate rules being broken, if they do not see that they are fair or just rules.
		6. Universal ethical principles	This last stage was in some ways an unclear one for Kohlberg and was difficult to test. People at this stage are extremely principled and not swayed by society. People in history who may have reached this level have been persecuted, as they are often seen as troublemakers (consider Jesus).

Observation

Try out the following story by Kohlberg on a group of children you work with. (The story has been simplified and adapted so that you can use it with children aged four or over.)

A man was trying to save his wife's life. He could not afford to pay for the special medicine she needed. He asked the only chemist who sold it, but the chemist would not give it to him. Later the man broke into the chemist's shop and stole the medicine. Should he have stolen the medicine?

Personality

It is fascinating to see babies quickly develop their own characteristics and personalities. Theories of personality are interesting. One of the most influential is that of Sigmund Freud. He is particularly famous for his psychosexual theory of development, which is often used to explain unconscious thoughts and actions. He was one of the first people to consider the ways in which personalities are constructed.

Freud's structure of personality

Freud suggested that there were three parts that made up our personality: the id, the ego and the superego. Not all of these parts are present at birth but develop with the child.

- *The id.* This is the instinctive part of the personality. It is governed by the drives and needs of the body, such as hunger or finding pleasure. The id does not consider how meeting desires and wants will affect others and so is often thought of as the selfish and passionate component. Freud suggested that babies had only the id when they were born; hence a baby will cry and cry until it gets fed, regardless of how tired the carer is or whether there are other children that also need feeding. Getting the desire or need met is known as 'gratification'.
- *The ego.* The ego has a planning role. It works out how to meet the id's needs and desires in the best way. The ego develops from the id in the first few months. Babies might learn that by smiling in some situations they are more likely to get their needs met, while in others it is better to cry. In some situations the ego may make the id wait for its demands to be met. For example, children may learn that if they snatch a cake from a tray they may have it taken away from them, but by waiting to be offered they will eventually get it. The term 'deferred gratification' is used when this happens. The ego is often thought of as being the common-sense part of our personalities.

- *The superego.* The superego develops later in childhood. It tries to control the ego. It comprises two elements: the conscience and the ego-ideal. The conscience will punish the ego if it misbehaves. This is the source of guilt. The ego-ideal will reward the ego if it shows good behaviour. This is the source of pride and confidence.

Erikson's theory of personality development

Erikson was influenced by Freud's work, but considered that the social environment (e.g. parenting, friendships) also affected personality. He accepted Freud's theory of the structure of personality being divided into three (the id, the ego and superego) but did not feel that Freud's work went far enough. He considered that personalities were not fixed but kept on changing over the course of a lifetime. His stages of personality development are 'life stages', linked to social stages. He considered that, at each stage, people face a dilemma or conflict, and that the outcome at each stage determines personality.

Erikson suggested that the way in which children are treated by adults and later by their peers affects development. Children in the stage known as 'initiative versus guilt', for example, need adult encouragement so that they feel they can explore their environment and be more independent; criticising or restricting children will lead to them feeling incapable. This highlights the importance of encouraging the children you care for and trying not to shame them (e.g. not saying things such as 'I'd better do it for you, because last time you got into a right mess!'). Erikson also looked at children's play, and this is examined in Unit 312.

Self-concept, self-esteem, self-reliance and independence

The way in which children develop a sense of identity is linked to personality. It is important that you gradually help children to learn that they are capable and can become independent. This area is explored further in Unit 310.

A key way in which you can help children to gain in confidence is by encouraging them to be independent. This process should start as early as possible and should carry on until children are ready to join the adult world. Developing children's self-reliance has added bonuses in terms of behaviour: it can prevent tantrums and other behaviours associated with frustration.

Did you know?

Freud believed that people's personalities are based mainly on biological needs or drives, of which the main ones were sexual and aggressive. He shocked Victorian and Edwardian society by suggesting that the sexual drive was present in babies and children. The energy behind these drives Freud called 'libido'. He suggested that there were five stages through which we pass in childhood, linked to physical development of the body, and that if people did not pass through these stages satisfactorily, part of their energy or libido would become stuck, or 'fixated'. This would affect their behaviour and personality.

Table 303.9. How self-reliance skills can be developed

Age range	Examples of how self-reliance skills can be developed
0–1 years	Encourage babies to push their arms through clothes Give older babies something to hold while you change a nappy Provide finger foods from nine months Encourage older babies to pull off their socks or hats when undressing Put out a choice of toys
2–3 years	Begin providing choices where appropriate (e.g. choice of coloured beakers, toys or activities) Build choice into the routine Encourage children to take off coats and hats Play games to help children to learn to tidy up Encourage children to serve and feed themselves Provide simple cooking activities Support children in their play, encouraging them to develop their own ideas Organise areas where children have free access to equipment and toys without needing an adult's help
4–8 years	Provide open-ended activities which give children the scope to solve problems Give children small areas of responsibility (e.g. plants to care for, wiping tables, playing with younger children) Provide opportunities for children to learn everyday skills (e.g. using scissors and other tools, washing up) Encourage children to evaluate risks (e.g. playing outdoors)
8–12 years	Encourage children to choose and prepare simple meals Provide opportunities for children to plan their own activities and to solve their own problems Praise and encourage independent behaviour Encourage children to ask for support (but avoid taking over) Provide opportunities for children to organise themselves (e.g. thinking what they need to pack, put out, consider)
13–16 years	Provide a small budget for an event (e.g. a party) Encourage young people to plan and organise Listen and use questions to help young people think things through rather than give advice and solutions Provide opportunities for young people to demonstrate their skills, knowledge and achievements (e.g. asking young people if they wish to take part in fundraising)

The principles of promoting and supporting children's development

By using observations as a tool, you should be able to look at children's development and then work out how best to support children. This section outlines some of the broad ways in which adults working with the different age groups can support development. This section is subdivided into four broad age ranges: 0–3 years, 4–7 years, 8–12 years, 13–16 years.

Supporting the development of children aged 0–3 years

The early years of children's lives are extremely important for their later development. This means that if you choose to work with this age range, you will need to be extremely good at attending to children's needs and also at observing them. Babies and children under three years are completely reliant on the adults who work with them to keep them safe and to meet their physical and emotional needs. This is not always an easy task, as children's ability to communicate and to understand is still developing.

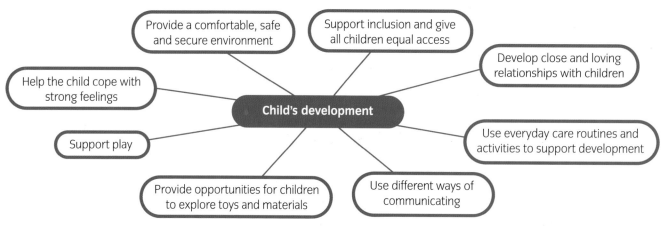

Provide a comfortable, safe and secure environment

Support inclusion and give all children equal access

Develop close and loving relationships with children

Help the child cope with strong feelings

Child's development

Use everyday care routines and activities to support development

Support play

Provide opportunities for children to explore toys and materials

Use different ways of communicating

• *Key principles of supporting the development of children aged 0–3 years.*

Provide a comfortable, safe and secure environment

Children need to feel comfortable and safe. For very young children, this is critical. Babies and toddlers will respond very much according to the way they are feeling. If they do not feel comfortable and safe, they will be unsettled and unhappy. This has both short- and long-term effects. They may cry, refuse to eat or generally be unresponsive to activities. In the longer term, this can be a reason why children fail to thrive and also develop poor patterns of behaviour.

For babies and toddlers, you must also think about providing a varied environment. While older children are able to move easily and can change room or go outside, babies and toddlers need more help to get enough stimulation.

Support inclusion and give all children equal access

Inclusion is about making sure that all children are valued and also that their needs are met. This means thinking hard about the way you care for children and also observing them. It means checking that what you are providing for them is working and, if necessary, changing the way you plan and work. Children's development can vary dramatically, and so what you need to provide for one child may be very different to what another child of a similar age needs.

Develop close and loving relationships with children

When you care for babies and toddlers, you are providing them with a substitute for their primary carers. For them to thrive without their parents, they need close reassurance (see the section on Attachment, page 138). You need to spend time with individual children so that they can develop a special relationship with you. They also need physical contact. This acts as reassurance and helps the child to settle in and feel valued. Physical contact means hugs and sitting on knees as well as holding hands when the child shows signs of wanting it. This can happen early on, as babies, for example, are able to indicate that they want picking up, while slightly older children try and 'snuggle in' or may follow an adult closely. In the same way that children can signal that they need physical reassurance, they can also show that they do not want it. They may put their hands behind their back or move away. These signals must not be ignored as otherwise the physical contact is inappropriate.

Use everyday care routines and activities to support development

While adults can find everyday routines dull, babies and toddlers can learn from them and be stimulated by them. This is because adults are fascinating for young children and most routine care activities allow babies and toddlers time with an individual adult. Routines such as changing nappies, feeding and washing hands are therefore potential learning activities that will be hugely enjoyable for the child. The key is that the adults are able to talk, make eye contact and play little games as they carry them out. In the same way, going out for a ride in a pushchair or a holding an adult's hand during a walk around the garden can stimulate babies and toddlers. The change in environment means that they have new things to observe, smell and feel.

Use different ways of communicating

To support children's language development, adults must spend plenty of time communicating with young children. This means talking, singing, making eye contact and, crucially, listening and responding to children.

It also means helping children to learn about gestures, facial expressions and simple signs. Children need adults to be physically close to them for this. For babies this means picking them up so that they can see the adult's face, while for older children it means adults getting down to their level. As babies and toddlers make sounds and even their first few words, it is important that adults show that they are interested and respond positively. Interest and response will help them make progress. From six months onwards you can introduce babies to simple books. Starting off early is hugely important for children's later interest in reading. You can maintain this early interest by encouraging toddlers to curl up with a book and an adult.

Provide opportunities for children to explore toys and materials

Babies and toddlers need toys and materials to help stimulate their development. What to give them is very dependent on their interests and also their stage of development. As this can change quickly, good practitioners use observations to work out what children will need. It is essential that anything chosen is safe and that you play or supervise children carefully. While there are many toys that help children to be stimulated, it is also useful to look at creating collections of materials that will help children to explore. Creating the right environment in which to use toys, equipment and materials is also important. Children must not feel hurried or under pressure. As children are trying to learn about their world it is also important that they are given opportunities to try to do things in their own way.

Support play

Play appears to come quite naturally in children, but only if adults encourage and support it. With babies this means playing simple games such as peek-a-boo or trying to engage a baby with a smile. From this early start, children then need adults around them who are able to play with them at times and to give encouragement. Children also learn by imitating and so at times your role will be to play with materials in a way that children may find interesting and wish to try out for themselves. This may mean putting out an animal set and pretending to move the animals or pretending to drink a cup of tea from a bowl. When you play with children or supervise play, you should be noticing what children enjoy doing. This will help you to provide future play opportunities.

Help the child to cope with strong feelings

One of the reasons why working with children under three years is such a skill is that they have difficulty both in expressing themselves and in understanding what is happening. Babies, for example, may cry until their needs are met. If their needs are not apparent, it can be very hard for the

Did you know?

Research has shown that watching television, videos and DVDs is not good for children under three years. There are many reasons for this, but particularly important is language development. Children are not actively using their language while watching and are not learning how to communicate with people. There are also some suggestions that children's brains may be affected by the rapid changes in light and images.

early years worker to know what to do. This is why observation is so important. Practitioners who are used to being with certain babies are quick to 'read' the messages the baby is sending out and so can calm the baby down. As physical skills and understanding develops, so toddlers begin to know what they want to do, see and touch. What makes this next stage difficult is that they cannot predict dangers, understand the needs of others or see why they cannot do what they want. This can result in toddlers from as early as 15 months feeling very frustrated and angry. This leads to temper tantrums, as well as toddlers snatching from others and throwing items. Interestingly, a few minutes later, the same child can be laughing and giggling. Such changes in emotions and feelings are hard for the child and demanding for the adult. Practitioners who know the children they care for are able to predict which situations will be hard for the children and to look for ways of avoiding them. They use distraction and are good at being calm and patient so that the children are relaxed.

Supporting the development of children aged 4–7 years

This is an exciting time in children's lives. They are likely to start school and in doing so gain some independence. Children are starting to make friends and develop their own interests. They may also find new interests and learn new skills. This is also a period in which children are keen to take on a little more responsibility. Adults need gradually to look for areas in which children can take some control. Supervision of children may become more discreet and children may be encouraged to set some of their own boundaries.

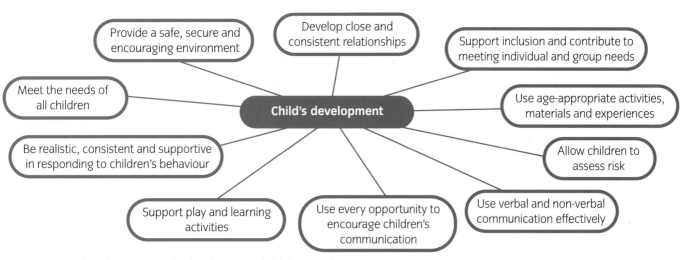

● *Key principles of supporting the development of children aged 4–7 years.*

Provide a safe, secure and encouraging environment

Children in this age group continue to need a safe and secure environment. This helps them to play freely and enjoy learning. Children need opportunities to play both indoors and outdoors. In a good environment children can be allowed more freedom and independence. This is essential, as children now need to gain confidence and use their skills. Supporting children means checking equipment, good supervision and also being aware of dangers (e.g. strangers, animals and litter). Children need adults around them who praise and support them in trying out new skills and activities.

Develop close and consistent relationships

Children should always be able to turn to someone when they are upset, disappointed or dealing with problems. They need familiar, friendly and supportive faces. You therefore need to be a good listener for children. Children also need opportunities to play with each other. Some children will need help in playing with others. They may find it helpful if you organise small-play activities with one or two other children.

Support inclusion and contribute to meeting individual and group needs

Children in this age range become increasingly aware of differences between them. They may notice that some are drawing with more skill or have different lunches, and may comment upon the appearance of other people. It is therefore important that children learn from adults about respecting others. One of the key ways in which children learn is through modelling. They will pick up on the language and the way in which adults approach children who have different needs and talents. It is therefore important that early years workers act as good role models and treat all children and their families with respect and courtesy. Children will also learn about others' needs and differences through activities and resources.

Use age-appropriate activities, materials and experiences

Children in this period are beginning to evaluate and consider their own strengths and weaknesses. From around the age of six years, some children start to 'give up' in areas where they feel they cannot achieve. This means that it is essential that you plan activities that will help them feel successful and that they enjoy. Children also need opportunities to try out new activities and experiences. This will help them to develop new skills and will also give them confidence. You can use observations to check that children are enjoying activities and can ask children about what they enjoy doing.

Allow children to assess risk

Children in this period need to gain some independence and confidence. They also need to be able to evaluate risks and consider safety. While you must provide safe environments, you must also provide some challenge. In outdoor play, this may mean encouraging children to think about how high they would like to climb or how fast they think that they can go on a bicycle. You can help children gain an awareness of safety by talking through with them how they might manage an activity safely. They may, for example, say that they will wear cycle helmets or would like to climb only up to a certain point.

Use communication effectively and encourage children's communication

Many children in this age range have good language skills. They need now to develop their language use so that they are confident in a range of situations. They may need to use language to socialise with their friends and also to explain their thoughts and feelings. You can help children by modelling the skills of language. Children will need to see you listening to them, using language to explain your thoughts and also making jokes and socialising. It is also important that you look for opportunities to encourage children to talk. This may mean simply asking children for their thoughts or opinions. Remember that children often talk best when they are alone with adults or in small groups.

Support play and learning activities

Many children in this period will have started formal education, but this does not mean that they no longer need to play. Play remains a key way in which children learn and also socialise. Play can be linked to the curriculum, but it is also important to ensure that children can play with materials and resources in the way that they want. Supporting play for this age group does not mean organising every aspect of it. Children can tell you what they want to do and what help they need. They may prefer for you just to be 'around' rather than directing their play.

Be realistic, consistent and supportive in responding to children's behaviour

Children in this age group need boundaries, but they also need to understand the need for them. Children respond well when they are given responsibility for maintaining their own boundaries. They also need to be praised and acknowledged when they resist temptation or control their feelings. Children who find it hard to manage their behaviour need very sensitive support. During this period, children will start to develop a view of themselves. Those who learn that they are not 'good' will start to live up to the label. This is why it is better to work with children rather than to confront them. It is also important that children support each other in maintaining boundaries. Children as a group need to be praised for the way in which they work together and to celebrate, as a group, individual children's success.

Meet the needs of all children

This is a crucial time for children's emotional development. They need to see themselves as strong, capable and good at persevering. Your role is to ensure that activities, opportunities and the way you work with children give them this confidence. Meeting the needs of all children means observing what you do and what is provided for children. Practitioners need to think about whether each child is benefiting. This may mean that activities and approaches need to be changed or adapted for individual children so that they are able to achieve.

Case study 4: Adapting activities to meet the needs of all children

Karl finds it hard to socialise with other children. He gets easily excited and this can lead him to be physically rough with the others. As a consequence, the other children tend to avoid him. Today a large tent has been put out for children to enjoy exploring. It has been suggested that Karl should go in the tent alone, to avoid any problems with other children.

1. *How can this activity be adapted so that Karl can go inside with other children safely?*
2. *Why is it important that Karl gets the opportunity to play with other children?*
3. *Explain why observing children can help you work out how to adapt activities.*

Supporting the development of young people aged 8–12 years

Children in this age group are continuing to develop their independence. They need adults who can support them in this. They also need opportunities to take part in new experiences and to develop new skills. This can be an age at which children begin to lose confidence in their own abilities and so adults should be ready to support them.

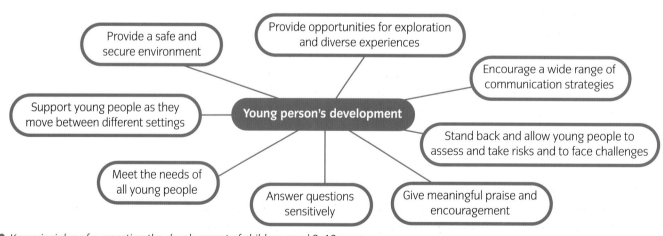

● *Key principles of supporting the development of children aged 8–12 years.*

Provide a safe and secure environment

Keeping children safe remains important. The way in which you provide a safe and secure environment does change slightly, though. One of the key changes is to ask children increasingly to take some responsibility and to set some of their own boundaries. Practitioners also need to do 'background' work, for example by checking premises and equipment and by ensuring that only 'safe' people have access to the children.

Provide opportunities for exploration and diverse experiences

Children in this age range are increasingly making decisions about how they see themselves. To help them find their talents, it is important that they have the opportunity to join in as many different activities and experiences as possible. This might mean children going on outings, trying new foods or having a go at a new sport.

Encourage a wide range of communication strategies

Most children of this age will have developed good language skills but will now need to know how to communicate effectively and confidently with a range of people. This will help them when they change schools or meet other children of a similar age. Children also need to learn the effect that language can have in different situations. A good example of this is swearing or calling names (which many children in this age range might be tempted to try). It is important that practitioners model appropriate communication so that children can learn some of the skills from them.

Stand back and allow children to assess and take risks and to face challenges

Children's physical and cognitive skills have developed considerably. They now need the opportunity to solve problems, assess risks and to set their own boundaries. Asking children how they intend to make a play activity safe or encouraging them to talk through potential problems is the key way in which adults can help children develop confidence and independence. You also need to be able to stand back and be ready for children to come to you (although, obviously, where children are in serious danger adults should intervene).

Give meaningful praise and encouragement

Towards the end of this period, children's body shapes will be changing. They may also be more frequently in competitive and formal situations. This can mean that some children are in danger of losing their confidence. You can help children by positively acknowledging them and by looking for ways of encouraging them. Children also need to know that you value them for who they are, not just for what they do.

Answer questions sensitively

In this period, children are getting a glimpse of the adult world. They need opportunities to ask questions about sex, drugs, relationships and other issues that they start to be aware of. Children need reassurance and also information. Their questions should be answered sensitively and also honestly. The way in which you answer is also important. Children need to feel that you are comfortable with them and ready to talk to them, otherwise they may not return to ask further questions.

Meet the needs of all children

All children need to be valued and to be given opportunities to fulfil their potential. Children in this period are increasingly aware of how well they are doing compared with their peers. They are likely to avoid situations in which they feel they might fail. It is essential that adults observe children and notice their feelings and behaviour. They need to provide activities and encouragement so that children feel successful and good about themselves. In practical terms this might mean adapting activities, putting children in smaller groups or providing different resources. It is also important for children to be given new experiences and opportunities so that they can develop their own talents.

Support children as they move between different settings

Most children between the ages of 8 and 12 years will change school. Some may also move home or have other changes to their lives. Change can make some children anxious. They may worry about 'fitting in' or having friends. They may also feel a sense of loss for their old friends. Adults can support children by being ready to listen to their fears and needs. You can plan activities, outings and experiences to encourage small groups of children to get to know each other.

Supporting the development of young people aged 13–16 years

This is a period of great change for young people. Their bodies are maturing and they are in the process of moving from childhood into adulthood. This passage is exciting but can also be daunting. Young people need adults who are sensitive and supporting and in whom they can trust.

● Key principles of supporting the development of young people aged 13–16 years.

Support young people's learning and development

Young people are likely to come under pressure to gain qualifications. This means that they need to be supported and encouraged. They also need plenty of alternative experiences so that they can gain opportunities to achieve outside the school system. This is essential as there is otherwise a danger that some young people will become disaffected and anxious about their futures.

Encourage positive communication

There are huge pressures on people in this stage of their lives. Positive communication is therefore essential so that young people can feel supported. Adults need to be good listeners and to be ready to avoid making judgements. Young people also need information so that they can make informed decisions.

Support opportunities to assess and take risks and to face challenges

In order to be able to cope successfully in the adult world, young people need to be prepared. They have to be able to consider risks, such as alcohol and drugs, and to know how to manage them. They also need to know how to set their own boundaries in terms of behaviour. Adults need to provide information and also to give young people opportunities to be independent and in control. This may mean that they organise their own activities and environments.

Give meaningful praise and encouragement

All children need reassurance and praise. Young people are no different. They need to know that they are valued and that the adults in their lives will be there for them. Young people need meaningful praise and encouragement so that they feel they can take control.

Meet the needs of all young people

Some young people will have complex needs. They may present challenging behaviour or have attitudes and values that you do not share. Adults working with young people need to be non-judgemental and able still to look at ways of meeting young people's needs. This will mean talking to young people and asking them about what services, provision and support they need.

Observation

Observe a child on five different occasions using at least two different observation methods. Write a summative assessment, based on your observations, that considers:

- the child's interests
- the child's development
- suggestions for future activities based on the child's needs and interests.

Reflect on your own practice

As you have seen, ensuring the promotion of children's development is an essential part of your role. Have a look at the statements below to assess whether you match up to the levels of care needed. The statements all refer to the performance criteria for CCLD 303.3.

Performance criteria statement	Always	Sometimes	Never
Do I plan provision for individual children based on my assessment of developmental progress and on consultation with appropriate adults?			
Do I implement plans flexibly and evaluate their effectiveness in promoting development?			
Do I regularly review and update plans for individual children?			

End-of-unit knowledge check

1. Give four reasons why you might observe a child.
2. Why is it important to ask for parents' permission before carrying out an observation?
3. What is the advantage of being a participant observer?
4. Explain why it is important to observe children several times.
5. What is meant by the term 'formative' assessment?
6. List three factors that might influence a child's development.
7. Explain why play is considered to be important in children's development.
8. What is meant by the term 'attachment'?
9. Explain why Bowlby's work has been influential.
10. Why are key workers used in many early years settings?
11. Explain what happens in the pre-linguistic phase of language development.
12. Give an example of a positive reinforcer that might be used to encourage a young child to repeat wanted behaviour.
13. Explain what is meant by the 'nature versus nurture' debate.
14. Describe one way in which Vygotsky's work has shaped educational practice.
15. Why is it important that children develop skills to help them become independent?

Reflect on and develop practice

Working with children is rarely dull. Every child has different needs and these are likely to change as they grow and develop. This means that, as an early years worker, you need to be quick thinking, as well as being ready to change your overall approach to meet the needs of children. The sector, too, is changing in a variety of ways. There is now more provision, such as wrap-around care, holiday clubs and full day care for babies. Approaches to working with children have also changed. Record keeping, following a curriculum and involving parents are examples of this. Overall, such changes mean that to work effectively within the sector you must be ready to reflect and also develop your practice. This unit looks at ways in which you can do this.

What you must know and understand:

- Why reflection on practice and evaluation of personal effectiveness is important (K3P222)
- How learning through reflection can increase professional knowledge and skills (K3D223)
- How reflection can enhance and use personal experience to increase confidence and self-esteem (K3D224)
- Techniques of reflective analysis (K3D225)
- Reflection as a tool for contrasting what we say we do and what we actually do (K3P226)
- How to use reflection to challenge existing practice (K3D227)
- The difficulties that may occur as a result of examining beliefs, values and feelings (K3P228)
- How to assess further areas for development in your skills and knowledge through reflection, feedback and using resources such the internet, libraries and journals (K3P229)
- How to develop a personal development plan with objectives that are specific, measurable, achievable, realistic and with timescales (K3P230)
- The availability and range of training and development opportunities in the local area and how to access these (K3P231)

- The importance of integrating new information and/or learning in order to meet current best practice, quality schemes or regulatory requirements (K3M232)

Reflect on practice

Reflective practice is relatively new to the sector. It is a new way of working and one that can improve the quality of your work considerably. Finding ways of developing and maintaining this quality has not been easy. Inspections, reports by line managers and sending staff on training are tools that have been tried. Today, it is realised that the best person to help you work effectively with children is yourself. The term 'reflective practitioner' is used to describe people who are aware of their limitations and gaps in their knowledge as well as their strengths and qualities. More importantly, reflective practitioners are also ready to do something about their limitations to become more effective in their work. This section looks at the importance of reflecting on practice and gives some practical guidance to help you begin to consider your own practice.

Key terms

Reflective practice is the process of thinking about and critically analysing your actions with the goal of changing and improving occupational practice.

Why reflection on practice and evaluation of personal effectiveness is important

Reflecting on your practice should help you in many areas of your work. Like most adults working in this sector, you may find that there is a lot more to your job than just working with children. You may, for example, have significant involvement with parents and other professionals, including colleagues. Reflective practice means looking at all the areas that encompass your job. The diagram shows the ways in which reflecting on your practice can develop your work further.

Changing children's behaviour
By thinking about the way in which you have responded to children's behaviour, you can develop new strategies.

Working with parents
By thinking through how you work with parents, you may be able to develop stronger partnerships.

Working with colleagues
Reflecting on the way in which you interact with colleagues can help you to create better relationships and teams. This can help you to enjoy your work more.

Reflective practice

Meeting individual children's needs
By reflecting on the way that children are learning and your role in this, you should be better able to meet children's needs.

Your role with children
By thinking about the effectiveness of the way in which you work with children you can tailor your approach to suit their interests and needs.

Planning to meet children's needs
By considering the effectiveness of your plans, you may be able to develop new systems of planning and recording that are faster or more effective.

- *Aspects of work that may benefit from reflection on practice.*

The use of best practice benchmarks for self-evaluation

What is considered to be good practice can evolve over time. It is therefore important that you evaluate your own performance against current **best practice benchmarks**. This is why it is important to read articles, take up continued professional development through training and also be aware of changes in the legislation and National Standards. Good practice is at the moment being benchmarked by the National Standards for care in your ~~~~ne country. These are the standards against which your setting will be ~~~~d and therefore need to be adopted in your work practice.

The benefits of reflective practice

The way you work with children will have a significant effect on them. You therefore have a professional duty to reflect and develop your practice because by doing so you are more likely to 'get it right' for individual children and their families.

While children and their families will benefit from you taking time to review your work, so will you. Knowing the reasons why an activity has worked means that you should be able to repeat it successfully. Identifying areas where you need further knowledge and support means that you can ask for time and training. Within each area of your work that you review, you can become more competent and in turn more confident. Overall this tends to mean that you can take on more responsibility and develop your career. There are also benefits if you take time to think about how you interact and work with colleagues. This can lead to stronger professional relationships, which can make the work environment more enjoyable.

Case study 1: Confident and competent practitioners

Moira has been working part time in a playgroup for three years. She loves her job and is interested in taking on more responsibility. Her supervisor has asked her to attend a training course on children's creativity. Moira is a little unsure about whether or not she wants to go. She does not really enjoy doing 'those kinds' of activities with children, as she was not good at art and music at school. During the training day, Moira enjoys herself and learns how to develop children's creativity. She feels more confident and enthusiastic and is keen to try out some of the ideas and approaches she has learnt about. She also realises that her own fear of art and music was probably affecting the way in which she worked with children. She asks the supervisor if she could attend a training day on maths, as this is another area in which she feels unsure.

1. *Explain why Moira is beginning to become a reflective practitioner.*
2. *How might Moira benefit from becoming more aware of her practice?*
3. *Explain how the children will benefit from Moira's confidence and enthusiasm.*

Techniques of reflective analysis

The starting point is to be ready to question what you do and to think about it rather than simply doing it. It can be helpful to begin by considering different areas of your job role and to look at them one by one. This may mean carefully observing the reactions of children and others to help you think about your effectiveness. In situations where you feel you are doing well, consider what skills, knowledge or practice are helping you achieve that success. Where you feel that you have weaknesses, think about what you need to do in order to improve. Generally, most weaknesses are down to skill, experience or knowledge. Viewed in these terms, you can then go on to draw up a plan of action (the personal development plan is considered in detail below).

Ways in which you might approach reflective analysis are set out in the diagram. The principle behind them all is to keep an open mind.

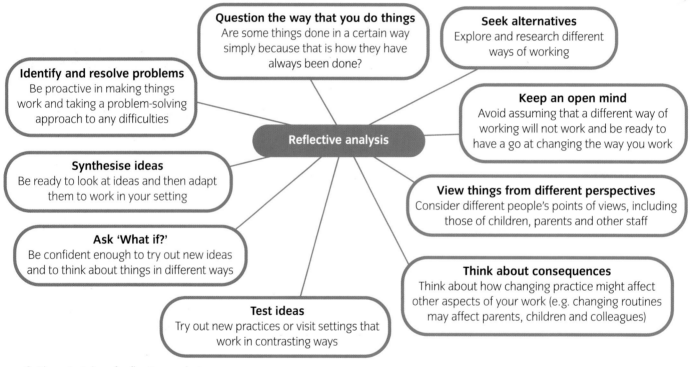

Question the way that you do things
Are some things done in a certain way simply because that is how they have always been done?

Seek alternatives
Explore and research different ways of working

Identify and resolve problems
Be proactive in making things work and taking a problem-solving approach to any difficulties

Keep an open mind
Avoid assuming that a different way of working will not work and be ready to have a go at changing the way you work

Synthesise ideas
Be ready to look at ideas and then adapt them to work in your setting

View things from different perspectives
Consider different people's points of views, including those of children, parents and other staff

Ask 'What if?'
Be confident enough to try out new ideas and to think about things in different ways

Think about consequences
Think about how changing practice might affect other aspects of your work (e.g. changing routines may affect parents, children and colleagues)

Reflective analysis

Test ideas
Try out new practices or visit settings that work in contrasting ways

● *The principles of reflective analysis.*

Keeping an open mind

There are few areas in child care and education where only one single approach is right. To be able to reflect in any depth means thinking about other possibilities and approaches, even when they are unfamiliar. It is easy, especially if you are relatively experienced, to fall into the trap of 'that's the way we have always done it'. While it is important to recognise past success, it is also important to understand that new curricula have been developed as well as new legislation and new theories about how best to work with children.

Case study 2: Inspection, reflection, review

Little Cherubs Day Nursery recently had an inspection. Overall, the results were very good, but the manager was a little disappointed to find that their work with parents was graded only as satisfactory. She had always thought that this was a real strength of the nursery and was confident that it would be graded as outstanding. Her first reaction was to blame the inspectors but, after a couple of days, she began to think hard about the practice in the setting. She realised that there had been very little staff training on working with parents and that the setting had not revisited its policy and ideas about parents for a few years. The reason why this area had been overlooked was mainly that she had assumed that it was an area that was working well.

1. *Why is it important for a setting to review its work regularly?*
2. *How might the nursery benefit from reviewing this area of work?*
3. *How might individual staff benefit from focusing on this area of work?*

Reflection as a tool for contrasting what you say you do and what you actually do

Reflection is an important tool with which to improve practice. You may have knowledge, policies and procedures to work with, but it is important that you think about how these are put into practice. The process of reflection is like holding a mirror up to your work. You can then check that what you ought to be putting into practice is actually happening.

Check it out

Find out how your setting's planning and organisation have changed in the past five years.

Case study 3: Reflection as a tool

Jennie is proud of her nursery and her staff. They have good policies about settling in children and making parents feel welcome. Recently, she visited another nursery and noticed how welcoming it felt, especially as the manager personally greeted many of the parents. She went back to her nursery and started to look at things in a new light. She realised that she did not know many of the parents' names and, on reflection, most mornings she was quite busy and so not available to talk to parents. As she had always felt that she had an 'open door' policy, this came as a bit of shock. She began to organise her day a little differently and made sure that she was around as parents came in to drop off and pick up their children.

1. *How has Jennie's reflective practice benefited the nursery?*
2. *Why is it important to contrast what you do with what you say you do?*

When contrasting what you say you do with what you actually do, you might reflect on the following areas:

- how you respond to children's behaviour
- play opportunities and activities
- the effectiveness of sessions

- your work with colleagues
- your work with parents.

These usually form a significant part of practitioners' work. (Note that these are starting points only, and are not intended to act as a comprehensive list of what you should reflect upon.)

How you respond to children's behaviour

Practice has moved on considerably in terms of children's behaviour over the past few years. It was commonplace for adults to see children whose behaviour was challenging as being the problem. Today, as part of the thinking on behaviour, the focus is turned away from the child and onto the adults. The emphasis is on thinking about the workers' responses and considering whether these are the most effective. To reflect on your own responses often means observing children carefully. Children's behaviour is closely related to their needs. As part of reflecting on this area of work, it is important to think about how you are meeting the child's particular needs. You might also notice how other adults, including children's parents and family members, work with the child. The 'Active knowledge' exercise might help you to consider the way in which you work with a child.

● *Reflect on how your interaction with children can affect their behaviour.*

Active knowledge

Take a close look at your work with a particular child over the course of a session. Then answer the following questions as the beginning of a process of reflection on your practice.

- How often do you smile or acknowledge the child positively?
- How much time do you spend listening to and talking to the child?
- What type of activities does the child most enjoy?
- How do you use these activities to help the child learn?
- To whom does the child respond well?
- How does this person react and work with the child?
- In what type of situations is the child likely to show unwanted behaviour?
- How do you work to avoid these situations?
- How do you encourage the child to take responsibility for his or her own behaviour?
- Is the child showing unwanted behaviour in response to being bored, frustrated or anxious?
- Are you reacting or taking a proactive approach to preventing unwanted behaviour?
- How do you react to situations when the child shows unwanted behaviour?
- Does this reaction make a long-term difference to the child's behaviour?
- What alternatives have you tried?
- What are the issues that are affecting the child's behaviour (e.g. boredom, need for attention, lack of understanding, language development)?
- How are you addressing these?

Mark is working with a small group of children in a nursery. He is finding one child's behaviour quite challenging. In these types of situation he usually asks a child to leave an activity. Today he is thinking through his usual responses and trying to evaluate them. He decides to give the child more responsibility and attention. He is pleasantly surprised to find that the child responds well. He wonders whether this approach would work with all children or just with some. Mark is also beginning to consider whether his approach to dealing with unwanted behaviour is linked to the way he was treated as a child.

1. *Why is it important for adults to reflect upon the strategies they are using with children?*
2. *How might children benefit from adults who can reflect on their practice?*
3. *Suggest one way in which Mark might develop his practice further.*

Play opportunities and activities

Children need a good range of resources and activities in order for them to enjoy playing and learning. Reflecting on how well an activity has worked for individuals and groups of children can help you to plan for the future. It is important to focus on the role of the adult during the activity as well as the responses of the children. This can help you to think about the contribution that you are making to children's enjoyment and learning. Consider the following points:

- Did most children appear to be engaged and interested in the activity?
- Can you identify what it was that helped children to be interested? (Perhaps for example the activity was sensory and children were active.)
- Were children encouraged to take control and be active during the activity?
- How much input from you was needed?
- Why was this input needed?
- How did you encourage children to be active in their play and learning?
- What did the children learn from the activity?
- Was this learning planned or spontaneous?
- How could this learning be reinforced or built upon?
- What did individual children gain from the activity?
- What was your role in helping children to learn?
- What types of resources were used?
- Were there sufficient resources?
- Which resources attracted children's attention?
- What further resources could have been used?
- What were the limitations of this activity?
- How could these limitations be addressed?

Observation

Plan an activity that you have used in the past with children. Carry out the activity. Use the questions listed to help you analyse why it is a successful activity. Give four reasons why this activity appeals to children.

The effectiveness of sessions

As well as looking at individual play opportunities and activities, it is also helpful if you can reflect upon the effectiveness of a session. This is particularly important if you have responsibility for the overall running of a setting. You might consider the following:

- Were the adults in the setting aware of the aims and the plan for the session?
- Were the adults aware of their own role and responsibilities for the session?
- What systems do you use to ensure that everyone gets the information that they need?
- How could these systems be changed to make them more effective?
- Do the timings and routine of the setting cause any difficulties?
- Are children 'rushed' or asked to tidy up before an activity has reached its natural end?
- Were there any difficulties with children's behaviour as a result of the timings and routines of the setting?
- How could the structure of the session be changed to address these issues?
- Was there a balance of activities to engage children's interests?
- What was the balance between child-initiated and adult-initiated activities?
- Which activities and resources were the most popular with children?
- What made them popular?
- Was the space in the setting fully used?
- Were there any areas or pieces of equipment that were not used effectively?
- What changes could be made to make better use of the space or resources?
- Were there any children who were not engaged or participative during part or all of the session?
- What changes could be made to engage their interest?

Your work with colleagues

At whatever level you work within an organisation, it is important to reflect upon your work with colleagues. This is particularly important if you have a supervisory position. Thinking about the way in which you interact and work with colleagues can make a difference to the services you provide for children and their families.

- How do you acknowledge colleagues at the start of the session?
- Do you respond to their acknowledgements positively?
- How does your work affect the smooth running of the team?
- How could these aspects be improved?

Continuing professional development

How to develop a personal development plan

Throughout society, there has been a shift in the way that people work. Most people can no longer expect to stay in the same job until retirement. There is also more focus on employees taking responsibility for their own careers and much less on people following a career structure that has been mapped out for them by their employer. This means that it is sensible for you to develop your own skills and to be aware of your strengths, weaknesses and training requirements. A personal development plan will help you to do so.

Did you know?

Personal development plans are used in many sectors of business as well as in education.

Advantages of having a personal development plan

There are many advantages to drawing up a personal development plan. First, you are taking responsibility for your own career and development. This is important because, although some employers are good at helping staff build on their skills, even they are likely to be limited by their own needs and interests. For example, a setting that does not work with babies is less likely than a setting that has a dedicated baby and toddler room to send a staff member on a training course about heuristic play.

Second, having your own plan also means that you can set your own timescales and goals. Taking responsibility for your own training and development is likely to motivate you more than simply being told what you need to do next.

Finally, a personal development plan can help you to think through what type of work you might like to do in the future and so prevent you from becoming 'stuck' and demoralised in a few years' time.

How to draw up and use a personal development plan

A personal development plan should not just be a piece of paper that means nothing to you. To make it work does require some time and effort. You will need to spend time thinking about what you want to do in the future as well as your own strengths and weaknesses. There are six main steps in creating and using a personal development plan, as set out in the diagram.

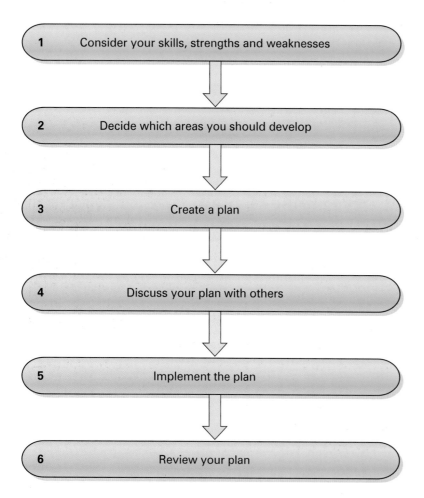

1	Consider your skills, strengths and weaknesses
2	Decide which areas you should develop
3	Create a plan
4	Discuss your plan with others
5	Implement the plan
6	Review your plan

● *Six steps to creating and using a personal development plan.*

Step 1. Consider your skills, experience, strengths and weaknesses

Before you can work out which areas to develop, you need to analyse your current skills. People often have more skills than they give themselves credit for. While some skills are job specific and can be used only in certain situations, such as feeding a baby, others are more transferable, such as being able to use a computer. It is also important to rate your skills so that you know which skills need further development.

Table 304.1 shows a grid that might help you to begin this process. The first two rows have been filled in as an example of how you would complete it. Note that it is not a comprehensive list of skills, as the child care and education sector is a wide area. The grid looks mainly at transferable skills across the sector. You will need also to analyse your current job role and work out what skills you are using.

The grid is divided into five columns. Column 1 shows some of the key competencies that are useful in the child care and education sector. Column 2 is where you give yourself a rating: 1 would mean that you need to work on this area, while 5 would mean that you feel that you are very competent. Column 3 is where you provide evidence of having used this skill. Column 4 is where you indicate how much you enjoy using this skill. You should also think about what this means for your future career. Column 5 is for writing down how you might develop this skill if you decide to focus on it. This is a column that you might need to leave until later on, as it might be important to talk it through with a line manager, assessor or colleague.

Table 304.1. A grid for recording skills, experience, strengths and weaknesses

Competency (skill, knowledge or experience)	Self-rating (1=low, 5= high)	Evidence	Enjoyment of using this competency (1=low, 5= high) and implication	How can I develop this?
Knowledge and experience of working with children of different ages, with different needs and in different settings	3	Worked in a nursery for 3 years with children aged 3–5 years. Worked as a midday supervisor for 1 year with children aged 5–11 years. Now working in day care with children 3–4 years	5 I enjoy working with children who have particular needs. I definitely want to work with children for most of the day. I will not be interested in becoming a manager	Learn more about children's learning and behaviour. Have responsibility for a child with particular needs`
Planning, assessing and record keeping	1	I fill in activity sheets and checklists, but am not responsible for the planning	3 I quite enjoy this and will need it for other jobs	Ask Sandie to show me how she does it. Ask if I can do more training days
Knowledge of the curriculum/framework				

continued on next page

Competency (skill, knowledge or experience)	Self-rating (1=low, 5= high)	Evidence	Enjoyment of using this competency (1=low, 5= high) and implication	How can I develop this?
Working in partnership with parents				
People and leadership skills				
Managing a budget				
Information technology skills				
Writing skills (e.g. letters, reports, newsletters)				
Health and safety				
Knowledge of legislation affecting the sector				
Multidisciplinary working				

Step 2. Decide which areas you should develop

This step requires a great deal of thought. First, you need to think about your current job. What do you need to do in order to develop and become more competent in your role? You also have to try to think ahead. Are you likely to want to stay in the same role or are you interested in moving on? Remember that moving on does not necessarily mean taking on more responsibility, but can mean simply working with a different age group or in a different setting. If you are not sure what job opportunities are available in the sector, look at some of the vacancies that are advertised locally and also in the specialist press. This will also give you an idea of the type of skills that are involved. Focus on what you want to achieve rather than any limitations, such as your age or family circumstances. Usually it is possible to find a balance between these limitations and what you want to do.

Step 3. Create the plan

Once you have considered the areas in which development might take place, you need next to think about how best you might achieve your objectives. Common approaches include training, asking to take on responsibility or shadowing a colleague. This should include a timescale for the achievement of your objectives, which might affect how you prioritise

Check it out

- What would you like to be doing in three or five years' time?
- What is preventing you from doing it now?
- What skills, knowledge or experience could you build now to help you towards this?

them. For example a college course may enrol students only once a year, and so while waiting to enrol you might look at a different area.

Large areas of development can be broken into smaller ones. This will have a bearing on the timescale. Setting yourself realistic goals is essential, as it will help to ensure that your plan works. The term 'SMART' is often used when setting goals. The aim of SMART goals or targets is to help people focus clearly on what they want to achieve and to avoid unrealistic objectives.

Specific
Try to make sure in your planning that you have thought clearly about what you need to learn, experience or develop.

Measurable
Consider how you will know whether you have achieved this part of your plan. You may, for example, need a qualification or certificate or want others to recognise that you have become more skilled.

Timescale
Thinking about how long each part of the plan will take is essential. Many people need a start and an end time to help them work effectively. Working out a realistic timescale will help you to remain motivated.

S = Specific M = Measurable A = Achievable
R = Realistic T = Timescale

Achievable
When thinking about your plan, make sure that it is possible to complete each target. This will include thinking about how you will organise it and whether it will meet your needs.

Realistic
There is always a danger of being over-enthusiastic and over-optimistic at the start of any project. Think about how you normally cope and check that your plan will meet your needs and the way in which you learn and work.

● *Your goals should be SMART.*

There are no set formats for a personal development plan, but any plan should show when and how you intend to implement it. You should show how you intend to check your progress. It's also a good idea to record what the objectives are for each part of your plan. Table 304.2 gives an example of a format for a personal development plan; it may give you some starting points for your own. It would be important to adapt it so that it suits your own needs and circumstances.

Table 304.2. Example format for a personal development plan

Area	Why?	How?	By when?	Update
Working with children with particular needs	To gain a qualification	Local college	September 2006	

Step 4. Discuss your plan with others

It is helpful to discuss your plan with other people, such as your employer, tutor or assessor. They may be able to offer support and advice. An employer may, for example, be ready to pay for some training or have other suggestions as to how you might gain experience or knowledge. In some cases your personal development plan may be used as part of the staff review and appraisal process. A tutor or assessor may know of a suitable qualification that will meet your needs. As a result of such input you may need to revise your plan.

Case study 7: Mark's personal development plan

Mark enjoyed visiting another nursery and also attending a day's training on children's behaviour. He realised that this was an area of working with children that he was particularly interested in. He began the process of drawing up a personal development plan. He realised that while he had experience of working with a variety of children of different ages, he was now ready to specialise. He presented his draft plan to his manager and asked whether the setting would be ready to fund a course he had found. He particularly wanted to attend this course because it led to a nationally recognised qualification. The manager could see the benefits for the nursery and agreed that the nursery would fund 50% of the cost. In return, Mark agreed to work with staff on a training day with a view to looking at the behaviour policy. Mark was pleased to do this as he realised that it would give him some experience of managing a project. Mark's manager also suggested that he should learn more about special educational needs. She found out that there was a course that led to a qualification at the local college. They agreed that to do both courses at the same time would be unrealistic, but that it would be worth doing the special educational needs course later on in the year.

1. *Why can it be helpful to talk through a personal development plan?*
2. *In what ways might Mark's nursery benefit from his plan?*
3. *Why is it important to establish some priorities when producing a plan?*

Step 5. Implement the plan

If your plan is realistic and you have taken time to do the necessary research, implementing it should be quite straightforward. It is, however, likely that within the first few weeks you will need to revisit the plan. You may find that a course that you wanted to do is not available or that an opportunity to gain experience has not materialised. This may result in a change to the plan and a reordering of priorities.

Step 6. Review your plan

It is also important to review the plan every six months or so. If you do not do so it may become an irrelevant piece of paper. Think about what you have achieved and consider whether circumstances have changed. You may, for example, have gained a promotion or been offered the chance of some training that was not originally scheduled.

Training and development opportunities

Continuing professional development is an important component of a personal development plan. It is important to think carefully about the kind of training that you need because there are many different types in the child care and education sector. Returning to training can also be hard if you have not done any recently.

Key terms

Continuing professional development means ongoing training and professional updating.

• *The types of training that might be available in your area. Over the past few years, a growing number of training courses have been developed.*

Finding out about training and funding

There are many ways of finding out about the training that is available in your area. Talk to local colleges, the careers service and an early years advisor as well as looking in magazines for the sector. In some areas there are forums for people working in early years (e.g. the Early Years Development and Childcare Partnership and the Pre-school Learning Alliance).

As well as various types of training being available, various funds are sometimes allocated to training. It is always worth beginning by talking to your employers, as they may have a staff development training fund that they are happy to use towards your training. Many qualifications are also subsidised or in some areas free, especially for people under 25 years of age. In addition, local forums for early years often provide free training sessions. If you are returning to the workforce and have claimed benefits, it can be worth asking at the local job centre if any training can be paid for. Finally, there are sometimes discretionary grants available in some areas. Finding out about these can be difficult, but it is always worth asking the organiser of the training you are interested in.

Will my time be paid?

Whether or not your training is paid for or your time is paid for depends very much on what you are doing and where you live. In some areas, employers are reimbursed for the cost of replacement staff for short courses in the day, whereas in other areas this is not available. Some qualifications are structured so that you can work and learn at the same time, although they often rely on you studying in the evenings.

If you are not being paid for training, it is worth asking if you can pay in instalments. It is also worth trying to see the long-term view and consider the financial and other benefits that the training will give you.

Courses, conferences and workshops

Many practitioners attend training that does not lead to qualifications. Much of this type of training lasts only a few hours. It is valuable nonetheless, as it can give you a taster or update your knowledge if you already have a qualification. A good example of this is training that focuses on one area of a curriculum or child protection training. This type of training is also useful because you can meet other practitioners in your area. Ideally you should try to undertake at least four days a year of this type of training.

You should keep a record of the courses and workshops that you have attended. You can then show a potential employer that you have kept your professional knowledge up to date. It is a good idea to keep a balance in the type of courses that you do. It is easy to be enthusiastic only about certain aspects of working with children, while ideally you need to be able to master them all. Short bursts of training are useful if you wish to find out about a new area of work. They also enable you to see what is involved before undertaking a longer period of study.

● *Training can be in the form of attendance at a one-day workshop.*

Full-time and part-time courses leading to a qualification

Most short courses do not lead to qualifications, with the exception of those on first aid, lifting and handling, and food hygiene. While short bursts of training can be very motivating and interesting, they may not be sufficient in themselves.

Do I need a qualification?

A good starting point when thinking about training is to consider whether or not you need a recognised qualification. Qualifications are often required if you wish to work in some jobs. A manager of a day care setting or of a nursery would, for example, need to have an appropriate level 3 qualification. If you wish to work as a nanny or childminder you should also gain a level 3 qualification, as you will be working with children alone. A recognised qualification will also help you to gain or change employment.

Case study 8: Choosing a recognised qualification at the right level

Annie wants to start her own business as a childminder. A glossy brochure has come through the post advertising a range of courses. She flicks through it and sees that there is one about caring for children. She notices that it says that no previous experience is necessary and that the entire course can be done from home. It seems a little too good to be true, especially as the brochure promises that no examinations or assessments need be undertaken. She telephones the number and asks if the course is nationally recognised and whether it will meet the requirements for registration as a childminder. The salesperson does not appear to know. She telephones the national organisation for childminders. They are very helpful and tell her that there is a difference between just doing a course and actually getting a qualification. They give her the number of the local organiser of the childminding network in her area. She telephones this number and finds that a range of courses is available locally. She also finds out that while she will eventually need a qualification at level 3, most people begin on a level 2 course so that they can build up their experience and knowledge. She puts the glossy brochure in the bin.

1. *Why is it unlikely that a nationally recognised qualification can be gained without any assessment taking place?*
2. *What is the danger of doing a course without knowing whether or not it will lead to a qualification?*
3. *Who would you contact in your local area if you wished to find out more about qualifications?*

Checking that qualifications are nationally recognised

It is essential before enrolling on any course that you check that the qualification is nationally recognised. Sadly, some students have taken a course of study only to find that their 'certificate' is not recognised and that they have paid for a worthless piece of paper. For a qualification to be nationally recognised, it has to be presented by an awarding body such as CACHE, Edexcel or City and Guilds. Awarding bodies are responsible for the syllabus and the assessment of the course. When candidates successfully complete a course, the awarding body issues the certificate. Most awarding bodies have websites and contact numbers that you can ring.

Finding out what the qualification covers

It is a good idea to find out exactly what a qualification will cover. Some qualifications do not cover looking after babies or working with older children, for example. It is also worth finding out whether or not the qualification covers practical work with children as well as covering the theory. You may also find that the qualification that you are looking at covers more than you need. This in the long term can be useful, as it will allow you to diversify if you wish.

Understanding how to achieve the qualification

All nationally recognised qualifications require candidates to do some form of assessment. Understanding the type of assessments that you will need to complete is important when choosing a qualification (see Table 304.3). Some qualifications use a range of methods to assess whether a candidate is at the level required to pass. The best way to find out how the qualification is gained is by asking the organisation that is providing the training or by checking with the awarding body.

Table 304.3. Methods of assessment for a qualification

Method	Nature of assessment	Advantages and disadvantages for the candidate
Examinations	Some examinations involve writing while others are about reading questions and selecting the most appropriate answers (multiple choice).	Some people can cope well with the stress of examinations, while others find it difficult. You will need to consider this carefully.
Written assignments	Many courses have written assignments for candidates to complete. These are either marked by the course tutors and checked by the awarding body or sent away to be marked externally.	Assignments work well for people who are good at writing and planning their time. Organisations offering training will help you with written assignments, although you will still need to complete the work yourself.
Portfolio	Some qualifications are based on candidates collecting material or evidence and presenting it in a portfolio.	This type of assessment works well for people who are well organised and self-disciplined.
Practical assessments	Some qualifications are designed to show that you are competent in addition to having the background theory. Qualifications that show competency will probably involve some type of practical assessment.	You are likely to be visited by an assessor at an agreed time and watched as you work. This type of assessment suits people who know that they are good when they work with children.

● *Many people are surprised to find they enjoy returning to study. It is important, though, to consider carefully what types of assessment a particular qualification will involve.*

How do I choose if several places are offering the same qualification?

It is worth doing a little research if you are not sure where to do your course. A good starting point is recommendation by other students. You could find out what the success rate was and how many students dropped out. It is also worth finding out how the training organisation intends to deliver the qualification. Some organisations expect students to do more self study at home than others. This might suit you well if you are self-disciplined and organised, but may not be right for you if you are someone who likes being 'taught'.

Active knowledge

Below is a list of areas in which people often need update training. Choose three of them:

● health and safety
● food handling
● working with babies
● understanding children's behaviour
● working with parents
● first aid
● management.

For each area of training find a course in your area. Write a brief summary of the training, to include cost, length and whether it leads to a qualification.

Getting the most out of training

For many people, returning to study can be daunting, especially if it has been a while since they have written anything down. The good news is that mature students can be very successful and many often find themselves getting quite addicted to learning. Regardless of the type of training that you undertake, you should aim to get the most out of what you choose to do.

If a course is popular, it is likely to be filled quickly. Once you know that you want to do it and if necessary have checked with your employer, try to enrol as soon as possible. If you find that the course is already full, try asking if you can be on a waiting list.

Always arrive on time. Ideally, try to be there a few minutes beforehand so that you can talk to other practitioners and meet someone to sit next to. In terms of qualifications, attendance is a fairly good predictor of success. Students with poor attendance tend to drop out and also do less well in assignments and examinations.

If you are given handouts, do take the time afterwards to read them. It is also important to keep some notes so that if you need to revise, to write an assignment or to pass on the information to colleagues, you have some way of remembering them.

Training can challenge your current practice or knowledge. You need to keep an open mind and think through carefully what is being said or suggested. If you try a new approach give it sufficient time before rejecting it. It is also worth remembering that both curricula and what is considered to be good practice evolve. This is an important reason why it is essential to attend training events frequently.

Case study 9: Keeping an open mind

Jane has been childminding for over 20 years. She recently went on a course about speech and language development. During the course, the tutor talked about the role of the television. She said that the latest research suggested that it should be used with great caution with children under three years old, as it might affect their language development. The tutor also recommended a website that she felt was helpful for practitioners to look at to find out more about this area. Jane was quite surprised, as she had often had the television on (she felt that it made the atmosphere more homely). Her first reaction was to dismiss the idea that it might be detrimental. Later on in the day, she thought more about it and decided to follow the advice and to note whether she could see any difference in children's language and behaviour. She also decided to read what was on the website.

1. *Why is it important for practitioners to have an open mind when they go on training?*
2. *Explain why it is important for practitioners to be aware of recent research.*
3. *How might children benefit when practitioners take the time to update their knowledge?*

Obtaining any qualification is a success in itself. Remembering this is quite important if you are already juggling a lot of other things in your life. Do not fall into the trap of working so hard that, after a few months, you have to stop because you have become exhausted.

Many mature students need support with their writing skills or even understanding some of the jargon at first. If you know that this is going to be a hurdle, do not be afraid to ask for help. No one will mind or think any the less of you. Be ready, too, for times when you might not be able to hand work in on time. Explain to your tutor how far you have got and when you think that you will be able to manage it. You might even be surprised at how many other students are in exactly the same position.

Most mature students juggle family, work and study. This means that you need to set yourself realistic goals about what you can and cannot do. Build in some time each week when you can study. If it is hard to study at home, think about whether you can do so during a break at work or get to the college or training centre early, so that you can spend some time studying there before the course begins.

Finally, it is a good idea to keep a record of the training that you have undertaken. Some people keep a file which contains notes and handouts from short courses as well as certificates of training. Your record of training is important when you apply for jobs, as it shows how you have kept up to date and also extended your professional knowledge. Remember to keep any certificates safe so that you can find them easily. It is now common practice for employers to ask to see the original of any qualifications.

Check it out

Talk to two people who have recently finished a qualification and find out the following:
- What did they enjoy most about doing the qualification?
- How has their learning affected their practice?
- What problems did they encounter doing the course?
- How did they overcome these problems?

 Keys to good practice: Training

- ✓ Register early
- ✓ Have good attendance
- ✓ Read handouts and keep notes
- ✓ Keep an open mind
- ✓ Try not to be a perfectionist
- ✓ Be ready to ask for help
- ✓ Set yourself realistic goals
- ✓ Keep a record of your training

The importance of integrating new information

Once you have completed some professional development such as training, it is important to consider how you can integrate your new information so that it is reflected in your practice. This may mean looking again at the care standards or the early years curriculum that your are working with and thinking about how you now need to change your practice. If you are leading a team or have responsibility for specific areas of a curriculum, it may mean devising an action plan or sharing your information with colleagues. In some cases, small adjustments to the way you work or plan activities might be required, such as changing the layout, while in others it can mean a significant overhaul of policies and procedures. A good example of this is child protection, where, over the past ten years, there have been significant changes to the procedures adopted in settings.

End-of-unit knowledge check

1. What does the term reflective practitioner mean?
2. Why is it important for practitioners to update their skills and knowledge?
3. What is a personal development plan?
4. What does the term 'shadowing' mean?
5. What is the difference between a level 2 and a level 3 qualification?
6. Why is it useful to meet with other local practitioners?
7. Give examples of two different types of assessment.
8. How do children and their families benefit from reflective practitioners?
9. What are SMART targets?
10. Give two ways in which you might gain feedback about your practice.

Protect and promote children's rights

An essential part of your role is to help to ensure and protect the rights of children. You need to be fully aware of how these rights influence practice in early years settings. All children have the right to a voice and to be protected from abuse. It is the role of a worker in children's care, learning and development to promote equality of access to relevant services. You need to be fully conversant with the legislation, policies and procedures that promote inclusion for all children, families and communities. It is essential that you are aware of the individual needs of all children and that your setting can contribute to meeting them. Protection of children from abuse is a vital part of any child care worker's role and you must be able to maintain and follow the relevant policies and procedures.

What you must know and understand:

- Legislation covering children's rights, laws covering equality and inclusion, and the UN Convention on the Rights of the Child (K3P233 and K3P234)
- The various forms of discrimination, the groups most likely to experience discrimination and the possible effects of discrimination on the children and families (K3P235)
- How inequalities are embedded in our society in all geographical areas and the negative effects of inequalities on all children, including those who are not experiencing inequality directly (K3P236 and K3D237)
- Difficulties in accessing provision and services that might be experienced by children and families and how procedures and practices can work to overcome these and improve services (K3C238)
- What barriers to participation might be and how you would ensure these were recognised and removed (K3D239)
- The kinds of community resources and support that are available, the scope of opportunities for referral if necessary and sources of information for children and families (K3D240)

- How to ensure your provision aims to meet current guidance for implementing inclusion and anti- discriminatory practice (K3P241)
- How to assess and plan for children's needs drawing on available resources and support services (K3D242)
- Organisational strategies and practice issues to ensure equal access and compliance with legislation for disabled children and children with special educational needs (K3P244)
- Techniques of monitoring to assess the effectiveness of provision in implementing inclusive and anti-discriminatory practice and the need for accountability (K3P245 and K3P247)
- The requirements of legislation, regulation and codes of practice for children's protection (K3P246)
- The importance of partnerships with parents and families (K3D248)
- Definitions and indicators of child abuse (K3S251)
- What increases a child's vulnerability to abuse (K3S250)
- The importance of following procedures without forming premature judgements regarding abuse (K3S249)
- Policies, procedures and the lines of reporting in the setting or service concerning suspected or actual abuse (K3S252)
- Safe working practices that protect children and adults who work with them (K3S253)
- The importance of promoting children's assertiveness, self-confidence and self-esteem to enable them to protect themselves (K3D254)
- The benefits of a multi-professional, multi-agency approach in maximising children's experiences and learning (K3M333)

Support equality of access

Legislation covering children's rights, laws covering equality and inclusion, and the UN Convention on the Rights of the Child

There is a raft of equal opportunities and diversity legislation relevant to children that every setting will be bound by. The National Standards for each home country reflect these (see pages 48–49). There are also Acts relating to sex discrimination, disability discrimination, race relations and special educational needs. In addition, the UK is a signatory of the United Nations Convention on the Rights of the Child, which is an international treaty that sets out the human rights of children and sets out the basic principles of working with children in all countries.

 It is an undeniable right that all children are fairly treated, loved, protected and helped to develop to the best of their ability.

Race Relations (Amendment) Act 2000

This Act places a responsibility on public organisations to encourage racial and social harmony and requires schools and nurseries to:

- promote equality of opportunity
- promote good relations between persons of different racial groups
- eliminate racial discrimination
- prepare and publish a race equality policy
- monitor and assess the effect of their **policies**.

Special Educational Needs and Disability Act 2001 (SENDA)

Before SENDA, children and young people in education did not have the same protection from discrimination on the basis of **disability** as in their everyday lives. There is now a requirement to make reasonable adjustments to the **provision** where a child or young person may be disadvantaged without it. The implications of SENDA are discussed in the section on special needs below.

Key terms

Policies are what your organisation has agreed its staff should or should not do in certain situations.

Disability means a physical or mental impairment which has a substantial and long-term adverse effect on the child's ability to carry out normal day-to-day activities.

Provision can be a physical setting or a peripatetic service based in the community, or other service.

The UN Convention on the Rights of the Child

The United Nations Convention on the Rights of the Child was signed by all countries of the world (except the USA and Somalia), including the United Kingdom in December 1991. It is an international human rights treaty that applies to all children and young people under the age of 18 years. It gives children and young people a set of comprehensive rights, including: the right to express and have their views taken into account on all matters that affect them; the right to play, rest and leisure; and the right to be free from all forms of violence (see Table 305.1). Some groups of children and young people – for example those living away from home, and young disabled people – have additional rights to make sure they are treated fairly and that their needs are met.

Table 305.1. Some key rights set out in the UN Convention on the Rights of the Child

Article	Essential feature of article
Article 3	• In all actions concerning children, whether undertaken by public or private social welfare institutions, the best interests of the child shall be a primary consideration.
	• The government must ensure the child such protection and care as are necessary for his or her well-being.
	• All services and facilities responsible for the care or protection of children shall conform with the requirements of safety, health, number and suitability of staff.
Article 6	• Every child has the inherent right to life.
Article 7	• A child has the right to a name, a nationality and, as far as possible, the right to know and be cared for by his or her parents.
Article 9	• Children shall not be separated from their parents against their will, except when such separation is necessary for the best interests of the child (e.g. where there is abuse or neglect of the child by the parents).
	• A child who is separated from one or both parents must be able to maintain regular personal relations and direct contact with both parents, except if this is contrary to the child's best interests.
Article 12	• Children who are capable of forming their own views have the right to express those views freely in all matters affecting them, and these views should be given due weight in accordance with the age and maturity of the child.
Article 13	• A child has the right to freedom of expression, including freedom to seek, receive and impart information and ideas of all kinds, orally, in writing or in print, in the form of art, or through any other medium of the child's choice.
Article 14	• A child has the right to freedom of thought, conscience and religion.

Key terms

Children with **special educational needs** learn differently from most children of the same age. They may need extra or different help.

Check it out

Have a look at the policies and procedures in your setting relating to inclusion.

- How are legislation and standards referred to?
- How is it made clear that there are legal requirements to work in certain ways?
- What reference has been made to equal opportunities?
- How could the policies and procedures be developed to make them easier for staff to understand?

Article 15 • A child has the right to freedom of association and to freedom of peaceful assembly.

Article 18 • Both parents have common and primary responsibilities for the upbringing and development of the child.

Article 19 • Government must take all appropriate measures to protect a child from all forms of physical or mental violence, injury or abuse, neglect or negligent treatment, maltreatment or exploitation, including sexual abuse, while in the care of parent(s), legal guardian(s) or any other person who has the care of the child.

Article 23 • All mentally or physically disabled children should enjoy a full and decent life, in conditions that ensure dignity, promote self-reliance and facilitate the child's active participation in the community.

• Disabled children have the right to special care with assistance appropriate to the child's condition and to the circumstances of the parents or others caring for the child.

Article 24 • Children have the right to the highest attainable standard of health and facilities for the treatment of illness and rehabilitation of health.

Article 26 • Every child has the right to benefit from social security, including social insurance.

Article 27 • Every child has the right to a standard of living adequate for the child's physical, mental, spiritual, moral and social development.

• The parent(s) or others responsible for the child have the primary responsibility to provide, with government help if necessary, within their abilities and financial capacities, the conditions of living necessary for the child's development.

Article 28 • All children have the right to free primary education and secondary and higher education should be available to all.

Article 32 • Children must be protected from economic exploitation and from performing any work that is likely to be hazardous or to interfere with the child's education, or to be harmful to the child's health or physical, mental, spiritual, moral or social development.

Article 37 • No child shall be subjected to torture or other cruel, inhuman or degrading treatment or punishment. Neither capital punishment nor life imprisonment without possibility of release shall be imposed for offences committed by persons below 18 years of age.

• No child shall be deprived of his or her liberty unlawfully.

Active knowledge

Talking about the UN Convention on the Rights of the Child sounds very formal. However, if you look at Table 305.1, can you see how you should be working to the Convention in your day-to-day practice with children? Think about it and list some examples of how you meet the provisions of these articles.

Discrimination, the groups most likely to experience it and its effects on children and families

What is discrimination?

Discrimination means telling things apart – knowing the difference between similar things. It is quite alright to discriminate between, say, a pair of shoes that you do not like and a pair that you do, but discriminating against people is very different. Discrimination does not mean 'telling people apart'. It is important to realise that people are all different. Discrimination does mean giving people an unequal service or treatment because of their differences.

If an employer did not want to appoint a woman to a job, because she might leave to have children, the employer would be illegally discriminating against her. The discrimination would not be simply that the employer realised she was female. The discrimination would be that she was treated differently from a man who might want to start a family. A man in the same situation would be appointed while the woman would receive unequal treatment because the employer thought she might leave the job or take maternity leave to have a baby.

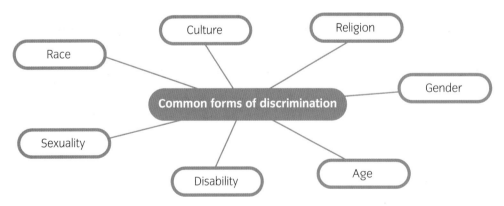

● *People who belong to any group can be discriminated against.*

How does discrimination come about?

All those who work with children and young people have to be interested in learning about other people – interested in diversity and difference. You cannot divide children and young people into 'types that I like' and 'types that I don't like'. Children and parents must never be excluded from receiving a good service because they belong to a different race, culture, religion, gender or age group, or because of their sexuality or abilities.

Seeing the world in terms of 'us and them' leads to certain kinds of thinking. Discrimination sometimes comes about because of assumptions that people make in their thinking. People will sometimes stereotype or label others.

Stereotyping

Life can be very complicated and sometimes people try to make it easier by seeing people in certain groups as being 'all the same'. One traditional stereotype is that people with red hair are bad tempered. A stereotype is a fixed way of thinking about a group of people. When people say 'All women are…' or 'All black people are…' or 'All gay people are…' they will probably go on to describe a stereotype of these groups.

Skilled work with people of all ages starts from being interested in their individual differences. Stereotyping lumps people together as if they were all the same. Thinking in stereotypes usually stops a person from being a good worker with people.

Check it out

What would you do in these situations?

- You are asked to line up the children ready for outdoor play with the girls in one line, the boys in another.
- Mrs Smith complains because her daughter has been playing with a little girl with cerebral palsy.
- A boy in the reception class uses abusive racist language.
- The owner of the nursery insists that all children wear shorts in nursery, although there are many children who are Moslem.

These are all incidents that have occurred in child care settings, and all are discriminatory.

Case study 1: Labelling

Some years ago there was a school for children with learning difficulties. When it came to mealtimes, the children had to sit down. The 'slow' children were allowed to start first because they took longer. Staff would label these children 'slows'. The 'slows' knew who they were and sat down when 'slows' were called for. Some children were not very skilled at holding their plates and so on, and these were labelled 'clumsies'. Children would describe themselves as 'slows' or 'clumsies'.

1. *What effect do you think describing themselves as a 'slow' or a 'clumsy' would have on children's development of self-esteem?*
2. *Can you think of an example of labelling a child that you have observed? If so, how did it affect that child and what would have been a better way of working with the child?*

Labelling

Labelling of individuals and groups is another form of discrimination. With labelling, instead of having a set of fixed opinions about a group to which a person belongs (which is stereotyping), the person is summed up in just one word or term. Labels can be used to claim that a group of people are all the same. They may say that people are all only one thing, such as aggressive, emotional or very clever. When individuals are labelled, it is almost as if they stop being people – labels take away people's dignity and individuality.

Prejudice

The word 'prejudice' derives from the Latin for 'previous judgement' and means judging other people without the knowledge to judge properly. Moreover, new information is unlikely to undermine a prejudice. If people believe stereotypes about groups, they may go on to make judgements about individuals. For instance, an employer who believes that 'women don't really care about work, they only care about their family' may develop a prejudice that women are not suited for promotion to senior positions. Employers with such a prejudice might try to promote only men. Once people develop prejudices against groups of people they are likely to discriminate against them when in a position to make decisions.

The consequences of prejudice and discrimination

People who work with children have to make decisions about how to help others all the time. If you have prejudices or if you label or stereotype children or parents, you may discriminate against them in the way that you work.

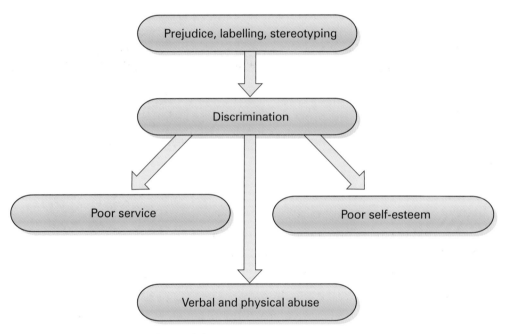

● *The consequences of prejudice and discrimination.*

Discrimination is not always obvious. It is often easy to make the same assumptions that everyone else does and this can come out in conversation. Children's and parents' rights can often be ignored as a result, and they can receive a worse service than others. When services or workers make assumptions about people, discrimination can easily follow. For example, the assumptions that everyone eats the same food or celebrates the same religious festivals results in people being excluded and discriminated against.

It is important to find out about individuals and try to check that your own behaviour and the service you provide meet the needs of people.

Where services do not provide equal quality to different groups of people it is important to challenge discrimination, first by raising the issue with managers. There should be a policy in every setting that works with people to help prevent discrimination.

How inequalities are embedded in our society and their negative effects

Poverty

The biggest single cause of inequality in the UK is poverty. There are a number of other reasons for inequality of **access** to services and provision but most of them are related in one way or another to poverty. The following children are at great risk of living in a low-income household:

- children in lone-parent households
- children in workless households
- children in large families
- children in families with one or more disabled persons
- children in families where the mother is aged under 25
- children in households headed by someone from a minority ethnic group (particularly of Pakistani or Bangladeshi origin or children of asylum seekers)
- children in inner-city areas.

Key terms

Access means opportunities for participation.

Geographical location

People who earn a good salary and are in secure jobs can choose their lifestyle. They can also choose where they would like to live. People in the professional classes tend to live in more expensive housing, in areas with good facilities for travel and education. People with lower incomes tend to live in more densely occupied areas and are often forced to rent rather than buy their homes. Different social class groups often live in different neighbourhoods. This is why marketing companies can use postcodes to work out what materials to send to different areas.

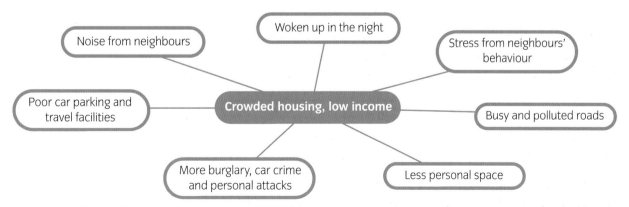

● The possible effects of living in high-density housing on a low income.

Child poverty and education

Studies show that children from poor backgrounds do not perform as well at school. A variety of reasons have been given for this, including:

- their language (children from better-off homes are more likely to use language in a similar way to their teachers)
- lack of access to books and other resources at home
- lack of suitable places in which to do homework
- lack of access to educational visits and materials
- there is less parental encouragement, partly because the parents are less familiar with the education system.

Child poverty and life chances

Poverty in childhood increases the likelihood of low income in adulthood. There is a strong link between children's earnings (as adults) and those of their parents. Only a third of boys whose fathers were in the bottom quarter of income made it into the top half when they grew up. Men whose fathers were unemployed are twice as likely to be unemployed for a year or more between 23 and 33 years of age (Department of Social Security, 1999).

Did you know?

Children from poor backgrounds lag significantly behind better-off children in educational development at 22 months. In 2000 in England and Wales three-quarters of pupils whose parents were in the highest professional group achieved five or more GCSEs at grades A–C, compared with only a third in the lowest group.

(Source: Sparkes, 2003)

Difficulties in accessing provision and services, and barriers to participation

Families who are poor often lack the means to search out services and facilities. For example, they are unlikely to have access to cars or the internet. Access to services may be further hampered by barriers of language and culture.

Better-quality early education delivers results for children. A child with pre-school experience has higher scores on pre-reading and number skills on entry to reception class compared with one without such experience. In turn, reception class attainment has an effect on attainment at Key Stage 1.

More and better child care improves life chances and helps to tackle child poverty:

- 23% of non-working parents mention lack of access to affordable child care as a reason for not working.
- 51% of non-working lone parents mention lack of suitable child care as a barrier to work.

Research shows that low achievers from higher social backgrounds overtake high achievers from low social background by the age of 6–7 years unless intervention helps children from poorer backgrounds to realise their potential. Reaching children early through integrated services can help stop inequality blighting their chances and narrow the achievement gap.

Case study 2: Accessing services

Jamilla lives on the fourth floor of a block of flats with her three-year-old twins. Her husband has a chronic health problem and cannot get out very much. The lifts in the flats are often not working and when they do they are dirty and smelly. It is a 30-minute walk to the local shops and community centre. The community centre has a SureStart centre, which Jamilla would like to use so that she could perhaps work part time, but she is too nervous to go. She worries that there will not be anyone she can talk to, and her husband is not happy at the thought of other people looking after their children.

1. *What is stopping Jamilla going to the centre?*
2. *How could she be helped to access the services at the centre?*
3. *What could be done by the centre to reach out to families like Jamilla's?*

Accessible and affordable child care and early years services are critical for all children and key to reducing some of the serious social class differences. Parents cannot move out of poverty and into work or training without high-quality, affordable child care.

Black and minority ethnic families tend to experience more barriers to access of child care and early years services than white families and so do not take up places on offer. Do not forget that minority ethnic families also include 'new communities' of asylum seekers, refugees and Travellers and Gypsies – groups that have very different needs due to very differing circumstances. However, it is important not to stereotype all such communities as being unable to access child care.

What are the barriers?

● *There are many complex barriers to the take-up of services.*

There are many complex barriers to the take-up of services and they vary according to ethnic community and, often, location. However, there are some common issues that were identified by research by SureStart. (SureStart is discussed on page 197.) These related to the type of provision, its costs, a lack of sensitivity to language and culture, and a lack of information. More information about the work done on inclusion by SureStart can be found on its website (www.surestart.gov.uk).

Type of provision available

- Families want flexible child care that helps with the education and socialisation of their children.
- Some families need access to child care only when they require it, for example, when a family member cannot offer support, or when work patterns demand it.
- Many families feel that most child care settings cannot offer the level of flexibility or the type of programme that they require.
- Many minority ethnic families prefer community-based provision (e.g. within local schools or community centres) but there is a perception that staff are not as well trained.
- Research shows that the take-up of places in the private and voluntary sector by black and minority ethnic families is much lower than the take-up of places in the maintained (mostly school) sector.

The cost of child care

- The cost of child care is seen as a problem for many families.
- The location of child care settings outside their area can give the impression that they are only for the rich.
- There is a high level of take-up of free educational places for three- and four-year-olds by black and minority ethnic families.
- Families may not be aware of the Working Tax Credit to support child care costs among black and minority ethnic communities.

Lack of sensitivity to language, culture and religion

- Many families feel that the child care available is not sensitive to their language, culture or religious beliefs.
- Child care staff are seen as having a lack of knowledge of, and sensitivity to, diverse cultures, especially in relation to food, language, dress and prayer.
- There is a lack of child care staff from black and minority ethnic communities in many settings, which gives the impression that the setting is not reflective of their community and its cultures, or that it is tokenistic.

Settings that do accommodate diversity in the language, dietary, religious and cultural requirements of their communities, and that recruit ethnic minority staff are generally very popular.

Lack of information

- Some local child care information services are not effective in getting the message into local communities.
- There can be a lack of knowledge about different types of provision, for example what childminders or private day nurseries can offer.

Observation

Take a long, objective look at your setting.

- Are the children and staff representative of your local community? If not, why not?
- What are the barriers to all the local community using your setting?
- What could be done to improve this?
- How could you start to work to improve access and remove barriers?

Overcoming barriers

The most important way to overcome barriers is to empower local communities to define their own ethnic description and to identify where, and from what, they feel excluded and where included. Communication is essential to improve links between providers and communities. Successful methods used in the SureStart projects included:

- using recognised community workers who can communicate directly, in community languages, with enthusiasm, empathy and clarity
- developing 'child care champions' in the local community
- running information surgeries
- using community radio advertising
- using community press advertising
- being aware of the power of the spoken word (e.g. 'word of mouth' to relatives and friends)
- promoting 'child care fairs' within community venues
- using more targeted mailing
- using local community and faith centres
- using high-profile and high-status venues for events, to attract interest
- ensuring catering at events is culturally appropriate
- avoiding religious days and holidays for events
- use of interpreters
- literature in community languages
- face-to-face interaction in community and faith venues, at local festivals and community events
- developing promotional videos and audio CDs
- billboard advertising
- training 'information ambassadors' to work in black and minority ethnic communities
- targeting fathers and extended families with information
- outreach/home visits.

Other important points to consider to reduce barriers include:

- having culturally sensitive resources
- better on-site support and using local authority designated Equal Opportunities Coordinators (EOCs) and Equality Named Coordinators (ENCOs), where they are available
- more training in racial equality, and specifically 'race'/cultural awareness, to improve awareness of the requirements of the Race Relations (Amendment) Act and good practice in working for equality.

Keys to good practice: Removing the barriers to participation

✓ Include all relevant members of the community.

✓ Make sure the right forms of communication are used.

✓ Listen to what people say they want.

✓ Make sure the setting is part of the community.

✓ Never make assumptions about anyone.

✓ Always review your resources to be sure they reflect the community your setting serves.

Reflect on your own practice

As you have seen, it is important that you promote equality of access to settings and services for children and families. Have a look at the statements below to assess whether you match up to the levels of care needed. The statements all refer to the performance criteria for CCLD 305.1.

Performance criteria statement	Always	Sometimes	Never
Do I provide information and implement procedures about access to provision to meet the needs of all children?			
Do I welcome children from all backgrounds ensuring that barriers to participation are identified and removed?			
Do I seek and respect the views and preferences of children and adapt my practice to the child's needs, age and abilities?			
Do I involve all relevant local community groups in the setting and provide information on local resources?			
Do I provide information about equality of access, and children's rights and responsibilities, in the context of my setting?			

Implement strategies, policies, procedures and practice for inclusion

Community resources, support and information, and the referral of children and families

SureStart

Most communities have a range of services available to help children and families in need of support. The crucial service, which encompasses health, education and social care, is SureStart. All four countries in the UK have their own SureStart programmes. Links to these can be found on the SureStart website (www.surestart.gov.uk). As an early years worker you should be familiar with your local SureStart provision, especially the information services.

● *SureStart is a crucial initiative in the area of child care.*

Observation

- What sources of information are there for parents and children in your area?
- How accessible is the information?
- Could it be improved? If so, how?

SureStart is the cornerstone of the government's drive to eradicate child poverty. There is a range of different programmes aimed at widening access and improving children's chances. SureStart programmes aim to:

- improve children's life opportunities by working with parents and parents-to-be in deprived areas
- provide better access to family support and advice on nurturing, health services and early learning
- identify babies and toddlers at risk of failure and help families to make sure that their children are ready to learn before they start school
- be responsive to local needs and preferences
- work closely with other local provision to offer a wider range of innovative services, including family learning.

By April 2003 in England, 450 SureStart programmes had been established, and a further 74 were due to be running by summer 2003. It is planned that the centres will provide services for about a third of children (400,000) under four years who are living in poverty in England. In Scotland £61 million has been used since 1999 on SureStart programmes.

SureStart services include:

- early excellence centres, which offer high-quality practice as a one-stop-shop for integrated education and day care for young children, and services and opportunities for parents, carers, families and the wider community, both directly and in cooperation with other providers
- children's centres, which provide integrated health care and education based on previous good practice
- neighbourhood nurseries
- children's information services, which provide free information on SureStart services for parents in every local authority
- ChildcareLink, which is a national helpline and website (www.childcarelink.gov.uk/)
- extended schools that offer a range of services for children, young people, their families and communities, including child care, family and lifelong learning, parenting support, some health and social care services, and access to information technology, as well as sports and arts facilities.

Local authority social services departments

In a typical week in England in 2003:

- 384,000 children were in need (82% of these were residing in families and the other 18%, or 69,100, were being looked after)
- 224,000 (58%) of children in need were in receipt of local authority social services

Did you know?

The US Head Start programme was an early project in the US to improve the lives of deprived children. It showed that, at the age of 30, people from the programme who had had two years' early family help far outstripped those who had had no help. Every $1 spent on early years saved the state $7 later in crime, welfare, mental health and unemployment payments.

- abuse and neglect counted as the single main reason for children receiving social service intervention (55% of looked-after children and 26% of others in need).

Active knowledge

Make a chart for your setting with the contact details of all the following services, and a summary of their services, either nationally or, if relevant, in your area, for children and young people and their families:

- local social services
- Childline
- Children in Need
- local children's trust
- local SureStart unit, including the programme manager
- local Connexions office if you work with young people
- local area child protection committee
- local contact for the National Society for the Prevention of Cruelty to Children (NSPCC)
- regional Commission for Racial Equality
- local Citizens Advice Bureau
- any local refugee support agencies
- local childcare information service
- any specialist support group for any individual needs of children you work with (e.g. Asthma Campaign, Autistic Society, Deaf Children's Society).

Identify any of these that you have had contact with. Finally, are you working with any children or families that these services could help in any way?

There are twice as many services for families of children under five as for families of children aged five to ten years. Only 2% of services are specifically aimed at minority ethnic groups, yet 8% of the total population are from minority ethnic groups and the proportions of under-16s in this group are almost double those in the white population.

Child development services

Children with multiple special needs often require specific, individual services, many of which are provided by community child development services organised by the National Health Service. Some examples are shown in the diagram overleaf. In addition, there are often a number of specialists for children with difficulties with their hearing or sight.

Specialist health visitors
Provide specific support to the family, especially in relation to monitoring the development and well-being of the child and family

Physiotherapists
Work to improve physical mobility and function of the body

Speech therapists
Work to improve communication skills

Social workers
Aim to provide coordinated service to families who have a range of issues to deal with.

Specialists working with children with special needs

Occupational therapists
Advise on equipment and home adaptations to help and work to promote independent living skills

Community consultant paediatricians
Doctors who specialise in children's health

Psychologists
Look at improving behaviour or helping people to come to terms with situations

Specific services for children with multiple special needs.

Observation

- What services are available in your area for children with multiple special needs?
- Find out where your nearest child development service is and how referrals are made.

Children's Rights Director

If you work with children or young people who live in children's homes, family centres, foster care, boarding schools, residential special schools, or colleges of further education, or who are going through adoption, who are getting any sort of help from social services, or who have just left care, you need to be sure that they are aware of the support or 'championing' available to them. In some countries there are children's directors in each region but in England there is just one national one. All of them work with social care inspectorates and check that children are being looked after properly in all of these places. The Children's Rights Director for England works in the inspectorate with the people who visit and inspect settings and services. He or she spends a lot of time listening to what children and young people have to say, and telling inspectors and the government what children think and want. The website is a good way for children in these circumstances to access the Director (www.rights4me.org.uk).

How to ensure your provision aims to meet current guidance for implementing inclusion and anti-discriminatory practice

Inclusion means children, young people and adults with disabilities and/or learning difficulties being included in mainstream society. Inclusive schools help the development of communities where all people are equally valued and have the same opportunities for participation. Think about what exclusion helps to promote – racism and sexism, for example – and you can see that inclusion is the exact opposite. True inclusion also involves making sure that all support systems are available to those who need them.

The key to making sure that your provision meets its responsibilities for promoting inclusion is simply to treat all children as individuals and assess and support their individual needs.

Recent changes in legislation now clearly support the needs of children with a disability even if they do not have special educational needs. A children's setting that considers all children as individuals, and seeks to welcome all children and parents, should not have difficulty in keeping to the law. It is useful though to think about the definitions of disability and special educational needs (SEN), and to know which legislation covers them.

● *Inclusive education is a human right.*

The Disability Discrimination Act 1995 (DDA) and the Education Act 1996

The DDA covers all four UK nations. It defines a disabled person as 'someone who has a physical or mental impairment which has a substantial and long-term adverse effect on his or her ability to carry out normal day-to-day activities'. This definition covers pupils with physical (including sensory), intellectual or mental impairments. The definition is broad and would include children with a learning disability, sensory impairment, severe dyslexia, diabetes or epilepsy, pupils who are incontinent, or who have AIDS, severe disfigurements or progressive conditions like muscular dystrophy.

In England, the Education Act 1996 says that 'a child has special educational needs if he or she has a learning difficulty which calls for special educational provision to be made for him or her'. This is provided under the SEN framework, which can include a statement of special educational need. Children in Scotland are covered by the Disability Strategies and Pupils' Educational Records (Scotland) Act 2002.

Thus, a disability might give rise to a learning difficulty that calls for special educational provision to be made if it prevents or hinders the disabled child from accessing education. The SEN framework is there to identify and meet any additional educational needs of children. There is a duty under the DDA to make sure that disabled pupils are not discriminated against and to seek to promote equality of opportunity between disabled and non-disabled pupils.

Many children who have SEN will also be defined as having a disability under the DDA. However, not all children who are defined as disabled under the DDA will have SEN. For example, those with severe asthma, arthritis or diabetes may not have SEN, but may have rights under the DDA. Similarly, not all children with SEN will be defined as having a disability under the DDA.

National Standards

The National Standards for early years provision laid down by the Department for Education and Skills and monitored by Ofsted include Standard 10, which relates to special needs (including special educational needs and disabilities). The registered person (that is, the person registered with the local authority as a 'fit' person to be in charge) must be aware that some children may have special needs and so be proactive in ensuring that appropriate action can be taken when such a child is identified or admitted to the provision. Steps must be taken to promote the welfare and development of the child within the setting in partnership with the parents and other relevant parties.

The Special Educational Needs and Disability Act (SENDA) 2001

The Special Educational Needs and Disability Act 2001, supported by the 2002 Code of Practice, strengthened the right of children with disabilities to attend mainstream educational facilities. All education in England and Wales is covered by the Act, from nursery to higher education provided by local education authorities, education authority maintained schools and classes, and independent schools and grant-aided schools. Some private, voluntary and statutory providers of nursery education that are not constituted as schools are still covered by duties in Part 3 of the Act, which relates to access and 'reasonable adjustments'. A reasonable adjustment is something that can be changed – for example, to enable a wheelchair user to access facilities, or a person who is deaf to follow lessons. It is against the law not to make reasonable adjustments.

- It is unlawful for any school to discriminate against any disabled pupils and parents can lodge a complaint to SEN and disability tribunals and via admissions and exclusions appeal panels. Ofsted inspect to check that schools, nurseries and so on are complying.

- The Act covers all education and associated services for pupils and prospective pupils. In essence, all aspects of school life are covered, including extra-curricular activities and school trips.

Less favourable treatment

If a setting treats disabled children less favourably than others because of their disability without justification, it may be breaking the law.

Case study 3: Children with a disability

Parents who want their son with epilepsy admitted to a nursery school are told that the school cannot take him unless he stops having fits.

A girl who uses a wheelchair is on a trip with her school. The teachers arrange for the children to go on a walk over a very rough and rocky path, but, having carried out a risk assessment, they decide that the disabled girl cannot go on the walk for health and safety reasons.

1. *Do you think that either case is justified?*
2. *What do you think should happen next in each case?*

Keys to good practice: Inclusion and anti-discriminatory practice

✓ Do all senior members of the setting take their responsibilities under the DDA seriously?

✓ Are all other staff aware of their responsibilities?

✓ Has the setting reviewed its policies, procedures and practices to ensure that it does not discriminate against disabled children?

✓ Has the setting made 'reasonable adjustments'?

✓ Have staff had training on the new SENDA requirements and the broader issues of disability equality?

✓ Are there procedures in place to ensure that discrimination by staff will be identified and dealt with properly?

✓ Has the setting got an effective complaints procedure?

How to assess and plan for children's needs drawing on available resources and support services

There are two very different views of disability:
- A **social model** recognises that any problems of disability are created by society and its institutions. If someone is a wheelchair user, problems

are caused not by the wheelchair but by the fact that some buildings do not have ramps and buses are difficult to access. The solutions to problems of disability are therefore in society's hands, and involve changing the attitudes of able-bodied people. The DDA is clearly a tool to help to improve the response of society in this manner.

- A **medical model** views the disability as the problem. Disability is seen as a tragic, incurable fact that leaves the sufferer with little chance of a normal life. It focuses on the disability the person has, rather than his or her abilities. Under this model, people with severe disabilities are cared for in institutions and have little hope of independence. Until the 1980s, disabled children were seen as uneducable (which is totally at odds with the view today) as a result of a medical model approach.

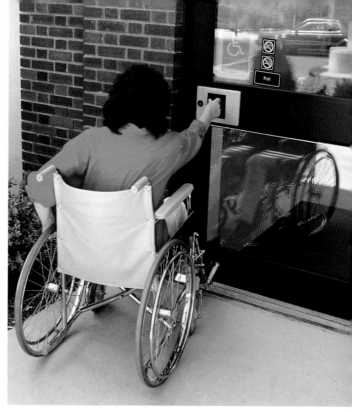

● *Is it the wheelchair that is the problem, or is it the door?*

In your settings it is essential that you work from a social model perspective.

Case study 4: Children with a disability

Lee, aged seven, was born prematurely after a pregnancy of 30 weeks. As a result of problems during his delivery, Lee has cerebral palsy. He uses a wheelchair to move around and a voice synthesiser to communicate. Although he cannot play sports he loves watching football and enjoys playing games related to football. Lee and his friends spend a lot of time together playing games at weekends. School swimming sessions are his favourite. With the support of a personal assistant, Lee attends a mainstream primary school and is looking forward to moving to senior school with his friends.

Leila, aged six, was also born with severe cerebral palsy and relies on her wheelchair to move around. Her parents were never encouraged to hope that Leila could attend a mainstream school. She attends a special school with children who all live a long way from Leila. Her parents are not happy to let her visit the one friend she has nearby, as they worry she will not cope without them. Although Leila loves shopping, her parents do not take her very often as it is hard work, and they find it difficult to cope with people staring at her. They are thinking that Leila will eventually live in a residential unit with care assistants looking after her.

1. *Compare these two children. Why do you think they have different lifestyles?*
2. *Why do you think this has happened in each case?*
3. *How could you support Leila's parents to help them to encourage her to have a more normal lifestyle?*
4. *What sort of support services do you think might be useful?*

Observation

Look carefully at your setting and imagine you were a child who had some type of disability. Think about wheelchair users, children who move with difficulty, those with reduced vision or hearing, or any other type of disability you have seen or heard about.

- Are all parts of your setting accessible?
- Can equipment be accessed by all children?
- Are there some areas of the setting that cannot be accessed by some children? How can this be addressed to avoid disadvantaging these children?
- Were any of the outings or activities held in the past months restricted to particular children? What could have been done to enable access for all?

It is important for child care workers to ensure that a child is not discriminated against in terms of the opportunity to reach his or her full potential. Look at these three examples:

- Jodi has hearing difficulties and as a result her speech has been delayed. She experiences communication difficulties unless alternative methods of communication are considered. When her group at nursery has story time, the nursery nurse always makes sure that Jodi sits at the front and that the story has a lot of visual appeal, to which end she uses puppets, pictures and miming.
- Samir has cerebral palsy, which means he has difficulty in controlling his movements without shaking. Playing in the home corner was difficult because it was a small area and he tended to knock things over. His teacher has re-sited the home corner so that it is in a bigger area and Samir can now play safely in it. His teacher has also realised that the new home corner is much better for Lucy, who uses hearing aids. The new site is much nearer to the main classroom area and Lucy can hear what is happening much more easily.
- Ramjet uses a lightweight wheelchair. He previously had difficulty getting into the playground as access to it was via two small steps. However, after the DDA came into force the school had a good-quality ramp installed and now Ramjet can get out into the playground easily and move very quickly around it. With the help of one of the staff, Ramjet's friends have invented a new form of football that allows him to use his arms instead of his feet.

There are many other ways to overcome difficulties. It is essential to structure activities and opportunities for the entire group of children in your care, taking needs into account. All children can benefit when activities are adapted – for instance, making story time a wider experience, and learning new ways of playing traditional games.

Adapting equipment for children with special needs

Sometimes special equipment may be needed to allow children with special needs to practise and develop all their skills.

- A child who has poor fine-motor skills and difficulty with fine hand and eye coordination may benefit from the use of thicker pencils and other tools.
- Children with delays in developing gross motor skills (large body movements such as walking or running), or sensory problems (vision, hearing, etc.) may enjoy large-scale toys such as ball pools and soft foam cushions.
- A child with a visual impairment may be able to read large-print books, and will enjoy listening to stories recorded on tape.

- *Equipment for children with a disability can also benefit other children.*

Some centres are equipped with multi-sensory rooms that provide opportunities for children with a wide range of specific needs. These rooms feature a range of lights, sounds, smells and touch sensations that stimulate (or in some cases soothe) the senses.

Any activity, game or toy designed to develop an aspect of a child's skill should aim to allow the child to use the skills that already exist, and encourage him or her to extend them. For example, when a child reaches the stage of being able to turn the pages of a book, make sure he or she has books with thick pages, showing pictures of interesting objects.

Sometimes there is no need to adapt equipment, but instead a need to change your methods of promoting an activity. A child who has difficulty sitting still for long will struggle to take part in a modelling activity lasting 15 minutes. However, you could, for example, sit with the child and keep up the encouragement, or ask to look at progress at frequent intervals, or you could give a child some responsibility for drawing all the children's efforts together, say for a display. This may help to prevent a child's behaviour becoming unacceptable.

Techniques of monitoring to assess the effectiveness of provision in implementing inclusive and anti-discriminatory practice

The regulations of the Race Relations (Amendment) Act of 2000 require settings that are receiving funding to monitor participation by minority ethnic groups. The maintained early childhood sector has statutory obligations but the obligations of the non-maintained sector, in which settings may be receiving direct or indirect funding, are not yet clear. The Department for Education and Skills does, however, require settings in the non-maintained sector to implement equality strategies and the effective collection, monitoring and analysis of ethnic data are seen as good practice.

The monitoring of the effectiveness of provision in children's settings is often not done well. Monitoring is important to check the effectiveness of your hard work as a setting to widen access. It is very difficult for authorities to get an accurate picture of minority ethnic participation in child care services across all sectors, especially in the private and voluntary sectors.

Information that needs gathering includes the following:
- characteristics of the setting's catchment area – ethnic mix, age profile, social class, rural, urban mix and so on (such information is available from the Office for National Statistics at ward and postcode level)
- detailed statistics about the geographical spread of children who attend
- the ethnic status of children
- the number of children with registered disabilities
- the number of lone parents.

This type of information will help you to focus on where action is needed to make the children attending the setting more representative of those in the locality. Once the base information has been gathered, regular checks can be made on the population of both staff and children to see if initiatives have worked. Information of this type can be very interesting. You can start to look for patterns in the way your setting is developing, and most importantly ask why this may be so, and how and what you can do to make things even better.

Remember that there are restrictions on collecting and keeping data about people. The basic tenet is that anyone can request to see information that is held about him or her.

Keys to good practice: Collecting information

✓ Let people know why you are asking for the information.

✓ Tell them that they can see the detail of information on record about them.

Reflect on your own practice

As you have seen, it is important that you can implement strategies, policies and procedures and practice for inclusion. Have a look at the statements below to assess whether you match up to the levels needed. The statements all refer to the performance criteria for CCLD 305.2.

Performance criteria statement	Always	Sometimes	Never
Do I use inclusive and anti-discriminatory practice in planning and delivering provision?			
Do I provide an environment, activities and experiences that promote positive images of all children and reflect the wider society?			
Do I assess and contribute to meeting the individual needs of children?			
Do I organise the provision to facilitate access and participation for disabled children and those with special needs?			
Do I monitor and evaluate how effective my setting or service is in implementing inclusive practice and implement change to improve the service offered?			

Maintain and follow policies and procedures for protecting and safeguarding children

In 2000 the NSPCC published the results of a national survey of 3000 young people aged 18–24 about their experience of a wide range of issues (Cawson, 2002) and found that:

- 7% had been physically abused by a carer
- 6% had suffered emotional and psychological maltreatment as children
- 6% had been seriously physically neglected

Did you know?

At the end of March 2003 there were 25,700 children on child protection registers in England. The most commonly recorded risk was for neglect (39%), followed by physical abuse (19%) and emotional abuse (17%).

(Source: Department of Health, 2003)

- 4% had been sexually abused
- 80% of physically abused children have also known domestic violence
- a significant number of children face repeated pathological and multiple forms of abuse at the hands of parents or carers.
- abuse is more common in families with drug or alcohol abuse problems.

The requirements of legislation, regulation and codes of practice for children's protection

Children Bill 2004

The tragic death of Victoria Climbié at the hands of her carers resulted in an independent inquiry into her death, which, in common with other inquiries into child deaths over the years, criticised the approach to protecting children in our society (Laming, 2003). The difference with Victoria was that the Laming report resulted in a green paper, *Every Child Matters*, which in turn led to the Children Bill 2004. The key features of the Bill are aimed at improving the protection afforded to children by providing for the following.

- An independent children's commissioner for England will be established to protect the rights of all children and young people.
- A sophisticated tracking system will keep a record of England's 11 million children. Databases of local children will be set up by 150 councils. Every child will have an electronic file that includes their name, address, date of birth, school and GP. This states whether they are known to social, education or welfare services, or to the police or youth offending teams.
- Children's directors are to take strategic responsibility for local authority education and children's social services.
- Lead councillors for children's services are to take political responsibility for local child welfare.
- Councils, primary care trusts and other agencies will be able to create children's trusts, new organisations that formally integrate children's health, education and social services.
- A new duty will be put on local agencies to work together to improve child welfare.
- New local children's safeguarding boards with statutory powers are to ensure that social services, the NHS, education services, the police and other services work together to protect vulnerable children.
- Ofsted is to set the framework for monitoring and inspecting children's services and new joint inspections of local children's services will be conducted by inspectorates such as the Commission for Social Care Inspection, the Healthcare Commission, the Audit Commission and the chief inspector of constabulary.
- New powers will be made for the government to intervene in children's social services where the quality of care has fallen below minimum standards.

Did you know?

In November 2004 a man was arrested and charged with actual bodily harm for smacking a child. The incident, which involved a child of about four, was alleged to have happened outside a store in Sutton, Greater London. The police said such cases were unusual and may have been prompted by publicity around the smacking debate. In the same month MPs backed an amendment to the Children Bill passed by peers that allows parents to give their child a 'light smack' only.

(Source: Guardian, November 2004)

Observation

- How is your local area responding to the Children Bill 2004?
- Has a children's director been appointed?
- What is the role of the children's director?
- What does your setting know about the new joint inspections of children's services?
- Have you had any information or dealings with the children's database?

The Children Act 1989

The Children Act 1989 places a duty on local education authorities to work with social services departments acting on behalf of children in need or enquiring into allegations of **child abuse**. England and Wales later produced *Working Together to Safeguard Children* (1999), which emphasised the responsibilities of professionals towards children who are at risk of harm. The All Wales Child Protection Procedures were amended in 2004 after consultation with every Welsh Area Child Protection Committee.

Key terms

Child abuse is where a child is suffering or likely to suffer significant harm from physical, emotional or sexual abuse, neglect and failure to thrive not based on illness, or bullying and harassment.

The importance of partnerships with parents and families

The important of partnerships with parents and families

Parents should be seen as the child's main educators, and clear communication with them, and understanding, are therefore essential if children are to develop to their full potential.

Keys to good practice: Partnerships with parents and families

✓ Provide parents with understandable curriculum plans.

✓ Encourage parents to carry out activities at home (e.g. finding a topic object, sharing a book).

✓ Ask parents to help in the setting.

✓ Ask parents to share the observations of their children.

✓ Have regular formal and informal meetings with parents.

✓ Hold information evenings where parents can experience the curriculum.

✓ Give parents time to talk about their child's learning where possible.

The definitions and indicators of child abuse

It is important that you are aware of the indications of child abuse. However, not every sign means a child is being abused. Have you cared for children who always appear a bit grubby and maybe smell a little, but are happy and loved by parents? Some physical signs such as darkened areas can be birthmarks and not bruising; for example, some infants of Asian or African heritage can have a dark bluish area on their lower back or buttocks, sometimes known as a Mongolian blue spot.

Sometimes the first signs that you observe are not physical but a change in behaviour. Recording your concerns and monitoring that change can be extremely useful.

Physical abuse

Physical abuse is when a child is physically hurt or injured. Hitting, kicking, beating with objects, throwing and shaking are all physical abuse, and can cause pain, cuts, bruising, broken bones and sometimes even death.

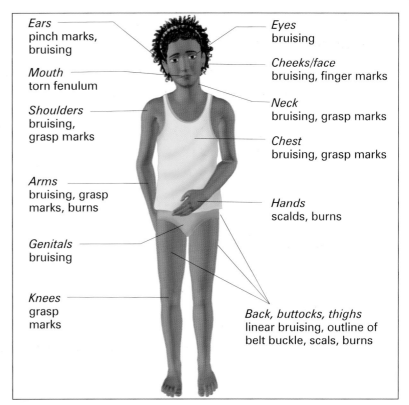

Ears
pinch marks, bruising

Mouth
torn fenulum

Shoulders
bruising, grasp marks

Arms
bruising, grasp marks, burns

Genitals
bruising

Knees
grasp marks

Eyes
bruising

Cheeks/face
bruising, finger marks

Neck
bruising, grasp marks

Chest
bruising, grasp marks

Hands
scalds, burns

Back, buttocks, thighs
linear bruising, outline of belt buckle, scals, burns

● *Usual position of injuries in cases of child abuse.*

Signs and symptoms

- Unexplained recurrent injuries or burns.
- Wearing clothes to cover injuries, even in hot weather.
- Refusal to undress for games.
- Bald patches of hair.
- Repeated running away.
- Fear of medical examination.
- Aggression towards self and others.
- Fear of physical contact; shrinking back if approached or touched.

Case study 5: Physical abuse

Jason, aged eight, has been away from school for two days; a note from his mother said that he had been unwell. You are helping him to get changed for PE in the hall and he jumps as you help him to pull his top off. The back of his upper arms and his back are covered in deep purple bruising. When you gently ask how they happened, he shrugs and says he fell off his bunk bed.

1. *What should you do now?*
2. *Who should you talk to about this?*
3. *How should you handle this with Jason and his parents?*

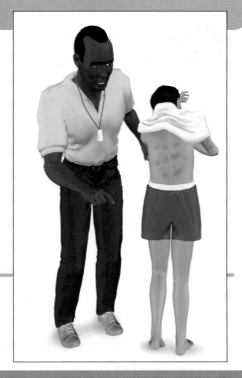

Many signs of physical abuse can be confused with genuine accidental injuries, but they are often not in the places or distributed as you would expect, or the explanation does not fit, or you may see the outline of a belt buckle or cigarette burn. Suspicion should be aroused if the parents have not sought medical advice soon after the injury occurred.

Case study 6: Accidental injury

Elaine was very upset when she took her nine-month-old son Harry to the accident and emergency department. She had slipped on the stairs while carrying him downstairs and he had obviously broken his upper leg as she fell with him. An X-ray confirmed that Harry had a fracture to his femur and would need several weeks in hospital. To Elaine's horror the doctor and nurses started to suggest she had deliberately hurt her son and called in the social services department. In her distress, Elaine did not immediately remember that her neighbour had been in the house when the accident happened and luckily could confirm how it had happened.

1. *Why do you think the doctor involved social services?*
2. *What do you think they should have done?*

Emotional abuse

Emotional abuse is when children are not given love, approval or acceptance. They may be constantly criticised, blamed, sworn and shouted at, told that other people are better than they are and rejected by those they look to for affection.

Signs and symptoms

- Delayed development.
- Sudden speech problems such as stammering.
- Low self-esteem ('I'm stupid, ugly, worthless').
- Fear of any new situation.
- Neurotic behaviour (rocking, hair twisting, self-mutilation).
- Extremes of withdrawal or aggression.

Neglect

Neglect, which can result in failure to thrive, is when parents or others looking after children do not provide them with proper food, warmth, shelter, clothing, care and protection.

Signs and symptoms

- Constant hunger.
- Poor personal hygiene.
- Constant tiredness.
- Poor state of clothing.
- Unusual thinness.
- Untreated medical problems.
- No social relationships.
- Stealing food.
- Destructive tendencies.

Case study 7: Neglect

Leanne is six years old and has an older sister, Jess, who is 11. Their mum and dad both have drinking problems. Sometimes there is nothing to eat in the house. Jess is often left alone to look after her sister. The school they both go to has noticed that they are always tired and appear very thin. Their clothes are often dirty and Leanne is often in the same clothes for a few days. One day when Jess comes to collect Leanne from the classroom to go home, Leanne bursts into tears and says she does not want to go home.

1. *What do you think Leanne's teacher should do?*
2. *What do you think should already have happened?*
3. *What structure should be in place in the school to deal with this incident?*

Sexual abuse

Sexual abuse is when a child is forced or persuaded into sexual acts or situations by others. Children may be encouraged to look at pornography, be harassed by sexual suggestions or comments, be touched sexually or forced to have sex.

Signs and symptoms

- Sexual knowledge or behaviour that is inappropriate to the child's age.
- Medical problems such as chronic itching, pain in the genitals, venereal disease.
- Depression, self-mutilation, suicide attempts, running away, overdoses, anorexia.
- Personality changes, such as becoming insecure or clinging.
- Regressing to younger behaviour patterns, such as thumb-sucking or bringing out discarded cuddly toys.
- Sudden loss of appetite or compulsive eating.
- Being isolated or withdrawn.
- Inability to concentrate.
- Lack of trust or fear of someone they know well, such as not wanting to be alone with a babysitter or childminder.
- Starting to wet or soil again, day or night.
- Becoming worried about clothing being removed.
- Suddenly drawing sexually explicit pictures.
- Trying to be 'ultra-good' or perfect; over-reacting to criticism.

Bullying and harassment

Bullying and harassment are also a form of abuse; it affects older children particularly. It can continue for a long time.

- **Emotional bullying** is the most common type and can involve not speaking to and excluding someone ('sending them to Coventry'), tormenting, ridicule, humiliation.

- *Bullying – groups pf people may gang up on one person.*

- **Physical bullying** can include pushing, kicking, hitting, pinching and other forms of violence or threats.
- **Verbal bullying** includes name-calling, sarcasm, spreading rumours and persistent teasing.
- **Racist bullying** can involve racial taunts, writing graffiti, gestures.
- **Sexual bullying** involves unwanted physical contact or abusive comments.
- **Homophobic bullying** involves hostile or offensive action against lesbians, gay males or bisexuals or those thought to be lesbian, gay or bisexual.

Bullying can be carried out by one person against another, or by groups of people 'ganging up' on a person. Bullying is not always delivered as a personal, face-to-face attack, but can also be delivered through technology, such as mobile phones and the internet (known as cyber-bullying).

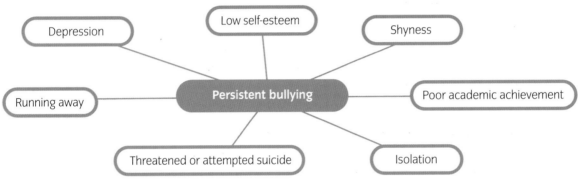

- *The possible results of persistent bullying.*

Case study 8: Bullying and harassment

Jim, aged 13, eventually contacted a telephone support service about all his years of constantly being bullied at school. He had often had things stolen from him, especially new school bags or trainers. The two boys who were bullying him had started it at primary school by calling him names and following him home. More recently they had started to push him over if he walked past them and were spreading rumours about his father. Jim had started to play truant to avoid meeting the bullies. The telephone counsellor explained to Jim that it was his right to be educated without fear and encouraged him to ask a friend to go with him to talk to the head of their year.

1. *Why do you think it has taken so long for Jim to tell someone?*
2. *How do you think this has made Jim feel about himself?*
3. *What do you think you could have done if you were working at Jim's school?*
4. *What should the school do now that this has come to light?*

What increases a child's vulnerability to abuse

Most of this unit focuses on your role in protecting children and keeping them safe in the setting you work in. One very important part of keeping children safe is recognising when they are not safe outside that setting. In order to do so you will need:

- good observation skills (noticing when a child's behaviour has changed, for example)
- a thorough knowledge of normal patterns of development and behaviour
- to know when to be concerned for a child's welfare and safety
- to understand your role and responsibility when abuse is suspected.

The National Standards require that 'all registered persons comply with local child protection procedures that are approved by the area child protection committee and ensure that all adults working and looking after children in the provision are able to put the practices and procedures into place'.

It is one of the most important responsibilities of a child care worker to report suspicion of abuse to an appropriate person. You are most likely to be the worker in close contact with a child on a daily basis, so will be the most likely person to spot the warning signs of possible abuse. It is vital that you deal with any suspicions promptly and appropriately.

Abuse can be a one-off incident or a regular feature of a child's life. Abuse can take place anywhere and be perpetrated by anyone, but the majority of abuse is carried out by someone the child knows.

Remember the UN Convention on the Rights of the Child? Article 19 states: 'Government must take all appropriate measures to protect a child from all forms of physical or mental violence, injury or abuse, neglect or negligent treatment, maltreatment or exploitation, including sexual abuse, while in the care of parent(s), legal guardian(s) or any other person who has the care of the child'. A child has an inherent right not to be abused and to be supported when abuse is identified.

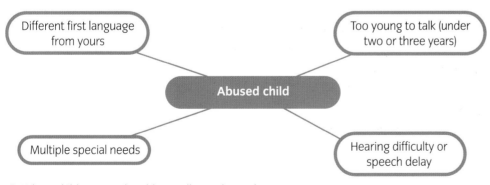

● *Why a child may not be able to tell you about abuse.*

It is not easy for abused children to voice their hurt, especially as it may be a parent who they still love who is causing the abuse. But think about children who have communication difficulties: how much more problematic is it for them? In fact, disabled children are even more at risk from abuse than children generally, the rate being 1.7 times higher. They are particularly vulnerable for the following reasons:

- they may have a greater need for intimate physical care for longer than normal, and this may be carried out by someone of the opposite sex
- they may have communication difficulties
- they may have low self-esteem, making complaining less likely
- the demands are great on parents of children with severe behaviour problems
- some of the signs of abuse may be mistaken for complications of the condition.

Furthermore, there are some types of abuse that are particular to a disabled child, including:

- lack of stimulation or supervision
- over-protection
- confinement to a chair or bed using physical restraints
- intrusive or insensitive medical procedures or photographs
- incorrect drug use
- poor physical care, including forced feeding
- withholding of essential aids, such as frames or wheelchairs.

Keys to good practice: Possible abuse of children who do not communicate normally

✓ Engage the child's trust.

✓ Encourage 'conversations' in alternative forms about the child's body.

✓ Promote self-esteem.

✓ Devise codes for saying 'No!'

✓ Be sure that you know when a particular child is unhappy.

Support for those caring for vulnerable children is an important part of your role. Have parents got the support they need, especially respite support to allow them to catch up on sleep if that is a problem or to spend time with other children? Does the family have the support of a key worker?

Just being alert for abuse is not enough as part of the attention to a child and their family, overall support and referral to appropriate agencies are key.

Policies, procedures and the lines of reporting for suspected or actual abuse and the importance of not forming premature judgements

Lines of reporting

The basic tenet of reporting concern about a child is to do this from the most important level upwards. If you ever suspect abuse, you should report directly to the designated person, who then passes the information up the chain ultimately to the Area Child Protection Committee.

Area Child Protection Committees

Local authorities are required to have an Area Child Protection Committee (ACPC) covering their area that brings together representatives of each of the main agencies and professionals responsible for helping to protect children from abuse and neglect. The ACPC is a multi-agency group who agree how the different services and professional groups should cooperate to safeguard children in their area, and who make sure that arrangements work effectively to the benefit of children. This is done by:

- raising awareness within the wider community (including faith and minority ethnic communities, and among statutory, voluntary and independent agencies) of how everybody can contribute to safeguarding children and promoting their welfare
- working together across agencies to identify and act upon concerns about a child's safety and welfare
- working together across agencies to help those children who have suffered or who are at continuing risk of significant harm, in order to safeguard such children and promote their welfare.

Membership should be decided locally, but should include as a minimum representation from:

- local authorities (education and social services)
- health services (covering both managerial and professional expertise and responsibilities)
- the police
- the probation service
- the NSPCC (when active in the area)
- the domestic violence forum (when active in the area)
- the armed services (where appropriate, and especially where there is a large service base in the area).

Guidelines for schools, nurseries and other settings

Schools, nurseries and other settings have responsibility, legally and pastorally, for their pupils and to promote their fundamental right to be protected from harm. Children cannot learn effectively unless they feel secure. Every setting should have a **child protection** policy that reflects its statutory duties and pastoral responsibilities.

A circular from the Department for Education Skills stated that:

- Staff should be alert to the signs and symptoms of abuse and know to whom they should report any concerns.
- All schools should have a designated teacher with the responsibility for coordinating action within school and liaising with other agencies.
- Designated teachers should have the appropriate training.
- Schools should follow county guidelines.
- Schools should have procedures for handling suspected cases of abuse, including where a member of staff is involved.
- Parents should be made aware of the school's child protection policy and the fact that this may require cases to be referred to the investigative agencies in the interests of the child.

The role of the designated person is:

- to ensure that the local ACPC guidelines and procedures are followed in school
- to ensure that all staff, including non-teaching staff, are aware of these procedures
- to ensure that all staff have training to enable them to know to whom they must pass their concerns
- to develop effective working relationships with other agencies (e.g. social services, police)
- to make referrals where child abuse is likely to occur, or is suspected or disclosed
- to attend case conferences, or ensure that the appropriate member of staff attends and is aware of the purpose and procedures of the child protection conference
- to ensure that a written report is prepared for the conference and participate in core groups as required
- to meet with the education welfare (or social) worker for the school to monitor children at risk.

Policies and procedures

Record keeping

When abuse is disclosed or suspected the member of staff should make brief notes as soon as possible, giving quotes if they can be recalled. Dates and times should be recorded. These notes must not be destroyed, even if a more detailed report is written later. They may be needed by a court. It is advisable to draw a diagram to indicate any marks or injuries observed.

Observation

- Have you had any involvement with a suspected case of child abuse during your career so far?
- If not, do you feel informed enough of procedures to handle such an event?
- If so, how effectively was the event handled? How did you feel about the incident?
- If you were closely involved, did you have the opportunity to discuss your feelings with a superior? What else, if anything, could have been done to improve operations?

The avoidance of premature judgements

Evidence of the signs and symptoms of abuse do not necessarily mean that a child has been abused but such evidence can help responsible adults to recognise that something is wrong. The possibility of abuse should be investigated if a child shows a number of these symptoms, or any of them to a marked degree. It is important to realise that a child may be the victim of a combination of different kinds of abuse.

Think about children who are neglected. Perhaps they are not properly clothed and fed. Do you think they can feel loved and protected? They may well be suffering from emotional abuse as well as neglect.

It is also possible that a child may show no outward signs and be trying to hide what is happening from everyone.

If you have any suspicions about the welfare of a child in your setting, share them with your supervisor or designated person. Your fears may be unfounded but it is better to be over-cautious in passing information on than ignore warning signs. It is very important to handle the issues in a sensitive manner and not upset the child concerned.

Check it out

- What is the procedure for your setting when abuse is suspected?
- Who is your designated person?
- Where is your ACPC?
- Is everyone aware of the procedure or is more training needed?
- How are parents informed about your child abuse procedures?

Observation

- What are the procedures that are followed in your setting when there is suspicion of abuse of a child?
- How do these fit into the local ACPC?
- Have you seen the procedures in action? How effective were they?
- Can you think of any changes needed?

Safe working practices to protect children and adults who work with them

The Children's Rights Director for England produced a report (Morgan, 2004) about keeping children safe and asked children of all ages for their views about this important aspect of children's lives. The children identified many different risks they feel exposed to, with the commonest being bullying, illness and accidents. Many children felt that the risk of abuse was greatest when they were being looked after by people they do not know (although this is not the case). The children all felt good about being asked for their views and these are some of their statements:

- Pay attention and talk seriously to children.
- Don't patronise us – explain so we can understand – don't talk complex.
- Don't always believe an adult over a child.
- We want to be looked after by adults we can trust.
- Treat us individually – children are not all the same.

These views of children and young people are worth bearing in mind whenever you work with them. Following these suggestions should help considerably in keeping children safe.

In keeping children safe, it is important to remember that staff working with children need protecting as well.

Keys to good practice: Safe working practices

✓ Never compromise on staffing levels.

✓ Never compromise on standards.

✓ Only employ well trained, appropriately qualified and experienced staff.

✓ Always check references, by talking to the referee as well as reading the reference and listening for any concerns.

✓ Never be tempted to employ or use volunteers before they have had full clearance for their suitability to work with children.

✓ Make sure that all staff are well trained in their job, and in child protection issues especially.

✓ Pay a good salary to reflect the important job staff carry out.

✓ Have very clear policies and procedures that staff are active in developing and so owning, with very clear sanctions for not following them.

✓ Provide and promote an open, responsive working environment where staff are valued for their expertise and contribution and the quality of their work with children.

✓ Welcome outside assessment of your provision.

✓ Be alert to the signs of stress in staff.

✓ Always make sure that staff are never left alone with children.

✓ Make sure that staff have the opportunity to share concerns about children or staff with someone and have good supervision sessions.

✓ Provide a well resourced, pleasant working environment, in which the children's welfare is paramount.

Helping to protect children

Babies, children and young people need protecting by adults, and when abuse occurs the carers responsible need support and help. Abuse happens for all sorts of reasons and one of the best ways of preventing it is to ensure that all parents feel good about themselves, and have the support they need when things go wrong.

Enabling children to protect themselves

Those children and young people who have the following characteristics are less likely to be vulnerable to abuse:

- they are assertive
- they are self-confident
- they are self-aware
- they have high self-esteem.

To feel safe and protected, children need to feel good about themselves. They need to have a good level of self-esteem and you can work to help a child develop this. A child who has a high self-esteem will do better in many aspects of development. Self-esteem can be helped by:

- giving lots of praise and encouragement
- encouraging independence, with many opportunities to try things out
- teaching children how to be assertive (which means having their own needs met but still respecting those of others)
- encouraging cooperation, respect and tolerance between children, and giving a positive example yourself.

It is important to be available to talk with children about any concerns they may have. If they are upset by a reported case of abuse, be as reassuring as possible. These cases are very rare, even though this may be hard to believe when they are constantly in the media. Stress that almost all children lead safe and happy lives and only very few adults want to hurt children in any way.

To be able to tell someone that they are unhappy with someone else's behaviour, children need help to use the right language or to be able to draw pictures or show an adult what happened, using a doll for example.

Using correct anatomical language, at a level appropriate to the child, is important when you are talking about bodies. However, you also need to be aware of the many different terms used by people for a part of the body such as the genitalia or functions such as passing urine.

● *Simple, age-appropriate sessions, linked to other activities, on how the human body works help children to understand what their bodies can do and raise awareness of what is normal and what is not.*

Simple, age-appropriate sessions, linked to other activities, on how the human body works help children to understand what their bodies can do and raise awareness of what is normal and what is not. Delivery as part of the normal activities of the setting – the curriculum in schools for example – 'normalises' sessions rather than making them seem unusual. Indeed, sessions on 'body maintenance' should be part of child's education, not just to warn them of the dangers of misuse.

The Keepsafe Code

1   *Hugs.* Hugs and kisses are nice, especially from people we like. Even hugs and kisses that feel good and that you like should never be kept secret.

2   *Body.* Your body belongs to you and not to anyone else. This means all of your body. If anyone harms you or tries to touch your body in a way which confuses or frightens you, say NO, if possible, and tell.

3   *No.* If anyone older than you, even someone you know, tries to touch you in a way you don't like or that confuses you, or which they say is supposed to be a secret, say NO in a very loud voice.

4   *Run or get away.* Don't talk to anyone you don't know when you are alone, or just with other children. You don't have to be rude, just pretend you didn't hear and keep going. If a stranger, or a bully, or even someone you know tries to harm you, get away and get help. Make sure you always go towards other people or to a shop, if you can.

5   *Yell.* Wherever you are, it is all right to yell if someone is trying to hurt you. Practice yelling as loud as you can in a big, deep voice by taking a deep breath and letting the yell come from your stomach, not from your throat.

6   *Tell.* Tell a grown-up you trust if you are worried or frightened. If the first grown-up you tell doesn't believe or help you, keep telling until someone does. It might not be easy, but even if something has already happened that you have never told before, try to tell now. Who could you tell?

7   *Secrets.* Secrets such as surprise birthday parties are fun. But some secrets are not good and should never be kept. No bully should ever make you keep the bullying a secret and no-one should ask you to keep a kiss, hug or touch secret. If anyone does, even if you know that person, tell a grown-up you trust.

8   *Bribes.* Don't accept money or sweets or a gift from anyone without first checking with your parents. Most of the time it will be all right, like when you get a present for your birthday from your grandma. But some people try to trick children into doing something by giving them sweets or money. This is called a bribe: don't ever take one! Remember, it is possible that you might have to do what a bully or older person tells you, so that you can keep yourself safe. Don't feel bad if that happens because the most important thing is for you to be safe.

9   *Code.* Have a code word or sign with your parents or guardians, which only you and they know. If they need to send someone to collect you, they can give that person the code word. Don't tell the code to anyone else.

● *The Keepsafe Code (source: www.Kidscape.org.uk).*

Older children need more detailed information such as:

- lessons on normal sexual function, related to adult behaviour (relevant to your setting's policy)
- information about misuses of their bodies, through smoking, alcohol and illegal drugs
- the risks of HIV infection, through sexual and drug misuse.

There are many useful organisations that can help with information and guidance on these topics. It is important to use them properly and not risk information being incorrect or not used to best effect. Ask your local health contact for suggestions. A SureStart group will have good links.

Children need to understand that they have a right to be safe, and to have people they can tell if they are not feeling safe. The citizenship programme being developed in schools offers a useful opportunity for children to look at safety, not only on a wider basis but also about themselves.

What is safe though? What is acceptable behaviour and what is not? Child care settings – along with agencies such as the NSPCC, Childline and Kidscape – are very important in educating children about looking after themselves. The important fact for all children is that they should never feel uncomfortable about someone they are with or something being done to them.

Have a look at the Keepsafe Code from Kidscape. Do you think it could be useful for all children?

Active knowledge

- Try to adapt the Keepsafe Code for children of the age you work with, particularly if you have children who have communication difficulties.
- Could you put it into a picture format with titles?
- Can you think how you could get the children to practise actions for the Code?
- What else might you need to do with the children so that they understand about hugs and touching that they are not comfortable with?

Keys to good practice: Helping to keep children safe

✓ Teach children how to keep themselves safe.

✓ Encourage them to share worries about abuse with their friends.

✓ Encourage them to tell a trusted adult.

✓ Make sure they know that being abused is never their fault and that abuse is never right.

✓ Promote services such as Childline or the NSPCC Child Protection Helpline to older children.

The principles of responding to disclosure taking into account the child's understanding and stage of development

Disclosure of abuse by a child can occur at any time, and can be a shock to the recipient. The way a disclosure is received can be very important in the outcome to a child, even many years later. Think about all the examples of abuse in the past, when the most shocking thing to us now is that they were not believed at the time.

Key terms

Disclosure of abuse is when a child tells you he or she has been abused.

If a child discloses that he or she has been abused, you should:

- Listen to what the child says carefully and attentively.
- Try not to display shock or disbelief and do not ask direct or leading questions.
- Communicate at the child's own pace and without undue pressure.
- Accept what is being said.
- Stress that it is right to tell.
- Reassure and support the child.
- Inform the child that the information cannot remain confidential.
- Do not criticise the perpetrator – the child may well still love him or her.
- Promptly follow the procedures for your setting.

Keys to good practice: How to respond to a child's disclosure of possible abuse

✓ Find out to whom you should report any concern you may have about the safety of a child in your setting.

✓ Make sure you understand your setting's child protection policy and procedure.

✓ Always pass on any information that may be related to possible abuse to the correct person.

✓ Never promise to keep a child's disclosure a secret.

Sources of information and support for children, workers and settings

There is a wealth of organisations that offer support and guidance for all participants in the child care arena when abuse is experienced or encountered. The first line is the next level of manager or supervisor. However, further professional help and guidance may be needed, and children may not be comfortable talking to their carers, particularly if they are involved in the abuse. Publicising the services available to children (e.g. the NSPCC, Childline and Bullying Online) is essential, especially for older children.

Your child protection policy should clearly identify the chain of reporting in your setting, through to the area child protection committee. If you feel in need of more information, then the NSPCC, BASPCAN, Childline or Kidscape have good sections aimed at professionals:

- NSPCC www.nspcc.org.uk – the national charity working to eradicate child abuse (also a good educational resource).
- ChildLine www.childline.org.uk – provides telephone support and guidance to children being abused (also a good source of information for child professionals).
- Kidscape www.kidscape.org.uk – a registered charity committed to keeping children safe from harm and abuse.
- Bullying Online www.bullying.co.uk – offers advice on bullying
- BASPCAN (British Association for the Study and Prevention of Child Abuse and Neglect) www.baspcan.org.uk.
- Local area child protection committee (for all county and metropolitan councils).

If you are ever involved in a child abuse case you will need support, depending on the level of your involvement. Good supervision from your line manager is important in allowing you the opportunity to talk through your feelings about the whole episode.

Observation

- What are the arrangements for supervision for staff in your setting?
- Have you taken advantage of supervision?
- How useful was this?
- Can you make suggestions for any improvements?

Reflect on your own practice

As you have seen, it is important that you can maintain and follow policies and procedures for child protection. Have a look at the statements below to assess whether you match up to the levels needed. The statements all refer to the performance criteria for CCLD 305.3.

Performance criteria statement	Always	Sometimes	Never
Do I maintain and follow procedures for the protection of children?			
Do I recognise indicators of possible abuse?			
Do I help children to protect themselves from abuse?			
Do I respond sensitively to a child's disclosure of abuse?			
Do I promote an environment of openness and trust allowing children to express themselves in their chosen way?			

Performance criteria statement	Always	Sometimes	Never
Do I follow safe working practices that protect children and practitioners?			

End-of-unit knowledge check

1. List ten of the rights of the child under the UN Convention.
2. Describe the meaning of discrimination.
3. What is meant by stereotyping?
4. Give three reasons why a family may have difficulty accessing provision.
5. What is the key method to reduce barriers to access?
6. Which agencies does SureStart work with?
7. Give a definition of inclusion.
8. Why is evaluation of provision important?
9. Give three key features of the Children Bill.
10. List three signs of possible physical abuse.
11. Why should you never promise to keep a child's secret?
12. What is the role of a setting's 'designated person'?
13. Name an organisation involved with helping children to be safe.
14. List four key principles to consider when a child discloses abuse to you.

Plan and organise environments for children and families

Children play and learn well when they are comfortable and relaxed and feel that they belong. This means that understanding how to plan and organise an environment that meets children's needs is an essential part of learning how to work with children. This unit looks at the importance of providing a good environment for children as well as ways in which you might provide such an environment for the children you work with.

What you must know and understand

- Legislation and regulations covering the provision of an environment for children, health and safety and equality (K3D255,K3H256/257)
- Principles underpinning the organisation, layout and planning of the environment for children (K3H257/258)
- How to adapt the environment to meet the diverse needs of children (K3D259)
- Routine safety checking of and maintenance of equipment (K3H260)
- Legislation covering quality of access including children who are disabled or who have special educational needs (K3D261)
- Safe and effective practice underpinning the organisation, layout and planning of the indoor and outdoor environment (K3H262)
- When and how to use safety equipment (K3H263)
- Materials and equipment, including ICT, that can be used to promote play and development (K3D264)
- The range of different activities that should be available to maximise learning and development and support a planned curriculum (K3D265)
- How the development of children is facilitated by a positive and enabling environment and consistent routines (K3D266)
- New ways of supporting children and their families who are new to the setting (K3D267)
- The needs of children for quiet periods and privacy as well as opportunities for social interaction with adults and other children (K3D268)

- The implications of children's attachment needs within the environment (K3D269)
- How to support positive behaviour and deal positively with conflict (K3D270, K3C271)
- The importance of respecting children's background and culture and of encouraging families to participate within the setting or service (K3D272)
- The importance of protecting children in the setting (K3S273)
- The importance of ensuring that adults who work with children are suitable (K3P274)
- The importance of protecting adults who work with children (K3S275)
- The nutritional needs of children and the requirements of children's special diets including allergies (K3H277, K3H279)
- The government's guidelines on healthy eating and nutrition and their importance (K3H280)
- The importance of physical exercise for positive mental and physical health (K3D281)
- Appropriate skin and hair care and the need for good oral hygiene (K3H282/283)
- How to deal with medicines, inhalers or drugs for long-term conditions (K3H284)
- The importance of sensitivity in supporting toilet training, not rushing or expecting children to have control before they are ready (K3D285)
- Good hygiene practice including appropriate systems to deal with different types of waste, food handling (K3H286)

Plan and provide an enabling physical environment for children

The way children feel when they enter a building affects them greatly. If they feel relaxed, safe and comfortable, they can settle down easily. This in turn means that they are able to enjoy playing and being with others and can benefit from what the setting offers. Especially with children who spend many hours a day in a setting, it is vital that you get it right for them. This is especially important to remember if you are working in a less than ideal building. Stressed and anxious children find it harder to learn, show inappropriate behaviour and may not cope with separating from their families. For children's families, the environment that you create is important. If they are leaving their children, they need to know that they are going to be happy and safe. As with their children, the **environment** that you create will also affect families. It may make a difference to how often they come into the setting and how long they stay. As parents and professionals need to work closely together, it is essential that they, too, feel welcome and relaxed in the setting.

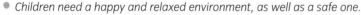 *Children need a happy and relaxed environment, as well as a safe one.*

Legislation and regulations covering the provision of an environment for children

National Standards

In recent years, it has been recognised that children need to be cared for in the best possible conditions. This has resulted in legislation that has allowed each of the nations of the United Kingdom to draw up a set of minimum standards. These are often referred to as the National Standards. It is important that you understand the care standards that apply to the home nation in which you are working, as there are differences between each of the countries. It is also important to check that you are using the care standards that apply to your setting, as there are different ones for day care, childminding and sessional care. The National Standards are compulsory and your setting will be inspected to ensure that you comply with them.

● *Areas that are included within the National Standards across the home countries.*

Finding out more about the National Standards in your home country

- In England, Ofsted is responsible for regulating settings. You will find the care standards for your setting on its website, www.ofsted.gov.uk.
- In Scotland, the Care Commission inspects and regulates care services and you will find the National Standards by searching www.scotland.gov.uk/publications.
- In Wales, the Care Standards Inspectorate for Wales (CSIW) is responsible for regulating settings. Standards can be found by searching www.wales.gov.uk.
- In Northern Ireland, at the time of writing, minimum care standards for the child care sector are still in consultation. To find out more visit the Department of Health, Social Services and Public Safety's website, www.dhsspsni.gov.uk.

Legislation covering health and safety within your setting

While there are differences in the National Standards across the home countries, health and safety legislation is fairly universal. The National Standards reflect this legislation. It is important when following health and safety that you keep up to date, as European Union directives in particular are likely to change the advice and current regulations. When looking at health and safety legislation, it is important to appreciate the differences between **guidance, approved codes of practice** and **regulations**.

Health and Safety at Work Act 1974

The Health and Safety at Work Act is the main piece of legislation that affects day-to-day provision of health and safety in workplaces. In order to provide a safe environment, you need to be familiar with this Act. It is

Check it out

Look at the National Standards for two of the home countries for the type of setting in which you work. Notice whether or not the layout is the same. See whether the adult–child ratios are the same.

Key terms

Guidance is advice that is given to help those responsible for health and safety comply with the law. Guidance is not compulsory.

Approved Codes of Practice give examples and advice as to how the law should be complied with. They also have special legal status and employers can be prosecuted for a breach of health and safety law, if it can be shown that they have not followed the provisions of the relevant Code of Practice.

Regulations are approved by Parliament. They are usually made under the provisions of the Health and Safety at Work Act 1974. They are legally binding.

considered in some detail in Unit 302 (see page 46). The Act was designed to protect employees and additional regulations have been added to it since its introduction. The legislation is fairly comprehensive, so settings that implement it carefully will be sure they are providing a safe environment for both employees and children. The main features of the Health and Safety at Work Act affect both employers and employees.

Keys to good practice: Health and safety

✓ If you are responsible for the health and safety procedures of your setting, you will need to make sure that you keep up to date. To check the current regulations, you can contact the government agency responsible, which is the Health and Safety Executive (www.hse.gov.uk).

Duty of employers

There are important duties for employers under the Act. Essentially, it requires employers to ensure, so far as is reasonably practicable, the health, safety and welfare at work of all employees. In practice, this is done by providing safety equipment and training and by writing and implementing safety procedures. Employers with more than five employees also need to carry out a risk assessment on their workplace and to write a safety policy that shows how risks are to be minimised.

Duty of employees

Under the Act, employees must make sure that their actions do not harm themselves or others. They have a duty to comply with their employer's safety procedures and to use the equipment provided, and to act with due regard for their own and others' safety.

Health and safety regulations

Since the original legislation, the Health and Safety Executive has also added regulations that employers must follow. It is important for supervisors and managers to understand the principles of these regulations. The most important of these for the early years setting is considered separately below.

Control of Substances Hazardous to Health Regulations 2002 (COSHH)

Hazardous substances are anything that can harm your health when you work with them if they are not properly controlled (e.g. by using adequate ventilation or providing protective clothes such as disposable gloves). They can include: substances used directly in work activities, such as glues, paints and cleaning agents; and naturally occurring substances, such as dust, blood, bacteria and urine.

Most settings use cleaning products or have other materials that could be hazardous. In addition, while caring for children, early years workers may have to handle nappies or clean up after toileting or other accidents. The COSHH make settings consider how they can limit the risks from these activities. This might mean that all cleaning materials are stored carefully in a locked cupboard. It might also mean that disposable gloves are provided to prevent infections such as hepatitis or HIV being passed on. It is important to remember that, as an employee, you will have a duty to use any protection that is provided and also to follow the guidelines of the setting.

Under the COSHH, employers have to take steps to minimise risks (see the diagram below).

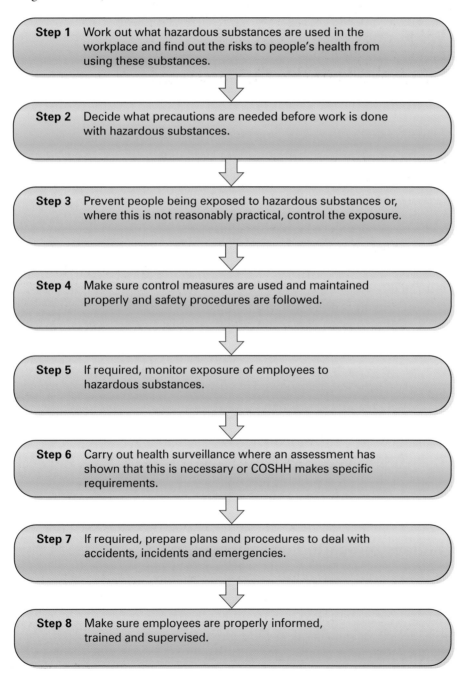

Step 1 Work out what hazardous substances are used in the workplace and find out the risks to people's health from using these substances.

Step 2 Decide what precautions are needed before work is done with hazardous substances.

Step 3 Prevent people being exposed to hazardous substances or, where this is not reasonably practical, control the exposure.

Step 4 Make sure control measures are used and maintained properly and safety procedures are followed.

Step 5 If required, monitor exposure of employees to hazardous substances.

Step 6 Carry out health surveillance where an assessment has shown that this is necessary or COSHH makes specific requirements.

Step 7 If required, prepare plans and procedures to deal with accidents, incidents and emergencies.

Step 8 Make sure employees are properly informed, trained and supervised.

● *The steps employers must follow under the COSHH.*

● *A well set-out changing area.*

Good hygiene practice

In order to minimise the risk to health, it is important to be aware of hazards in the environment. Table 306.1 outlines common hazards and suggests ways in which they might be managed.

Table 306.1 shows how settings working with children might the minimise risks arising from hazardous substances.

Potential hazard	Dangers of hazard	Methods of reducing risk
Cleaning materials	Accidental poisoning	Lock all cleaning products in a cupboard (e.g. in kitchen)
	Fire risk	Ensure all products are labelled
	Unstable if mixed together	Follow manufacturer's instructions
	Skin irritant	Wear protective gloves. Do not use products near children
Changing nappies, toileting	Infection	Wear disposable gloves and aprons when changing nappies or assisting children with toileting
		Put soiled nappies into bags provided and dispose of them in separate bin
		Clean changing areas after use
		Wash hands before and after nappy changing or assisting children with toileting
First aid treatment	Infection	Record all accidents in the accident report book
		Keep separate books for staff and for children in office
		Use disposable gloves
		Dispose of items used during treatment in bags provided

continued on next page

continued from previous page

Potential hazard	Dangers of hazard	Methods of reducing risk
Bodily fluids	Infections such as HIV, hepatitis	Wear disposable gloves, protective aprons Dispose of waste (see page 262)
Cross-infection	Viral and bacterial infections spread	Ensure good ventilation Wash hands Wear protective aprons, disposable gloves Wipe children's noses Good food hygiene (see page 260)
Disposal of waste	Puncture wounds, cross-infection	Waste to be sorted and disposed of according to setting's procedures (see page 262)
Food handling	Food poisoning	Follow good food handling procedures (see page 260) Ensure good storage of foodstuffs, including fridge temperatures

Reporting of Injuries, Diseases and Dangerous Occurrences Regulations 1995 (RIDDOR)

As part of these Regulations, workplaces must provide an accident report book. Most settings keep separate books for employees and children. All accidents should be recorded, preferably on a special form such as the one shown overleaf. Any injuries to employees that mean they cannot work for three days or more must be reported to the Health and Safety Executive, as must more serious incidents.

Keys to good practice: Reporting accidents

✓ Maintain separate accident report books for staff and children.

✓ Keep accident report books in a central place.

✓ Ensure accident report books are kept up to date.

✓ Report serious accidents to the Health and Safety Executive; also report when a staff member has been off work for three or more days because of an injury sustained at work.

WAVERLEY NURSERY STAFF ACCIDENT REPORT FORM

Report of an accident or injury to a person at work or on duty

This form must be completed in all cases of accident, injury or dangerous occurrence and submitted to the Health and Safety Officer

Name of injured person _____

Date of birth _____

Position held in organisation _____

Date and time of accident _____

Particulars of injury/accident _____

Activity at time of injury/accident _____

Place of injury/accident _____

Details of injury/accident _____

First aid treatment (if any) given _____

Was the injured person taken to hospital? If so, where? _____

_____

Names and positions of persons present when the accident occurred

_____

Signature of person reporting incident _____

● *A form for reporting accidents involving staff.*

Fire Precautions (Workplace) Regulations 1997

It is important that all settings have plans and procedures for action in the event of a fire. Most settings have regular fire drills (see also Unit 302, pages 81–82) and equipment such as fire extinguishers and smoke detectors, and fire alarms are tested regularly. Records of fire drills and tests should be kept, and signs showing what to do in the event of a fire should be placed in every room.

Fire officers can give advice about evacuation procedures and it is good practice in early years settings to make sure that these are rehearsed with the children. In some settings, doors and windows may have to be locked to ensure children's safety. In such cases, it is important that they can be opened easily and quickly by an adult in the event of an emergency.

Keys to good practice: Fire precautions

✓ Fire exits must be kept unlocked and unobstructed at all times.

✓ Fire exits must be easily accessible.

✓ Regular checks should be carried out to make sure that fire alarms and extinguishers are working.

✓ Rehearse evacuation procedures regularly with the children.

✓ Advice about evacuation procedures should be obtained from a fire officer.

Health and Safety (First Aid) Regulations 1981

First aid skills are always important when working with children, but there is a legal duty for employers to keep a first aid box and appoint at least one person to be responsible in the event of an accident. Most early years settings also need at least one trained first aider. It is important to remember that first aid qualifications need to be updated and that it is sensible to have several staff trained in first aid. Unit 302 also considers first aid and suggests what should be included in any first aid box (see pages 67–68).

Keys to good practice: First aid

✓ Ensure several members of staff have first aid training.

✓ Keep first aid boxes out of reach of children but still accessible to staff.

✓ Take first aid boxes on outings.

✓ Check first aid boxes regularly to see whether the contents are complete and that items are not out of date.

✓ Display signs around the setting to show where the nearest first aid box is kept.

Regulations covering the safety of toys, equipment and materials

Choosing safe toys and equipment for children is important. Fortunately, there is legislation in place to prevent toys, equipment and materials being sold that could be dangerous for children. From the Consumer Protection Act 1987, there are the Toys (Safety) Regulations 1995. The Regulations define a toy as: 'any product or material designed or clearly intended for use in play by children of less than 14 years of age'. Under the regulations, third parties, as well as the actual users of toys, must be protected against health hazards and physical injury when the toy is used.

Various symbols are used to indicate that toys and equipment are safe and suitable for children of particular ages. This is covered in Unit 302 (see pages 46–47).

✔ Keys to good practice: Toys and equipment

✓ When taking donations or buying second-hand toys and equipment, extra care is needed to ensure that they are safe and meet the current regulations.

✓ Remember that the way in which children play with toys and are supervised are just as important as the age range suggested by the manufacturer. Always think about children's level of development rather than their age when choosing toys.

✓ Avoid toys with loose pile fabric or hair which sheds easily and thereby presents a choking hazard.

✓ Avoid toys with small components or parts which detach, on which a child could choke.

✓ Avoid toys with sharp points and edges or finger traps.

✓ Avoid loose ribbons on toys and long neck ties on children's costumes.

✓ Check toys to see that they have not become dangerously worn (e.g. revealing sharp points and edges or filling materials). Record when toys and equipment have been checked so that it can be done systematically.

✓ Encourage children to be tidy and put toys away after play. Accidents can be caused by people and children tripping over toys.

Maintaining and using safety equipment

Many items of equipment are used to keep children safe in early years settings. Regular checks on all safety equipment should be carried out, and the manufacturer's instructions should be closely followed, especially if items need maintaining or cleaning. In general, it is considered good practice to buy new equipment, as it will conform with the latest safety regulations. Second-hand or older equipment needs to be carefully checked. Table 306.2 shows examples of safety equipment and when it might be used in settings.

Check it out

- Find out about the safety policy and risk assessment that have been carried out in your workplace.
- Who is responsible for reviewing the policies?
- How does your setting conform to the first aid and fire regulations?
- Carry out a risk assessment on your workplace, using either your own sheet or one from your workplace. What are the main risks? How are these risks minimised?

Did you know?

If you are unsure about whether a toy is safe or suspect that you have bought something that is not, you should contact your local trading standards officer. The trading standards department is responsible for enforcing this type of safety legislation.

Table 306.2. The safety equipment commonly found in early years settings

Equipment	Purpose
Stair gates	Prevent babies and children from falling downstairs or from having access to certain areas
Reins and harnesses	Prevent children from straying onto a road or dangerous area when they are outside. Also used in pushchairs and highchairs to prevent children from falling out
Electric plug covers	Prevent children from putting their fingers or objects into plug sockets
Highchairs	Help young children to sit safely at mealtimes. Harnesses may be used to strap children in
Bath mats	Prevent children and babies from slipping in the bath
Window locks	Prevent children from opening windows and falling out or leaving premises
Cupboard locks	Prevent children gaining access to dangerous materials
Corner protectors	Protect children from sharp edges on furniture
Cooker guards	Where it is not possible to prevent children from being in the kitchen (which is the best safety measure), a cooker guard prevents children from tipping over pans
Car seat/booster cushion	Helps to protect children and babies if a car suddenly brakes or is involved in an accident. Car seats have to be correctly fitted and must not be bought second hand. Seats must be correct for the age of the baby or child
Fire guards	Used to put around heaters and radiators to prevent children from being burnt

Legislation covering the equality of access and provision for children

It is essential that we plan to ensure that all children can enjoy and take part in settings. While we have a moral duty to do this, there is also legislation in place. Key legislation includes the Disability Discrimination Act and also the United Nations Convention on the Rights of the Child. This legislation, as well as suggestions for improving access, is considered in detail in Unit 305.

● *Stair gates will benefit younger children especially.*

Organise space and resources to meet children's needs

Creating an environment for children requires much thought. You need to think about the layout, routine and staffing. It is also important to review the environment regularly and to consider whether it still meets the needs of children. This is particularly important when hours have been extended or there are changes in the age ranges of children that you are looking after.

Principles underpinning the organisation, layout and planning of the environment

Planning the layout of a room

The way in which furniture and activities are laid out affects the activities that can be carried out and even the mood of the children. A good room layout will allow the children to move from one area to another easily, while helping them to feel secure. If items of furniture cannot be moved, at least the equipment and activities set on the tables and elsewhere can be changed.

Sometimes the weather may affect room layout. For example, if children have been unable to go out they will benefit from some kind of physical exercise and movement indoors.

Changing the room layout periodically can also help to stimulate children's interest in activities and can mean that some equipment that is under-used becomes more valued by children.

If you decide to change a room's layout, make sure that you liaise with colleagues and lift and handle furniture safely. Consider also the needs of children who may need assistance in being mobile or who have particular requirements such as the need to be playing and working in good light.

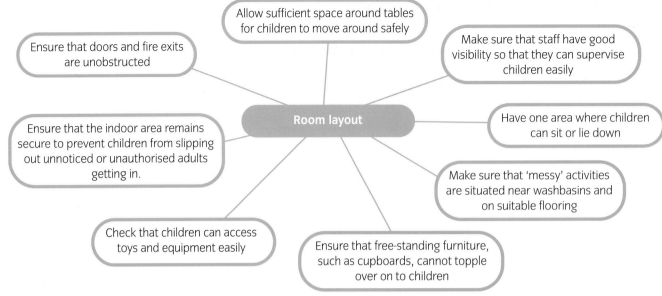

Ensure that doors and fire exits are unobstructed

Allow sufficient space around tables for children to move around safely

Make sure that staff have good visibility so that they can supervise children easily

Room layout

Ensure that the indoor area remains secure to prevent children from slipping out unnoticed or unauthorised adults getting in.

Have one area where children can sit or lie down

Make sure that 'messy' activities are situated near washbasins and on suitable flooring

Check that children can access toys and equipment easily

Ensure that free-standing furniture, such as cupboards, cannot topple over on to children

● Basic principles that you should consider when planning a room.

Laying out activities attractively

An important part of preparation is to lay out materials, equipment and toys attractively. Children will then be more interested in them. Making the environment welcoming and attractive is particularly important for children who are starting in a new setting as well as for children who find it difficult to start playing. In some cases this may mean starting off an activity to give children an idea of how to use the materials or toys. For example, a floor puzzle or collage may be begun.

● Would children find this tabletop inviting?

Table 306.3 gives some ideas of the routine tasks involved in preparing for sessions.

Table 306.3. Routine tasks involved in preparing for sessions

Activity/area	Preparation
Painting table or easels	Put out fresh paint, a variety of brushes, printing equipment, paper and a pencil to write children's names on their work. Prepare an area to receive wet paintings. Children will need aprons.
Water tray	Make sure that toys such as boats, jugs and cups are clean before putting them out. Children will need aprons. A cloth and towel may also be put nearby. Water must be changed at least once a day.
Sand area	If outside, check that the sand has been covered to prevent animals from soiling it. Rake sand and check that toys are clean. Put a dustpan and brush near the area, as sand on floors can be slippery.
Home corner/ dressing-up area	Make sure that clothes are clean and arrange them in an inviting way. Dress dolls, lay out home equipment such as the table. Make sure that there are enough props. Consider changing the props in this area from time to time to stimulate different roles, for example a shop.
Book corner	Sort through books and remove any that need repairing. Present books attractively by standing them up. Check that cushions and seating are clean. Consider choosing books about a current theme for display.
Jigsaws/construction area	Check that jigsaws are complete. Remove any that have parts missing. Set out construction toys and attract children's interest by partly building something.
Dough	Make up enough fresh dough for the numbers of children who are likely to choose this activity. Check that boards and tools are clean.

Adapting the environment to help children with special needs

Where settings are working with children who have special needs, some adaptations to the environment may be necessary (see above – it is now law that children should not suffer discrimination in their care and education because of a disability). The types of adaptations will depend on the individual needs of children. Before making any changes to an environment, it will be important to talk to parents and other professionals about how best to adapt the environment.

● *Adapt the environment to meet the needs of all children.*

Early years workers can help children by thinking creatively of how to enable them to take part in activities. In some cases helping a child with special needs is an exercise in problem solving. For example, rather than struggling to take a child to an activity, the activity could be taken to the child. This might mean putting construction toys on a table rather than having them on the floor, or taking some of the sand out of the sandpit and putting it into a tray so that the child does not have to stand.

Case study 1: A less noisy setting

Isabella has just begun in a nursery class. She has partial hearing. Grace, her teacher, asks her parents what might be done to help Isabella in the classroom. They explain that Isabella will benefit from the background noise being reduced during activities when she must listen carefully to instructions or others talking.

1. *Suggest two ways in which the layout or organisation of the classroom might be changed to accommodate Isabella's needs.*
2. *How might this be of benefit to the other children?*

Using outdoor areas with children

If you have an outdoor area, there is no reason why it should not be used all year around. The ideal for young children is that there should be free flow play rather than fixed playtimes outdoors. This is not always possible, as in some settings there is no immediate access from the indoor environment.

Unit 302 looks at the safety aspects of the outdoor environment (see pages 57–59).

Flexible outdoor area

While the outdoor area can be used to promote physical exercise, it is also worth thinking about how it can be used to promote learning. Consider putting out tables so that activities that were traditionally carried out indoors can be done outside. Large-scale painting and marking are, for example, easy to carry out. In the same way role-play can be integrated outdoors by bringing out props from the home corner and giving children opportunities to build dens with fabric. With the emphasis on outdoor play, it is important to make sure that there is some storage outdoors.

Supervising outdoor play

As with all work with children, it is important to provide a layout where children can be supervised. You have a duty of care towards children and so it is important that you supervise children carefully, according to their age

Did you know?

The outdoor area is increasingly seen as being as valuable as the indoor environment, partly as a result of concerns over children's level of fitness and activity. The term 'outdoor classroom' is now being used to encourage early years settings to see the outdoor environment as one where children can also learn. Most inspectors looking at opportunities for children's play and learning now focus on how effectively the outdoor area is being used. This means it should be integrated into any curriculum plans.

and the activity that they are undertaking. The level of supervision therefore depends enormously on your individual setting. It is always worth having an adult on hand where children are using large-scale equipment as well as tricycles, wheeled toys and so on. Ideally, the adult supervising should have a first aid qualification or at least some basic knowledge of first aid. Some settings use mobile phones or walkie-talkies so that an adult outdoors can always have instant communication with a member of staff indoors.

● *Why is it important for a supervisor to have direct communication while outside?*

Offering a range of activities for children

The National Standards across the home countries consider not only the organisation of the setting but also whether children are getting effective opportunities to play and learn. It is important to offer a range of activities for children. For further information about meeting the needs of babies and young children see Unit 303.

Basic principles

There are some simple and quite basic principles underlying the provision of a range of activities for children's play and learning. Observing the type of play and interests that children enjoy is essential and it is good practice to build on these. This means that a toddler who is enjoying dropping objects into a post box might also enjoy sending a ball down a piece of drain pipe. It is also important to be ready to respond quickly when children's interests begin to change.

Some aspects of children's unwanted behaviour can be linked to boredom. Children need to find new challenges. Especially for a child who spends many hours a week in the setting, toys and activities should be changed each day or even during the sessions. Play and learning activities are often grouped into areas such as construction play, imaginative play or creative play. This is because each area of play helps children to develop in different ways. Building a den outdoors helps children's gross motor movements, thinking and maybe also social skills, while playing in the sand tray may encourage children's small hand movements.

Look for a range of opportunities that will interest children while also promoting their development. Activities, toys and equipment are also needed in order to support the curriculum where a curriculum is appropriate. A writing area and a quiet book area might support literacy while activities that encourage children to touch, feel and notice changes might support early science.

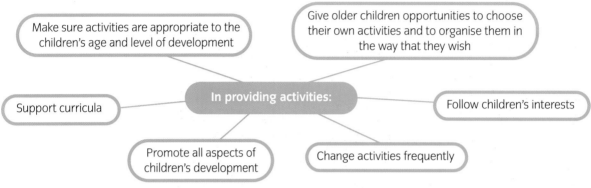

● *Providing a range of activities*

Dividing the environment into areas

Many settings find it helpful to divide large spaces into particular areas (Table 306.4). This can help children to focus more easily and (especially for younger children) help them to feel more secure. A large area that is noisy and busy can be intimidating for young two- and three-year-olds. Dividing the environment into areas can help with supervision and helps children to play in different ways. This may apply to the outdoor as well as the indoor environment.

Table 306.4. Examples of different types of areas commonly found in early years settings

Area	Contents/activities
Imaginative play	Dressing-up clothes, home corners, pushchairs
Small-world play	Farm sets, dolls' houses, Playmobil, toy cars, train sets
Creative play	Glueing, painting, collage, musical instruments, junk modelling, tools, sewing
Exploration	Items for sorting, scales for measuring, magnifying glasses
Literacy	Book corners, mark-making tables, chalks, white boards, story tapes
Natural materials	Sand tray, water tray, peat or mud, pasta, dough
Physical play	Climbing frames, balls, hoops, tricycles, wheeled toys, wheelbarrows
Construction	Duplo, Lego, large wooden bricks, jigsaw puzzles
ICT	Remote-controlled cars, programmable toys such as Roamers, Pixies, computers, gadgets and toys that have microchips in them, e.g. singing birthday cards, toys that light up and make sounds

In addition to providing different types of activity areas, most early years settings also look at providing a balance between adult-directed activities and child-initiated ones. Interestingly, this approach was considered to be the most effective in stimulating children according to the latest findings of the EPPE project (Effective Provision of Pre-school Education). Adults in the setting might for example carry out a cooking activity with children or play games to help children recognise their names.

● *Contrast the types of learning that the areas shown would most benefit.*

Reflect on your own practice

As you have seen, sound knowledge of the legislation bearing upon the setting is required, alongside an appreciation of the importance of a well-organised space with adequate resources. Have a look at the statements below to assess whether you follow the principles. The statements all refer to the performance criteria for CCLD 306.1 and 306.2.

Performance criteria statement	Always	Sometimes	Never
Do I ensure that the physical environment meets health and safety requirements?			
Do I ensure that barriers to participation are addressed?			
Do I carefully organise and structure the physical environment?			
Do I encourage children to be actively involved in decisions about their environment?			
Do I ensure there are comfortable areas where children can go for quiet and privacy?			

Provide a caring, nurturing and responsive environment

How the development of children is facilitated by a positive and enabling environment and consistent routines

The idea behind providing an enabling environment is to help children gain independence skills, make choices and gradually take responsibility. This helps children to learn that they are competent and can be trusted and so supports their self-esteem. It also encourages them to gain a sense of belonging. Many children spend a large proportion of their time in child care and education settings, and there is a danger of them becoming institutionalised.

As well as making sure the physical environment supports children's independence, the role of the adult is also essential. The type of environment that you plan for children must support children's moves towards independence. For example, shelves and furniture must be chosen that will allow children to be able to take toys and also tidy them away. As suggested above, if the furniture and layout within the setting are well thought out, older children should sometimes be able to be supervised from a distance rather than having an adult on constant standby.

The way in which adults interact with children makes the environment a positive one. Children need adults to help them 'have a go' and also to support them when they are having difficulties or becoming frustrated. A positive environment means that children do not worry about making mistakes as they know that adults will be on hand to support them without 'taking over'. Children can learn to make choices and take responsibility only if they are feeling secure and know that adults' reactions will be supportive. For example, children who pour a drink and spill it needs to know that they will not be told off, but will be helped to get a cloth and wipe it up.

Did you know?

The EPPE project (Effective Provision of Pre-school Education) provides early years practitioners with some interesting insights into how best to support young children's learning. Find out more about the key findings of the EPPE project on the website www.ioe.ac.uk/schools/ecpe/eppe/.

Keys to good practice: A positive and enabling environment

✓ Most shelves and storage should be at children's height.

✓ Labels and photographs can be used to show children where things are kept.

✓ Provide opportunities for children to talk about what they want to do and then to collect the necessary items, toys and materials.

✓ Aprons and protective clothing for outdoors should be accessible.

✓ Give children time in which to try to do things for themselves.

✓ Acknowledge children's success when they are able to organise their play.

Harry and Jodie have just begun in a pre-school group. They enjoy playing together, especially in the home corner. The pre-school supervisor shows them where various props are and suggests to the children that they can use whatever they like. She asks them why it might be important afterwards to tidy up and they agree that they will do so. Harry and Jodie are excited and have a lovely time choosing things and playing with them. Afterwards, they do tidy up, although things are not put back perfectly. The supervisor praises their efforts and helps them finish off.

1. *Why is it important for children to organise their own play?*
2. *Explain how Harry and Jodie will benefit from being able to choose and take responsibility for their play.*
3. *Why is it important for children to tidy away at the end of their play?*
4. *Why was it important for the supervisor to praise their efforts and help them tidy away rather than doing it herself?*

How routines can support care, learning and development

The setting's routines can have a strong impact. A good routine can help children to feel secure and develop a sense of belonging. This is essential for the youngest children as well as for older children who have experienced many upheavals. Some children with additional needs such as autism also rely on a routine in order to cope. A good routine can also be used to help children learn. It is now recognised in the *Birth To Three* framework (see Unit 309, page 330) (for England but also the similar ones being developed in the other countries of the United Kingdom – again, see Unit 309) that everyday care routines for children under three years can provide wonderful opportunities to stimulate language and social skills (see also Unit 303, pages 146–149).

The test of a routine is how the children respond to it. Where children are showing examples of unwanted behaviour at key points in the session or day, it is likely to be a result of the routine not meeting their needs. Routines should not create stress for either children or staff.

As children grow they do have changing needs. This means that a routine that once worked in a childminding setting may no longer be as successful. In large settings similarly, there is often a danger that a well-established routine will, increasingly with time, fail to meet children's needs: staff have moved on, times have changed, but the routine has not. It is always worth periodically reflecting upon the way in which a routine is working and, if needed, adapting it. This is part of reflective practice, as discussed in Unit 304.

Examples of routines

Greeting and saying goodbye to children

The way in which children settle in at the start of any day or session is extremely important. A good routine here can help young children to find their feet quickly and make parents feel comfortable. It is good practice for children's key workers to greet children and their parents and it is helpful if some sort of personal routine for the child is established.

In the same way, the end of the session or day is important. Saying goodbye is a way of 'signing off'. It is essential for children to go home on a happy note. Some settings find it useful to have a group song to round off the session. The end of the session or day can be an opportunity to talk about what might happen the next day. In some settings children begin to choose and put out some of the equipment and toys they might like to use when they arrive the next day. This can work well in a childminding setting, where children put into a fabric bag the toy that they want to use. Children then come into the setting the next time looking forward to what they are going to do.

Meal and snack times

Meal and snack times can sometimes be problematic. This is sad because it is an ideal opportunity for children to chat, relax and learn social skills. The key to getting meal and snack times right is often to have small groups and to find ways of staggering the times. A lunchtime with 20 children at once is usually riotous and can result in children showing unwanted behaviour, while an adult sitting quietly down with five children at a time is more manageable. During meal and snack times, children should be encouraged to talk and enjoy themselves. It is also good practice for children to serve themselves – it encourages their fine manipulative skills and builds their confidence and independence.

Nappy changing, toileting and other physical care

While some practitioners find this part of their role arduous, it is extremely important for the child. It is often a good chance for the child to gain individual attention, away from others. Some children spend quite a while in the toilets, as they like chatting away to the accompanying adult. For babies and toddlers, this time is precious and they rely on being with a responsive adult. It is good practice for nappy changing, bathing and other aspects of physical care to be carried out by the child's key worker (partly because they will be able to report any concerns such as significant changes to the skin directly to parents and partly also to facilitate good attachment – see page 138).

Ways of supporting children and families new to the setting

Starting off in a new setting can be difficult for both children and their families.

Looking for ways to help them make the transition is therefore important. In Unit 303 we looked at ways of helping children to make a transition and also at the importance of key workers. As well as making sure that children have developed a good relationship with you before they are left in the setting. You can also help the settling-in process in other ways.

Opportunities for parents and children to learn about the setting

Parents and children will find it easier to settle into a setting if they have had the opportunity to familiarise themselves with it. This may mean asking parents if they would like to visit the setting and meet the people who will work with their child. It is also helpful if parents can learn more about the aims of the setting and the type of activities provided. Children will also be helped if they can join in, use and see the toys and equipment and also get used to what happens while they are feeling secure in the presence of a parent or carer.

Meeting other parents

It can be useful for parents to meet with other parents. This can be reassuring for them and also helpful if they are new to an area. Some settings do this by inviting parents to stay on and have coffee or by introducing one parent to another at home time.

Providing feedback

If parents are leaving leaving their children with you for the first time, it can be reassuring for them to have some contact with you straightaway so that they know whether their child has settled down. Some settings encourage parents to wait outside or will contact them after five minutes by phone in order to let them know how the separation is going. It is also important for parents to be given plenty of feedback at the end of sessions, until the child has fully settled in. this feedback might include who the child has played with, what activities he or she joined in with and any minor glitches. Providing good feedback to parents early on can foster good relationships and usually encourages parents to feel that they can share information with you.

✓ As children need to build up a relationship before they can truly settle, staggered admission arrangements should be considered. Trying to settle several new children in all at once may seem a good idea, but is actually difficult to do well. If one or two new children are taken at a time, children will often settle in more quickly.

The needs of children for quiet periods and privacy

As part of the routine and layout of the setting, it is important that children are given opportunities to rest and simply be quiet, as well as opportunities for privacy. Rest and sleep are essential for younger children, but older children too may sometimes need time and space to themselves. This is especially true where children are spending many hours a day in the company of lots of other children. It is therefore important to identify places where children can rest or sleep, or areas to which they can go to 'escape'. Some settings are able to put aside a quiet room or area. This is a more effective approach than trying to enforce a 'quiet time' on whole groups of children. Playing relaxing soft music and dimming the lights can be soothing. In settings that cannot put aside a separate room, it is important to look for ways of creating a special area. This might mean fencing off part of a room and creating a tent-like environment.

Quiet times and rest are considered further in Unit 307 (page 277).

The implications of children's attachment needs

It is often said that children are adaptable. This is not wholly true, as children do need routine and also need to be with familiar faces. Young children, especially those under three years, find it hard to have constant changes of carers, as they need stability in order to feel secure. This is explained in Unit 312 (see pages 386–444).

Children's attachment needs have implications for staffing. For younger children it is essential that there is a key worker system in place and that when key workers are on holiday, sick or absent, thought is given to how to provide some continuity. In day care, for example, two staff members might spend time with babies and toddlers so that if one is not available children are still able to cope. When absences are planned, such as holidays, some parents may arrange to take theirs at the same time.

Change of carers

There will be times when a member of staff leaves the setting or moves room. As there is usually some notice of this happening, it is important to prepare children. Ideally, another member of staff should make sure that children are comfortable with him or her before the staff member leaves. It is also important that parents are told about staff changes so that they know who will be responsible for their child's care. As children can get very attached to adults who care for them, particularly if they have spent a lot of time with them, it is important to understand that some children will often go through a grieving process. You can support them by providing photographs of the carer, encouraging them to talk about how they feel and providing opportunities for them to write letters or paint pictures. It is also important that children are not left thinking it is their fault that their carer has left. Children will need to hear that the adult is sorry that he or she had to leave and if possible some contact should be continued, even if this is just an odd note or postcard.

Case study 3: Change of carer

Mark is four years old. He has been with the childminder since he was six months old. He has now started school, but still enjoys being picked up and spending time there after school. The childminder is moving house to another area and so has told Mark's mother that she will need to find a new childminder for his after-school care at the end of the summer. The childminder is part of a network and knows some other childminders well. She helps Mark's mother to find a new childminder. They decide to tell Mark about the changes gradually. The childminder invites the new childminder round for the afternoon so that Mark can meet and play with her. The new childminder invites them both back to tea at her house the following week. This is a success and is repeated. Mark's mother tells him that his childminder has to move house. Mark is upset, but is also interested as the childminder lets him pack some boxes and shows him pictures of her new house. Mark's mother lets him choose a present and they make a card for the childminder. On his last day, the childminder gives Mark a small present and promises him that she will write. A letter duly arrives and his new childminder helps Mark to make a picture to send back. After a couple of weeks Mark is quite settled and, while he does miss his old childminder, he is quite happy.

1. *Explain why it is was important for Mark to meet his new carer in the company of his childminder.*
2. *Why is it important for parents and practitioners to work closely together when preparing children for change?*
3. *Why is it important to prepare children for changes in their care?*

How to support positive behaviour

As mentioned at the start of this unit, the term 'environment' describes the atmosphere or emotional climate of the setting as well as its physical aspects. The way in which children's behaviour is managed is therefore an essential ingredient. Ideally, children need early years workers to be consistent, fair and calm. You need to create a sense of belonging and unity within group settings so that children look for ways of helping each other, rather than competing for attention. Unit 337 looks in detail at the strategies to promote positive behaviour (see especially pages 460–462).

How to deal positively with conflict

How you respond to children's behaviour requires close thought. Angry loud voices can make other children feel very uncomfortable. This is sometimes called the 'spill-over effect'. Where possible, adults should avoid taking a confrontational approach with children. Try to ensure that your voice remains calm and that you talk to rather than interrogate children. With younger children you might find that distraction will work well, while with older children a sense of humour or giving children time to reflect or take responsibility for their actions might be the way forward.

Case study 4: Dealing with conflict

Carlos is eight years old. He has just snatched Kylie's drawing and has ripped it up. Faith sees his actions and goes over to him. She decides that he is already in quite a rage and thinks about ways to defuse the situation rather than inflame it. She quietly says, 'Carlos, I think that you have gone too far. Talk to me about why you needed to do that.' Carlos shouts back 'She took my pens and wouldn't give them back when I asked!' Faith sits down at the table. She slows her actions and speech down. 'Oh dear, that doesn't sound like a happy start to the afternoon does it, you two? Where are we going to go from here then?' Kylie looks down and says 'Sorry'. Carlos picks up the bits of paper from the floor and says 'I could try and stick them if you want'. Kylie smiles and says 'It wasn't very good anyway. I was going to do another.' Faith asks them if she should find a few more pens if there are not enough and suggests that maybe they could help her to order some more from the catalogue.

1. *Why is it important for adults to stay calm when working with children?*
2. *Explain how Faith defused the situation.*
3. *How did Faith involve the children in resolving the conflict?*

Respecting children's background culture and encouraging families to participate

A major part of who children are is their home background. Children need to be able to talk to you about their home and what they enjoying doing. They may, for example, want to show you photographs or bring in things that they have made or been given. Finding out about and valuing children's home lives helps children to feel more settled. It also shows parents that you are keen to work with them and to avoid a 'them and us' atmosphere (see also page 210).

Wherever possible, you need to look for ways of encouraging parents to feel that they can participate in and indeed shape the setting. This might be anything from encouraging parents to sit in at the end of a session through to parents coming in and acting as helpers on either a one-off or regular basis.

● *Look for ways of encouraging parents to feel that they can participate in your setting.*

Protecting children

Children have a right to safety. This means that as well as taking physical safety measures (e.g. the use of stair gates – see Table 306.2 above), you must also ensure that they are safe from abuse. Today there is a greater awareness of child protection, but where procedures are not followed children can still be put at risk. Unit 305 looks at the detection and reporting of abuse (see pages 210–214) as well as the vetting procedures for the employment of staff (see page 218).

You have a legal duty to protect children and so if you suspect that a colleague, helper or any adult within the setting may be abusing or may have abused a child, you must act. You should begin by consulting the child protection policy in your setting. If it is not possible to follow the policy's procedures (e.g. because it is the manager of the setting that you have concerns about) you should contact outside services such as the National Society for the Prevention of Cruelty to Children or the local social services team.

Protecting children during care routines

There may be times when you have to care for children in potentially intimate situations, such as changing nappies, supervising them in the toilets or helping them if they have accidents. Only members of staff who

Check it out

Within the terms of the National Standards in your home country, your setting should have a child protection policy. That policy should set the procedures to be followed. What does the policy in your setting say you should do if you suspect a child is being abused? What does it say in connection with the appointment of staff?

have been vetted should have access to children during intimate care routines. It is important to take steps to protect children and also yourself from allegations. In this connection it is essential that children are given as much privacy as possible, dependent on their age and needs. This means that, where possible, children should be able to close the toilet doors; while adults might be on hand, they should be discreet. It is also important for children to take as much responsibility for their care needs as possible. A two-year-old may need help with fastenings on clothing, but may be able to pull up and down his or her own pants. Similarly, older children who have had an accident may be able to change most of their own clothing.

Protecting against accusations of improper behaviour

Many adults who work with children fear that they are vulnerable to accusations of abuse. While such allegations are rare, it is a good idea to avoid putting yourself and the child in situations where they might be made. As part of your child protection policy, you should have guidelines on how to work with children. It is also essential that volunteers, helpers and other parents in a setting also know and follow these. This can form part of an **induction period**, so that all adults in a setting understand the policies relating to child welfare, including those on confidentiality and behaviour, as well child protection.

Key terms

An **induction period** is a time during which new staff and volunteers learn about the policies and procedures in a setting.

Keys to good practice: Avoiding allegations of improper behaviour

✓ Never leave anyone who has not been given clearance alone with a child (i.e. out of the view of others).

✓ Make sure during nappy changes or intimate care routines that doors are kept slightly ajar.

✓ Always encourage children as much as possible to do their own personal hygiene.

✓ Do not play games involving blindfolding children.

✓ Do not play games involving secrets.

✓ Do not give children your address or personal details.

✓ Do not give children your home address, telephone number or email address unless there is a particular reason to do so; if so, ensure that parents and colleagues know about it.

Check it out

How does your setting help volunteers and new members of staff find out about policies relating to child protection?

Case study 5: Protecting children and adults

Margaret is a retired teacher. She has offered to help out at a local pre-school as she is missing being with children. It is a few years since she last taught. The manager of the setting is delighted. She tells Margaret that she will need to be supervised while she is with the children and that she will need permission for a police check to be done on her. She explains that all volunteers also have some induction training about child protection, confidentiality and behaviour management. Margaret is surprised and feels insulted. The manager explains the reason behind this policy is not just to protect children but also to protect staff and volunteers. Margaret understands and says she is happy to sign the disclosure papers and also to bring in evidence of her identity.

1. *Why is it important that volunteers and staff are checked in this way?*
2. *Explain why volunteers should not be left unsupervised with children.*
3. *Discuss the advantages of having an induction period for volunteers.*

Reflect on your own practice

As you have seen, part of your role is to provide a caring, nurturing and responsive environment. Have a look at the statements below to assess whether you match up to the levels of care needed. The statements all refer to the performance criteria for CCLD 306.3.

Performance criteria statement	Always	Sometimes	Never
Do I show that I value children and families and respect their culture?			
Do I explain any foreseeable changes to the child's environment clearly and honestly?			
Do I deal positively with conflict that may arise between children?			

Facilitate children's personal care

Children can relax and settle only when all of their needs have been met. As part of organising an environment for children, you have to ensure that their physical needs have been met. The extent to which you support children's personal care will depend partly on their age and partly on your role. Childminders or nannies may find that they need to care for children's hair and skin, while if you work in a pre-school you may find that your role involves providing food and drinks. This is an important part of their care and you will need to know how to ensure that children are eating a balanced and nutritional diet. Providing food and drinks is covered in detail in Unit 307.

Appropriate and safe care for children's skin, hair and teeth

Hygiene

In some situations, adults working with children may be required also to meet their hygiene needs. It is important that this is done with parental consent and that you work closely with parents to ensure that individual children's needs are met. For example a child may have an allergic reaction to certain skin products or parents may ask you to care for children in a way that meets their religious beliefs. It is essential that information that parents give is written down so that there is no confusion. This is particularly important where more than one person needs to take care of a child.

Keys to good practice: Children's hygiene

✓ Make sure that information about how children's needs are to be met is recorded.

✓ Always check before using any skin products on children.

✓ Make sure that each child has a separate face cloth and towel, or use disposable products.

Check it out

Look at the two meals below and consider how each of them might meet children's nutritional needs.

- Lamb stew made with carrots, swede served with mashed potatoes, broccoli and peas, with yoghurt for dessert.
- Vegetarian lasagne made with lentils, tomatoes and spinach, served with salad and fresh tomatoes, with fresh fruit salad and fromage frais for dessert.

Are there any groups of children for whom either or both of these meals would not be suitable?

Safe care for children's skin

Children's skin is particularly sensitive and so needs to be well cared for. Skin products should not be used without checking with parents. Skin must always be dried thoroughly by being patted rather than rubbed, especially if children have eczema. This avoids sore areas and also can reduce the risk of infection.

Hand washing

Washing hands frequently is a key way in which you can prevent infection from spreading. Children generally handle objects but also often put their fingers and hands into their mouths. This means that bacteria, viruses and parasites can directly enter a child's body.

● *Encourage children to take responsibility for their own hygiene.*

Before eating or touching food

After using the toilet

Hands should always be washed:

After touching animals

After playing outdoors

● *Hand hygiene.*

Hands need to be washed with warm water and soap and thoroughly dried. It is important to use mild soap and also to check with parents that their children are able to use it, as children with eczema may need special soap that is moisturised. Disposable towels are thought to be the most hygienic method of drying hands. As early as possible, you need to encourage children to wash their own hands. It can be seen as an activity in its own right, although you do need to create pleasant environment. As children become older, you may need occasionally to remind them to wash their hands, as it is not uncommon for them to 'skip' this. Explaining to them the importance of hand washing can help and you may wish to look at resources from your local health promotion team (which can usually be found by contacting your local NHS trust).

Noticing changes

When caring for children, it is important to keep an eye out for rashes or changes to the skin. A child might have a fungal infection such as athlete's foot or dry skin. Concerns need to be reported to the parents and no treatment can be given until parental consent is obtained. It is also important to think about whether bruises or marks that you notice might be the result of abuse (see Unit 305, pages 210–214).

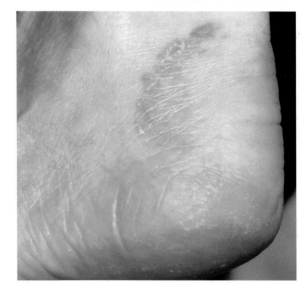

● *Athlete's foot.*

Caring for skin in the sun

It is now recognised that skin cancers can be avoided if care is taken in the sun. Advice about how best to prevent skin cancer has changed over the past ten years and so it is important to keep up to date. The danger from UV (ultraviolet) rays is still not wholly understood and increasingly parents are warned that children must be kept covered up and out of direct sunlight. Children who have pale skin are particularly at risk, as it would now appear that being sunburnt as a child can cause permanent skin damage. At the time of writing the advice set out in Table 306.6 was being

given by the Department of Health. It applies to all children regardless of skin tone, as UV rays penetrate the dermis. Note that sun lotion should not be applied without the parents' consent.

Table 306.6. Safe sun for children

Age range	Advice
Babies	Avoid using sunscreen or products as their skin is sensitive
	Keep them out of the sun
	Babies' skin burns faster than that of older children or adults
Older children	Cover up with loose fitting T-shirts with long sleeves
	Should wear 100% UV-blocking sunglasses
	Put sunscreen on half an hour before going outside
	Apply sunscreen generously every two hours
	Use at least factor 15 sun lotion
All	Avoid having trips outside in the summer between 10.00 a.m. and 2.00 p.m.
	Offer children frequent drinks to avoid dehydration
	Children's skin can still burn on cloudy or windy days
	Limit the amount of time children are outside on hot sunny days, even if they have sunscreen on

● *One of the best ways to protect children from the sun is to dress them appropriately.*

Caring for children's hair

Childminders and nannies may have responsibility for looking after children's hair. Advice from parents needs to be taken regarding how often they wish their child's hair to be washed and also how the hair should be groomed. This can depend on hair type as well as religious customs.

As part of ongoing care, it is important to keep watch for head lice. These are very small parasites that live on the hair. Signs that a child has head lice include scratching, small red marks on the scalp (where the child has been bitten) and white egg cases (nits) on the hair. They do not move even after they have been brushed or combed. The lice themselves are small and translucent and so can be difficult to spot. If you do suspect that a child you are caring for has head lice, you must talk to the parents about the treatment that they wish to use. Do not apply any lotions without their consent. It is also important to reassure children with head lice that they have not done anything wrong and are not dirty. Children can often

● *Watch out for head lice.*

sense from adults the revulsion associated with head lice. It is important, however, that the head lice are dealt with before the child has contact with other children.

As early as possible, you should involve children in the care of their hair. They might hold a brush, choose a style or look in the mirror. As they become older, they should gradually take on responsibility for their hair.

Caring for children's teeth

Babies' first teeth usually arrive at around six months. From this point onwards, it is important that the teeth are regularly brushed. Guidelines about how often brushing should take place have changed; currently, most dentists consider twice a day sufficient, but one brushing should certainly be after the last food and drink of the day. This means that the teeth can be 'food free' for a few hours. As with other aspects of children's physical care, it is important to talk to parents. Even when you are not directly involved with the brushing of teeth, you can help children's teeth to be kept healthy by thinking about the types of food and drink that children are given (see above, and see also Unit 307, page 283).

How to deal with medicines, inhalers or drugs for long-term conditions

Some children you work with may need medicine or have access to an inhaler. It is important that you can meet these children's needs as otherwise those children might not be able to attend the setting. This would be a form of discrimination against the child (see page 188).

As incorrect dosages or medicine given to the wrong child could have serious consequences, it is essential that good procedures are in place in the setting. The National Standards consider how best to manage medicines and so it is important that you also look at the guidance that accompanies the Standards in your home country. It is essential that you have the written consent of parents *before* administering any medicines or drugs, even if they have verbally asked you to do so (see also Unit 302, page 79).

Before giving any medicine, always double check your records. Look also to see that the inhaler or medicine is still within date.

Written instructions

Make sure that parents give written instructions as to when, how and in what circumstances the medicine should be offered. Details of why the child may need medication are also required. Storage instructions should also be provided.

Record keeping

Records must be kept of when, how much and why medicine (including an inhaler) has been given. The records should also show who administered it and in what dosage. Records should be dated and signed. Parental signatures showing that they have been informed may also be required.

Food handling and storage

If your setting prepares food for the children, it must comply with the Food Safety Act 1990. Although the Act focuses on businesses selling food, it also covers settings that prepare foods for members of the public. There are five main points under this Act, two of which are particularly relevant to settings looking after children:

- the food must be fit for people to eat
- the food must not be dangerous to health.

Handling and preparing food safely is looked at in detail in Unit 307.

Did you know?

Information about food safety can be found by contacting the Food Safety Agency. It provides advice about legislation and also practical tips and guidance on preparing, storing and serving food. Its website is www.food.gov.uk.

Toilet training

As indicated in Unit 303 (see page 128), toilet training cannot take place until the child's nervous system has matured so that a full bladder or bowel is recognised (from about 18 months to three years) and the child's communication skills are developed so that he or she can indicate a need for the toilet. On starting toilet training, the child will need a potty, or a toilet seat, and a step for access and safe use of the toilet.

Approaches to toilet training

As children become physically able to gain control of the bladder and bowel, they are at the same time becoming aware of their control over others. Sensitivity is needed to prevent toilet training from becoming a battleground between a child and the carers.

Encouraging recognition of a full bladder and offering the use of a potty or toilet, combined with lots of praise when used, is one approach. Children should never be made to feel they have done something wrong if they wet or soil themselves. Great care should be taken to avoid embarrassing the child in front of others.

If you are involved in the toilet training of a child, as with everything else you must consult and cooperate with the parents. Some parents may have quite fixed views on how they wish to approach the issue, while others may value your advice and support. Consistency between home and setting is essential, to avoid confusing the child.

There is a wide range in the age at which a child will become dry during the day and at night. Toilet training is often discussed among parents of children aged between 18 months and three years. You will always hear of the child who was dry day and night within two weeks of reaching 18 months, while another at the age of three still had accidents, especially when busy playing or at night. Always remember that both are normal. Night-time dryness can take a long time to develop. Many children are still wetting at night at the age of seven years, and can take until their late teens to develop night-time bladder control.

Equipment for toilet training

Good hygiene should be encouraged from the very start. Appropriate equipment is essential. Toilets and sinks at the right height for the children are vital, with soft toilet paper, paper towels, soap and water at the right temperature. Care must be taken to ensure a child's privacy, although you should be on hand to help if needed.

Privacy is especially important for a child with special needs, who may require more assistance. An older child who is still using nappies, for example, needs very sensitive care routines, to recognise his or her relative maturity. Equipment for children who are wheelchair users should be of the right type, with wide doors for easy access and to ensure the child's maximum independence. No child who uses a wheelchair should ever have to be helped to the toilet simply because the toilet cubicle is too small. The Disability Discrimination Act 1995 covers issues such as this (see Unit 305, page 201).

Keys to good practice: Toilet training

- ✓ Make sure that the child is ready for training – there is a wide variation in the age at which a child may be ready (14–36 months).

- ✓ Make the potty a familiar part of a child's environment and let the child sit on it with a nappy on as part of play.

- ✓ Let the child see other children using a potty as much as possible, as an example.

- ✓ Try to introduce toilet training in warm weather, when the child can run around without a nappy on.

- ✓ Always praise the child when a potty is used appropriately, but do not show disapproval if accidents happen.

Did you know?

Until about the 1950s it was thought that a baby could be toilet trained from birth, by sitting him or her on a potty while feeding. All that happened was that the potty caught the automatic reflex action of the gut and bladder during feeding. By the time the child was about one or two years old and starting to recognise his or her own individuality, there was often rebellion and the training 'failed'.

Check it out

Children cope with toilet training far better if they have the right equipment. Does your setting have the following equipment?

- Potties.
- Small toilets. There should be a minimum of one small toilet for ten children, with the same number of sinks. Water should be at 63°C, with germicidal soap and paper towels provided.
- Box steps to help children reach large toilets.
- Seats to set on top of toilet seats.

Case study 6: Beth's toilet training

The parents of 18-month-old Beth have asked Leah to help them with her potty training. She is at Leah's nursery from 9 a.m. to 5 a.m. every weekday.

1. *How should Leah help Beth's parents with this stage of development?*
2. *Make a note of the steps Leah would take, including the equipment that would be needed.*
3. *How should Leah plan to meet her general hygiene needs?*

Appropriate systems to deal with different types of waste

It is important when working with children to ensure that the environment is kept clean and tidy. Part of this work is to consider how you dispose of waste. Some types of waste have the potential to cause injury or cross-infection (see Unit 307, page 293). In addition, as a society we are also moving towards recycling waste.

Under the Environmental Protection Act 1990, businesses are required to dispose of waste properly. This means that it is likely that your setting will have a trade waste agreement and will be provided by the company with different types of bins in which to dispose of waste. Waste products that could cause cross-contamination (e.g. nappies, blood-stained cloths) will have a designated bin and glass products are likely to have a separate recycling box. It is important that the right type of bin is used as, under the law, settings have a duty of care to ensure that waste is kept safely. This means that you should always check that the bin is properly closed and that when it is full a collection is organised.

Observation

With the permission of your supervisor or, where appropriate, parents, choose a child to focus on for a session or day. Observe the child at key moments during this time, such as at the start of the session, during meal or snack times and at the end of the session. Notice how quickly the child settles into the setting, who the child enjoys being with and what kind of activities he or she participates in. Critically evaluate to what extent the setting is meeting the child's needs.

Check it out

Ask a selection of parents of children aged approximately three to four years about the toilet training of their children. Did they encounter any problems? If so what were they and how did they deal with them? Were there similarities between the different children?

Did you know?

It is illegal to place black dustbin bags on a pavement. Householders and businesses have a duty to ensure that rubbish is disposed of safely and is unlikely to be scavenged or burnt or cause litter.

Check it out

Who is responsible for waste disposal in your setting?

Is there a recycling policy in action?

What is the procedure if the outside waste bins are full?

Reflect on your own practice

As you have seen, promoting children's personal care is an essential part of your role. Have a look at the statements below to assess whether you match up to the levels of care needed. The statements all refer to the performance criteria for CCLD 306.4.

Performance criteria statement	Always	Sometimes	Never
Do I ensure that personal care routines support children's protection and that of the adults who work with them?			
Do I meet children's nutritional needs during the time they are present?			
Do I handle and store food safely?			
Do I set up systems to deal with waste according to the procedures of the setting and regulatory requirements?			
Do I deal with children's medicines according to procedures?			

End-of-unit knowledge check

1. Explain one duty that an employee has under the Health and Safety Act 1974.
2. What is the difference between guidance and regulations?
3. Why is it important for settings to have procedures in place before children are given food and drink?
4. What is meant by the term 'spill-over effect'?
5. Why is it important to talk to parents about children's skin care?
6. At what temperature should chilled foods be kept?
7. Why is it important to be aware of child protection procedures in your setting?
8. Why is it important to lay out activities attractively?
9. Why is it important to consider the age/stage of a toy before providing it for children?
10. When must an accident be reported to the Health and Safety Executive?

Promote the health and physical development of children

This unit is concerned with the health and physical development of children and the planning of routines and environments to meet children's physical needs. It includes the role of the practitioner in educating children and their families about their health and promoting healthy lifestyles.

What you must know and understand

- How you adapt your practice to meet the health and physical development needs of children taking into account age, gender, ethnicities, and individual needs and abilities (K3D287)
- The type of indoor and outdoor activities that will encourage balance, coordination, gross motor skills and hand–eye coordination (K3D288)
- In what circumstances you might change routines or activities; how you would adapt existing or planned activities or routines (K3D289)
- What the organisation's policies and practices are regarding risk assessment and safety and why it is important to follow these (K3H290)
- How to carry out risk assessment that takes all reasonable precautions without restricting opportunities for development; how organisational policy can support this (K3H294)
- What is meant by challenging activities for individual babies and children and the link between challenging activities and developmental progress (K3D291)
- How you encourage children to extend their range of skills and achievements (K3D292)
- How to provide opportunities for children to rest and recover from physical activity and why this is important (K3D293)
- The government's guidelines on healthy eating and why it is important that these are followed by childcare practitioners (K3H295)
- What are appropriate foods to give to children, what foods are unsuitable and why (K3H296)
- Special dietary requirements related to culture, ethnicity, religious beliefs or illness (K3H297)

- Why it is important that all dietary information is documented and shared with others (K3H298)
- How you can encourage healthy eating practices in children (K3H299)
- The need for good oral hygiene and how and why this should be encouraged (K3H300)
- Principles of cross-infection and basic hygiene (K3H301)
- Correct disposal of different types of waste according to procedures and why this is required (K3H302)
- Activities that can be undertaken by children to raise awareness of their own bodies and health needs (K3H303)
- Details of health surveillance of children and young people, the role of immunisations and information on regimes for children (K3H304)
- How chronic illness may affect physical development and how to access further information (K3H305)

Plan and implement physical activities and routines for children

Adapting practice to meet the health and physical development needs of children considering all aspects of diversity

This unit focuses on how you as a practitioner can help to promote children's health and physical development through daily routines and activities. In any of your work with them, it is always important to remember that all children are individuals. Trying to use a 'one size fits all' approach to planning will result in a less than ideal situation for all the children you are working with.

There are several aspects of a child that you must think about. It is fairly obvious that age and ability matter – planning a physical activity for an 18-month-old child that includes strenuous climbing is of little value, for instance. Planning meals for a child must take in to account cultural variations. For example, you'll need to cater for children who are vegetarian or have cultural or religious dietary needs.

Keys to good practice: Considering children's diversity

For every planned activity or general contact with children, use this checklist. As you become more experienced, you should not need to use a written checklist

Have I considered each child's:

✓ age

✓ gender

✓ ethnicity

✓ experience

✓ abilities

✓ specific needs?

Indoor and outdoor activities that encourage coordination and motor skills

Given the right environment, resources and encouragement, children of all ages will play. As a worker in children's care, learning and development you need to understand the benefits of different types of play and how to help children experience play that will support their overall development. Some children may need particular support for one aspect of their development, for example improving their **fine motor** development.

Key terms

Fine motor skills give the ability to perform small, accurate movements, for example using the fingers to draw or sew.

Gross motor skills give the ability to move the whole body well, for example running and jumping.

Hand–eye coordination is the ability to direct hand movements (generally unconsciously) in relation to an object (often moving), for example hitting a ball with a bat.

● *Consider the benefits of different types of play.*

Observation

Spend some time observing children playing, both in groups and individually. Note what they are doing and identify which aspect of their development is being assisted. (You will need to refer to Unit 303 on children's development.)

Case study 1: Activities and skills

Jess, a childminder, noted the main activities of each child in her care:
- *Lou, 15 months old, building a tower of bricks*
- *Lee, aged two years, kicking a ball*
- *Riana, aged three, drawing with crayons*
- *Brian, aged six, making a sandwich.*

1. *Which skills was each child developing?*
2. *What could Jess have suggested to extend the benefit of each activity?*
3. *How far could each activity have been used for the other children?*

The developmental benefits of a range of **activities** are presented in Table 307.1. As you can see, there are few activities that concentrate on only one aspect of development. The list does not include a whole host of everyday activities such as sitting, personal hygiene and helping with household tasks and cooking. Many activities an adult might think of as work or chores have immense value to a child in terms of development. If you are working in a child's home, think of how these activities could be made fun.

Key terms

Activities are purposeful conduct engaged in by the child to satisfy curiosity or to achieve an objective. Activities can include planned or unplanned, structured or unstructured play with or without equipment, as well as interactions with others.

Table 307.1. Activities to encourage development for children aged 3–8 years

Activity	Balance and coordination	Gross motor skills	Hand–eye coordination
Push-and-pull toys, for example a trolley weighted with bricks. Toys and chairs to climb and sit on	✓	✓	
Climbing equipment, slide, swing, rope swings, adventure playground	✓	✓	
Bat and ball games, throwing, bouncing, catching, stretching, hitting	✓	✓	✓
Hoops (hoola-hoop, throwing bean bags into hoops, rolling hoops, hoop obstacle races)	✓	✓	

continued on next page

continued from previous page

Activity	Balance and coordination	Gross motor skills	Hand–eye coordination
Banners and streamers (running, whirling and pattern games, circle games, playing with a large parachute)	✓	✓	
Riding tricycles, scooters, bicycles	✓	✓	
Running, skipping and jumping	✓	✓	
Dancing and moving to music	✓	✓	
Swimming, gymnastics	✓	✓	
Jigsaws and puzzles			✓
A variety of books, including 'lift the flap' books			✓
A variety of wooden bricks and stacking beakers		✓	✓
Playing with tea sets		✓	✓
Drawing and making marks with crayons, pencils, paints			✓
Threading wooden beads			✓
Duplo, Lego and other construction bricks			✓
Bubbles (for blowing and making shapes)			✓
Self-dressing, including buttoning and unbuttoning own clothing		✓	✓
Cutting out with scissors			✓
Computers (use of mouse and keyboard)			✓
Water toys and sand		✓	✓
Playdough		✓	✓
Junk modelling		✓	✓
Board games involving shaking dice and moving objects (e.g. snakes and ladders)		✓	✓

Observation

Can you think of other activities that are not listed in Table 307.1?
Make a note of any activity you see children engaged in and identify
which skills they are promoting. How could each activity be used with
different age groups?

When you might need to change routines or activities

Activities are usually planned with a group of children in mind, with due regard to individual needs. This is essential to ensure that all children are included and feel that they belong to the group. However, additional children may join the group at the last minute, or a child may, for example, have broken a leg and no longer be able to participate. It is important always to have thought about how an activity could be extended or adapted if needed at the last minute.

Case study 2: Change of plan

In the middle of summer John had planned a full day of activities outside for the children aged four to eight years in the summer play scheme. There was a shaded area to make sure the children did not get too hot, and plenty of drinks would be provided. The children all had their sun hats and sun lotions and were looking forward to the day, which was presented as a sports day. At 9 am the sky clouded over and it started to rain heavily.

1. *What do you think happened next?*
2. *What could John do to avoid disappointing the children?*
3. *List the types of sports day activities John might have planned and suggest how they could be adapted for indoors.*
4. *What health and safety implications would the move indoors have and how could they be dealt with?*
5. *Apart from rain, what else might have caused the sports day to be called off?*

In case study 2, John's predicament could not be avoided in relation to the weather, but he should have planned an alternative. Any outdoor activity needs an alternative indoor plan; it may not always be possible to adapt the plan for indoors and so a totally different plan may be needed.

Active knowledge

Play therapists are specially trained professionals who can advise on how objects can be adapted for children with special needs, such as cerebral palsy, visual impairment and so on. Try to arrange to find out about how a play therapist works with children.

Risk assessment: policies and practice, safety and opportunities for development

Risk and challenge are vital for social and physical development (see Unit 302, pages 64–65). Children need to be given the freedom to experience controlled risk, but the activities offered must take into consideration their age, gender and inclinations. Early years workers need to be able to see the risks and benefits of an activity. Any activity can offer dangers (a child could, after all, choke on a piece of a jigsaw), and children may never be completely safe. This is why risk assessment is important. The practical steps of risk assessment are covered in Unit 308 (see pages 308–309). Risks and benefits come to the fore in outdoor play.

The benefits and risks of outdoor play

The outdoor environment presents a balance of risk and benefit. A free flow of movement from inside to out and outside to in is highly desirable. However, children often face difficulties playing outside. A recent report by the Children's Society hit out at the 'culture of intolerance' towards children's play in public, with grumpy grown-ups keeping the proverbial balls to themselves and whose backyards are certainly not for playing in, and petty play bans and regulations outlawing play opportunities for youngsters in public spaces that, in all probability, were initially designed for those very members of the public to play in.

The spider diagram below illustrates the importance of providing opportunities for outdoor play. Draw a similar diagram to show the risks associated with play outdoors.

● *Children can face many barriers to outside play.*

As children spend more time in front of television and video games, outdoor play at school or nursery becomes even more important.

Many young children are overweight, to the possible detriment of their future health. Healthy habits are best introduced in childhood, in order for them to be continued through to adulthood. Inactive children are more likely to become inactive adults.

Physical activity helps build and maintain healthy bones, muscles and joints.

How children benefit from outdoor play

Where supervision is a problem, parents become concerned about stranger danger, traffic and are reluctant to let their children play out.

Research shows that being outside is good for the immune system.

Children need to take risks and explore their own boundaries.

● *The importance of providing opportunities for outdoor play.*

Safety, supervision and utilising space

When you are supervising indoor and outdoor activities that develop gross motor skills, it is vital that equipment is of the highest safety standard, to minimise the risk of a child being injured. Space must be allowed for children to run, hop, skip, throw and so on. Space will obviously vary according to availability but no room should be overcrowded. This may mean a setting needs to allow small, supervised groups of children to use a large area to develop their gross motor skills freely and without inhibition.

Safety of equipment

All equipment must be made to specific standards and display one of the following symbols:

- the Kitemark, which means that the British Standards Institution (BSI) has checked the manufacturer's claim that the product meets specific standards
- the Lion mark, which is found only on British-made toys and means they have met the British safety standards
- the CE mark, which means that the product complies with European and British safety standards.

You can see what these marks look like by turning to Unit 302 (page 47).

Every setting should have a health and safety policy and procedures for checking equipment used by the children. Registration and inspection officers who regularly inspect provision for the under-eights will want to see detailed evidence of health and safety procedures.

Most equipment can be adapted for children with special needs. If equipment cannot be adapted, alternative equipment should be used. Parents, colleagues and other professionals who work closely with a child with specific needs should be able to advise upon suitable equipment and where it can be purchased.

Check it out

Read the health and safety policy of your setting. How you would implement it when checking the safety of planned activities?

Think about:
- equipment safety
- children's personal safety
- space for each child to move freely without bumping into other children or objects
- appropriate adult–child ratios
- all children being visible to their supervisors
- safety of the environment
- surfaces (are they soft and safe, to encourage freedom of movement?)
- giving children the freedom to develop their skills, with adult support but not too much intervention.

Challenging activities and how to encourage children to extend their skills

Some children need encouragement to explore the range of movement and limits of their bodies. This may be for a number of reasons:
- recent illness or injury limits strength and activity
- the child has a long-term condition that limits movement or skills
- the child lacks self-confidence
- lack of opportunity
- over-anxious parents have restricted exploration.

● *Help the children understand what they are doing.*

It is important to remember that observing children's development will help you to assess the type of opportunities you need to provide in order to develop their confidence in different aspects of development. This observation may be recorded as part of your setting's record keeping.

With all activities that promote development, the early years worker will need to help children understand what they are doing. Therefore it may be necessary to demonstrate a task in order for children to develop a particular skill appropriately. It does not matter if you are not very good at the skill – in fact it can encourage children to see that not everyone is good at everything.

Keys to good practice: Encouraging children to extend their skills

- ✓ Play alongside the children – throwing a ball, skipping etc.

- ✓ Show the children how to throw and catch. For example, hold out arms ready to catch a ball.

- ✓ Ensure that each child takes a turn or takes a leading role in an activity such as throwing in a circle.

- ✓ Encourage both boys and girls to join in all activities, individually and together.

- ✓ If a child has a special need you must ensure that the equipment is adapted so that he or she can take part.

- ✓ Give plenty of praise and encouragement.

Experimentation and equipment

When providing opportunities for children to develop their confidence in movement, remember that they love to experiment and that through this they can extend their experience and develop their skills. For example, a floor cushion given to a group of three-year-old children might encourage them to:

- roll it
- push it
- jump on it
- pick it up.

Many everyday pieces of equipment can be used by children to explore and enjoy, and to develop confidence in their movement. Specialised equipment is not always necessary to help children develop new movements, but there are many items that are useful for this purpose, for both indoor and outdoor play in any setting, such as the following:

- push-and-pull toys
- cushions and other soft play objects
- climbing frames
- slides
- balls, bats, bean bags
- bicycles and trucks
- trampolines (carefully supervised).

Every child must develop his or her skills of locomotion (moving along) and balance (maintaining an upright posture) in order to reach full potential and develop other skills, such as hand–eye coordination. These skills are naturally developed through play. Your role as an early years worker is to provide suitable activities and equipment, using your knowledge of the stages of physical development (see Unit 303). You will also need to be aware of the importance of enabling children with special needs to take part in any activities you provide.

One of the most important roles of an early years worker is to ensure that children enjoy developing all their skills and that they are secure in the activities available to them. The environment you help to create, the activities provided and the communication you have with children all have to be carefully considered in order for them to develop confidence in their movement skills. Close supervision, praise and encouragement will help children to move safely and independently.

Remember that a child of seven may need as much encouragement as a child of 18 months. Older children can develop a self-conscious attitude towards activities and often feel that they are not as good as other children at certain types of activity, such as running.

Encouraging children to participate in activities

It is essential that children at every stage of skill development are offered a range of activities, both indoors and outdoors. You will need to ensure that all children have equal access. As children mature, they are influenced by the society around them and may begin to show gender preference. For example, boys may not want to skip if they feel it is too feminine, and girls may refuse to play football if they view it as a 'boy's game'. By being a positive role model you can discourage gender preference and other stereotyping. If certain children rarely use a piece of equipment, such as the climbing frame, it may be advisable to discuss with your team how they can be given appropriate encouragement to do so.

Keys to good practice: Developing children's confidence

✓ Treat children equally and do not discriminate against them because of their gender or culture. For example, boys can learn to sew as well as girls.

✓ Build on a child's previous experience. For example, a six-year-old who has learned to walk along a line on the floor can then learn to balance and walk on a wooden bench.

✓ Encourage children to repeat actions such as throwing a ball in a circle. Skills will develop with practice.

✓ Understand which particular physical skill a movement is developing, for example a gross motor skill or a fine motor skill.

Case study 3: Gross motor skill development

Andrew was supervising a group of three- and four-year-olds who were playing in the garden of a nursery. They had taken a ball from the equipment box and were running around trying to play football. One of the children, Tarik, aged three, began to get upset as he did not often have a chance to kick the ball, and when he did he missed it. Andrew gently took him to one side and showed him how to practise kicking another ball forwards into a goal. They took it in turns and had great fun. Andrew was aware that Tarik, like most three-year-olds, was beginning to want to play with his peers, but was only just competent in kicking a ball forward. He knew about the stages of children's gross motor development and therefore created the right opportunity for Tarik to develop the skill of kicking.

1. *Why was it important for Andrew to intervene?*
2. *How did Andrew's actions help Tarik?*

If the opportunities for outside access are limited, furniture can be cleared away to give children appropriate opportunities to catch soft balls, spin hoops, throw bean bags and so on. Even in a small space such as a living room, children can climb over cushions and balance during games such as 'Simon says'. In settings that have more space, play houses, tunnels and indoor slides can be used. Games such as musical statues encourage balance and locomotion, as do songs such as 'Head, shoulders, knees and toes'.

Observation

Choose an appropriate time indoors or outdoors and observe a child in your care developing either gross motor skills or hand–eye coordination during play. In your evaluation, consider whether the child follows a broad pattern of development. What other opportunities would you provide to extend their skills? Use research to validate your conclusion.

Did you know?

Most children can throw a large ball at the age of three, but not bounce and catch until the age of four. The skill of aiming a throw does not normally develop before four years of age.

Most children can steer and pedal toys at three years old, but do not develop confidence in this until the age of four.

Walking balancing bean bags can help develop posture and balance; getting children to walk along a chalk line on a floor can develop balancing skills.

Outdoor apparatus should always be an extension of equipment provided indoors to encourage free floor play. However, an outdoor play area often has different surfaces to facilitate a variety of activities, and older children can enjoy surfaces marked for hopscotch, stepping stones and so on.

Children should be encouraged to understand the difference between various locomotion skills and activities. This may be done simply by labelling the activity as it is occurring, for example by saying 'Tom, you are jumping high', or by giving children instructions in more structured activity sessions, according to their stage of development. A lesson in primary school might encourage children not only to use a variety of locomotion skills but also to control the way they start and stop, and their speed. They might be asked to start walking with large strides slowly around the room, and stop when told, wherever they are. In this way children will become aware of the way they can best use different locomotion skills.

It is important that children have a positive attitude towards those with needs to develop specific skills, and that they play appropriately together. Consider the following case study.

• Consider the picture from the social model of disability outlined on pages 203–204.

Case study 4: Inclusion

Jamie is in a primary class of six- to seven-year-olds. He uses a wheelchair and is able to develop locomotive skills only in the upper part of his body. His local education authority follows an inclusion policy, which means that children with special needs are integrated into mainstream schools wherever possible. The children are playing a game with a ball in a circle. When the children throw the ball to Jamie they are aware that they have to throw at his level. Sometimes he wheels his chair to collect the ball if it has been thrown out of the circle – his classmates do not run to collect the ball for him. The teacher encourages Jamie to throw and catch the ball just like the other children, always aware that Jamie cannot move his legs. While his teacher always tries to treat Jamie like his peers, he is aware of the fact that Jamie has limited mobility and must concentrate on developing the locomotion and balance of the upper part of his body.

1. *Why is it important that the other children let Jamie collect the ball himself?*
2. *Why is it important for all the children that Jamie is included in the game?*

Keys to good practice: Encouraging children to extend their skills

✓ Be a good role model yourself – join in with the activities and be active; children will enjoy seeing adults playing football or balancing on a bench or doing puzzles.

✓ Check that the activity chosen is suitable for all the children in the group; for example, a child in a wheelchair will enjoy playing catch with a ball, but may feel excluded if you choose a moving ball game like football.

✓ Choose games that involve sharing and teamwork – relay races, team board games or crawling through tunnels in turn can be great fun – but make sure no one wins until the whole team has finished.

✓ Praise children who share and help each other, and explain clearly why you are giving the praise, so that the children can understand the advantages of being considerate to each other.

✓ Talk about all types of activities, arts, games and sports. You could use famous people as good role models, especially in non-gender-specific activities such as art and writing, and in games such as tennis and swimming.

Your involvement may be to support an activity that is already taking place, or to set up an activity for the children in order to develop a particular area of physical development. There are children who are naturally able to throw, catch, kick or bounce and will need only the minimum amount of support. However, other children may be less confident, agile or dexterous, and it is the role of the early years worker to ensure that they are given time to develop their gross manipulative skills without feeling daunted by comparisons with their peers.

Case study 5: Freddy and the ball

Fiona, an early years worker, was playing in the garden with two-year-old Freddy. He was very unsure about a ball. Fiona used a large foam ball and took time to encourage Freddy to gently roll the ball to her. They also rolled the ball to Freddy's teddy, who, with Fiona's help, sent the ball back to Freddy.

1. *Which large muscles was Fiona helping Freddy to develop?*
2. *Why was Freddy being encouraged to roll rather than throw the ball?*

Consolidation:

What sort of activities would you provide for:
- a three-year-old child to help develop locomotion and balance
- a four-year-old to develop hand–eye coordination
- an eight-year-old to improve coordination?

How to provide opportunities for children to rest and recover from physical activity

Rest and quiet periods

The body needs time each day to recuperate, through sleep and rest. Few children will spend all day running around actively playing. Most will enjoy some time to sit down and watch the world go by, or hear a story, or watch television for a short time. These are all resting or quiet periods. Most nurseries and reception classes have a designated 'quiet' time in their daily routine to allow children to recoup their energy. A skilled early years worker will build these times into the children's routine (see Unit 306, page 250).

When and for how long a setting has a rest or quiet period will depend on the ages of the children. Babies and toddlers will follow their own body clock, and you should discuss the child's routine with parents to find out the usual pattern.

There are three 'levels' of quiet period:
- sleep times – especially needed by babies and toddlers, for example in a day nursery
- rest periods – for toddlers and pre-schoolers
- quiet activities – essential for all age groups as a break between other activities and a chance to recuperate. Quiet activities include story time, watching a television programme or video and listening to music, all of which should use material that is soothing and not stimulating. Older children may enjoy relaxation exercises.

It is important to try to comply with parents' wishes relating to sleep. A late afternoon nap that results in a child not being ready for sleep until very late in the evening may not be popular with some parents, but others who wish to spend time with their children in the evening may prefer this. Older children will usually fit within an overall plan of changing levels of activity.

Keys to good practice: Encouraging rest and sleep

✓ Follow a routine that encourages children to relax into sleep or rest.

✓ Allow children time to unwind after vigorous activity, to have a drink and prepare for a rest.

✓ Deal with children's toilet or nappy needs before settling them to rest.

✓ Check that the room is at a pleasant temperature, check the position of cots and chairs, and draw the curtains if necessary.

✓ Ensure that any comforters such as toys or blankets are readily to hand for the children. Make sure you know the individual needs of children in your care. Some children like their hair to be stroked as they relax, while others need a cuddle.

✓ Minimise unnecessary noises and distractions.

✓ If the quiet time is part of story time, make sure books, pictures etc. are ready by your seat.

✓ Make sure you are in a calm, reassuring mood during quiet time. A child will not rest if you are rushing around in a frenzy of activity.

✓ Do not insist on a child having a rest if he or she is not ready for one. Instead, offer a quiet activity such as reading a book or doing a puzzle or drawing (for an older child). Younger children should be quietly played with in another room if possible. The important point is not to allow a child who is not ready for a rest to disrupt those who are.

Reflect on your own practice

As you have seen, ensuring that the physical environment meets the developmental needs of children is an essential part of your role. Have a look at the statements below to assess whether you match up to the levels of care needed. The statements all refer to the performance criteria for CCLD 307.1.

Performance criteria statement	Always	Sometimes	Never
Do I plan indoor and outdoor activities to provide opportunities for children to practise physical skills?			
Do I assess the risk of activities without limiting opportunities and ensure that activities are inclusive?			

continued on next page

continued from previous page

Performance criteria statement	Always	Sometimes	Never
Do I provide activities that develop balance, skill and coordination?			
Do I provide activities that develop hand–eye coordination?			
Do I provide activities that encourage cooperation and sharing between children?			
Do I encourage children to extend their own abilities and reward their efforts?			
Do I plan routines that allow children to rest and recover from physical activity?			

Plan and provide food and drink to meet the nutritional needs of children

It is important for early years workers actively to promote a healthy diet, to both children and parents. Children's diets have an important influence on their future health. You have a key role as a health educator. Although children are heavily influenced by the meals they have at home and the family approach to eating, you can make a difference by showing or reinforcing the principles of healthy eating. If your job involves out-of-school activities or work with parents it may be possible to have an even greater effect.

Why it is important to follow government guidelines on healthy eating

There has been a huge amount of research into the problems of childhood obesity – caused by a combination of eating too much (especially fatty and sugary foods), frequent snacking between meals and not having enough exercise. It has been proven beyond doubt that diet and physical activity in a child's early years can affect health in later life. Childhood eating habits tend to determine adult food tastes and the body's metabolic rate. Fat adults who were fat children find it more difficult to lose weight than those who were thin as children.

There are eight guidelines for a healthy diet:

- Enjoy your food.
- Eat a variety of different foods.
- Eat the right amount to maintain a healthy weight.
- Eat plenty of foods rich in starch and fibre.
- Eat plenty of fruit and vegetables.

Did you know?

In the past 10 years the level of obesity in six-year-olds has doubled (to 8.5%) and trebled among 15-year-olds (to 15%).

Maturity-onset (type 2) diabetes is now being seen in school children who are obese; previously it was only seen in middle-aged and older adults.

(Source: Health Survey for England, 2001)

- Do not eat too many foods that contain a lot of fat.
- Do not have sugary foods and drinks too often.
- If you drink alcohol, drink sensibly. (Obviously this guideline doesn't apply to children.)

The *Balance of Good Health* is a pictorial food guide produced by the Food Standards Agency to help people understand and enjoy healthy eating. It should be visible in schools, workplaces, health centres and supermarkets. It shows the proportions and types of foods that are needed to make up a healthy balanced diet. The guide shows that all foods can be part of a healthy diet.

Foods from the largest groups should be eaten most often and foods from the smallest group should be eaten least often. The guide is shaped like a dinner plate, which has been designed to make healthy eating guidelines simpler to understand. The plate is divided to show five food groups. These are set out in Table 307.2.

- *Balance of Good Health.*

Table 307.2. The five main food groups

Group	Main nutrients provided	Role of nutrient
1. Bread, other cereals and potatoes	Carbohydrate (starch)	Needed to provide energy. Starchy carbohydrates are broken down and converted to glucose, which is either stored as glycogen in the liver and muscles or is circulated in the bloodstream, where it can enter cells and be used as energy.
	Calcium (some)	Has a role in the development and maintenance of teeth and bones.
	Iron (some)	Needed for the formation of haemoglobin in the blood. It is also a component of many enzymes.
	B vitamins	Principally involved in energy metabolism (see also opposite).
	Dietary fibre	Not absorbed but passes through the gastrointestinal tract, helping to keep it healthy.
	Protein	Essential for the growth and repair of the body; any excess is used to provide energy.
2. Fruit and vegetables	Vitamin C	Needed to help in the structure of connective tissue and bones. It is required for wound healing and helps the absorption of iron from non-meat sources. It may help to prevent the risk of chronic diseases such as heart disease and cancer.
	Carotenes	Contributes towards the formation of vitamin A (see opposite).
	Folates	Needed for the formation of blood cells.

continued on next page

continued from previous page

Group	Main nutrients provided	Role of nutrient
	Carbohydrate	As above.
	Dietary fibre	As above.
3. Milk and dairy foods	Calcium	As above.
	Protein	As above.
	Vitamin B12	Needed for the formation of blood cells and nerve fibres.
	Vitamin A	Needed for the maintenance and repair of tissues necessary for growth and development. It is also essential for the immune system to function and to help night vision.
	Vitamin D	Helps with calcium and phosphate absorption from food and is essential for healthy teeth and bones.
4. Meat, fish and alternatives (e.g. pulses)	Iron	As above.
	Protein	As above.
	B vitamins (especially vitamin B12)	As above.
	Zinc	Needed for growth of tissues, immune function and wound healing.
	Magnesium	Needed for bone development and nerve and muscle function. It is also helps in the function of some enzymes involved in energy use.
5. Foods containing fat and/or sugar	Fat	Provides energy, but only moderate amounts of fat required.
	Carbohydrate (sugar)	As above.
	Some also provide other nutrients (e.g. fat-soluble vitamins) and some contain salt	

Why is a balanced diet important?

No single food contains all the essential nutrients the body needs to be healthy and to function efficiently. The nutritional value of a person's diet depends on the overall mixture, or balance, of foods that is eaten over a period of time. The correct diet will be determined by the needs of the individual. Everyone needs energy to live, but the balance between carbohydrate, fat and protein must be right for good health. Too little protein can interfere with growth and other body functions, while too much fat can lead to obesity and heart disease. Adequate intakes of vitamins, minerals and dietary fibre are important for health, and there is growing evidence that a number of bioactive plant substances (also termed phytochemicals) found in fruit and vegetables are also important. This is why a **balanced diet** is recommended.

Observation

- How much information on healthy eating is visible in your setting?
- Have you seen the *Balance of Good Health* picture in use before?
- Try to monitor the nutritional intake of a small group of children in your setting. You could produce a table that shows both actual intake and the recommended daily intake for that age group.

Did you know?

Children attending nursery sessions of two hours or more are eligible to receive (free) a third of a pint of milk on each day they attend. This is known as the Nursery Milk Scheme and is operated by the Department of Health. Children under five whose parents receive Income Support or Jobseekers' Allowance are currently eligible to receive a free pint of milk daily under the Welfare Food Scheme. This scheme is currently under review.

- *Schools are now required to ensure their lunches meet minimum nutritional standards.*

School meals

In 1980 the government ceased to require schools to provide meals of a set nutritional standard, with the result that in many schools lunch provision became far from satisfactory. On 1 April 2001 the government reintroduced regulations in England and Wales on national minimum nutritional standards for schools that provide lunches, in recognition of the importance of the contribution that school lunches can make to the health of children. The government has also announced a minimum amount that must be spent on school meals. Some schools offer advice on packed lunches as part of a 'whole-school approach' to healthy eating, through which the food consumed at school is linked to the principles of healthy eating taught in the classroom.

Appropriate and inappropriate foods

Food requirements change according to age, size, activity levels and gender. As you work with children at different ages it is of course important to understand their dietary needs. The added complication is that, apart from age, many other factors will affect the child's diet.

Children over five years of age start to take some responsibility for their own food intake, so it is important that they understand the need for a healthy diet. If children are offered a range of foods, they will tend to eat a balanced diet. Even when a child seems to want to eat only beans on toast, for example, a 'food diary' kept over a few days will usually reveal that they are also drinking some milk and eating small amounts of other foods, which, in total, provide all the required nutrients. It is perfectly normal for a child to have a 'fad' for a particular type of food for a time. Problems tend to be the result of parents or carers turning food into a battle ground over what the child should eat.

As with adults, children's appetites vary. Some seem to eat huge amounts of food, while others may hardly seem to eat enough to survive on. If you are concerned about a child eating enough, ask yourself the following questions:

- Is the child healthy?
- Does the child have a lot of energy?
- Does the child sleep well?
- Is there a healthy balance in the diet?

Check it out

Think about your own food intake and what you like and do not like to eat. What has influenced these tastes?

Discuss your own preferences with a group of colleagues. What are the differences between you?

Did you know?

Iron deficiency anaemia is a problem in some young children, such as those who have a poor iron intake from solid foods and, to an extent those who have been given cows' milk (as a main drink) too early (i.e. before 12 months of age). Anaemia can result in frequent infections, poor weight gain and delay in development.

What sorts of food do children need?

Childcare books from the 1920s and 1930s were very clear about the range of suitable foods for a child: 'if he is unsuitably fed, with too much butcher's meat, or starchy foods, his health inevitably suffers from the poisons which are circulating in his blood' and 'the child prefers and thrives on a simple and monotonous diet' (*Every Woman's Doctor Book*, Amalgamated Press, 1930). Views are a little broader in our multicultural society, and there is little that a fully weaned child cannot eat.

Babies

During pregnancy the foetus obtains nutrients from its mother via the placenta. Once the baby is born, energy and nutrients are supplied by breast milk or formula milk, generally for the first six months of life.

● *There is little that a fully weaned child cannot eat.*

From six months of age a baby needs:

- foods in addition to breast milk or infant formula
- a first 'solid' food that is sloppy and smooth (baby rice is the most common first weaning food in Britain)
- food that has been softened by cooking and then pureed, mashed or chopped
- foods of a variety of textures, so that the child learns to chew
- slow introduction of new foods, including vegetables, meat, fish, dairy products and fruit
- iron, in a form that can be easily absorbed
- supplements of vitamins A, C and D (in the form of liquid drops).

A baby under one year should not be given:

- wheat or other cereals that contain the protein gluten (giving gluten to young infants increases the risk of coeliac disease)
- cows' milk
- nuts
- salt added to food
- sugar unless it is necessary (e.g. with sour fruits).

Pre-school children

Care is needed when following healthy eating guidelines with pre-school children (one to five years of age). A diet that is low in fat and high in fibre may not supply enough energy for a young child. However, a healthy family lifestyle will encourage a child to eat more healthily; this is important, as food preference will begin be established during this stage of life.

Did you know?

Most fast foods have an extremely high energy density. Studies show that humans are innately poor at recognising foods with a high energy density and regulating the amount of food eaten appropriately in order to maintain energy balance. This inability induces so-called 'passive over-consumption'.

(Source: Prentice and Jebb, 2003)

- *Pre-school children are likely to need a high-energy diet.*

Pre-school children are:
• growing quickly and becoming more active
• developing teeth and bones

And they have:
• high energy requirements for their size
• small stomachs

So they need:
• foods which are high in energy (and also rich in nutrients)
• small and frequent meals
• protein, calcium, iron and vitamins A and D
• whole cows' milk, as it is a rich sources of a number of nutrients.

 Dietary requirements of pre-school children.

Schoolchildren

Schoolchildren, much like pre-school children, are also growing quickly and becoming more active, so they too have a high energy requirement for their size. They will similarly need foods that are high in energy and rich in nutrients, small and frequent meals (especially for the younger ones) and a good supply of protein, calcium, iron and vitamins A, C and D.

However, it is thought that between 5 and 15 per cent of school-aged children are overweight. They should not be expected to lose large amounts of weight but should be encouraged to remain at a constant weight or – if they are still growing taller – increase weight slowly while their height increases, so that they grow to be an acceptable weight for their height. Developing a healthy family diet and lifestyle is important in the weight management of children.

Food hygiene

While it is important that the diet of a child follows the guidelines on healthy eating, another aspect of healthy eating is about food hygiene (the regulations on which are covered in Unit 306 – see page 260). If you are involved in preparing or serving food to children it is important for you to take a food hygiene course to show employers that you are safe with food. There are thousands of cases of food poisoning each year in Britain, and in some cases deaths occur – simply as a result of poor food hygiene practices.

The micro-organisms responsible for food poisoning include bacteria, viruses, moulds and yeasts. Bacteria are found everywhere – in air, water, soil, animals, people and food. Most are not harmful and many even serve a useful purpose. A few types of bacteria, however, are harmful in food.

 Did you know?

A king-size chocolate bar can provide around a fifth of the daily calorie needs of a 10-year-old.

(Source: Chief Medical Officer, 2002)

 Did you know?

Schoolchildren in the UK are spending more than £1.3 billion a year on food. Almost a third of their pocket money goes on snacks eaten while travelling to and from school. Of those who eat school meals, 84% say they enjoy them, with pizza ranking as their favourite dish.

(Source: Survey by catering company Sodexho, 2002)

These fall into two types:

- *Spoilage bacteria*. These cause food to rot and decay, but do not necessarily make people ill. They hasten deterioration of food and are likely to change its smell, taste, colour and texture. These effects are usually sufficient to alert people to the fact that the food is no longer fit to eat.
- *Pathogens*. The few types of bacteria in food that are responsible for causing illness are referred to as pathogens. They may be present in food in large numbers and still not cause obvious changes to the food, so that it still looks, tastes and smells wholesome.

Viruses are even smaller than bacteria and can be seen only through an electron microscope. Most viruses that can cause food poisoning multiply only in human cells. Viral food poisoning can be caused by contamination of food by infected food handlers (e.g. from faeces or vomit). If the food is cooked these viruses are destroyed, but contaminated ready-to-eat foods or undercooked foods can cause illness. Reports of viruses associated with food-borne illness rose from approximately 320 in 1986 to 2050 in 1997.

Keys to good practice: Food hygiene

To prevent food from becoming contaminated by bacteria or viruses, and so causing illness, you should always:

✓ avoid using raw eggs in foods such as mayonnaise and uncooked desserts

✓ cook foods thoroughly

✓ reheat food soon and thoroughly

✓ avoid reheating foods more than once

✓ keep foods at correct temperatures

✓ keep animals away from foods

✓ practise good personal hygiene (pay particular attention to hand washing before food preparation involving direct handling of foods)

✓ cover cuts with clean plasters

✓ avoid sneezing or coughing near food

✓ always keep cooked food covered

✓ keep cooked and raw foods separate, even in the fridge

✓ ensure all surfaces are cleaned at least once per day and are easy to clean

✓ ensure equipment such as can-openers, slicers and food processors are regularly cleaned and sterilised

✓ ensure all rubbish bins are kept well away from food, and are regularly disinfected.

Did you know?

The National Diet and Nutrition Survey: Young People Aged 4–18 Years (2000) found that:

- Children eat less than half the recommended five portions of fruit and vegetables a day. In an average week, one in five 4–18-year-olds ate no fruit at all.
- Chicken and turkey were the most popular types of meat, with over 70% of the sample eating these foods.
- Under half the boys and just over half the girls ate raw and salad vegetables (excluding tomatoes and carrots) during the seven-day study period, while 40% ate cooked leafy green vegetables and 60% consumed other types of cooked vegetables.
- Four per cent of the sample did not consume any vegetables during the seven-day survey period.
- The most commonly eaten fruits, consumed by over half the sample, were apples and pears, followed by bananas.
- Carbonated soft drinks were the most popular drink, with three-quarters of the group consuming standard versions and just under half drinking low-calorie versions.
- Generally, the quantities of foods eaten increased with age, with the exception of whole milk and vegetables, which both decreased with age.

Special dietary requirements related to culture, ethnicity, religious beliefs or illness

The importance of understanding diversity – respect for the child's culture and family setting – emphasised throughout this book. This naturally extends to children's dietary requirements, which are often determined by the family's culture, ethnicity or religious beliefs. Examples of religious dietary requirements are set out in Table 307.3. It is important, however, not to make assumptions here, as elsewhere, and it is always advisable to discuss diet with the parents.

Table 307.3. Examples of religious dietary requirements

Religion	Dietary requirements
Buddhists	Many Buddhists are vegetarian as they respect all life and avoid killing animals
Hinduism	The eating of meat is generally forbidden, but especially beef, as the cow is a sacred animal. Many Hindus will not eat fish or eggs.
Islam	Muslims will not eat pork or pig products, and all animals must be killed according to Islamic regulations (producing what is known as halal meat). Halal food must be cooked with separate utensils and should not be stored or cooked with non-halal food.
Judaism	Food acceptable to the Jewish religion is known as 'kosher'. Jews may not eat fish without fins or scales, shellfish, pork, birds of prey or rabbits. Meat and milk may not be eaten together, and the same utensils may not be used for each of these.
Rastafarians	Rastafarians tend to prefer to eat natural foods and many avoid pork. Fruit and vegetables are important and are called I-tal. Many Rastafarians are vegetarians.
Sikhism	Beef is forbidden and dairy products are important; many Sikhs, though, are vegetarian.

Observation

- What types of dietary needs are there among the children in your setting?
- Are you aware of all the particular needs of those diets? If not, where can you find the information?
- How could you make sure that all the children are receiving a diet that meets all their needs?

Vegetarian diets

A good vegetarian or vegan diet requires planning to make sure that all of the nutrients needed for rapid growth and development are supplied. It is a myth to think that a vegetarian diet is automatically 'healthy' or 'slimming'.

Most plant food proteins (with the exception of soya) have a low content of one or more of the amino acids needed by the body. Also, different amino acids are missing in various plant foods. These therefore need to be combined to provide high-quality protein. If proteins from different plant sources are eaten together or over the course of a day, the diet should contain enough of the right sort. The main food nutrients that are usually supplied by meat or dairy products can in this way be provided by plant sources (see Table 307.4).

Pulses and rice (e.g. bean casserole and rice, dhal and rice)

Pulses and cereal (e.g. baked beans on toast)

Nuts and cereal (e.g. peanut butter sandwich, nut roast)

● Good combinations of vegetarian food.

Table 307.4. Vegetarian alternatives to animal sources of nutrients

Nutrient	Animal sources	Vegetarian or vegan alternative
Protein	Meat, poultry, fish, eggs, milk, cheese, yogurt	Soya, pulses (lentils, chick peas and beans, including baked beans), bread, grains, seeds, potatoes, nuts
Calcium	Milk, cheese, yogurt, and tinned sardines and salmon, including the bones (the soft bones should not be discarded)	Fortified soya milk and tofu, seeds (e.g. sesame seeds), green leafy vegetables (e.g. spring greens), nuts (e.g. almonds), bread (especially white bread), dried fruit (e.g. apricots)
Iron	Liver, red meat, chicken, fish (haem iron), eggs (non-haem iron)	Fortified breakfast cereals (the label should be checked to see if iron has been added), bread, pulses (e.g. soya beans), green vegetables, dried fruits (e.g. apricots), nuts, plain chocolate

continued on next page

continued from previous page

Nutrient	Animal sources	Vegetarian alternative
Vitamin A	Liver, butter, whole milk, cheese	Yellow/orange vegetables (e.g. carrots) and dark leafy ones (e.g. parsley, watercress), yellow/orange fruit (e.g. mangoes and apricots – fresh or dried), fortified margarines and spreads, sweet potato
Vitamin B12	Liver, meat, poultry, fish, milk and its products, eggs	Fortified products only (check on the label)
Vitamin D	Oily fish, meat, whole milk and its products, fortified milk products (such as skimmed milk powder), eggs	Fortified margarine and spreads, fortified breakfast cereals (check the label to see if vitamin D has been added)

Young children

A vegetarian or vegan diet that is healthy for an older child or adult may not be appropriate for infants and young children, as this is a time of rapid growth and development, when a good supply of energy and nutrients is particularly important. Diets that are low in energy and fat and high in bulk may not be nutritionally good for young children.

Young children on a vegetarian or vegan diet need:
- a good intake of energy and nutrient-rich foods, such as milk, cheese, margarine, pulses and nut butters (e.g. peanut butter)
- one pint of cows' milk daily or its equivalent in yogurt or 'vegetarian' cheese (nearly all cheese is now produced using synthetic, non-animal-based rennet) or fortified soya milk
- adequate amounts of calcium, vitamin B12, vitamin D and riboflavin via supplements, or, in a vegan diet, fortified foods.

Case study 9: Summer party time

Jumala's setting is having a party for all the children and their parents. Jumala is in charge of the food for the party. There are 30 children, aged two to five years, plus at least one, if not two, members of the family for each child. Among the families and their children are several Muslim, Hindu and vegetarian families. Jumala is a bit daunted by the prospect of planning the food and seeks the help of the nursery cook.

1. *What sort of food do you think the cook might suggest?*
2. *What sort of foods might not be suitable for some or all of the party?*
3. *What type of party foods will provide a broad range of nutrients?*

Why it is important that all dietary information is documented and shared with others

Communication is crucial in all aspects of good childcare. The sharing of dietary information is part of that communication. This information might include parental preferences about their child's diet, the cultural reasons for those preferences, the child's own preferences, and health issues, such as allergies or diabetes. It is vitally important to have this information in writing and to share it with the appropriate people, such as kitchen staff and staff on different shifts. Allergies, for example, can be life-threatening. Written information will also be useful to check against while monitoring a child's intake of food and drink.

Did you know?

In April 2002 one childcare setting made headline news when a child died as a result of an allergy to dairy products, which staff had been informed about. A nursery nurse fed the child a product containing dried milk.

Observation

- List how many children in your setting have special dietary needs or preferences.
- Make sure you know what these involve.
- Do all staff know about these needs?
- Is there anything needed in terms of training or information for all involved?

How you can encourage healthy eating in children

The key to encouraging healthy eating practice in children is to get them involved in their food as soon as they show an interest. As with all aspects of development, there is an optimum age for a stage of progress: children under three years of age are responsive to experimenting and are not yet set in their ways.

Again, childhood diets very much set the scene for their future health. It is important to encourage from a young age an interest in how food is made and what can be enjoyable and good for you. Cookery classes are no longer part of the curriculum in schools, and many children do not have the opportunity at home to cook with their parents or family. It is valuable therefore to try to introduce an interest before school if possible.

Older children will enjoy greater involvement in choosing menus: they can help with the planning, shopping and cooking or preparation. These activities will also develop their vital numeracy and literacy skills and science concepts.

Vary the foods on offer

Introduce lots of foods with different tastes and textures

Encourage children to eat by themselves with finger foods, such as strips of cooked chicken or cheese cubes

Avoid making a fuss about food. Mealtimes should not involve a battle of wills between adults and children

Let them try self-feeding with a spoon and/or fork

New foods that are rejected the first time should be offered again later

Choose foods that are naturally brightly coloured to make meals more appealing

Eat as a group as much as possible, as it will encourage children to enjoy mealtimes

Encourage a fussy eater to eat by varying meal locations: try a picnic in the garden or eating in a playroom

Let children help to prepare meals (this can be simple things like stirring the jelly or arranging things on the plate) to help them learn about food

● *Encourage children to have an interest in food and feeding.*

Lack of appetite

The early years worker should be aware that a variety of factors can affect children's appetites. Over the course of the day, a child's appetite could be reduced by:

- excitement (e.g. about a forthcoming event such as an outing or holiday)
- diverting activities (e.g. a new toy, other children playing outside, recent skill acquisition such as walking)
- tiredness.

Over the longer term, appetite could by affected by stress and illness.

- Stress can have two effects on the appetite. It may lead to 'comfort eating', usually the less healthy types of food, or it may depress the appetite. If there are stressful events in a child's life – for example parental rows or divorce, bullying, school phobia, a change of schools or nursery – they will often be reflected in a child's eating habits.
- Illness will usually affect a child's appetite. Even having a common cold is enough to stop a child eating. This need not be of concern, as lack of food for a few days will not cause problems. Once the child is well and active again, the appetite will soon return, and any weight lost will be rapidly regained. It is important to ensure that adequate fluids are drunk – fresh juice, milk and water – to avoid dehydration.

Keys to good practice: Food and drink

✓ Refer to the government guidelines for healthy eating when you are planning food and drink.

✓ Follow the guidelines in your own eating habits, partly so that you act as a role model to the children.

✓ Encourage children to make healthy choices about food.

✓ Try to involve children in the planning and preparation of food.

✓ Have written information available on all children with special dietary needs.

Reflect on your own practice

As you have seen, you need to ensure that the children in your care are given appropriate foods. Have a look at the statements below to assess whether you match up to the levels of care needed. The statements all refer to the performance criteria for CCLD 307.2.

Performance criteria statement	Always	Sometimes	Never
Do I plan menus that meet children's dietary needs as identified by government guidelines and best practice?			
Do I involve children in the planning and preparation of food where possible and encourage them to make healthy choices?			
Do I provide food and drinks that are interesting and meet the dietary requirements of all children?			
Do I ensure that high standards of hygiene are maintained in the preparation and storing of food?			
Do I model healthy eating practices?			

Provide physical care for children

The need for good oral hygiene

Teeth need looking after as soon as they start to appear. Plaque, a sticky substance that encourages bacterial growth, will stick to the tooth and start the process of decay. Despite the rise in the use of fluoride toothpaste, and the presence of fluoride in most water supplies, many young children are having their milk teeth removed due to decay.

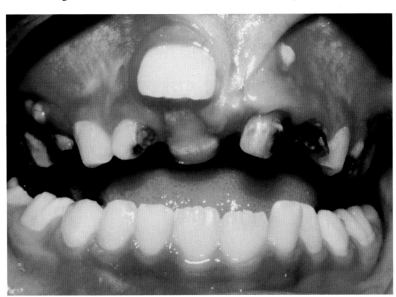

 Advanced tooth decay.

There are many things that can promote good dental health:
- regular and thorough brushing of the teeth
- never giving a baby fruit juices in a bottle or comforter (the acid will damage the teeth)
- limiting intake of pure fruit juices in all children (although they are nutritious, an excess can damage the enamel on teeth)
- avoiding sweetened drinks at any age
- encouraging a child to drink plain water after meals
- eating sweets only after meals, followed by brushing the teeth
- giving a child fluoride drops if it is not added to the water supply
- encouraging regular trips to the dentist as soon as teeth appear
- encouraging a diet with plenty of calcium, fluoride, vitamins A, C and D and foods that need chewing.

Cross-infection and basic hygiene

Hand washing and hygiene

The importance of careful hand washing cannot be over-stressed. Even hands that seem clean can have a mass of bacteria on them. Bacteria serve useful purposes in the right place in the body but some kinds can cause serious illness in the wrong place. Trips to the toilet transfer thousands of potentially harmful bacteria onto the hands, through wiping bottoms, touching handles and so on. Picking your nose will transfer *Staphylococcus aureus* to your hands and then potentially to food. A brief hand wash without soap will leave most bacteria still on the hands; if those hands subsequently go into a child's mouth, there is a serious risk of infection.

The bowel is full of bacteria called *E. coli*; these are essential bacteria which help to keep the bowel healthy. However, if they get into the upper digestive tract via dirty hands, they can be very harmful. *E. coli* can also cause vaginal infections in girls. It is important always to wipe a baby's bottom from front to back to avoid contamination in this way. In addition, little girls should be taught in this way when being toilet trained.

Hand washing can be made a game, with competitions for the cleanest hands. For older children, a science experiment in which bacteria from dirty and supposedly clean hands are cultured on plates can show them the results of poor hygiene.

Correct disposal of different types of waste

You will at some time in your career have to dispose of different types of bodily waste. It is essential that blood, vomit, urine and faeces are disposed of correctly. This is to avoid contamination of surfaces and materials that may be used to prepare food, or that children may work on. You also need to protect yourself from possible infection from waste. Make sure you know what the procedures are in your setting.

Keys to good practice: Disposing of waste

✓ Always wear disposable gloves and apron when dealing with waste.

✓ Dispose of waste promptly, in the appropriate bin – do not leave it lying around.

✓ Always wipe surfaces that waste has been in contact with, using the correct fluids and cloths.

✓ If children's clothes are soiled with waste, put them in a plastic bag and wash separately from non-soiled clothes.

✓ Dispose of your gloves and apron and wash your hands thoroughly after dealing with waste.

Raising children's awareness of their own bodies and health needs

Learning about the body and keeping it healthy should be fun and exciting for children.

There are many books and games on the market aimed at doing just that. Have a look at some of them and develop your own ideas.

Consider how you would use some of the following activities:
- Singing songs involving parts of the body (e.g. 'Heads, shoulders, knees and toes')
- Children drawing round their bodies on a large sheet of paper and drawing where organs such as the heart and lungs are
- Teaching about the importance of healthy eating through shopping at pretend shops in nursery
- Holding food-tasting events for new healthy foods
- Looking at the work of well-known chefs with older children
- Conducting quizzes about health for older children
- Encouraging children to visit websites for children with information on health.

Health surveillance of children and young people

Not all children and young people benefit from good health as a matter of course. Health promotion aims to help them to look after themselves and help themselves to be as healthy as possible.

For babies and children this starts when, and in many cases before, their mother becomes pregnant. All expectant mothers and their children are entitled and encouraged to take part in a free surveillance programme to help the best possible development.

Expectant mothers attend regular checks as soon as the pregnancy is confirmed. Tests and checks are done to make sure that the mother is healthy and does not develop complications in pregnancy such as high blood pressure or diabetes. The growth and health of the baby are carefully monitored as well through:
- scans
- blood tests
- listening to the baby's heart beat
- monitoring movements
- more advanced tests if problems are suspected.

As soon as the baby is born, he or she is subjected to a range of test and checks (see unit 303). These tests give the baseline of the baby's health and condition and lead into the routine child health surveillance programme.

There are some regional variations but, in general, all babies have checks at approximately:

- 6–8 weeks
- 6–9 months
- 18–24 months
- 39–42 months.

These checks generally combine a series of physical checks with health education for the parents. Checks are made to see how the baby is developing compared with expectations and, if needed, the baby can be referred to an appropriate person (e.g. to an audiologist if problems are noted with a baby's hearing at 6–9 months).

The checks are carried out by a child's health visitor and/or general practitioner. Every family with children under five has a named health visitor who can advise on development and everyday issues such as teething, sleeping and feeding as well as **immunisation** programmes.

Active knowledge

The NHS publishes excellent material on immunisation, available at www.immunisation.nhs.uk

Find out the latest schedule of immunisations for all children and young people.

All babies should be immunised at two, three and four months against diphtheria, tetanus, whooping cough, polio and Meningitis C. At 13 months, they should be immunised against measles, mumps and rubella (MMR).

At the age of three to four years, children should be immunised against diphtheria, tetanus, whooping cough, polio and MMR.

At the age of 10–14 years, young people should be immunised against tuberculosis, and at 13 to 18 years they should receive a booster injection against tetanus, diphtheria and polio.

Older children have a range of health checks at school involving the school nurse. School nurses have an important role in child health including:

- assessing the needs of school children and school communities and agreeing individual and school health plans

- playing a role in immunization and vaccination programmes

- contributing to personal health and social education and to citizenship training

- working with parents to promote parenting
- offering support and counselling, promoting positive mental health in young people
- advising and coordinating healthcare to children with medical needs.

Active knowledge

Find out the exact child health surveillance programmed in your area, both for babies and young children and for young people at school.

What kinds of activities are promoted?

How chronic illnesses can affect physical development

Children develop well when they are healthy. In the long term, poor health can have a serious impact on a child's potential for development unless care is taken to prevent this.

Observation

Chronic illness takes many forms. Consider these examples:

- asthma – narrowing of the airways in response to an irritant (e.g. allergy to dust)
- arthritis – erosion of the covering of joints causing pain and deformity
- sickle cell disease – irregular-shaped red blood cells that can cause bouts of serious pain
- eczema – itchy, dry, patchy skin that can become raw and bleed
- cystic fibrosis – lack of vital enzyme in mucous surfaces of body (e.g. lungs and digestive tract) that affects digestion and lung function.

1. Research each of the conditions –either on the internet or in a book.

2. How do you think each of them would affect a child being able to take part in everyday activities?

3. How would the conditions affect the child's development?

4. Think of a child you have worked with who has suffered from a chronic health condition. How was he or she affected?

Finding out about a child's individual condition and the potential impact on a child or family is part of your role.

The internet is an excellent source of information, especially the website of the organisation Contact A Family at www.cafamily.org.uk, which features an extensive list of conditions to research.

Reflect on your own practice

As you have seen, ensuring the physical care of children is an essential part of your role. Have a look at the statements below to assess whether you match up to the levels of care needed. The statements all refer to the performance criteria for CCLD 307.3.

Performance criteria statement	Always	Sometimes	Never
Do I provide opportunities for children to learn about how their bodies work?			
Do I provide opportunities for discussion about healthy physical development?			
Do I support children in making positive health decisions?			
Do I ensure children with chronic illness or physical difficulties can participate positively?			

End-of-unit knowledge check

1. List four activities that each encourage balance, coordination, gross motor skills and hand–eye coordination.
2. Why might you need to change a planned activity?
3. What is meant by risk assessment of activities?
4. Why are rest and sleep essential for the body?
5. What is meant by a balanced diet?
6. List the five main food groups.
7. List five ways to encourage healthy eating in young children.
8. Why is good dental care important?
9. When do the permanent teeth start to form?

References

Prentice, A. M. and Jebb, S. A. *Fast foods, energy density and obesity: a possible mechanistic link.* (2003)

Chief Medical Officer *Annual Report.* Department of Health (2002).

Promote children's well-being and resilience

Over the past few decades, there have been many changes to how people live their lives. Some of these changes have created pressure and stress, which can sometimes affect children's lives. Helping children to cope with pressure and stress is therefore an important part of your work. It is also essential that you help children to learn their own coping strategies, and so there is an increasing awareness that you must work to develop in children a sense of well-being and resilience.

What you must know and understand

- How to carry out risk assessment that takes all reasonable precautions without restricting opportunities for development; how organisational policy can support this (K3H306)
- Factors that affect resilience in children and how to support children's resilience (K3D307/308)
- The link between children's ability to relate to others and their emotional well-being and resilience (K3D309)
- The concept of an emotionally and psychologically safe environment that allows children to express their feelings freely (K3D310)
- The importance of trust, openness and honesty in practitioners' relationships with children (K3D311)
- How you can help children understand, express and manage all of their feelings (K3D312)
- Why it is important for children to challenge and test their abilities and the relationship between this and self-esteem (K3D313)
- How you can encourage and support children to test and stretch their skills and abilities; how you can help them manage success and failure in ways that do not damage their self-esteem (K3D314)
- What is meant by focused attention, why this is important to children's self-esteem and how you provide such attention (K3D315)
- The importance of not judging children; why comments should be directed at behaviour rather than the individual and the link between this and children's resilience and self-esteem (K3D316)

- How you demonstrate empathy and understanding to children, including the language and expressions you might use (K3C317)
- How you recognise and manage your own negative feelings, such as lack of confidence and feelings of inadequacy (K3P318)

Self-reliance and self-esteem: enabling children to take risks safely in a supportive and challenging environment

Well-being, resilience and self-esteem

What children need in order to be resilient

All children (and indeed adults too) have emotional needs that underpin the way they act and how they cope with pressure. By ensuring that your practice with children meets their underlying needs, you can promote children's **well-being** and **resilience**.

Key terms

Well-being is used to describe children's physical and mental health, as well as their confidence and ability to cope in a variety of situations. In some ways it could be dubbed 'inner strength and confidence'.

Resilience is the ability to withstand normal, everyday disappointments, hurts and assaults on one's confidence, without it affecting self-esteem.

Security
Knowing that you are physically safe and protected

Self-esteem
Valuing yourself

Child's emotional needs

Belonging
Knowing that you are valued, accepted and needed

Agency
Feeling that you have some control in your life and having some freedom

Children's emotional needs can be grouped into four main categories.

The importance of fostering well-being and resilience in young children

There are times in everyone's lives when they feel under pressure or stress. How well they are able to cope with this will depend partly on the support that they are given at the time and partly on their own reserves of confidence and strength. Confidence and self-esteem have their roots in early childhood. By focusing on children's well-being and resilience in their earliest years, you not only help them at the time, but also lay down the foundations of later support for them.

Recognising the pressures that can affect children's resilience

If you think about the pressures that some children are under, you will realise just how important the concepts of well-being and resilience are to the early years worker. Children with high levels of well-being and resilience should be able to manage these pressures more easily.

Pressure to do well academically
Children become aware at an early age that there is a pressure on them to do well at school.

Drugs, alcohol and smoking
Some primary school children are experimenting with substance misuse and many others are under pressure to try.

Media pressure
Children are targeted by and influenced by the media. They can feel under pressure to have certain foods or toys, or to behave in a particular way. Media pressure is also sometimes linked to children's feelings about body image.

Family breakdown
Family structures have become less stable and more fluid. Some children will be separated from a family member who is important to them.

Growing up in a deprived area
Some children are growing up in areas that have few amenities and facilities. There may also be high levels of anti-social behaviour and crime.

Formation of new family units
As well as family breakdown, some children are also adjusting to new family units and relationships.

● *Examples of pressures that affect children.*

There are many ways in which adults can help support children's resilience. Children even in circumstances that are difficult can sometimes find a way through with the help of a supportive adult.

Listening

All children need adults to listen to them and to be there for them. Children under pressure will particularly need someone that they can talk to.

Consistency

When a child's life is turbulent, it is important that adults are consistent with them. They need to know that support will always be available and that they can count on consistent reactions. This may include the setting of boundaries. Boundary setting can help children to feel secure and safe, especially if they are in situations where boundaries are unclear.

Check it out

How many children do you work with who have experienced family breakdown?

High expectations

We can support children's resilience by showing them that we believe in them and that we have every confidence in them. This means showing them that we have high expectations of them, although it is essential that these expectations are realistic.

Affection and warmth

Everyone needs signs of affection and warmth. Children who are under pressure particularly need to know that they are wanted, cared for and liked.

Why self-esteem is important in building children's well-being and resilience

The term 'self-esteem' is used a lot in connection with well-being and resilience. This is because self-esteem is about the way that you feel about yourself. If children have good feelings about themselves, they are likely to be positive and confident. Self-esteem helps children to overcome setbacks and cope with difficult situations. This makes a difference to their overall resilience.

Self-esteem is not something that people are born with. It begins early on in childhood and the first step in this process is for children to learn about who they are and what they are like.

Self-concept

What you learn about yourself is sometimes referred to as self-concept or self-image. This process is linked to what other people around you say and do. Babies, for example, quickly learn to react to smiles and expressions, and three-year-olds are already aware of whether they are a boy or a girl. By watching and thinking about how others respond to them, children start to develop some ideas of what they are like: a young child who is often praised, cuddled and told that he is wonderful is likely to learn that he is lovable and popular, whereas a child who is often reprimanded and made to feel bad may come to the conclusion that she is worthless and not capable of being 'good'.

Comparison

By the age of about six years, most children also start to learn about themselves by comparing how they are doing with others. They may see that another child makes adults smile or is good at doing something. From comparing the reactions of others and also the achievements of other children, they may again come to conclusions about what they are like. A child who sits next to another child whose drawings are often praised and put on the wall may decide that she is not good at drawing, whereas the other child may at the same time be learning that he has a talent.

Did you know?

Feeling good about yourself affects your physical as well as mental health. Positive feelings generate a range of chemicals in the brain. Some of these are responsible for mood while others appear to make a difference to the immune system.

How self-concept affects young children's responses

Children's self-concept quickly begins to affect how they behave and what they do. Children who realise that they are slower than others at finishing jigsaws may stop choosing to do them, while those who learn that they can do them easily may often get them out. Similarly, children who are not given opportunities to do things for themselves may become completely reliant on adult support, having failed to develop the idea that they are competent or capable.

● *By the age of six children will be comparing how they are doing. At what age might they stop doing so?*

The ideal self

During children's primary school years, they begin to think about what they would like to be like. This is sometimes referred to as the 'ideal self'. The ideal self can be based partly on how they think adults would like them to be and partly on what they admire in other children. For example, a child who sees that her friend runs quickly and gets a lot of praise from adults may, as part of her ideal self, want to be a fast runner. Children can also form their concept of an 'ideal self' by watching television and reading magazines and books.

Check it out

Think back to when you were a child. Did you ever stop doing something because you came to the conclusion that you were not good at it?

How the ideal self is linked to self-esteem

A current theory of self-esteem links the ideal self to the self-concept. It is suggested that people with high self-esteem have an ideal self that is quite similar to how they view themselves. People with low self-esteem do not see themselves as being anywhere near how they would like to be. This theory can explain why people whom others regard as being successful can still have low self-esteem: they may not feel that they measure up to their own image of what is successful. An extreme and dramatic example of the interaction between self-concept and the ideal self is, perhaps, the disease anorexia. Those with this disease have an ideal self who is thin, but their self-concept is that they are fat. The internal judgement is so strong that, regardless of friends and family telling them that they are fine, they still feel a long way from their ideal.

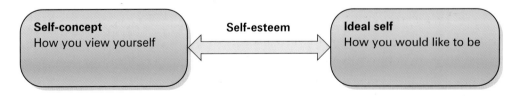

Self-concept How you view yourself	**Self-esteem**	**Ideal self** How you would like to be

● *Self-esteem links the ideal self to the self-concept.*

Carl is one of three children in the family. He has an older sister and a younger brother. He is six years old. He finds learning to read a struggle. There are plenty of books at home and both his parents enjoy reading. His younger brother has already begun to catch up. Family members as well as staff at the school often talk about how well his older sister is doing. His younger brother often comes home with certificates and stickers. Carl rarely gets anything, partly because he does not try very hard. When he is meant to be reading or looking at books, he often messes around and looks for other things to do. On some days he 'forgets' to take books home.

1. *Is Carl's self-esteem in this area high or low?*
2. *Explain the reasons for your answer.*
3. *How might Carl's self-esteem affect his future learning?*

Influence of adults on children's self-esteem

It is essential that early years workers are good at helping children to feel positive about themselves. Children who grow up hearing criticism or believing that they are helpless are likely to have a lower self-esteem. In turn they will be likely to set themselves fewer challenges and to have less ambition. They may also find it harder to cope with pressure. Some children with low self-esteem will go on to try destructive behaviours such as drug taking, or settle into abusive relationships. Adults who work with children should therefore help them develop a strong self-concept and, in older children, a realistic 'ideal self'.

Providing a supportive and challenging environment

One of the ways in which you can help foster well-being and resilience in children is by providing them with the right environment. This can help them to develop strong and positive feelings about themselves. Children need not only to feel safe when they are with you but also to be able to express their feelings, as well as learn about their capabilities; in addition, they should have opportunities to try out new skills and activities without worrying about failure.

Most adults looking back on their childhood talk about playing, taking risks and having a sense of freedom. This is particularly true where adults have had opportunities to play outdoors and have had times when adult supervision was kept to the minimum. Today, many children do not get those same opportunities (see Unit 307, page 270). Fears among parents about letting their child play outdoors or alone in parks and among practitioners worried about the consequences of having an incident in their setting have meant that control of play has shifted increasingly from children towards adults. While adults have to take an overview of risk and are responsible for children's safety, it is important that they get the balance right.

Why children need to take control and risks

One of the ways in which you can help children become resilient is by teaching them to take control of situations. Some autonomy or control over parts of their lives is one of the four fundamental emotional needs that children have (see page 301). A key factor in whether people can cope with stress is whether they feel that they can control it. Children who have had opportunities from an early age to take responsibility and make decisions are therefore more likely to cope in stressful situations. If children always have others making decisions for them, they may learn that their views and actions are not important. This in the longer term may teach them to become dependent and needy (a state that is sometimes called 'learned helplessness').

As well as learning to take control, children also need to learn to assess risks for themselves. While it is only natural for you to want to protect children, it is also important that you think about how you can help them identify and manage risks for themselves. Obviously, this needs to be a gradual process and one that reflects children's age and stage of development.

 Case study 2: Confidence is linked to the experience of being in control

Habib is seven years old. He is used to people taking care of him and also telling him what to do. He is not used to taking decisions or responsibility. His early experiences of play were very structured and he has become used to being organised. His school is arranging a residential trip. Habib does not want to go because he is afraid that he might get lost. He is also worried because he does not like changes to routines and not knowing what is happening next.

1. *Explain why Habib might miss out if he does not go on the trip.*
2. *How might Habib's early experiences be affecting him now?*
3. *Why is it important that children gain confidence in their early years?*

Ways in which children may be given control

Some of the ways in which you can help children to take control are quite simple and are about adults allowing children to do things for themselves. A baby who is crawling, for example, can be given a basket that contains several different toys covered by a cloth. By pulling the cloth back, the baby learns that he or she can be responsible for finding and choosing things to play with. This is a good lesson for the child, who may otherwise learn that adults are always responsible for choosing what they play with. This idea of encouraging children to choose what to play with should be continued and developed as they get older. Four-year-old children could, for example, collect together the props and equipment that they think they would like to use in the home corner or take out things to play with outdoors.

● *Choice can be offered from a very young age.*

In addition to choosing what to play with, children should also have opportunities to explore and play in their own way. Six-year-olds may, for example, choose to use large cardboard boxes to hide in, but then decide to see whether they can climb on them. The cardboard boxes are likely to collapse, but the children need to learn this for themselves. By trying things out, even if they do not work very well, children learn not just skills but also how to be responsible and to think of solutions. Look at the situations presented in Table 308.1 and work out how you might give the children more control (the first row has been completed, by way of illustration).

Table 308.1. Giving children control

Situation of low control	How control might be given to children
At snack time, drinks are poured ready for the four-year-olds	Children are given small jugs to pour from and encouraged to wipe up spills with a cloth
Paints are chosen by adults and put out ready in containers	
Outdoor toys are put out ready for children at playtime	
Materials are put out on the collage table and an adult shows the children what to stick and where	

Duty of care is not about restricting children

You have a duty of care when you work with children. You therefore need to know what the potential dangers are in the environment and be sure that they are managed safely. You must not, however, become so cautious that children are completely restricted or that risk is used as an excuse for children to be constantly controlled. Ironically, in the longer term, creating completely risk-free zones for children is counter-productive. Children without any challenge often show unwanted behaviour and also fail to develop some important physical and cognitive skills (e.g. balance, awareness of height, judgement of speed).

Supervising and supporting children

One of the key ways in which you can manage risk is by providing good supervision of children. Supervision can take many forms, from the complete involvement of the adult through to more distant and discreet watchfulness, which will give children some privacy in their play. Good supervision should be supportive for children rather than restrictive. It might mean distracting toddlers and encouraging them to try out something new and then discreetly removing an offending item. For three-year-olds it might involve offering new pieces of equipment if a squabble does not look like it is going to be resolved easily. For older children, it might be about asking them if they need any help and making it clear that you are on hand.

How to carry out risk assessment

Risk assessment is about being aware of potential dangers in the children's environment and then taking steps to minimise the risk. It is neither possible nor desirable to eliminate every risk. This would mean stopping children from running as there is, of course, always a risk that they might fall over. Good risk assessment should look at every area within your setting, both indoors and outdoors. It involves thinking about the types of activities and play that children engage in. Ideally, it is worth attending health and safety training, to help you to see potential dangers. Once you have noted the potential dangers, the next step is to consider how best to minimise the risks and the next is to take appropriate action.

Key terms

Risk assessments must be carried out in order to identify hazards and find out the safest way to perform certain tasks and procedures.

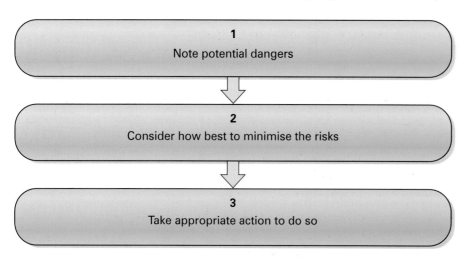

● *The three steps to risk assessment.*

Allowing children to set their own limits

Once you have a good understanding of the potential dangers, you should aim to work with children to keep them safe. This needs to be done according to children's level of understanding and development. Five-year-olds, for example, could be asked how they might play safely on the slide (i.e. not go down head first or run up it), while older children could be increasingly encouraged to set and keep their own boundaries. The advantage of working in this way is that children learn to be more self-disciplined.

● *Would you feel it necessary to set limits for these children? What risks are they taking?*

Case study 3: Helping children to set their own limits

Three children aged five and six years are playing outdoors. They want to build their own camp. Sarah, who is supervising, agrees that this is a good idea and says yes. She asks them to talk to her about the areas of the garden that cannot be used. One of the children points to an area where there are some flowers, and another tells Sarah that they should not go over to the steps, as they might fall down them. Sarah praises them for thinking in this way. The children go off and get some fabric and build a 'camp'. She asks them if they would like some logs to hold down the fabric for the den. The children are keen. Sarah asks them to work out why they must not be thrown. The children tell her that they might land on someone's foot. They suggest that they might roll them over to their 'camp'. Sarah watches them as they roll the logs and use them to weight down the fabric.

1. *How did this approach help children to learn about responsibility?*
2. *Why is it important that children learn to set their own limits?*
3. *Explain why this type of activity can help children to gain in confidence.*

An emotionally safe environment for children

As well as getting the physical environment right for children, you must also look at the emotional environment. Children need to learn to express and control their feelings. They need to learn that adults are there for them and value them unconditionally. An emotionally safe environment for children is one where they know that there will be consistency and that the adults are there for them. It is also one where children know their feelings will be acknowledged, even if they are negative ones. Creating this emotional environment is especially important for children who are undergoing changes in their lives or who are under particular stress.

Creating an emotionally and psychologically safe environment

The responsibility for creating an emotionally safe environment lies with the adults. Openness, trust and honesty underpin the way we create this environment, and there are many factors that mesh together.

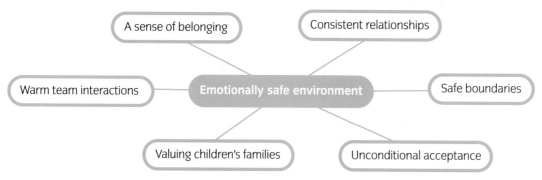

● *The factors that mesh together to create an emotionally and psychologically safe environment.*

A sense of belonging

First, you have to make sure that children feel that they belong in the environment. Belonging is one of the four fundamental emotional needs that children have (see above). Children should feel that they are actually a part of the setting, and quite often this will involve giving them some responsibility and control over it (see above). With older children this might mean encouraging them to help put up displays, or asking their opinion about toys and equipment. Children can also be made to feel that they belong through the use of routines. For example, some settings develop their own song that children sing at the start or end of the day. Some early years workers develop their own way of greeting children, which helps them to feel special and engenders trust.

Consistent relationships

Continual change can make children feel uncertain and on their guard. For children to feel secure, it is important that they have some relationships that are consistent. This is particularly important with very young children or those who experience a great deal of change or upheaval outside the setting. Going into a nursery, pre-school or holiday club and knowing that the same faces will be there to greet them can be very reassuring for children. Another aspect of consistent relationships is that the adults should be predictable in the way that they react and behave. Knowing what to expect helps children to relax and be themselves.

Safe boundaries

Knowing what they can and cannot do is important for children. Boundary setting is about making sure that children know what is expected of them. Again, this helps them to relax and settle, although some children will of course want to get the feel of what the limits are.

Boundaries need to be focused on children's safety rather than adult convenience. There should be as few as possible, as children who are in over-structured environments can easily become anxious that they might not be 'getting it right', and are less likely to develop the independence skills that will help them gain a sense of 'agency' or control.

Where boundaries are set, you should try to explain their purpose. Openness and honesty about why the boundaries are there will help children accept them. As soon as children are ready, the boundaries need to be established with them so that they can take some ownership of them. This can start from as young as four years, when some children will be starting to understand the need for cooperation, respect and simple rules.

Unconditional acceptance

Unconditional acceptance is extremely powerful and helps children's self-concept, as it makes them realise that they are lovable and liked. They understand that they are liked not because of what they can do or achieve, but just because they are themselves. Children who feel unconditionally accepted are often able to express their emotions more easily, because they are not afraid of being judged or of saying the 'wrong' things. Adults must make sure, therefore, that they do not limit praise and encouragement just to achievement (see also page 318).

Valuing children's families

Children notice the way that early years workers interact with their parents, families and other carers. For children to feel comfortable, it is essential that they see family and practitioner working together: part of children's identity is linked to their cultural, religious and family background. If you were to ignore this aspect of your work, you would effectively be ignoring one essential part of the child and giving the child an underlying message that that part is not important.

Warm team interactions

If you work with other early years workers, it is important that children hear and see you responding well to each other. Children are quick to sense atmospheres that are slightly strained or negative. This can make them unsure. Team members should aim to acknowledge each other and look for ways of showing appreciation. While this might seem quite a small step, it can have a significant effect on children.

Key terms

Unconditional acceptance of children is when they know that they are valued not for what they do but simply because they are there. It allows them to feel safe and nurtured.

Check it out

Think about an adult you enjoyed being with when you were a child. Why did you enjoy spending time with him or her? Did you feel safe and loved in the company of that person?

● *When working with colleagues, it's important to respond well to each other.*

Helping children to understand, express and manage all of their feelings

Part of growing up is understanding and also controlling impulses, feelings and emotions. For the very young child this is difficult. As with other areas of child development, the ability comes gradually and children need to be supported.

Acknowledging children's feelings

It is important that adults recognise and acknowledge children's feelings. Although many adults are good at talking to children about positive feelings such as happiness and acknowledging them, they may sometimes ignore children's negative feelings. Children do feel jealous. They also can feel immensely angry, disappointed and resentful. These are strong feelings and although it can be tempting to try to cheer children up, it is actually important to acknowledge how they are feeling. This is partly because it will help them later to be able to empathise with others and partly because it is vital for children's self-concept (where children's feelings are denied, children may learn that they are 'bad' to have such feelings). You must therefore help children to feel that they are normal in having negative feelings and that this does not make them less valued. Once feelings have been explored and acknowledged, children are often able to move on and are less likely to harbour such feelings.

Case study 4: Acknowledging feelings

It is Mark's birthday. His brother, Simon, watches him get a lot of attention as the nursery sings happy birthday and everyone claps. He does not join in. He is finding it hard because Mark has had a lot of presents and cards. Later in the afternoon, he goes over to one of the cards that Mark has been given and pulls off the badge. He is told that was not a nice thing to do and that he should say sorry. When Simon bursts into tears, he is told that he is spoiling Mark's birthday. Later on a member of staff sees Simon and spends a little time with him. She asks him if it is hard for him when it is Marks' birthday. Simon nods but does not look at her. She tells him that many children find it hard when it is someone else's birthday. Mark looks up. She tells him that the feeling inside that is making him feel cross and angry is called jealousy. She tells him that this feeling does not stay but even grown-ups get it sometimes.

1. *How are Simon's feelings affecting his behaviour?*
2. *Why is it important for adults to be aware of the feelings that children may have?*
3. *Explain why adults need to acknowledge honestly children's feelings.*

Adults as role models

One way in which children learn about managing feelings is by watching adults. If you are quick to lose your temper, show frustration or are impatient, children will learn that this is acceptable. This is one of the reasons why aggressive acts by adults such as smacking, shouting or threatening are considered to be harmful. Ideally, children need to see how adults can manage feelings appropriately. They need to learn that feelings can be vocalised rather than acted upon.

The role of language in controlling and expressing feelings

One of the major turning points in children's development is the acquisition of language. Language is often the key to helping children manage their feelings and impulses. Language helps people to organise and process their thoughts. Most adults will say that they have an inner 'thinking voice'. This voice often helps to rationalise what is happening and can increase impulse control. For example, stuck in a long queue and short of time, you might feel frustrated, but your inner voice would calm you down by reminding you that other people too have the right to shop, helping you to think whether there are alternatives to staying in the queue or making you realise that being five minutes late will not make much of a difference. You can help children develop this thinking voice by encouraging their language.

Did you know?

Developmentally, it is not until most children are around six or seven years old that they are able to internalise their thoughts fully. This is not an automatic process and depends on how much language the child has developed. Older children whose language is not developed can sometimes find it hard to control their feelings.

Supporting children's language and putting their feelings into words

Words are powerful tools in helping children to think through what they are feeling. You need to help even young children learn the vocabulary of emotions and feelings. This can be done by 'labelling' both children's feelings and your own. 'Were you disappointed when you missed your go?' or 'I am feeling quite excited today because I am expecting a parcel' are examples of the everyday ways in which you can help children to learn the language of emotions and feelings. It is also useful if you can begin to help children see the link between their feelings and how they might want to behave: 'Because you are so excited, you are finding it hard to sit still' or 'Because you are sad at the moment, you might not feel like joining in straight away'.

It is important that you use the language of emotions regularly. Focusing on it just now and then will not give children the exposure that they need to absorb the words and begin to imitate it. As well as working with groups of children, it is essential to spend time working with individual children (see the section on focused attention on page 323).

Keys to good practice: Helping children to feel valued

✓ Make sure that all children feel welcome.

✓ Encourage parents and families to be part of the setting.

✓ Ensure that children's emotions are recognised and accepted.

✓ Look for ways of helping children to learn the language to express their feelings.

✓ Avoid giving children the impression that you are interested only in their achievements.

✓ Help children to gain confidence in everyday skills.

Activities to help children to express their feelings

As well as promoting children's language, you can also help them by looking for activities that will help them to explore their feelings in a safe context. This is important, as children often need to explore some of the 'darker' feelings, such as anger, jealousy, resentment and impatience.

Imaginative play

Children of all ages benefit from using imaginative play to explore and express their feelings. Interestingly, this type of play comes fairly naturally to most children: toddlers from around 18 months begin to cuddle toys and 'put them to bed'. Older children can also use this as a way of understanding what other people are feeling and how they might react.

There are different types of imaginative play. Some children are keen to take roles and are essentially acting a part. This is called role play. Young children often repeat scenes from their own lives and so ideally you should provide role play areas that reflect this. This means providing a home corner, shops and a 'mini' nursery or pre-school.

As well as role play, children also enjoy small-world play. This might be anything from playing with farm animals through to small figures or play people. This is slightly different to role play, as children are controlling others, which can help them to feel powerful and also helps them to imagine different points of view. It is interesting to watch how children often create characters and have favourites within their small-world play. They can also be quite destructive (it is not unknown for play people to be 'drowned' in the water tray or pushed head first into the dough). Although you may be tempted to stop children from playing in this way, it can actually be beneficial. It allows them to develop a sense of power and is a way in which negative and angry feelings can be explored and safely released. If you carry on watching rather than intervening, some children may go on to 'save' or have 'mercy' on the hapless small figure.

Puppets and cuddly toys

Some children respond well to puppets or cuddly toys that are animated in some way. Many practitioners are surprised that children who are normally quite reserved are keen to talk to puppets and toys. With some children a good technique is to ask them, for example, if they would like to show their teddy their favourite activity in the nursery or to comfort teddy because he is feeling a little bit lonely.

Puppets and cuddly toys can also be used to open up discussions about feelings. Teddy may come into the nursery feeling very cross because he has been told that he cannot wear his favourite jumper. Children are then often able to make connections between what teddy is feeling and what they have experienced themselves. They may tell teddy about what happened to them. Some children are also good at explaining to teddy why he was not allowed to wear the jumper.

A puppet can be used to encourage quieter children to talk.

Sensory materials

Sand, water and dough are sensory materials that most children enjoy playing with. The materials can be moulded and moved, and give children a sense of control and freedom. Most often children will find calmness and relaxation as they repeat scooping, pouring or rolling movements. At other times they will use the materials to be destructive (e.g. pinching objects from others, knocking down structures or slapping the water). These materials are therefore thought to be useful in helping children who do not have good language skills, but who still need to find ways of controlling and expressing their feelings. Talking to children about what these materials make them feel can be useful. You might say to a five year old 'How does it feel when you squash down the dough?'

It can be a good idea to put some sensory materials into smaller trays so that children who do not feel like socialising and negotiating can play in their own way.

Mark-making and drawing

Emotions can also be expressed through mark-making and drawing. For young children this is a sensory experience and one in which they can again take control. Look out for areas where children might be able to use whole-arm movements to express themselves (e.g. chalking on an outside wall). Aim to ensure that this is a 'free' activity, rather than limiting children to using only certain colours or having to draw particular things. A good selection of objects for printing (e.g. sponges, pads, large brushes) can also help children to express themselves.

● *Many children gain a sense of release and enjoyment from painting.*

Music and dance

Music and dance are also powerful ways of getting in contact with emotions. Even babies respond to music. You can ask children which music they prefer and how the music makes them feel. Children also enjoy playing musical instruments. Shaking percussion instruments or tapping out a rhythm can help them to feel powerful and in control.

Dance for the youngest children may simply be about relaxing and moving to music in whatever way they choose. Scarves and ribbons can also be used as they add a visual component. Music and dance can sometimes be very structured activities, but for children to have an opportunity to express themselves, let them take the initiative.

Why children need to challenge and test their abilities

As well as learning to express their feelings, children also need to develop a sense of **agency**. A child may, for example, have seen another child climb up a wall and want to try it out too. Trying out something new and then achieving it gives children a sense of satisfaction. They learn that they 'can do' and that they can be responsible for what they achieve.

Key terms

Agency is control over your life. It is about being able to do things for yourself and setting your own challenges.

How you can encourage children to try new activities and challenge themselves

Adults have an important role in helping children to develop a sense of agency or the 'can do' mentality. From an early age, children need assistance to develop the self-help skills that they use every day (e.g. dressing, tidying up, feeding and organising their own things). This is a gradual process but, over time, you can encourage children to do more for themselves.

Alongside support for self-help skills, you need also to provide as many opportunities as possible for children to try out new things. This can be anything from cooking through to painting or rock climbing for older children. The more things children can try out the better, as this will help them to find out their interests and strengths.

Introducing new activities

Some children quickly learn that they do not like trying out 'new things'. This is sometimes because they lack confidence or are worried about not doing well. It is important therefore to plan activities in such a way that children begin by being successful. Small successes can lead to greater things, while early failure can stop children in their tracks and, worse still, teach them that they do not like trying out new things. It is also important that adults encourage children to enjoy the 'trying out' rather than focus on how well a child does.

Helping children to challenge themselves

While young children often challenge themselves because they are less worried about failing, some children after the age of four years or so become more cautious. They especially will need feelings of success when they start a new challenge. You can also talk to children about what they would like to do next and help them to break down the challenge into manageable steps.

It is important for some children to hear that you think that they can do a particular task. Although, in the long run, it is better if children have self-belief, such encouragement can in itself help children believe in themselves. Some children also need the physical presence of an adult before trying out something. Just being there can help them to feel that they are not alone as they try something out (e.g. an adult might stand underneath a rope bridge that a child wants to cross).

● *Achievement gives self-belief.*

Managing success and failure

Children who do achieve and are able to cope with pressures often have a strong sense that they are capable and competent. As outlined above, children should be given opportunities to try out new activities and to take control so that they gain a sense of agency. As part of this learning, children need to have plenty of opportunities to feel successful. They also need strategies to help them cope with failure or disappointment.

Being and feeling successful

Being and feeling successful are slightly different things. Someone can be a success in the eyes of someone else but not necessarily feel it. Children need to feel successful if this is to become part of their self-concept.

If children believe that they are successful this will have a huge influence on them. One study showed that when seven-year-old boys were asked to rate their ability to do a task before they tried it out, those who scored themselves very low did not perform well. His research followed the boys through into adolescence. The boys who rated themselves highly in the original experiment had gone on to do very well. Those boys who at seven years had lower self-esteem fared much less well.

Helping children to feel successful

Feeling successful is about having some inner satisfaction. Although it is important for you to praise children when they try hard or achieve a task, in the longer term it is important that they are able to recognise their achievements for themselves. In addition to giving praise, therefore, you need to ask children about how they are feeling. For young children this may mean modelling the language by saying something such as 'Did you enjoy doing that? I see that you have built a large tower. Were you pleased with yourself?' By talking to children about their feelings when they are doing something, you can teach them that it is good to acknowledge your own efforts.

For children to feel successful, they have to have opportunities to set their own goals and meet them. A four-year-old may want to complete a floor puzzle but a six-year-old may want to ride a bicycle without stabilisers. A toddler may want to copy an older child and make marks. You may need to help children to achieve their goals. If so, it is important that you do so in such a way that they do not feel that you are taking over: feeling successful is also about knowing that you did it for and by yourself. How you support children will depend on what they want to do and also on their age, experience and current skill level. In some situations, you may just need to be on hand, to encourage the child and provide the necessary materials and equipment.

You can help children to feel successful in other ways too.

Breaking tasks down into smaller steps

You may need to help the child to break tasks down into smaller steps. You might suggest to the child who wants to ride the bicycle that they try going along a straight path and concentrate on pedalling and not steering. You might let the child know that all children find it hard at first. You would have to be on hand in case of injury and to help the child feel safe.

Notice success

Children quickly tune in to the reactions of adults. They notice when adults are pleased. If your praise is always linked to achievement in some way, children might feel that they are failing even when they are doing very well. A good example of this is games in which there is a winner. If the focus is just on the winner, children who have tried hard and perhaps enjoyed the game may feel that they are not successful. In the same way, children might feel that they cannot draw if their picture is not talked about and put up on display.

Adults therefore need to notice what children are doing and how they are doing it, as well as their achievements. Giving children positive feedback rather than praise is often more useful. Children need positive feedback from adults when they have persisted or have tried out new ideas or are simply enjoying a challenge. Too much focus on achievement can also stop children from experimenting and setting high goals for themselves: they may decide not to take any 'risks', to be sure of getting the praise.

Helping children to notice their achievements

One of the ways in which you can help children to feel successful is by encouraging them to reflect on their achievements. Children often forget how much they can do, what they have learnt and how well they are doing. They often focus on what they cannot do and what they can see others doing. Helping children to notice and reflect on their skills is therefore important.

Did you know?

Noticing achievement is a technique that was often used to help Soviet athletes improve their performance. Athletes' performance was measured before and after film clips were shown them. The film clips contained highlights showing their best moments on the track. Their performance soared when they had seen themselves doing well.

Keys to good practice: Helping children to reflect on their skills

✓ Point out to children what they can now do.

✓ Ask older children to write down a 'can do now' list.

✓ For younger children talk about what they were like when they were babies or toddlers. This can help them to see how much they can now do.

Case study 5: Learning to see success

Carl has a new childminder. He enjoys going to the childminder because she makes him feel special. He is still reluctant to read and this is becoming a 'hurdle' for him. The childminder knows that if he continues to feel a 'failure' about his reading, it will become more of a problem. She gets out from a box several picture books that have only a few words. She asks Carl if he could choose one that he thinks would be good for her to read to the toddler that she also cares for. Carl looks through the books and recognises one that he used to have when he was little. He opens the book and flicks through it. He then settles down to read it. His childminder asks him if, when he has a moment, he might be able to read it to the toddler. Later on she spots him on the sofa reading the story through with the toddler.

1. *Why does Carl need to see himself as a reader?*
2. *How might this help Carl with his reading?*
3. *Why is it important to find ways of giving children confidence?*

Failure as a learning experience

As most adults know, life is not all about success. There are times when you might try something and find that it has not worked out for some reason. Children need therefore to learn about failure and, more importantly, how to cope with it. This is how children learn to become resilient and are able in the longer term to bounce back after small upsets.

Analysing failure

Many children decide that if they cannot do something, they are not good at it, and instead of persevering they simply give up. This often leads to a vicious circle where children 'know' that they are not good, stop trying and so do not develop the skills they need to do well at something. If they do try again their lack of skill affects how they do and so it confirms for them that they are no good at it. Personalising failure in this way is understandable, especially if a child can see another child who is able to do something.

It is therefore important that you help children to learn to analyse situations in which they have not been as successful as they had hoped. They need to realise that there are likely to be a variety of reasons for failure in a specific instance, and that they can control some of these factors, if not others. Children need to be able to work out what has happened and to think through what they can do about it.

Skill level

Children need to know that skill level is something that can affect how well they do. They might need to learn some new skills or practise existing skills so that they can achieve a task. A six-year-old who is learning to ride a bicycle will need to master several skills, including balance, steering and pedalling. For young children, you might have to explain that all children of their age struggle with tasks and that they will in time be able to achieve theirs.

Practice

Children often watch older children or adults and come to the conclusion that they are not good at something. A three-year-old might struggle with a coat but see an older child put one on effortlessly. Children need to learn that practice is often the key to success.

Equipment and materials

Sometimes failure can be the result of using the wrong materials or equipment. For example, plastic bottles are hard to stick together with glue, and so if they fall apart in a model children have made, the children should be encouraged to think about whether or not they were using appropriate materials for the job. They would then be focused on why the materials had failed, rather than on the fact that they themselves had failed.

Check it out

A survey of achievements in mathematics showed interesting results. Parents were asked which they thought was the greater influence on children's competency with mathematics: natural ability or hard work. American parents generally rated natural ability as far more important, while Japanese parents rated hard work more highly. Interestingly, Japanese children on the whole do better at mathematics than American children.

Knowledge

Some activities are based upon knowledge. There might be a step-by-step procedure that has to be followed, or knowledge from one situation may need to be transferred to another. When a child sees another child being successful, it can be helpful for them to realise that the other child has already done something similar or has been shown before how best to do it.

● *Skills, practice, knowledge and materials will all have a bearing on failure. And some factors are beyond control.*

Factors that cannot be controlled

Finally, sometimes there are factors that are not amenable to control: a kite will not fly if there is not enough wind, and a plant will not grow if slugs eat it. Children need to realise that there are often such setbacks. Nonetheless, in such circumstances a change of plan can get around the problem: a simpler type of kite may need less wind to fly, or a different plant may be less vulnerable to attack by slugs.

Talking about failure

The way in which children can learn to feel better about failure is to talk about it. First, you must acknowledge children's disappointment. Their feelings of hurt, anger or frustration are real. Children need to see that you take these seriously, otherwise they may not believe you when you try to talk about the reasons why something has not worked out. You should support by talking about what their next steps might be to achieve their goal. You may need to encourage them or even to give them practical help.

Role models

Children also learn about failure by watching other people's reactions when things do not go well. If you appear frustrated or take out your anger irrationally, children will learn that this is acceptable. Ideally, children should learn to hear how you can rationalise a difficulty or failure: 'I should have remembered that that surface is not flat. Next time I will put my cup down over there.'

Keys to good practice: Success and failure

✓ Help children to focus on what they can do.

✓ Encourage children to notice their own achievements.

✓ Look for some activities that are within children's skill levels.

✓ Plan activities that sometimes require children to persevere.

✓ Help children to break down activities into smaller steps.

✓ Use 'failures' as an opportunity to help children learn how to evaluate things.

Observation

Plan an activity that will help children to see that success is not always instant and that perseverance may be necessary (e.g. making bubble mixture, building a den or doing a jigsaw puzzle).

Implement the activity and write about how you supported the children.

Explain why it is important to ensure that the activity is fun and within the children's skill level.

Reflect on your own practice

As you have seen, the provision of a challenging yet supportive environment is an essential part of your role. Have a look at the statements below to assess whether you match up to the levels of care needed. The statements all refer to the performance criteria for CCLD 308.2–4.

Performance criteria statement	Always	Sometimes	Never
Do I encourage children to try new activities and experiences?			
Do I support children in managing failure and disappointment?			
Do I help children to predict the consequences of their actions?			

continued on next page

Performance criteria statement	Always	Sometimes	Never
Do I clearly agree boundaries with children and the reasons for these?			
Do I carry out risk assessment in line with organisational policy, without limiting opportunities to extend and challenge children's skills?			
Do I engage with and provide focused attention to individual children?			
Do I praise specific behaviour that I wish to encourage?			

Enable children to relate to others

Focused attention

Adult attention helps children to feel valued and nurtured. It is best when children receive this type of attention individually. A little time one-to-one with an adult can mean a lot to children of all ages. This is what is meant by focused attention. When you give children your focused attention, you are dedicating some time to being with them. It is special time in which children can feel close to you. This may mean listening to them, playing alongside them or just chatting.

When children have this time with an adult, relationships become stronger. You will be able to respond more sensitively to them as you become more familiar with them. You may notice that a child is not quite as lively or that their tone of voice is not as bright as usual. Strong relationships will also help you to know how best to work with individual children. You may recognise that a child needs a moment of quiet or is looking for physical reassurance.

Focused attention is important for all children, but especially for those who spend many hours a days as part of a group. Individual attention helps these children to gain a stronger sense of identity and to feel valued as individuals. This is important for their self-esteem.

How adults can give children focused attention

Focused attention is about listening to and responding to children. It is also about finding ways of encouraging and valuing children. This is done by showing that you enjoy being with them and allowing them to set the 'talk agenda'. You may, for example, go over to a three-year-old who is playing alone with some bricks and take the time to play alongside him or her. By showing an interest in what the child is doing and by just playing in a relaxed way alongside the child, you are giving individual attention. It is important here to note that focused attention is not about interrogating children by asking them lots of questions. It is about being there for children and being interested in them. It is important that you are relaxed and not hurried: children will sense this and know that it is not a good time to share their thoughts, worries and news with you.

Organising time for focused attention

Focused attention can demand a rethinking of the routine of the setting: the ways in which staffing and activities are organised and whether they allow children to have a little one-to-one time with adults. A nursery might put a member of staff into the quiet corner so that individual children can come and share books with an adult or simply talk to them. You might sometimes be able to encourage children to chat to you as you are doing some everyday tasks such as clearing tables, preparing snacks or laying out activities. Key worker systems should provide opportunities for children to have some individual attention.

It is also important to think of a system that will allow you to check that all children have the opportunity to have special moments with adults. Quieter children who are not demanding of adults and who play happily can sometimes be overlooked. Where older and younger children come together, such as in childminding settings, the older children should also have a chance to have some moments together with an adult. This may be straight after school or while a younger child is having a nap.

Check it out

How much time do you have to give children focused attention. How could you increase this time?

The importance of not judging children: separating the behaviour from the child

Children's self-esteem is precious: it allows them to be positive about themselves and to develop an inner confidence. Sadly, one group of children who often have low self-esteem are those who present challenging and inappropriate behaviour. It is easy for children to find themselves in a destructive cycle. Their low self-esteem means that they crave attention, but the type of attention they receive may even contribute to their low self-esteem. Attention-seeking behaviours range from children being uncooperative through to destructive and aggressive actions.

This type of behaviour must be addressed of course, but it is important for adults to see it for what it is and to 'depersonalise' it. Feeling frustrated and irritated with children is a normal reaction, but not at all helpful, as it can confirm to the children that they are not lovable and wanted. This is why it is important when addressing children's behaviour to make sure that they understand that you are unhappy with the behaviour – not with the child.

Tackling attention-seeking behaviour is usually about giving children more attention. Spending more time with these children so that they learn how to get attention in positive and appropriate ways can gradually reduce the amount of attention-seeking behaviour that they show. Overnight changes in children's behaviour are rare, however. Children often require sustained periods of 'positive' adult attention so that they can change their self-concept and come to believe that they are good at 'being good'. During this change-over period, their behaviour can fluctuate, as they 'test out' their self-concept. Early years workers must continue to give children positive feedback and to avoid coming to the conclusion that this strategy is not working.

Check it out

Does your setting's behaviour policy encourage you to separate behaviour from the child?

How you demonstrate empathy and understanding to children

Adults who are good at giving children focused attention make children feel that they understand them. You can do this by making sure that you avoid dominating and taking control of the conversation or play activity. Providing eye contact and also smiling at children can show them that you are giving them your full attention. It is also helpful to show children that you understand them, by saying things such as 'That must have been fun for you' or 'That sounds quite scary'. By making comments that sum up what the child might have been feeling, children can see that you have been listening and also that you understand them. Sometimes perceptive comments can also help children to acknowledge their own feelings (see above).

● *How do you show empathy?*

The skilful adult is able to make such comments, but not 'take the talk away' from the child by changing the focus of what the child wants to talk about. Good listening is essential. A child who says that he went to a birthday party and did not get a piece of the cake is unlikely to want to be asked 'How many candles were on the cake?'

How you recognise and manage your own negative feelings

The way you respond to children will be partly linked to your own experiences of childhood. It is important that you recognise this when working with children. Some adults find that they automatically want to cheer up children while others find themselves dismissing children's problems as petty, with an 'off you go and sort it out yourself' approach. Adults may work in this way because that is how they were treated as children. It is therefore important for adults working with children to think about their own childhood experiences and to reflect on how they may be influencing their practice. It is also important to think about how you cope with setbacks and changes, as the children will pick up quite a lot from simply watching you. Finally, it can also be worth thinking about people in your childhood who gave you support and warmth. Working out what they did and how they did it can give you some ideas about the way in which you work.

Case study 6: Recognising and managing your own feelings

Mick is working in a crèche for the first time. He is doing very well. Children, parents and staff members think that he will become an excellent practitioner. During his appraisal, which is very positive, the manager mentions one area of his work that he may need to reflect on. She has noticed that he can at times be a little unsympathetic to boys when they have, for instance, fallen over and want some comfort. She gives him an example from the day before. She asks him whether or not he feels that this is a fair comment. Mick thinks it over. He realises that this is true and that he tends to be more sympathetic to girls. He begins to reflect upon his own childhood. His own father tended to dislike 'scenes' and he remembered being encouraged to be 'brave'.

1. *How might Mick's childhood influence the way he works?*
2. *Why is it important for Mick to recognise this?*
3. *How might this knowledge help Mick to become a better practitioner?*

Observation

Think about one child you work with who might benefit from having some more adult input. Ask your supervisor if you can spend some time focusing on this child. Observe the child in a variety of situations. Find out about the child's interests and strengths. Look at whether the child is developing self-help skills.

Write an activity plan that will help this child to gain confidence and to express their feelings.

Explain why you have chosen this activity and describe your role in it.

Implement the activity and evaluate the child's responses.

Reflect on your own practice

As you have seen, enabling children to relate to others is an essential part of your role. Have a look at the statements below to assess whether you match up to the levels of care needed. The statements all refer to the performance criteria for CCLD 308.1.

Performance criteria statement	Always	Sometimes	Never
Do I demonstrate respect for children's views, opinions and feelings?			
Do I encourage children to consider the feelings of others?			
Do I help children to identify the boundaries of acceptable and unacceptable behaviour?			
Do I demonstrate respect for children's capabilities and strengths?			

End-of-unit knowledge check

1. What is meant by the term 'well-being'?
2. What is meant by the term 'resilience'?
3. Give one reason why resilience is important.
4. List three pressures for children today.
5. What is an 'ideal self'?
6. Explain the process by which self-esteem develops.
7. How might low self-esteem affect a child's future?
8. Give three activities that might help children to express their feelings.
9. Explain why children need focused attention.
10. Explain why children should be given opportunities to become independent.
11. Why is it important for children to learn how to evaluate failure?
12. Explain why adults need to acknowledge children's emotions, including negative feelings.
13. What is meant by the term 'unconditional acceptance'?

Plan and implement curriculum frameworks for early education

Any early years curriculum should have a clear balance of activities and experiences to enable children develop to their full potential. This requires clear planning. Planning involves monitoring, assessment and evaluation to ensure that the activities and experiences offered are appropriate. This unit will guide you in planning the curriculum in your role as part of an early years team. You will discover the importance of providing a wide range of planned activities and experiences that encourage children to experiment and explore their world through play. The focus is on children aged under eight years, but if you are working with older children who may be in the early stages of learning then some of this unit will be still be relevant. It is important to recognise that early education frameworks vary between the four home countries (England, Scotland, Northern Ireland and Wales) but that the principles of good curriculum planning in order for children to learn effectively through play are the same. You will also find out about the importance of unplanned learning activities for children in the early years and how you can support these.

What you must know and understand

- Details of the early education curriculum requirements in your home country (K3D319)
- Requirements of the relevant inspectorates (K3P320)
- Sources of support in respect of planning and curriculum development, drawing on available best practice (K3D321)
- The kinds of equipment, materials and activities that support the implementation of a learning curriculum, using play as a vehicle for delivery (K3D322)
- Effective use of ICT to support the curriculum (K3D323)
- Theoretical approaches to how children learn and develop and how these might influence practice (K3D324)
- How children's learning is affected by their stage of development (K3D325)
- The importance and implications of a differentiated approach to the provision of learning experiences for children (K3D326)

- The effects of low self-esteem and lack of confidence on learning (K3D327)
- The benefits to children of learning through play and not relying on formal experiences and activities that are inappropriate for the child's age, needs and abilities (K3D328)
- How to support and extend play opportunities to encourage learning (K3D329)
- That children learn in different ways and have individual learning styles and preferences (K3D330)
- Specific issues for children's development and learning in multilingual settings (K3D331)
- How you adapt your practice to meet the individual needs of all the children in your setting, including age, gender, culture, abilities and learning styles (K3D332)
- The importance of monitoring provision and the need for accountability to children, parents, families and other agencies (Kd013)
- The importance of partnerships with parents and families and how these partnerships can be developed and supported (Kd014)
- The benefits of a multi-professional, multi-agency approach in maximising the children's experiences and learning, drawing on local communities and external expertise (Kd015)

Develop curriculum plans according to requirements

Early education curriculum requirements in England, Scotland, Wales and Northern Ireland

In the UK children are expected to go to school earlier than in many other European countries. Early years provision has an increased focus and more places are being created for children in early years settings. While learning through play is a common focus, the four home countries have differing requirements.

Active knowledge

Did you know that the Children Act 2004 focuses on opportunities for all children? Parts of the Act apply to all of the UK. Log onto the website of the Department for Education and Skills (www.dfes.gov.uk) and read extracts of the *Every Child Matters* consultation document, or visit the website www.4children.org.uk to find out how early years care is planned to develop in your area. If you live in Northern Ireland, Scotland or Wales you can gain more information about the developments in early years from www.direct.gov.uk.

England

In England there is a separate curriculum for each of the three age groups in early years care and education, as set out in Table 309.1.

Table 309.1. The early years care education curricula in England

Age group	Curriculum/title of curriculum document	Website
0–3 years	*Birth to Three Matters*	www.surestart.gov.uk/ensuringquality/birthtothreematters/
3–5 years	Foundation Stage	www.qca.org.uk/223.html
5+ years	Key Stage 1 of the National Curriculum	www.nc.uk.net/index.html

Children aged up to 3 years

SureStart has produced a framework to support children aged up to three years. It is intended to be used flexibly by practitioners. The curriculum framework is called *Birth to Three Matters* and it is divided into four areas:

- a strong child
- a skilful communicator
- a competent learner
- a healthy child.

When being inspected by **Ofsted**, any setting that provides care for children under three years of age will be expected to provide an appropriate curriculum for them to learn through play.

Key terms

Ofsted is the Office for Standards in Education. It is the government department that is responsible for the inspection of childcare and pre-school providers, schools and local education authorities in England.

Children aged from 3 to 5 years

The Foundation Stage is a curriculum designed by the Department for Education and Skills for children aged three to five years. The Education Act 2002 extended the National Curriculum to include the Foundation

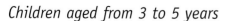

Stage. Under the Act children in pre-school settings are entitled to $12\frac{1}{2}$ hours of free education a week. These settings are inspected by Ofsted.

The Foundation Stage continues into the first year of primary school. It is based on learning through play, and the curriculum is based on six areas of learning:

- personal, social and emotional development
- communication, language and literacy
- mathematical development
- knowledge and understanding of the world
- physical development
- creative development.

Each area has a set of related 'early learning goals' as the expected areas of learning for the Foundation Stage (see Department for Education and Skills and QCA, 2000).

The Foundation Stage can be followed in nursery and reception classes, playgroups, pre-schools, day nurseries, and accredited childminders in approved childminding networks.

How children are assessed at the Foundation Stage is looked in Unit 310 (see page 374).

Children aged from 5 to 7 years

From five to seven years children follow the National Curriculum. This sets out ten subject areas for this age group, the first four of which are 'core' subjects:

- English
- mathematics
- science
- design and technology
- information and communication technology
- history
- geography
- art and design
- music
- physical education.

From September 2005 National Curriculum tests (**Standard Assessment Tasks, or SATs**) at the end of Key Stage 1 will be carried out on a more informal basis than previously. This will cater more for the individual needs of each child, as the teacher will be able to support each child more and make the process less daunting.

The change from the Foundation Stage to Key Stage 1 is referred to as transition. Children experience more formal learning at Key Stage 1 but there is still an emphasis on learning through play. Children with special needs are included where possible in mainstream education. Primary schools are inspected by Ofsted.

Scotland

Children up to three years of age are cared for in a variety of settings, mostly private. Guidance on their education is provided in the document *Birth to Three: Supporting Our Youngest Children* (Learning and Teaching Scotland, 2005). Learning through play is encouraged. Assessment is through a self-evaluation tool called 'Child at the Centre', which is considered in Unit 310 (see page 375).

A curriculum for excellence is to be implemented in 2007. It is intended to bring the curriculum guidelines for children aged three to five and five to fourteen years together, to ensure a smooth transition in children's learning. It will emphasise the importance of purposeful and well-planned play.

The current curriculum for children aged three to five years is based upon five areas of learning:
- emotional, personal and social development
- communication and language
- knowledge and understanding of the world
- expressive and aesthetic development
- physical development and movement.

It emphasises observation, equality of opportunity and supporting transitions, home and families.

Wales

In Wales, the language of instruction can be either Welsh or English. The Welsh Assembly has a ten-year strategy called the 'Learning Country'. A framework for children's learning is being introduced, under which the foundation phase will be for children aged five to seven years.

At present there is some government-funded nursery provision. Key Stage 1 is similar to that in England except it includes Welsh as a language. Children with special needs are integrated into mainstream education wherever possible.

In 2002 a less formal, play-based curriculum was introduced; however, the Welsh version of the 'Desirable Outcomes' is still being used (see Unit 310, page 375). This curriculum emphasises planning as a basis for an effective play curriculum.

Key terms

Key Stage 1 is the part of the National Curriculum that applies to children aged five to seven years.

Standard Assessment Tasks (SATs) are tasks set externally that are intended to assess a child's educational level at stages throughout their education. Key Stage 1 SATs take place towards the end of year 2 in primary school.

Northern Ireland

The Northern Ireland Executive is working towards the provision of one year of full-time pre-school provision (i.e. before age five) on a voluntary basis. Many four-year-olds are already in reception classes in primary school for five full days. There are plans to introduce a Foundation Stage for children aged from three to six years. At present, children are in Key Stage 1 from five to six years of age. The Key Stage 1 curriculum in Northern Ireland comprises five areas of study:

- English
- mathematics
- science and technology
- environment and society
- creative and expressive studies.

The assessment of children doing Key Stage 1 is currently under review.

Observation

Your setting should have a curriculum planning document. For example, in England for children under three the government gives guidance in *Birth to Three Matters*. Obtain a copy, along with the accompanying CD-ROM (which should provide suggested reading, video footage, discussion and case studies as well as useful contact addresses), and use it to help you plan an effective curriculum.

If you work in Northern Ireland, Scotland or Wales, ask your manager if he or she has a copy of the draft curriculum document for the early years.

The requirements of inspectorates in England, Scotland, Wales and Northern Ireland

Each country of the UK has a government department that is responsible for inspecting the early years services (Table 309.2). The examples used in this unit are based on the requirements of the English inspectorate, Ofsted, but the principles are similar for the other countries. If you check the websites given in Table 309.1, you can see how you will be expected to support the various curricula.

Table 309.2. Inspectorates of the home countries

Country	Inspectorate	Website
England	Ofsted	www.ofsted.gov.uk
Scotland	Her Majesty's Inspectorate of Education	www.hmie.gov.uk/
Wales	Estyn	www.estyn.gov.uk
Northern Ireland	Department of Education	www.deni.gov.uk/

The work of Ofsted

Ofsted states that those working with children under eight years of age in sessional day care will find the publication *Curriculum Guidance for the Foundation Stage* (Department for Education and Skills and QCA, 2000) an 'essential tool for helping children work towards the early learning goals' (see Unit 310, page 374, on the early learning goals) whether or not they have provided funded nursery education. Inspectors will visit each setting and look carefully at the curriculum offered to the children. It is accepted that curricula will vary but an inspector will always expect to see evidence that the **registered person** has planned and provided activities and play opportunities 'to develop children's emotional, physical, social and intellectual capabilities'. This is in accordance with the third of the 14 National Standards for day care (see page 48).

Foundation Stage

Nursery inspections will relate to the Foundation Stage and will include:

- evaluation and reporting of standards reached by children with relation to the early learning goals
- the quality of teaching and learning in the six areas of the Foundation Stage curriculum
- the quality of curriculum leadership.

Inspectorates will expect children to be assessed in the Foundation Stage. You can read more about this in Unit 310.

Key Stage 1

Since its introduction in 1998 there has been a move towards a more flexible approach to the National Curriculum; nonetheless, children in state-controlled schools are legally required to follow it. Key Stage 1 inspections extend the Foundation Stage inspections to cover the following:

- evaluation and reporting of standards reached by the pupils
- quality of teaching and learning
- quality of curriculum leadership
- core subjects and work seen in other subjects
- inspection across the whole curriculum.

Inspection of settings offering alternative curricula

Inspectors will also inspect settings where an alternative curriculum is offered. Three of the more common types of alternative setting in the UK that will receive inspections are considered in this section.

Key terms

Registered person is the term Ofsted uses to describe the person or organisation legally responsible for providing the childcare.

Check it out

Research the early learning goals for children aged three to five years. These apply to children in the Foundation Stage, which may start in a nursery setting and finish at the end of the reception class of school. Review the planning for the age group of children you are working with in your setting to see how the early learning goals are used. You might like to share planning models with other candidates in your tutor group. You will discover that all settings have their own versions of curriculum planning.

Highscope

This programme was designed for children in the USA in the 1960s. Children are expected to plan, do and review in a very organised environment. Children lead their planning and review their choice of activities in small groups with an adult.

A number of settings in the UK use some of the principles of Highscope but incorporate them into a more traditional model.

Montessori

● *Maria Montessori.*

There is a growing number of nurseries and schools based on the philosophy of Maria Montessori. The curriculum is based on structured rather than imaginative play. Children are encouraged to work independently. They are provided with specific natural materials to be used in sequence.

Steiner

Steiner nurseries and schools are often part of a community. Their founder, Rudolph Steiner, believed in healthy living in a community that fostered respect between child and adult. Children's temperaments are essential to the planning of the curriculum. Children with special needs are actively integrated into the community.

Sources of support for planning and curriculum development

The early years team

The team that you work in is key to supporting the curriculum.

Your supervisor will also have an important role in planning the curriculum and supporting you in the process. Your supervisor will have to ensure that:

- new concepts are introduced to children to expand their knowledge
- children are given the opportunity to work on a one-to-one basis
- the curriculum areas are covered
- you understand your role
- planning is reviewed and adapted.

Parents

Parents can also play an important role in the planning process. They are a valuable source of feedback, as they are the people who have the most knowledge about their child's interests and experiences. You can also ask them to bring in items for an activity or display, perhaps for an 'interest table'. Some parents may even be able to be involved in a curriculum activity, such as reading, cooking or talking to children about a subject of interest in group time.

Children

Children are also key to the planning of the curriculum. Their views and ideas should be respected. They can give information about their favourite activities, indicate who they would like to play with, or give ideas about how an activity can be extended. They can also be encouraged to bring relevant items in for the activity and share them with their peers.

Other sources

A range of other people can be drawn upon in supporting the curriculum:

- a special educational needs coordinator (SENCO) will be able to help you to create individual learning plans for children with special needs
- advisers from your local education authority or early years partnership, for example, may be able to advise your setting on planning and implementing the curriculum
- trainers may be asked to conduct some in-house staff training on delivering the curriculum.

In addition, visitors may be invited in to enrich the curriculum, such as a police officer when the children are learning about 'people who help us' or a trumpet player when they are learning about musical instruments.

Finally, there will be students and trainees (such as yourself), although they will need support in curriculum planning and delivery.

Reflect on your own practice

As you have seen, developing curriculum plans is an essential part of your role. Have a look at the statements below to assess whether you match up to the requirements. The statements all refer to the performance criteria for CCLD 309.1.

Performance criteria statement	Always	Sometimes	Never
Do I research and extract relevant information from curriculum documents?			
Do I cover each area of the curriculum, emphasising an integrated approach and using children's play as a key vehicle for delivery?			
Do I ensure that adequate resources are available for the implementation of the early education framework?			
Do I clearly define the roles and responsibilities of those who are involved?			
Do I include children, parents and families and external expertise in the planning process?			
Do I ensure my plans reflect inclusion and anti-discriminatory practice?			

Implement curriculum plans

Equipment, materials and activities that support a learning curriculum using play

A range of resources and equipment are essential to support children's play and learning. They may include:

- games
- books
- audio tapes/CDs
- story props
- story boards
- puppets/dolls
- sensory materials
- musical instruments.

Units 302 and 308 (pages 64 and 308) have separately looked at how to make a risk assessment of the resources and equipment used to support the curriculum.

While there are differences between the curricula of the home countries, they all endorse a play-led approach to children's learning. This means that the equipment, materials and particularly the activities that we provide need to support children's learning through play. In unit 312, we look at ways of promoting babies' and young children's development. Below is a chart outlining ways of providing key areas of the curriculum for children aged three to five years. Ideas for activities and equipment to support children's physical development can be found in unit 307.

Area of the curriculum	Examples of equipment and materials	Example of activities
Early mathematics	Sand, water, dough Measuring jugs, bottles Plastic and magnetic numbers, scales Birthday cards, straws	Hiding numbers in the sand tray Number lotto Making a birthday cake
Mark-making and early writing	Chalks, paints, pens, envelopes, pencils, registers Jotters, diaries and shopping lists in the home corner	Mark-making with large brushes and buckets of water outdoors Making letter shapes in gloop
Language and communication	Toy telephones, walkie-talkies Story tapes, tape recorders, puppets, props, dressing-up clothes, story bags	Role play areas e.g. shops, home corner Games such as 'Guess what is in this bag?'
Early reading	Selection of attractive books, catalogues Tents, benches and cushions for quiet reading Jigsaws	Opportunities for adults to read stories to individual or small group of children Story bags and story tapes Treasure hunt looking for names Snap, picture lotto
Creativity	Paint, collage materials, musical instruments, clay, dough, brushes, sensory materials gloop, staplers, tools	Collage and painting tables Playing musical instruments in small groups Making things for the role play area
ICT	Gadgets and toys with microchips e.g. speaking dolls, remote controlled cars, programmable toys such as Roamers, Pixies, digital phones	Steer the remote controlled car through the maze Take digital photos of friends
Early science exploration, investigation and awareness of environment	Sand, water and dough Construction toys and bricks Fabrics Magnifying boxes, glasses, wind chimes, staplers, sticky tape	Making dens outdoors Treasure hunts Making boats for water tray Digging, planting and playing outdoors

● Board game.

● Construction toys.

 Keys to good practice: Buying equipment and materials

When choosing what equipment and resources to buy, consider the following:

✓ Does it have a recognised safety mark?

✓ What age is it suitable for?

✓ Can it be stored appropriately?

✓ Is it versatile?

✓ Is it hygienic?

✓ How many children will benefit playing from it?

✓ Are spare parts easily available?

✓ Can the item provide a variety of play opportunities?

✓ Is the item suitable for children with special needs?

Planning the use of resources

In larger settings, equipment and resources may have to be shared and negotiation may be required over who will have what at a particular time. It is therefore important that the use of equipment and materials is properly planned as part of the curriculum provision. Table 309.3 indicates what a planning sheet might look like for a setting. A series of such planning sheets will allow everyone to know what is needed, when and by whom, and will fit well as part of the overall curriculum planning. In planning the use of resources, you should try to ensure that the equipment is used appropriately and that best use is made of the space available.

Table 309.3. Example planning sheet for use of resources

Planning sheet: 24 April, afternoon session, outside area			
Activity	**Learning goals**	**Equipment/resources**	**Group size**
Planting seeds	Physical development (fine motor skills) Creative development Knowledge and understanding of the world	Hand trowels Hand forks Watering cans Pots for seeds	4
Obstacle course	Physical development Social and emotional development	Hoops Tunnel Wooden blocks Bean bags	5
Chalk pictures	Physical development Creative development	Chalks	4

Equal opportunities and resources

Equality of opportunity is also important when providing resources and activities for children. Consider the diagram.

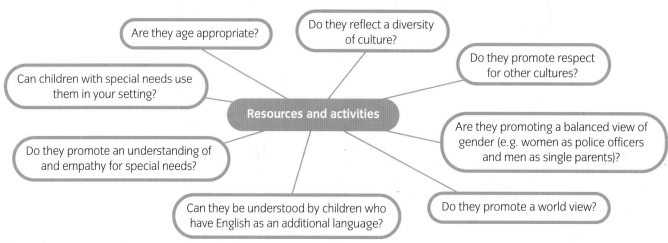

Equal opportunity and resources.

Effective use of ICT to support the curriculum

ICT (or information communication technology) is essential in this increasingly technological era. Children as young as two years can be encouraged to use the computer in a variety of different ways. This may be to:

- source information
- support an early learning goal, i.e numeracy and literacy
- create an individual piece of work such as a picture/plan.

Computers should be provided as part of a planned programme of play activities. A set of flat-screen computers at children's level, with appropriate programs, can be used in a group session for developing the appropriate skills. There is a range of early years programs available and children can quickly learn to use a simple program such as Paint, Other technology, including digital cameras and interactive whiteboards, can also be used to display photos or short fims of the children as well as to support literacy and numeracy.

Theoretical approaches to how children learn and develop

In order to plan an appropriate curriculum for the children in your care, it is important that you understand how children learn and what their thought processes are. You should observe children as part of the planning process (see Unit 303, page 86 on observation) but it is also essential that you understand the theory behind children's learning so that you can help to provide the appropriate curriculum. Unit 303 covers this area in some detail (see pages 84–156).

Did you know?

Children's learning is often described as cognitive development. This means the development of the way they think and learn. The activities and experiences that you provide are crucial to a child's cognitive development. You will need to consider the child's memory, perception and concentration in your planning and implementation.

● *Children learn from each other.*

Models of learning

There are four approaches to learning, as shown in the diagram overleaf. Children's education has been the subject of intense debate among psychologists as to where it fits in the nature–nurture dichotomy. Some psychologists believe that children's learning is more nature than nurture, which would imply that children can be allowed to progress and mature naturally, although of course with appropriate adult support.

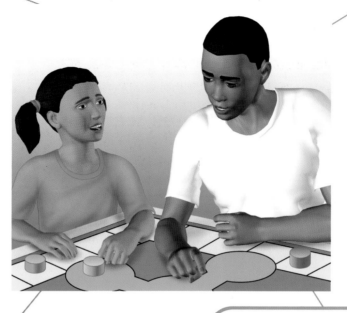

Social constructivist
The adult is the facilitator

Transmission model
The adult extends the child's learning by making it manageable

Adult-dominated learning
The child is largely occupied rather than learning

Natural learning
The adult supports the child's learning but does not always extend it

● *Four models of children's education.*

Observation

Plan an observation of a child in your setting playing with an experienced practitioner.

● Make sure your aim and rationale refer to the benefits of observing how a child might copy or imitate an adult who is playing with the child.
● Make a written record.
● Note how the child copies or imitates the adult.
● In your evaluation consider how the child benefited from playing with the adult.
● Refer to the relevant theory of children's learning. You might consider researching the theory in more depth.

How children's learning is affected by their stage of development

In order for children to learn effectively from play experiences, it is important that the curriculum offered is appropriate to their age and stage of development (see Unit 303, pages 105–120). Jean Piaget referred to three stages of learning that children under eight years of age will pass through (see Table 303.3, page 135). The research he did showed that children are at the centre of their own learning. This philosophy is fundamental to learning through play. While children must be supported by adults it is their needs that should influence the activities and experiences offered.

We can also observe how children become interested in exploring concepts through their play. Chris Athey developed Piaget's ideas of schemas and applied them to observing children's play. The table below shows some of the schemas that children might show us in their play and considers equipment and toys that might be used to support their learning.

Schema	Toys and equipment
Transporting Children are interested in moving things from one place to another, e.g. putting teddy in a pushchair, walking round with boxes	Pushchairs, wheelbarrows, wheeled toys, shopping bags, wheeled suitcases, handbags, brief cases
Connecting Children enjoy putting things together and separating them.	Construction toys, jigsaw puzzles, stickle bricks
Trajectory Children want to see how things move, e.g. they may throw objects or enjoy running themselves	Balls, bats, hoops, things that roll
Rotation Children are fascinated with things that go round or create patterns that rotate, e.g. putting their hands in the sand and making circles	Sensory materials including gloop, sand and water that will allow children to make circular marks. Toys and equipment that spin, e.g. tops, roundabouts
Enveloping Children are interested in containers and putting things inside each other. They may play with post-it toys or enjoy dropping things down drains!	Post-it toys, drainpipes for balls to be dropped down, tubes, bottles and funnels for water and sand tray, boxes with lids

The importance and implications of a differentiated approach to the provision of learning experiences for children

When providing a balanced curriculum for children you will need to be aware of their individual needs and ensure that they are met. This may mean adapting activities for some children, for example by allowing extra time or ensuring that they have extra adult support. This can apply to children who have a variety of needs, including those who are considered to be advanced in their learning. Differentiation should be clear in curriculum plans.

Some children may have an 'individual learning plan' (ILP), which can guide the practitioner as to how activities should be planned for them to meet their specific needs. When planning activities for children with an ILP so that they can benefit from the curriculum plan, the following need to be considered:

- equipment
- resources
- staffing
- adaptation of activities
- parents' wishes.

It is important to remember that although some children may have advanced skills for their age, their emotional needs are likely still to be age-appropriate. In this situation it is not always the best practice to move children to a higher age group, as they may find it difficult emotionally and socially.

Case study 1: English as an additional language

Natalia is Italian and has English as an additional language. She is finding it difficult to join in certain activities. She is also shy in her play with other children. Sue, her key worker, plans a cooking activity making a special kind of Italian biscuit. She makes notes about how she will encourage Natalia to talk about the biscuits, share some of the activity with another child, such as mixing, and help another child with a specific clearing up task. In this way she hopes to give Natalia the confidence to comment on the activity and to integrate with other children in a small group.

1. *Why do you think Sue chose to cook Italian biscuits?*
2. *How did Sue differentiate the activity to support Natalia's needs?*
3. *How do you think Sue might have involved Natalia's parents in planning the activity?*

Why formal experiences might be inappropriate

All the curricula of the home countries support the need for children's learning to be supported through play. This is because children find it easier to concentrate and learn when they are playing. Formally teaching young children is not considered to be good practice. This is because we know that young children need to be active in order to learn. They also benefit when activities and experiences are child-centred. Formal teaching requires children to be passive and so is usually ineffective. Interestingly, children show in their behaviour that formal experiences do not suit them. Most children fidget, lose concentration and may be unwilling in the first place to come and sit down.

The effects of low self-esteem and lack of confidence on learning

The importance of children's self-esteem and confidence in early years settings is considered in detail in Unit 308. In order for the curriculum to develop children's self-esteem, it should promote their independence. This might be done by involving children in any of the following ways:

- helping to set out and clear away activities
- putting on and taking off own aprons and shoes, and so on
- choosing resources and activities
- helping to plan activities
- having opinions listened to
- receiving praise
- having work displayed
- using resources independently if appropriate.

The benefits to children of learning through play

In order to devise an appropriate **curriculum plan** for children that is based on play, you will need to have an understanding of the theories about how they learn. You will also need to explore the benefits to children of learning through play. To understand the theories of how children learn, see the sections on pages 129–137 in Unit 303.

Key terms

A **curriculum plan** is an arrangement of activities and experiences.

● *A child learning through play.*

Table 309.4 summarises the way in which children learn through play at different stages of their development.

Table 309.4. Learning through play at different ages

Age	Developing through play
Birth to 6 months	• Watching adults closely • Exploration through mouth and hands • Playing alone with toys such as rattles and baby gyms
6–12 months	• Exploration through mouth and touch • Watching and copying adults • Repeating movements (e.g. dropping a rattle) • Playing games such as peek-a-boo • Exploring toys (e.g. treasure baskets) alone
12–18 months	• Learning through trial and error (e.g. banging two bricks to discover the sound they make) • Repeating actions that they have enjoyed (e.g. clapping) • Starting to play with adults and notice other children • Playing by themselves and chatting to themselves
18 months–2 years	• Learning through trial and error • Imitating other adults and children • Exploring through taste • Repeating actions (e.g. taking objects in and out of boxes) • Watching other children but not joining in • Enjoying playing with adults
2–3 years	• Starting to reason, although still using trial and error • Imitating adults and other children • Starting to use symbols in play (e.g. a yogurt pot becomes a teacup) • Starting to play alongside other children • Mostly pretend play (e.g. singing to teddies)
3–4 years	• Developing reasoning skills and asking questions (e.g. 'Why?') • Concentrating for longer periods on play activities that they are interested in • Recognising shapes and letters • Solving jigsaw puzzles through reasoning and trial and error • Taking turns • Playing cooperatively with other children • Playing imaginatively (e.g. dressing up, the home corner)
4–6 years	• Showing a clearer understanding • Using reason based on their own experience • Starting to use and understand symbols (e.g. reading and writing) • Starting to understand simple rules in games • Playing cooperatively, taking turns and enjoying table-top games

continued on next page

6–8 years	• Enjoying using rules and understanding the need for rules
	• Using reasoning skills but still sometimes learning through trial and error
	• Playing in small groups and making up own games
	• Not always coping with losing
	• Often preferring to play with children of their own gender

How children benefit by learning through play

Play is essential for children to develop into confident adults who are able to reach their potential. Play for a young child is essential to development. Every child needs to have the opportunity to explore and experiment. If appropriate play is encouraged, children can benefit by developing their self-esteem.

Carefully consider this statement made by Vygotsky, who believed in free play and who felt that adults had a significant part to play in extending a child's thinking: 'In play, a child always behaves beyond his average age, above his daily behaviour; in play it is as though he were a head taller than his normal self'.

● *A head taller than his normal self.*

Categories of play

There are two categories of play:
● *Spontaneous play* is when children play in their own way and, making their own choices, are able to build their own self-esteem and confidence.
● *Structured play* is when play is planned and supported by adults.

Consider the 'spiral of learning' as defined by Janet Moyles (1989): 'Rather like a pebble on a pond, the ripples from the exploratory free play through directed play and back to enhanced and enriched free play, allowed a spiral of learning spreading ever outwards into wider experiences for the children and upwards into the accretion of knowledge and skills.' You will recognise this approach to play and the fact that there is a clear link between children playing on their own and being directed by an adult. Free play often follows a directed play session, and gives children a chance to explore and challenge concepts they have learnt in an adult-led activity.

Children from birth to eight can benefit from positive structured and unstructured play experiences.

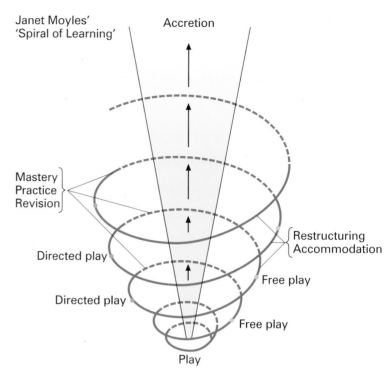

● *Janet Hoyle's Spiral of Teaching*

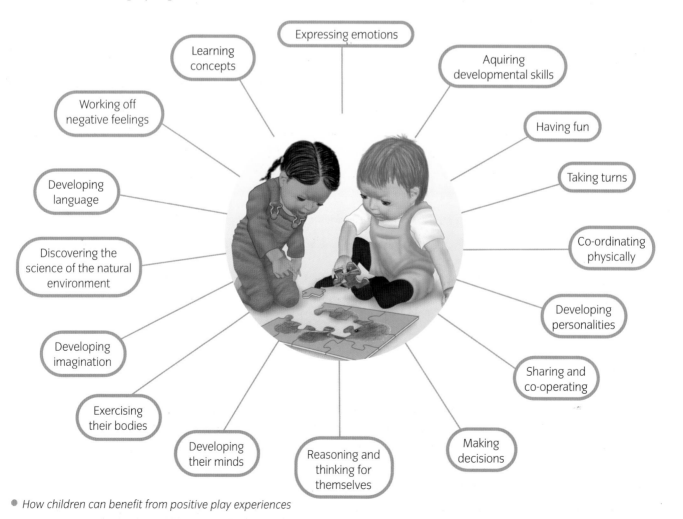

● *How children can benefit from positive play experiences*

Case study 2: Spiral of learning

Tia and Suanita, who are both two and a half years old, have been making small cakes with Alfie, who is one of the qualified practitioners in the pre-school group they attend. They had great fun stirring the mixture. The next day they are playing in the sand. Tia starts stirring sand in a large container. Suanita starts to copy her. Alfie sits alongside them and gently starts to remind them about the cake making. Tia gives Alfie a piece of 'sand cake' to taste. He pretends to eat it and to the delight of Tia and Suanita pats his tummy in appreciation.

1. *How do you think Tia and Suanita benefited from the cooking activity?*
2. *What were Tia and Suanita doing when they were making sand cakes?*
3. *Comment on how you think Alfie supported Tia and Suanita's play.*

Planning an integrated curriculum based on play

Planning is key to the effectiveness of any early years curriculum. Settings plan curricula in a variety of ways. Most find a way of planning that suits their needs. Plans will also vary according to the objectives or areas of development/learning to be considered. Each child will need to be considered and observed in order to be provided with appropriate activities and experiences in the setting.

Case study 3: Observation and assessment

The children at Ridings Children's Centre were enjoying the newly designed outdoor play space. It had a variety of wooden equipment, tactile surfaces, growing areas, activity areas, story circles and an area for bikes, trucks and scooters. The staff were excited about it but they noticed that the children were generally finding it difficult to use areas appropriately. Three children in particular seem daunted by the whole experience.

The early years team decided to observe the children using the area for two weeks. As a result of their observations the team decided that they needed to offer a variety of activities to introduce the outdoor areas, as they had previously done with indoor experiences. It was decided that individual staff members would be responsible for planning and leading activities in each area, supporting different areas of the curriculum. It was also decided to introduce a quiet covered willow area with benches that could be private but visible to adults.

In a curriculum review six weeks later the team were pleased that the area was more effective in supporting the children's learning.

1. *Why was the play area initially not as successful as the team had hoped?*
2. *How do you think observing the children using the area improved the provision?*
3. *How do you think the creation of the safe quiet area might have supported the small group of children who found the new outdoor play area daunting?*
4. *How did the team evaluate the new outdoor provision?*

Keys to good practice: Effective planning

✓ Ensure the planned activities are appropriate for the ages and developmental stages of the children involved.

✓ Take into account the interests of children.

✓ Cover all aspects of children's learning and development, with reference to the appropriate curriculum.

✓ Support children's individual needs, including special educational needs and English as an additional language (EAL).

✓ Consider and promote children's health and safety.

✓ Involve parents, visitors and other professionals.

✓ Encourage equality of opportunity and diversity.

An effective curriculum comprises many different tasks carried out by practitioners, children and their parents. Look at the planning of children's learning outlined below and consider what your part is in the **planning cycle**.

Key terms

The **planning cycle** is a constant cycle of planning, implementing and reviewing/evaluating.

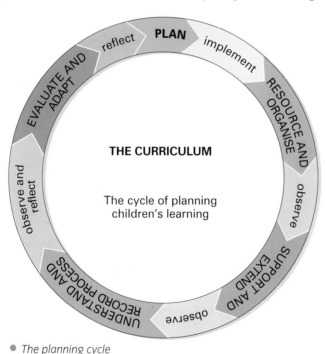

● The planning cycle

The five areas of play

Whatever the curriculum model you are involved in planning, it will consider the five areas of play shown in Table 309.5. When integrating these five areas into the curriculum, it is important to remember the following points:

● children develop at different rates

● children will have cultural as well as developmental needs

● children with special needs may require a play-based curriculum beyond the age of eight.

Table 309.5. The five areas of play

Type of play	Characteristics
Creative play	Children are encouraged to explore and experiment in their play
Physical play	Children are encouraged to exercise and develop the large and small muscles in their body through a variety of experiences and activities
Imaginative play	Children are encouraged to use their imaginations to play creatively and explore their own world
Manipulative play	Involves children using their hands
Social play	Children learn to interact and communicate with each other and with other adults

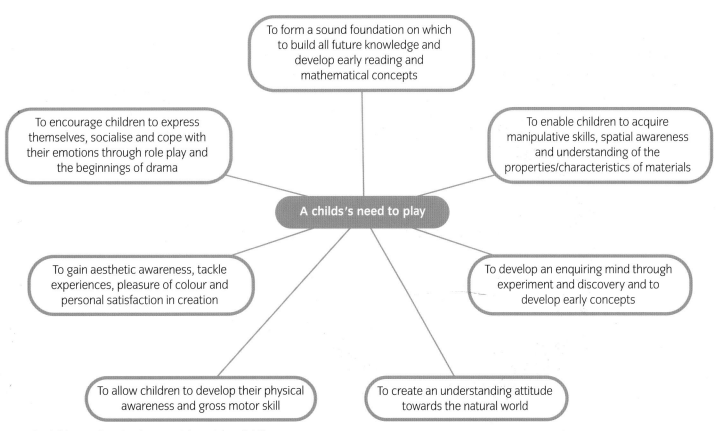

● *Children's play develops a wide variety of skills.*

Flexible planning

Flexibility can enrich the curriculum if you are aware of its value and relaxed about changes to your planning. It is dangerous to be so rigid in your planning that children's interests and spontaneous learning are not allowed for. In addition, children's reactions to a planned activity will not always be what you expect. The key to flexibility is to learn from any unplanned experiences that may arise and to consider the effect that they may have on any future planning.

Keys to good practice: Flexible planning

✓ Allow for spontaneity, such as the rare fall of snow or the visit of a parent with a new sibling.

✓ Do not discourage children if they bring in something to share that does not fit in with the curriculum topic (e.g. a child brings in a dried wasps' nest when the subject is transport).

✓ Do not worry if children react differently to a situation than you expected (e.g. a child cries when you use a dragon puppet and starts other children crying). It does not matter if you have to stop the activity to explore their reactions or even abandon the activity altogether.

Long, medium and short term planning

Most settings have separate curriculum plans for the long, medium and short term (Table 309.6), with each in turn being based on the wider objectives of the longer term plans.

Table 309.6. Long, medium and short term plans

Plan	Coverage/characteristics
Long term	Usually covers a three-month period, a term or a year
	Provides a curriculum overview
	Based on principles of good early years practice
	Reviews what children need to learn and how this will be implemented
	All areas of learning are considered
	Meets development plan or school improvement plan (SIP) as required by Ofsted
	Relates to policies and procedures of setting
	Ensures advance planning and consideration of specific activities (e.g. festivals, outings)
	Ensures effective use of resources and equipment
Medium term	Usually covers two weeks to a month
	Based on child observations
	Profiles and assessments are taken into consideration
	Differentiation is considered
	May focus on an area of the long term plan (e.g. a theme or an area of learning)
	Will need to be flexible and constantly reviewed
Short term	Daily plan
	Specific but flexible
	May be used to target children's specific needs
	Resources and role of adult specified

Keys to good practice: The curriculum plan

✓ Children's needs are observed and assessed.

✓ Parents, children, colleagues and other professionals are consulted.

✓ Reference is made to the appropriate curriculum.

✓ The aims and objectives of the plan are agreed.

✓ A timescale is established.

✓ Experiences and activities are planned that will meet the aim of the plan.

✓ Daily and weekly plans are produced.

✓ Plans are reviewed and evaluated.

The figure below shows a one-week curriculum plan for children aged three to five years produced by a trainee on placement at a state-run nursery school. This plan aimed to promote the children's creative development. The current theme within the nursery was Africa and so some of the activities were related to that theme. Within the plan, promoting learning of another culture is closely linked to creative development, but is also linked to knowledge and understanding of the world and social and emotional development. The table overleaf shows the detailed outline of the activities set out in the plan, and the table on page 355 shows the brief activity plans for four of the sessions indicated in the weekly plan. Finally, and in much greater detail still, the detailed activity plan for 'Table printing' is shown on page 356.

Time	Monday	Tuesday	Wednesday	Thursday	Friday
9.00 – 9.15	Settling in	Settling in	Settling in	Settling in	Settling in
9.15 – 11.15	Creative modelling	Drawing – variety	Painting – table printing	Sensory room available	Playdough – cutters/trays
11.15 – 11.45	Group time	Group time	Group time	Group time	Group time
11.45 – 12.30	LUNCH	LUNCH	LUNCH	LUNCH	LUNCH
12.30 – 1.00	Outside play	Outside play	Outside play	Outside play	Outside play
1.00 – 3.00	Textured materials	Musical instruments	Construction – Lego	African artefacts	Music and dancing
3.00 – 3.20	Group time	Group time	Group time	Group time	Group time
3.20 – 3.30	Parents arrive	Parents arrive	Parents arrive	Parents arrive	Parents arrive

● *One-week curriculum plan for three- to five-year-olds, incorporating the theme 'Africa' and aimed at promoting creative development in particular. (Courtesy of Michelle McElroy.)*

Activity and resources	Outcomes	Adult role
Creative modelling Empty boxes/cartons, card, paper, glue, tape, scissors, etc.	• Use available resources to create objects • Promotes creative use of resources	• Plan activities/experiences that support the childrens' learning • Provide a wide range of materials/resources • Consider health and safety issues, explaining if something is unsafe and why • Allow children time to complete activities at their own pace • Promote learning by making suggestions/asking questions • Introduce new vocabulary • Allow children to explore new sounds/sensory experiences • Introduce music or artefacts from a variety of cultures (in this case African) • Show interest in, but do not inhibit, children's play • Promote development of new learnt skills • Be sensitive to and encourage less confident children • Encourage and praise individual flair
Exploring textured materials Variety of materials with different textures, e.g. smooth, furry	• Use senses to explore colour and texture in 2 and 3 dimensions • Begin to describe the texture of materials	
Drawing – variety Variety of coloured paper and card, chalks, wax crayons, pencils	• Experiment with different media • Develops personal creativity by exploring texture	
Playing musical instruments/singing Range of instruments, including African, e.g. drums	• Use senses and explore different sounds of instruments • Promotes self-expression through music	
Painting – table printing Variety of coloured paints –table surface/tray, white paper	• Experiment with the colours and texture of paint • Develops personal creativity	
Construction – Lego Construction base boards/base cloth – Lego bricks, animals, cars, people	• Begin to construct and work creatively on a large and small scale • Promotes creative use of resources	
Sensory room Relaxing background music and equipment in sensory room	• Explore variety of media/materials using senses • Opportunity to respond to experience	
African artefacts (role play) Variety of artefacts – masks, native animals, cloths, jewellery, carvings	• Explore and experiment with artefacts from a different culture • Encourages role play/imagination	
Playdough – cutters / trays Range of coloured playdough and cutters, rolling pins, tea set etc.	• Explore variety of media that can be used for construction • Encourages role-play / imagination	
Music and dancing Selection of different types of music, CD/tape player	• Encourages and allows children to express themselves through creative movement and move to music	

● *Detailed outline of activities for the plan shown in Figure 309.1. (Courtesy of Gemma Hall.)*

Activity	Details	Early learning goals for creative development specifically related to activity
Exploring textured materials	A table will be set out with a variety of materials with different textures, e.g. smooth, furry. The children will be encouraged to feel the materials and describe them. They should use their senses to explore the new textures, and use appropriate language to discuss the materials. The children should be encouraged to describe what the materials look and feel like. If necessary, new language should be introduced, e. g. colours and textures. The children could be asked to think about items that are made from material, e.g. clothes, cushions, curtains, and say which material they think it is made from, e.g. a shiny fabric could be used to make a party dress.	• Exploring colour and texture in 2 and 3 dimensions • Responding to senses (sight, touch) • Allowing children with impairments, such as of sight or hearing, to participate in activities which promote the use of other senses
Table printing	There will be a large tray on the table. Several pots of different coloured paint will be set out alongside the tray, as will a pile of white paper. The children choose one or two colours and pour (with adult supervision) a little of the paint into the tray. They then mix the paint using their hands, moving it over the surface of the tray. Next they draw a picture or pattern in the paint. When they are happy with their design a piece of paper is laid on top. When the paper is lifted, their picture will be printed onto the paper.	• Encouraging self-expression and personal creativity • Responding to senses (sight, touch) • Exploring colour and texture
Sensory Room	The Sensory Room will be set up to its full potential. This includes the fibre optic lights, bubble tube, projector, UV light and music. The music will be appropriate to the desired atmosphere – in this case, relaxation and the use of senses. Other equipment can be introduced to encourage the use of senses, for example scented beanbags. The children will be guided to use their senses to explore their surrounding and the items within it.	• Responding to senses (sight, hearing, smell, touch) • Exploring a variety of media and materials • Allowing children with impairments such as sight, hearing, to participate in activities which promote the use of other senses
African artefacts	A table will be set up with a variety of artefacts, to possibly include masks, native animals, cloths, jewellery, carvings and instruments. An adult should be available to talk to the children about Africa and the artefacts, promoting learning of the world. However, if an adult is not present the children can use the artefacts as props for role play.	• Using imagination in imaginative and role play and stories • Stimulating different ways of thinking

● *Brief activity plans for four of the sessions from the plan shown in Figure 309.1. (Courtesy of Gemma Hall.)*

Activity: Table printing
Number of children: max. 4
Setting: Art table in 'Apple Tree'
Activity time: 9.15–11.00
Age of children: 3–5
Preparation time: 15 minutes
Cleaning up time: 15 minutes

Resources:
• Large tray
• 4 aprons
• Ready mixed paint (blue, red, yellow)
• 3 large paintbrushes
• A3 and A4 white paper
• Pencil
• Wipe-clean cloth to cover table
• Bowl of warm soapy water

Key learning intentions (aim):
self-expression
exploring the texture of paint
exploring colours
using senses to explore paint
(sight, touch)

Rationale:
This activity is designed to promote the children's creative development. Through exploring the texture and colour of paint, the children will use their senses in a variety of ways (touch and sight). They will also be shown a new technique that will enable them to express themselves without being restricted to a paintbrush or pencil. This technique will encourage creative flair by allowing the children to make an individual design. Their design could be a pattern, a picture or simply a swirl.

Preparation:
• Put the wipe-clean cloth on the table, placing the tray on top of the cloth
• Mix red, yellow and blue powder paints in a large container and pour a small amount into smaller containers, to be placed on the table
• Find A3 and A4 paper and place on the table
• Prepare a bowl of warm soapy water and put in the low sink in the painting area

Implementation:
• As children approach the table, ask them to put an apron on (max. 4 children)
• To demonstrate – explaining why:
• Pour a little paint into the tray
• Using both hands, move the paint around the tray so that it is spread thinly
• Draw a picture or pattern in the paint using a finger (or fingers)
• Gently place a piece of paper on the design, smooth down and carefully remove
• Hold up the paper up and show them the design, explaining what's happened
• If the children would like to participate, pour different paints in different areas of the tray, allowing them to mix them if they wish
• Encourage them to draw a pattern/picture, then help them write their name on a piece of paper before making a print
• Ask the child to put their paper on the drying rack
• As more children approach, supervise taking turns, telling them only 4 children can paint at a time
• Replenish paint and paper when necessary

Clearing up:
• When the children have finished at the table, direct them to the bowl of soapy water
• Ensure they dry their hands thoroughly
• Ask them to remove their aprons and hang them up, helping where necessary
• Remove the paint from the table and either wash out empty pots and brushes or cover pots with paint remaining
• Clean out the tray and wipe the tablecloth
• Put away and tidy all equipment

Creative development:	Personal, social and emotional development:
• Introduce a new painting technique • Encourage self-expression and personal creativity through paint • Responding to senses (sight, touch) • Explore the texture of paint • Experiment by mixing colours	• Sharing, taking turns • Working as part of a group • Concentrating on the activity • Building confidence in own achievements and abilities
Physical development:	Communication, language and literacy:
• Develop and promote hand–eye co-ordination through drawing pictures/patterns in the paint • Promote gross motor skills by walking round the table	• Talk about the texture and colours of paint • Talk and listen to others • Promote writing and drawing skills
Knowledge and understanding of the world:	Mathematical development:
• Learn about printing and patterns • Investigate materials using senses	• Experimenting with and learning about patterns • Counting the number of children round the table
Specific language to be developed:	
• Describing the feel of paint and the colours • Discuss the technique and children's work	

● *Detailed plan for the activity 'Table printing'. (Courtesy of Gemma Hall.)*

Preparing detailed plans

It would be unrealistic to fill in a very detailed plan for every activity, but plans can be useful on occasion and are certainly a good learning exercise. A detailed plan should cover the following points:

- the reason for the activity
- the number of children the activity is planned for
- group size
- the age of the children
- preparation time
- length of activity
- resources/equipment
- the intended learning outcomes
- how the activity is carried out (implementation).

Routines as part of the curriculum

Routines are integral to the implementation of the curriculum. They allow children to learn in a secure situation. Routines will vary from setting to setting but they are generally centred around meals, rest or sleep for younger children, and particular activities.

The outline below shows a routine plan devised for a five-month-old African girl, devised by a trainee. The child was her parents' firstborn and was being cared for at home by a live-in nanny. When planning such a routine it is important to remember that the times of the routine should be

OUTLINE OF 24-hour ROUTINE FOR BABY	
6.45 a.m.	Wakes up, her nappy is checked and changed if appropriate and she plays with her parents while her bottle is warmed.
7.00 a.m.	Morning bottle, 180 ml (given by either parent).
7.20 a.m.	Handover from parents to nanny.
7.30 a.m.	Wash (top and tail) and change of nappy and clothes.
8.00–9.30 a.m.	Play – swimming – 'free play' – activity frame, soft and musical toys etc.
9.30–11.30 a.m.	Morning sleep Nappy checked and changed on waking.
11.45 a.m.	Bottle, 180 ml.
12.15–1.30 p.m.	Play or outings – walk to park, baby group, baby gym etc.
1.30–3.00 p.m.	Afternoon sleep
3.00 p.m.	Bottle, 180 ml. Nappy checked and changed after bottle.
3.30 p.m.	Play – baby massage, treasure basket, activity frame etc.
6.00 p.m.	Bath and dress ready for bed.
6.30 p.m.	Bottle, 180 ml.
7.00 p.m.	Bed.
7.15 p.m.	Handover from nanny to parents – this is flexible as sometimes a parent may come home earlier or later depending on their daily work commitments.
10.00 p.m.	Final bottle, 120 ml. Nappy checked and changed if necessary. (Is given by either parents or nanny – depending on parents' routine)
10.30 p.m.–6.45 a.m.	Sleep. Child is seen to by the nanny should she wake during the night.

● Routine planned for a five-month-old baby. (Courtesy of Michelle McElroy.)

flexible and change in line with the individual needs of the child and parents. The activities and experiences included in this example are important to a baby's overall development. The toys and activities that are provided take into account her age and stage of development and her developmental needs. Therefore, as she grows and develops, these will change. The routine aims to take a holistic approach to the child's development by encouraging her physical development through activities such as nappy changing, bathing and hanging toys in her cot and pram. Exploring treasure baskets and other toys encourages her cognitive development. Listening to music and nursery rhymes and being around adults and other children at baby and toddler groups encourages language development. Her emotional development is encouraged through interaction with her carers and the security provided by the routine. Attending baby and toddler groups, going on outings and walks and interacting with her carers encourage her social development.

Case study 4: Routines

Consider the morning routine of a group of six children aged 18 months to three years in a day nursery:

- 8.00 a.m. Welcome. A choice of activities available indoors and out
- 8.45 a.m. Group time
- 9.00 a.m. A choice of activities and an adult-led activity
- 9.45 a.m. A snack and drink sitting around the table
- 10.00 a.m. Outdoor play
- 11.15 a.m. Book sharing and story time
- 11.45 a.m. Washing hands and going to the toilet
- 12.00 p.m. Lunch

During snack time, the children ate raisins and pieces of banana and apple. Jo, who was nearly three, gave all the children a bowl. Tom, aged two, helped Christine (a qualified practitioner) to offer children the fruit to put in their bowls. The children were given the choice of banana or apple or both. Chris encouraged the children to say thank you and praised Tom for helping her. The children were encouraged to pour their own milk or water from a small jug, although there was the odd spillage. Two of the younger children helped to clear the bowls away.

The nursery had started to use *Birth to Three Matters* as a basis to its curriculum planning. Obtain a copy of *Birth to Three Matters* and read in more detail about the four aspects of this curriculum.

1. *What are the four curriculum aspects?*
2. *Which aspects were covered during snack time?*
3. *How do you think the children were developing self-assurance during this snack time? Which component of the curriculum is this an aspect of?*
4. *Try to identify some other components of* Birth to Three Matters *that are being developed in this activity.*

How to support and extend play opportunities to encourage learning

How to support and extend play opportunities to encourage learning

The skill in working with children is often to know when to support, show and intervene in their play and when to step back. Ideally, the curriculum plan should contain a mixture of spontaneous as well as structured activities.

- Observe children carefully so that activities build upon their interests, knowledge and understanding.
- Help children make connections between what they are doing and what they have done before.
- Allow plenty of time for children to play and explore.
- Avoid interrogating children, but extend their thinking by asking interested questions.
- Encourage children to repeat activities, but sometimes vary them by adding in a new material or challenge.
- Look out for sensory activities such as sand, water and dough as these help children to concentrate.
- Avoid taking over children's play if they are already benefiting and learning
- Allow children to mix play materials as this allows for richer play.
- Encourage children to plan for their own play.
- Make sure that there are varied play opportunities to appeal to different interests of children.
- Show children how something works or how to play a game, but then give them an opportunity to do it for themselves.

One of the most important ways in which you can support the planning of any curriculum is through the way in which you support children's development. You should consider:

- how to extend children's attention span and memory
- how to promote children's language development
- how to develop children's awareness and understanding of sensory experiences
- how to develop children's understanding of mathematics and science
- how to develop children's imagination and creativity.

Attention span and memory

It is essential that children are given time to complete their tasks. Have a realistic idea of how long an activity will take and create the best possible environment to allow children to concentrate exclusively on the activity. Factors to consider are:

- lighting – either too little or too much can be distracting
- temperature of room
- noise

- room plan
- other people – for instance other children engaged in a different activity, visitors, adults talking.

Children's memory can be encouraged by careful questioning to prompt recall. Children easily muddle the order of events, but with support from early years practitioners they will learn to sequence events. To encourage this, ensure they have time to talk and give plenty of praise and encouragement. Use prompts, such as 'And what happened next?' Ask them about how they felt: emotions will often prompt the recall of events.

Language development

Early years practitioners can help children develop language by organising and planning a range of activities and materials that encourage the use and extension of language.

What type of adult support is required?

Will children with communication difficulties be able to join in?

Can the activity be developed to extend children's language if required?

Will the activity encourage children to listen to each other?

Planning a successful language activity

Is the activity appropriate for children's stage of development?

Will the activity generate stereotypical play?

Is the activity interesting?

- *A range of activities and materials encourage the use and extension of language.*

Ensure that the activity is at the right level. If it is too advanced it will end in failure and the children will become frustrated. Look for activities that will allow children of different abilities to participate equally. For example, cutting and sticking activities with a wide range of different materials (fabric, pasta, thread, ribbon etc.) will encourage children to learn new words.

The following activities and equipment are found in nearly all early years settings and can be regarded as core activities to develop language:

- dressing up and imaginative play areas
- sand
- water
- painting and drawing.

Dressing up encourages role play, allowing children to create their own worlds. A good selection of props allows them to explore a variety of situations, all with their own particular vocabulary.

Sensory development

Children are surrounded by sensory experiences – experiences that involve one or more of our five senses – and senses play a vital part in all areas of learning. Babies and young children in particular rely on taste, touch and smell. As we get older, sights, sounds and smells all prompt memory recall. When you are planning activities for children you need to ensure that you are using all their senses as part of the development process.

Case study

Olwen was playing in the nursery garden with some three- and four-year-old children. One of the children thought she heard a bird singing a nursery rhyme! Olwen used this imaginative opportunity to encourage the children to discriminate between different birds' songs by asking them to work out which other rhymes the birds were singing.

This extended the children's listening skills in an imaginative and fun way. Can you think of any other learning opportunities she could have made out of the experience?

Mathematics and science

Children are learning mathematical and scientific skills all the time. As an early years worker you can enhance that learning by providing suitable activities to introduce and reinforce concepts. Remember, mathematics does just not just mean numeracy; it includes concepts such as colour, size, pattern, sequencing and matching.

Case study

On her birthday, four-year-old Melissa brought some sweets into nursery to share among her friends. This provided opportunities for sorting, counting, sequencing and vocabulary such as 'more', 'less' and 'the same'.

1. *Suggest ways in which these opportunities could be used.*
2. *Describe some extension activities to build on what has been learnt.*

Science is an aspect of cooking, water and sand play, nature study and so on. Concepts such as prediction and observation are also the foundations of scientific thought and can be introduced into play very easily. For instance, in a cooking activity, you could ask the children what they think will happen when you add two ingredients together (prediction), then test their hypothesis by seeing what actually does happen (observation).

Creativity

Creativity should be integral to all children's play. Imagination cannot be taught, but it can be encouraged and stimulated by providing the right environment. As we have seen, dressing up is a prime example of promoting imaginative play, as are small world toys and a well-equipped home corner. Children should be encouraged to explore the world around them. Creative play can combine physical, social, emotional and intellectual skills.

Individual learning styles and preferences

Learning involves the processing of information. This can be done in different ways, and much research has been done into learning styles. These are outlined in Table 309.7. You will see that these styles are linked to the senses. Children (and adults) will have their preferred ways (i.e. those that best allow them to process information), but even these will be used differently by each child. Moreover, children may adopt different learning styles at different stages, or may combine styles.

Table 309.7. Styles of learning

Check it out

Consider a time recently when you have studied something for your Level 3 qualification. Carefully consider your own learning style.

- Do you have one clear learning style, or a combination?
- Do you think your learning style is always like this?
- Were you surprised at the results? Do you think they reflect your personality?

Learning style	Examples/characteristics of learners
Visual	Like to watch people speak as well as listen
	Look for shapes and forms in words and numbers
	Enjoy pictures in books
	Enjoy visual descriptions

continued on next page

Learning style	Examples/characteristics of learners
Auditory	Listeners and talkers
	Listeners retain and recall the spoken word
	Talkers have to hear a voice to process information
	Prefer the spoken word
	Love different kinds of voices
	Enjoy involved explanations
	Enjoy communication with others and themselves
	When auditory learners read, they hear themselves speak the word
Kinaesthetic	Need to sense relative position and movement
	Like to examine, touch and feel in order to learn
Tactile	Want to touch, experiment and handle
	Often perceived as disruptive

By familiarising yourself with the ways in which individual children learn and their preferences, you will provide a curriculum that helps them to develop to their full potential. Table 309.8 suggests how you can support children's learning styles and preferences through observation and curriculum planning.

Table 309.8. Observation of children's learning styles and preferences and the implications for curriculum planning

Area for observation	Examples of observations	Implications for curriculum planning
Play preferences	A small baby may really enjoy kicking on a mat	Build on preferences with experiences you offer in the curriculum
	A toddler may have a favourite soft toy	
	A five-year-old child may particularly enjoy Lego	Encourage child to make a Lego bus after a trip to town on the bus
Routines	Child likes to read a book or play a puzzle instead of sleeping at rest times, but is later drowsy	Ensure activities take place when a child is less tired
		Talk to parents and colleagues
		Be aware of the stage of the child's development
Development	Child is crawling	Provide appropriate resources (e.g. tunnel for child to crawl through)
	Toddler tantrums	Talk to parents
		Talk to colleagues

continued on next page

continued from previous page

Area for observation	Examples of observations	Implications for curriculum planning
Individual needs	Child is unsettled and needs a familiar routine	Talk to parents
	Child has cultural needs	Talk to child
	Child has special dietary, learning, physical or health needs	Consult colleagues and other professionals as appropriate (e.g. special educational needs coordinator)
		Follow individual learning plan (ILP) if appropriate
		Adapt curriculum as needed
		Understand stage of development
		Integrate needs of child
		Provide equipment and resources as appropriate

How you adapt your practice to meet the individual needs of all the children in your setting, including different ages, gender, culture, abilities and learning styles

When working with children in your setting you must carefully consider the following needs and ensure that your practice reflects this:

- ages of children
- gender
- culture and ethnicity
- learning needs
- learning styles.

Consider the Table 309.9 below:

Table 309.9

Children's needs	Good practice
Ages of children	Be aware of the way you communicate, the level at which children are involved and can take responsibility, the level of supervision, the type of activities you offer.
Gender	Ensure that children are not discriminated against in any way because of their gender and that they have access to all activities and experiences.
Culture	Communicate appropriately, reflect the culture of child in your setting, adapt activities to meet and respect child's cultural needs, work closely with parents.
Learning needs	Observe children, work closely with SENCO and parents, adapt activities and experiences accordingly, provide appropriate equipment and resources.

Keys to good practice: English as an additional language

Some children with EAL (English as an additional language) may not have any understanding of English at all. However, they should be given the same opportunities as other children. You can help by:

✓ providing good-quality picture books

✓ ensuring cultural messages in books, games and so on are appropriate and do not carry negative messages

✓ providing plenty of tactile experiences as a way of communicating and absorbing the English language

✓ providing appropriate role-play areas.

Reflect on your own practice

As you have seen, implementing the curriculum is an essential part of your role. Have a look at the statements below to assess whether you match up to the requirements. The statements all refer to the performance criteria for CCLD 309.2.

Performance criteria statement	Always	Sometimes	Never
Do I communicate curriculum plans to all relevant people?			
Do I provide planned curriculum activities and experiences that meet the needs of the children?			
Do I use everyday routines to enhance learning?			
Do I encourage children's participation, ensuring a balance between planned activities and freely chosen play?			
Do I support and extend play to encourage learning, drawing on my knowledge of individual children and their preferred learning styles?			
Do I seek additional support if children are not progressing as expected?			
Do I keep appropriate records?			

Monitor implementation of curriculum frameworks

The importance of monitoring provision and the need for accountability to children, parents, families and other agencies

It is important to monitor activities so that you can evaluate their success. This will in turn allow you to make any necessary changes to the curriculum. Evaluating the work you do with children can help you to plan more effectively in the future and help you to decide how future curriculum plans should be drawn up. Observations and assessments are ways in which the monitoring can be performed, and these are detailed in Unit 303 (see pages 89–94).

You may have to be accountable to a number of people when monitoring the provision in your setting. These could include:

- health visitors/workers
- educational psychologists
- advisers, mentors, monitoring groups
- Ofsted
- professionals from other settings
- co-workers
- parents
- the children themselves.

Asking children for their views

Simply listening to children can inform the process of monitoring provision. You can ask older children directly about their favourite activities and about those that have not held their interest. In some cases you may find that a strong indicator as to whether children are enjoying themselves is their friendships. This may mean planning some activities and experiences so as to allow children to work and play alongside their friends.

Older children can also give you ideas about extension activities. Most settings that take the time to ask for children's views find that it is rewarding and that children are pleased to be given the opportunity to talk about what they are doing.

Involving parents

Parents can provide you with valuable feedback, because often children will talk to them about what they have done and enjoyed. Children who are quiet in settings are sometimes talkative with their parents. Listening to parents' views may reveal which activities are particularly popular. Some parents may also be able to provide materials that will extend activities (e.g. items for the interest table or books).

Did you know?

An interesting technique has been developed to help very young children express their preferences. It involves taking a teddy into a setting and asking children what they think the teddy would like best about the setting if he were to stay for a day. This method encourages children to think through what they like most, and to use the teddy as an intermediary. The method has been used on children as young as two and a half.

Keys to good practice: Monitoring provision

✓ Did the children feel secure?

✓ Was there enough time for the children's care requirements?

✓ Were the children able to have individual contact with their carers?

✓ Were the children able to communicate and socialise?

✓ Was there an allowance for flexibility?

✓ Were individual needs supported appropriately?

✓ Could the activity have been adapted?

✓ Were the views of parents taken into account?

The importance of partnerships with parents and families and how these partnerships can be developed and supported

Parents should be seen as the child's main educators, and clear communication with them, and understanding, are therefore essential if children are to develop to their full potential.

Keys to good practice: Partnerships with parents and families

✓ Provide parents with understandable curriculum plans.

✓ Encourage parents to carry out activities at home (e.g. finding a topic object, sharing a book).

✓ Ask parents to help in the setting.

✓ Ask parents to share observations of their children.

✓ Have regular formal and informal meetings with parents.

✓ Hold information evenings where parents can experience the curriculum.

✓ Give parents time to talk about their child's learning where possible.

● *It is good practice to work with parents to ensure that their child benefits from the curriculum.*

The benefits of a multi-professional, multi-agency approach

Children can but benefit from a multi-disciplinary approach to their education. Mutual respect is hugely important for the benefit of both practitioners and children. As an early years practitioner you may work alongside:

- health visitors
- teachers
- nurses/doctors
- play specialists
- special educational needs coordinators
- members of voluntary organisations
- advisers
- social workers.

Check it out

The government is investing in children's centres, which have a multi-disciplinary team for both parents and children, providing for their health, education and welfare in one building. Log on to your SureStart website (www.surestart. gov.uk/surestartservices/ childrenscentres/) to find out whether a children's centre is set to open near you.

Reflect on your own practice

As you have seen, monitoring the curriculum is an essential part of your role. Have a look at the statements below to assess whether you match up to the requirements. The statements all refer to the performance criteria for CCLD 309.1.

Performance criteria statement	Always	Sometimes	Never
Do I develop monitoring strategies and documentation as required by the curriculum framework?			
Do I regularly communicate with parents, families and other adults to support monitoring of curriculum frameworks?			
Do I review health and safety procedures and make suggestions for improvements?			
Do I check that each area of the curriculum is implemented to a consistent level?			
Do I monitor the participation and learning of all the children in the setting?			

End-of-unit knowledge check

1. What is the early years framework for the country you work in?
2. Define 'cognitive development'.
3. What are the stages of children's learning referred to by Piaget?
4. What is structured play?
5. What sort of learning environment did Rudolph Steiner advocate?
6. What are the four aspects of the *Birth to Three Matters* framework?
7. What sort of timescale would a short term curriculum plan cover?
8. What does an appropriately planned routine give the child the chance to do?
9. How can you ensure staff, including supply staff, provide the appropriate activities for the children in your setting?
10. Name two types of professional you may work with to provide an effective curriculum.

References

Department for Education and Skills and QCA (2000) *Curriculum Guidance for the Foundation Stage*. Available at www.surestart.gov.uk/ensuringquality/foundationstage/curriculumguidance/.

Learning and Teaching Scotland (2005) *Birth to Three: Supporting Our Youngest Children*. Scottish Executive. Available at www.ltscotland.org.uk/earlyyears/Birthtothree.asp.

Moyles, J. (1989) '*Just Playing*': *The Role and Status of Play in Early Childhood Education*. Open University Press.

Assess children's progress according to frameworks for early education

Assessment is essential to meet each child's needs and to plan an appropriate curriculum. In Unit 303 (pages 84–156) you have already read about the importance of observing children and the different methods that you can use. In this unit you will find out about assessing children's progress within the appropriate curriculum framework of your country. It is important that you not only understand the assessment and recording process but that you are also aware of how to plan assessments. As you are studying for a qualification that allows you to work unsupervised, it may not be long before you care for a group of children who you are responsible for assessing.

What you must know and understand

- Specific issues for children's development and learning in multilingual settings. (K3D331)
- How children's learning is affected by their stage of development (K3D334)
- Current theoretical approaches to how children learn and develop (K3D335)
- Detail of the early education frameworks and curriculum requirements in your home country and the approach to assessment of children's progress (e.g. use of profiling) (K3D336)
- Requirements of the relevant inspectorates (K3M337)
- Safeguards that need to be in place when assessing children, and the need for objectivity (K3M338)
- The basic provisions of data protection legislation relevant to your work (K3M339)
- The possible effects of low self-esteem, lack of confidence and discrimination on learning (K3D340)
- How to use assessments of children's progress as part of the planning cycle (K3D341)
- Using assessments of children's progress to inform staff or personal development and improve provision (K3P342)

Identify and plan assessment requirements of curriculum frameworks

Why are assessments important?

In the past few years, there has been an increasing trend to assess young children's development. While assessment needs to be handled extremely sensitively, it can be helpful as a way of identifying children who need additional support or challenges. Assessment is also used as a way of learning more about groups of children so that the curriculum can be adjusted to meet their interests and needs. Unit 303 looks at different ways of observing children and so needs to be read alongside this unit. It is also important to realise that assessing children is not an exact science and that we should see any assessments only as a guide and a tool. Young children are ever-changing and their development and interests reflect this. A child who in September appears uninterested in books may just a few months later be begging his parents to read to him at home, while another child who is fascinated by any toy with a set of wheels may have developed an interest in gluing!

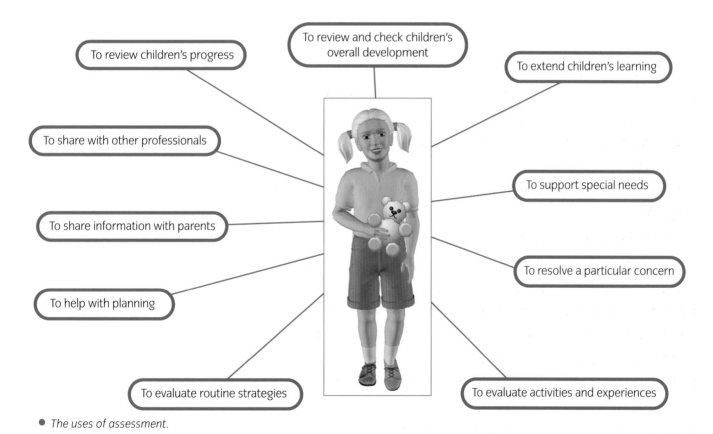

To review children's progress

To review and check children's overall development

To extend children's learning

To share with other professionals

To support special needs

To share information with parents

To resolve a particular concern

To help with planning

To evaluate routine strategies

To evaluate activities and experiences

● *The uses of assessment.*

Specific issues for children's learning and development in multilingual settings or where a child has English as an additional language

Some children whose progress we need to assess may be learning more than one language. This needs to be taken into account when planning assessments as otherwise there is a danger that assessments will not be accurate. A child may, for example, may be able to count up to 20 in the home language, but only count up to 5 in English. This may lead an observer who is unaware of the child's capabilities in their home language to assume that the child has a limited understanding of numbers. It is also worth knowing that young children often associate situations with a particular language and if asked about them in another language may have difficulty in responding. This again may give the impression that the child does not understand or cannot talk about things that have happened in the past.

In settings where more than one language is being used, it is important to remember to assess children in the language that they use for that area. For example, if children have heard a story in Welsh, they are likely to have a better recall of it if questions are in Welsh.

As well as understanding that children might respond differently according to the language that is being used, it is also essential not to make assumptions about the levels of the home language. A child whose speech is difficult to understand may not be speaking clearly in their home language either.

It may therefore sometimes be useful to carry out assessments using each of the languages that a child speaks in order to find out the extent of their knowledge and skills. This might be done by working with the child's parents or by using the services of an interpreter. In some areas, there are also teams who support children who have more than one language and who can provide advice.

It is also common to find 'gaps' in children's vocabulary, as early language depends very much on the context in which a child hears it. This means that words associated with home may only be known in the home language. Knowing children's strengths and gaps in a language should help us to plan particular activities so that they can become fluent in each of the languages that are being used.

Keys to good practice: Assessing children for whom English is an additional language

✓ Assess children's home language.

✓ Avoid making assumptions about the level of a child's home language.

✓ Carry out assessments in the language that the child associates with the activity.

✓ Plan activities that will widen children's vocabulary.

✓ Use visual cues to help children remember.

How children's learning is affected by their stage of development

Young children learn best when they can connect new information or skills to what they already know. A child who has a name that starts with an 'm' and who can recognise that letter, is more likely to find the letter 'm's that are hidden in the sand tray. In the same way a child who can catch a bean bag will find it easier to catch a soft ball than a child who can only catch objects that are rolled rather than thrown.

One of the reasons that assessment of children is so important is that by assessing children's knowledge and skills we can determine their stage of development in any given area and so plan activities that will be appropriate.

Case study

Selda is four years old. She enjoys counting, singing number rhymes and can sort things out into colours. As part of the regular observation cycle at the nursery Selda attends, Harvey watches her as she plays with a tray of buttons. He notices that she can group the buttons in different ways. He asks Selda if she has any favourites. Selda shows him a group of five buttons that she has separated from the others. He comments that she has quite a few. Selda tells him proudly that there are fifteen and proceeds to point to the buttons but does not touch them. As a result of observing Selda with the buttons, Harvey plans some activities that involve counting and encourages Selda to touch one object at a time while saying the number name. Six weeks later, Selda is playing again with the buttons. She shows Harvey a group of buttons and proclaims 'There are four buttons here. Look. One, two, three, four. That makes four!' Harvey notes that this time Selda touches each button in turn as she counts them.

1. *What progress has Selda made?*
2. *Why is it important to use assessments to work out what experiences a child needs?*
3. *Suggest one activity that could build on Selda's knowledge of numbers.*

Patterns and theories of children's learning and development

Children's development is comprehensively covered in Unit 303 (see pages 105–120), and in addition Unit 309 briefly looks at how this fits into a learning framework (see pages 342–344).

It is important to remember here that children develop at different rates and do not always achieve the same stages of development at similar ages. It is part of your role as a practitioner to reassure parents who are worried that their child is not developing at the same rate as other children. You should work with them to promote their child's development and assess the child's individual needs as appropriate.

Whatever the curriculum that you are following, good practice is to place children at the centre of their learning. Children are active learners who need a balance of free play and structured play that is supported by an adult.

Observation

To ensure that you understand that children will develop if they have the opportunity to make their own choices in their play, try to observe one or more of the following situations:

- a child engaged in role play
- children playing in the sand pit
- children at the water tray
- a child at bath time
- a child playing with a cardboard box
- children exploring a collection of musical instruments
- a baby exploring the contents of a treasure basket.

In your evaluation, consider how the children made choices and the role the adult played in the situation. Also reflect upon how much the children were able to benefit from leading their own play.

Education frameworks and curriculum requirements, and the approach to assessment

Unit 309 presents the curriculum frameworks for each of the home countries (see pages 330–333). Within these frameworks, some of the assessment requirements are more formal than others and are carried out at a specific time during the year.

England

Birth to 3 years: observation

There is no compulsory framework at this age but SureStart has developed a curriculum approach called *Birth to Three Matters* (see page 330). Practitioners are encouraged to observe, plan and reflect as a way of assessing the needs of children.

Foundation Stage profile

This framework, developed by the Department for Education and Skills, is firmly centred on play. All settings that receive government funding for three- to five-year-olds are expected to follow the Foundation Stage curriculum, which is based on six areas of learning (see page 331). Each area of learning has a set of early learning goals. These early learning goals relate to:

- personal, social and emotional development
- communication, language and literacy
- mathematical development
- knowledge and understanding of the world
- physical development
- creative development.

A single national assessment system for the Foundation Stage is in place. It is called the Foundation Stage Profile. The Profile has thirteen summary scales, which cover the six areas of learning. These need to be completed by the end of the Foundation Stage for each child who receives government funding.

Foundation Stage profiling takes place throughout the year and can be transferred if a child moves setting. Children with special needs and English as an additional language (EAL) are considered in the assessment material. Assessment material is externally moderated and the data collected and made available.

Key Stage 1 of the National Curriculum: SATs

The National Curriculum has to be taught in schools that receive government funding. Observation and assessment are encouraged as a way of planning an appropriate curriculum. Key Stage 1 is for children aged five to seven years. At the end of Key Stage 1, children are assessed by formal tests called SATs (Standard Attainment Tasks). These tests are externally moderated and a table of results is available. From September 2005 the SATs assessment will become less formal and cater more for children's individual assessment needs.

Scotland

From birth to three children are encouraged to learn through play. There is no formal assessment guidance for this stage.

Practitioners working with children aged three to five years have a self-evaluation tool for the practitioner called 'Child at the Centre'. A curriculum for excellence is to be implemented in 2007. It is intended to bring the curriculum guidelines for children aged three to five years and 5–14 years together to ensure a smooth transition in children's learning; it will emphasise the importance of purposeful and well-planned play.

The Scottish curriculum that presently applies to five- to seven-year-olds has been designed by teachers. It is they who assess when a child is ready for the next stage. Sample assessments are moderated to ensure similar assessment criteria are used. Results are made available to parents.

Wales

At present children are assessed on an early years curriculum based on Desirable Outcomes, which emphasise six areas of learning. In 2002 a less formal play-based curriculum was introduced; however, the Welsh version of the Desirable Outcomes is still being used.

Schools have to use an accredited baseline assessment, which helps the planning of the children's learning. Key Stage 1 is similar to England but includes Welsh as a language. Children who are assessed with special needs are integrated into mainstream education wherever possible.

Teacher assessment takes into account English or Welsh, mathematics and science. Teachers use a programme of study, discussion and observation as assessment tools at the end of Key Stage 1.

Northern Ireland

As in other countries, an early years framework from birth is being developed.

The curriculum framework at present for children aged three to five years is less dominated by language and literacy but emphasises a quality curriculum. There is no formal assessment although ongoing assessment is encouraged as good practice.

Like the English National Curriculum children are assessed at the end of Key Stage 1, using similar procedures.

Requirements of the relevant inspectorates

Each home country has a government body with responsibility for ensuring that early years settings meet the relevant assessment standards. This helps to ensure that each child will have equal chances and opportunities. The inspectorates themselves, as well as the curricula, are described in Unit 309 (see pages 329–334).

While each inspection process is slightly different across the home countries, there are many similarities. Inspectors will need to see that children are regularly observed and that records are kept. They will also want to see that everyone in the setting is familiar with the curriculum framework that is being used.

- Do all staff members have a good understanding of the curriculum framework?
- Are curriculum documents available and used for planning and assessment?
- Are links between the curriculum frameworks clearly shown in planning and assessments?
- Do staff attend training so that they are aware of curriculum developments?
- Who is responsible for ensuring that assessments are carried out?
- Where are records stored?
- Are observations carried out regularly?
- How are the observations recorded and used?
- How do the assessments feed into the planning cycle?
- How are parents involved in the assessment process?
- How do parents find out about the progress of their child?

England: Ofsted

Ofsted inspects early years settings and schools.

Birth to 3 years

Inspectors expect children under three to be assessed through observation and record keeping. They may review record keeping and observations while carrying out an inspection to see if settings are following Ofsted standards.

Foundation Stage

The Foundation Stage is inspected with a specific visit that focuses on the curriculum. Inspectors will expect practitioners to be basing activities and experiences on the early learning goals. They will also want to see Foundation Stage Profiles in progress. These Profiles will be externally moderated.

Key Stage 1

It is the role of the Qualifications and Curriculum Authority (QCA) to keep assessment systems under review, and from September 2005 Key Stage 1 assessments are due to become more informal.

The Ofsted inspectors will want to see a clear understanding of child assessment on the part of practitioners, as this will support children's transition from the Foundation Stage to Key Stage 1. Inspectors will expect a system of continual assessment to be in place.

All schools are expected to have an assessment policy, as effective assessment provides information to improve teaching and learning.

The aims and objectives of assessment in our school are:

- To enable our children to demonstrate what they know, understand and can do in their work

- To help our children understand what they need to do next to improve their work

- To allow teachers accurately to plan work that reflects the needs of the child

- To provide regular information for parents that enables them to support their child's learning

- To provide the Head Teacher and governors with information that allows them to make judgements about the effectiveness of the school.

● *Assessment policy of a small primary school.*

Scotland: Her Majesty's Inspectorate of Education

Her Majesty's Inspectorate of Education is responsible for inspecting schools and for monitoring the quality of assessment in schools.

Wales: Estyn

Estyn is responsible for inspection of both pre-school settings and schools. Baseline assessment takes place at children's entry to school.

The Curriculum and Assessment Authority for Wales (Awdurdod Cwricwlwm Asesu Cymru, or ACAC) emphasises the crucial role of observation in planning a curriculum and assessing a child's progress.

Northern Ireland: the Education and Training Inspectorate (ETI)

The ETI will inspect early years settings and expect them to reach certain standards of assessment.

Key Stage 1 is from five to six years. Assessment of Key Stage 1 is currently under review.

It is the role of the CCEA (Northern Ireland Council for the Curriculum, Examinations and Assessment) to monitor assessment arrangements.

Consolidation:

If you are working in a setting that is inspected by Ofsted, you are expected to be familiar with the appropriate regulations. Ask your supervisor if you can read a copy of the relevant standards and note what is expected of you with regards to the assessment of the children.

Reflect on your own practice

As you have seen, identifying the assessment requirements of the curriculum frameworks is an essential part of your role. Have a look at the statements below to assess whether you match up to the requirements. The statements all refer to the performance criteria for CCLD 310.1.

Performance criteria statement	Always	Sometimes	Never
Do I research relevant information from curriculum documents on which to base my assessments?			
Do I plan assessments according to local or national requirements?			
Do I review health and safety procedures and make suggestions for improvements?			
Do I clearly define the roles and responsibilities of those involved?			
Do I check that those involved are clear about assessment methods and requirements?			

Assess and record children's progress in consultation with others

Safeguards that need to be in place when assessing children, and the need for objectivity

One of the main dangers when carrying out assessments is that children may be labelled (e.g. as 'bright' or 'not capable'). The reality is that young children's development is not uniformly continuous, and many external factors can affect progress. A child who has, for example, been feeling poorly or who has not got any friends may find it hard to concentrate and learn.

The danger is that once a child has been labelled, adult expectations can take over. A child who is seen as 'gifted' may, for example, come under pressure to do more than the other children, while a child who is seen as 'ordinary' might not be given challenging opportunities. We also know that once adults have a view of what children can do, there is a danger that they will focus on those things that the child does that reinforce this view. A child who is seen to be keen on books may also be interested in other activities, but an adult might particularly notice the times when the child sits quietly in the book corner.

As well as being aware of the danger of labelling children, it is also important to remember that some observation methods are likely to change the child's natural behaviour. A child who knows that they are being watched or who is asked to do something might try a little harder or become more anxious and thus not perform as well. (See also unit 303.)

Active knowledge

Select a child who you know very well, perhaps out of the work setting (maybe even your own child), and consider:

- things you know about the child
- how the child reacts in a variety of situations
- your feelings towards the child
- things you may have heard others say about the child.

How do you think this knowledge would make it difficult to assess the child fairly? Perhaps you could discuss this in more detail in your study group.

Keys to good practice: Objective assessments

✓ Remember that children's development is neither continuous nor uniform.

✓ Consider whether children are happy, confident and relaxed.

✓ Be aware of external influences that might be affecting children, e.g. moving house, separation of parents.

✓ Avoid labelling children using terms such as 'bright' 'less able' or 'immature'.

✓ Talk to parents about what their child enjoys doing at home.

✓ Observe children in a variety of situations.

✓ Think about using a range of methods and also other adults to carry out assessments.

✓ Record what you see rather than what you think you know.

✓ Try not to make any assumptions, especially culturally or ethnically based ones.

✓ Avoid expressing personal opinions.

✓ Avoid giving children a label (e.g. 'a sensitive child').

✓ Do state how a child is feeling – comment on what you see (i.e. what it is that leads you to presume how the child is feeling).

✓ Ensure formal assessments are fair and that instructions are followed in detail.

There are a variety of people who may be involved in the assessment of children. Engaging different perspectives is another way of ensuring fair and objective assessment.

● *What sort of observational methods are being used here? Refer to Unit 303 (page 89).*

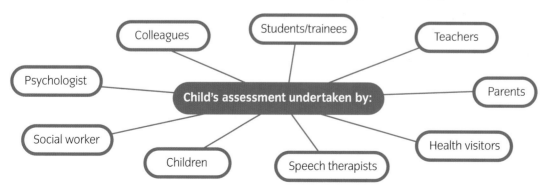

● *People who could be involved in the assessment of children.*

Confidentiality and data protection

Unit 301 considered the legal requirements for confidentiality and data protection (see pages 000–000). In relation to assessments, it is important to heed the following:

- Conceal the child's identity, to give each child full protection.
- Store information in a secure place, to ensure that information is shared only as appropriate.
- Do not identify the setting name, so that children cannot be identified in this way.
- Pass information on to the relevant people only when this is in the best interests of the child.
- Follow the setting's policy of information sharing, which will highlight the importance of confidentiality.
- Obtain permission to make assessments and ensure the results are shared only with the appropriate people and only for the purposes of the assessment.
- Gain permission from parents, as they are a child's main carers and have a right to know what information is being stored about their child.

● *Data protection in practice.*

The possible effects of low self-esteem, lack of confidence and discrimination on learning

Self-esteem is in some ways everything when it comes to learning. In terms of assessment, we should always consider whether or not a child's progress is linked to low self-esteem. Confident children who see themselves as capable are more likely to do well, try out new experiences and have friends. On the other hand, children who are worried about how well they are doing or who do not feel valued are likely to underachieve. Particular groups of children are at risk of developing low self-esteem and it is important that we consider assessing children's self-esteem and confidence. In Unit 308, we looked at how children's self-esteem is formed and also at ways of helping children to develop a strong self-image and self-esteem.

Using assessments to enhance self-esteem

In children's earliest years, this means that we need to think about how best to give children confidence and also how to plan activities so that they are challenging but do not put children in situations where they may fail. This is why assessment is so important. By observing children in a range of situations, we should be able to plan for them more effectively and build on their strengths and interests. We may, for example, notice that a child becomes easily worried and rarely contributes when playing a game with a large group of children, but is more relaxed in small group situations. Using this information, we might make sure that the child has more adult support when in a large group or might plan activities a little differently so that more small group work can take place.

Assessments may also help us to ensure that children are developing the social skills they will need to make and maintain friendships. We may, for example, look at children as they play and note whether children are beginning to form strong friendships. This is important, as self-esteem is linked to children's popularity, especially as they get older.

Check it out

- Does the child come into the setting happily?
- Does the child have friends within the setting?
- Does the child seem overly concerned with pleasing the adults?
- How does the child react if their activity is not working out as planned?
- How much initiative does the child show?
- How keen is the child to try out new activities, materials or equipment?
- Does the child seem relaxed and happy?

How to use assessments of children's progress as part of the planning cycle

Unit 309 presented the planning cycle (see page 350). Assessment has an important role within the planning cycle, as the diagram indicates. Children will be observed during the activities that are part of the curriculum. As a result, children's needs are identified. This information can then be used to plan further curriculum activities to support children's learning.

Case study 1: Assessment and routines

Nicola spent time over the course of a week carrying out a developmental check on 12-month-old Junama in a day care setting. Nicola used a series of observations with a checklist method while working in the nursery so that she could see Junama reacting naturally. She put a tick against the expected developmental norms in one of three columns, headed 'Yes', 'No', 'Sometimes'. One of the developmental checks was to see whether Junama could pick up food with her fingers. Nicola found that Junama liked to be fed by an adult, although she could pick up objects with her finger and thumb. Nicola talked to Junama's parents and discovered that she ate most meals sitting on her father's lap while he fed her: she seemed to enjoy the comfort of being cuddled up to her father when eating. Nicola and her colleagues planned meal and snack times as part of the curriculum and discussed with her parents how they could all encourage her to eat finger foods to gain independence. They decided to start the process by ensuring that Junama sat next to an adult while developing these skills, to give her a continued feeling of security.

1. *Why was Nicola assessing Junama?*
2. *How did Nicola's developmental assessment affect the planning of the curriculum and routines in the nursery?*
3. *Do you think that natural observation was a good way to assess Junama's development?*

Summative and formative assessment

The different methods used in assessments and observations of children are described in Unit 303 (pages 89–94). In brief they are:

- written records
- checklists and tick charts
- event samples
- target child observations.

The use of a variety of assessment methods will contribute to the objectivity of the process.

Think of an observation you have carried out using a written record method. List what you think were the advantages and disadvantages of that style of recording. You might consider:

- how the resulting data were used to assess the child
- the method of writing everything down
- the materials used
- the recording of spontaneous actions.

Assessments may be either formative or summative:

- **Formative assessment** is ongoing and does not draw overall conclusions. For example, a teacher may record a child's behaviour over a period of time. While no overall conclusion is drawn these records may form part of an eventual assessment of the child's behavioural patterns and the way in which they can be supported when planning curriculum activities and experiences.
- **Summative assessment** draws findings together and may have an overall conclusion. For example, the child whose behaviour has been observed over a period of time might have a number of other observations and records made that contribute to an overall picture of their specific needs. Academic records and assessments and contributions from parents might also be considered.

Thus, a series of formative assessments would contribute towards a summative assessment of a child.

Key terms

Formative assessment is ongoing and does not draw overall conclusions.

Summative assessment draws findings together and may have an overall conclusion.

Sharing assessments with others

Once we have assessed children, it is important to share information with other people who work or spend time with the child. The extent of the information that is shared will depend on their exact role. Sharing information is important as it can help other people to know how best to work with the child. This includes parents. Many parents are keen to help their child and to build on their child's interests. Parents of a child who has just started to read might be pleased to know the type of books that their child particularly enjoys at school, while parents of a baby in day care might be interested to know that their child is fascinated by bubbles.

Using assessments of children's progress to inform staff or personal development and improve provision

While assessments are largely used to help us focus on children's progress, we can also use them to think about the effectiveness of our practice and planning. We can look at the assessments and carry out a simple audit, noticing any trends in children's progress and achievement. The easiest assessment tool to do this with is probably the checklist or tick chart. If, for example, many four-year-olds were not able to recognise their name, we might need to think about this. On reflection, we might decide to make literacy the focus for staff training over a few weeks, or we might consider increasing the number of activities where children's names are used. Later assessments might then be used to see if this has affected children's learning.

Reflect on your own practice

As you have seen, identifying the assessment requirements of the curriculum frameworks is an essential part of your role. Have a look at the statements below to assess whether you match up to the requirements. The statements all refer to the performance criteria for CCLD 310.2.

Performance criteria statement	Always	Sometimes	Never
Do I draw on everyday observation and my knowledge of individual children to inform my assessments?			
Do I undertake ongoing formative assessment using agreed methods?			
Do I undertake summative assessments as required by curriculum frameworks?			
Do I liaise with others who will use my assessment information to inform planning?			
Do I share my assessment findings with those who need the information and maintain appropriate confidentiality?			

End-of-unit knowledge check

1. What are the two forms of assessment?
2. What are they used for?
3. Name two types of professional who may be involved in the assessment process.
4. Why would you share assessment information with parents?
5. Why are assessments useful as part of curriculum planning?
6. Describe three ways in which you could ensure that assessment is objective.
7. Why is it important to be objective when carrying out an assessment?
8. Give one example of an assessment record that you have used. What information were you required to collect?
9. The Data Protection Act stipulates that personal data must be processed 'in accordance with the data subject's rights'. Explain what this means.
10. Name one secure method of storing assessment data.

Plan and implement positive environments for babies and children under three years

This unit is aimed specifically at supporting you in providing optimal care and learning opportunities for babies and young children. Babies and young children need warm, consistent and responsive care from familiar adults. A tremendous surge in development occurs before three years of age, across all aspects of development; key shifts occur which 'signpost' important changes in the normally developing child's skills and abilities. The crucial role of the practitioner is in identifying individual children's needs, in partnership with parents.

What you must know and understand:

- When and how to carry out observations on babies, including the purpose of observations, the different methods that can be used and when you would use them (K3D386)
- When and how to carry out observations on children under three years, why a different approach from that used for babies might be necessary, and the reasons for carrying out observations on this age group (K3D387)
- What factors might affect the reliability or validity of your observations and why you would document this (K3D388)
- What is meant by baseline information, how to obtain such information and why it is necessary to facilitate children's development (K3D389)
- Why it is important to obtain permission from parents before carrying out observations on babies and children under three years and how this may be accomplished (K3D390)
- Theories of child development and frameworks of effective practice (e.g. *Birth to Three Matters*), and how you use these in your work with babies and children under three years (K3D391)

- The expected pattern of development for children aged up to three years, including the acceptable range and recognised limits (K3D392)
- Organisational policies and procedures that must be followed when reporting and referring any concerns about development and why it is important to report/refer concerns as soon as possible (K3D393)
- Why and how to record observations of development accurately and clearly, using accepted language and formats; what these are (K3D394)
- What is meant by a warm and respectful approach (e.g. tone of voice, expression, use of appropriate language) and how this affects relationships (K3C395)
- Legislation relating to the use of personal information (e.g. Data Protection Act), including the limits to confidentiality (K3M396)
- Who it is appropriate to share information with relating to the development of individual babies and children and why such information should be shared (K3M397)
- What methods you would use to engage the attention and interest of babies and what effect developmental competence will have on your choice (K3D398)
- Why it is important to allow children to initiate communication and how to recognise signals that indicate that the baby or child wishes to communicate, disengage from communication or does not wish to communicate at all (K3C399)
- The range of communication methods you can use with babies and young children, including non-spoken languages (K3C400)
- How to recognise communication differences and difficulties; the possible reasons for these (K3C401)
- Likely emotional and behavioural responses to communication differences of children under three years and how these can be managed in ways that benefit the child (K3D402)
- Activities that will support different areas of learning and development for babies and children and under three years (K3D403)
- In what circumstances you might change routines or activities; how you would adapt existing or planned activities or routines (K3C404)
- How to encourage children to communicate through their play and learning activities (K3C405)
- Patterns of communication development up to three years, covering listening/watching, talking, early interest in reading, early writing and mark-making (K3D406)

- What the organisation's policies and practices are regarding risk assessment and safety and why it is important to follow these (K3H407)
- What is meant by challenging activities for individual babies and children and the link between challenging activities and developmental progress (K3D408)
- Why it is important to carry out risk assessment, how you would do this and what action to take if the surroundings or equipment do not meet requirements (K3H409)
- Why it is important to share information with parents and the sort of information that can affect the care and well-being of babies and children under three years (K3M410)
- Why it is important to respect parents' preferences concerning the care routines for their children, and how you would reach agreement where these do not meet the requirements of good practice (K3D411)
- Sources of advice available to parents, locally and nationally and in different formats, including language (K3P412)

Observe, assess and record developmental progress

How to observe, assess and record the developmental progress of babies and children under three years

Observations provide the information you require in order to plan and implement high-quality, positive environments for babies and young children. You will therefore need to know and understand how babies and young children develop during this time and the importance of working closely with parents to ensure best care and best practice. The importance of observing children under three years is highlighted in the *Birth to Three Matters* framework in England and others that are being similarly developed in the other home countries (see below). Unit 303 covers child developmental aspects (pages 105–120) as well as the general principles of observation and assessment (pages 89–94).

Observations should inform the planning of the care and education of young children, in a cyclical fashion, as shown opposite. From your observations you should adjust your provision, thinking about safety needs as well as occasions when you need to support, encourage, soothe and reassure. You will need to have a sound knowledge of the broadly expected developmental shifts between birth to three years and beyond (see below), to help you reflect on what the baby is actually doing and what might be expected. This will help you plan your resources to meet children's changing needs. The diagram at the bottom of the page presents an example of such an observation cycle. It is taken from one of the many case studies in the *Birth to Three Matters* pack. It shows you what you could look for, what you might listen to and what you might note down. It also shows you how what you observe can help support a child's development.

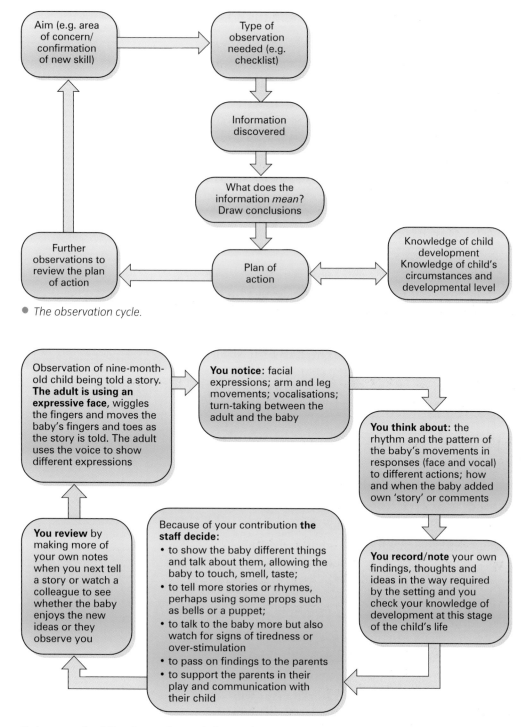

● *The observation cycle.*

● *An example of the observation cycle in practice.*

When to observe babies and children under three years old

The idea behind observing children is to meet their needs and unless you carry out regular observations you will not necessarily recognise these. It is important to observe children frequently, especially babies, as their interests, skills and needs are constantly changing. Frequent observations will also allow you to see the rate at which babies and young children are developing. Babies should ideally be observed daily, although some of these observations will be informal and not necessarily planned.

Check it out

How often are observations carried out in your setting? What methods are frequently used?

Types of observation method that may be used

There are no right or wrong methods of observation to use with babies and toddlers, although it is important that you use a range of methods and observe them in a range of situations. It can also be helpful to involve parents in the observation process and ask them to make some simple notes or use a checklist at home. This could allow you to collect some information about the interests and skills that children show in a completely different environment. Unit 303 looks at some methods that can be used to observe children's development. Below are some methods that are commonly used by practitioners working with younger children.

Checklists and tickcharts

These can be used to ascertain how children are progressing against the developmental milestones. Repeating these observations frequently can give you an indication of the rate of development. As babies and toddlers do not perform skills to order, it is a good idea to keep a checklist or tickchart for each child to hand and then fill it in as you see the skill or make a note of it and then fill it in later. The skills recorded must be dated, otherwise it is hard to evaluate the child's progress.

Free description, also known as running record

Many practitioners find it useful to jot down odd notes about what babies and children are interested in or have done. This can be done on sticky notes or in diaries, for example. It is useful to collate this information and to check that different areas of development are being focused on and evaluated.

Sound recordings

Evaluating a child's language development can be tricky. It is hard to write down what a babbling baby is saying or what toddlers are saying as they play. Recording speech using a tape recorder or dictaphone can therefore be useful. Consider having a tape for each child. To evaluate language progress, it is helpful to record babies and children regularly. This will make it easier to check that babies' babbling is becoming tuneful and that toddlers are beginning to increase their store of words.

Case study 1: Listening to babies' language development

Carla is a childminder. She has decided to keep regular recordings of Charlotte, a baby she looks after who is six months old. She tapes Charlotte for a few minutes each week. She is surprised to hear the way in which, over a period, Charlotte's babbling evolves. Charlotte becomes more tuneful in her babbling and also babbles in longer strings of sounds. Carla compares the tape recordings to the milestones of language development and is happy to see that Charlotte is making excellent progress. She shares the tape with Charlotte's parents, who are excited and delighted to have their daughter's early sounds captured.

1. *Why should assessments be repeated regularly?*
2. *Explain why it is essential to compare the development of children to normative development or 'milestones'.*
3. *Why is it important that parents are involved in observations?*

Focus for observations

An observation may need to be focused on any one or more of the following areas:

- how a child is settling into a new setting/placement
- whether a child appears contented and alert, interested and involved
- how a child is spending time
- whether a child has friends or is isolated (or whether a baby shows interest in other babies)
- what a child's attitudes and reactions to experiences are
- what knowledge, skills and understanding are being demonstrated by a child
- whether a child is making progress against developmental milestones
- whether a child's behaviour is influenced by context
- what a child is actually gaining from the provision
- how other adults who are with the child mainly spend their time
- the manner of the interactions between adults and the child (emotional quality, control, degree of turn-taking etc.).

Observation

Some interesting things to observe during a baby's first year include the following:

- physical development (include vision and hearing in your observation)
- how they react to and respond to different types of toys, including simple household items such as wooden spoons and a smooth bowl or pan
- their fascination with their hands and feet (note how the way they hold and use their hands changes over time)
- the rhythm of their kicking when lying down
- how they learn to follow, track and reach for objects
- how their reaching becomes more accurate over time
- when they start to roll from front to back/back to front
- their reactions to different people and how these change.

Keys to good practice: The principles of observation

✓ Obtain permission from your supervisor and parents.

✓ Decide carefully what types of observations, recording and reporting will be best suited to the purpose.

✓ Ensure the information gathered remains confidential.

✓ Incorporate observations as an *essential* part of daily practice.

Did you know?

It is possible to observe *situations* as well as children. This includes observations of other adults involved with the care of the child – it may be pertinent to assess the quality of interaction between them and the child. This is particularly important for the welfare of babies and young children. *Peer observations* (i.e. staff observing one another during day-to-day activities) are becoming a requirement for evidence of best practice in quality assurance (QA) schemes such as the national Investors in Children scheme and by Ofsted inspectors.

● *Who is being observed? Peer observations are an increasingly important feature of child care.*

The practicalities of carrying out observations with babies and toddlers

With babies, it is often useful to carry out observations as a **participant observer** so that you can gauge a child's level of interaction and social skills. This is partly because in any case with babies it can be hard to find opportunities to disengage; however, with toddlers it can be useful to observe them from a distance when they are playing in a naturalistic way.

Keys to good practice: Non-participant observation

✓ Position yourself so that the child can be seen and heard but so that you are not within his or her play area or personal space.

✓ Make detailed notes as soon as possible after the observation has taken place or, if you are extremely busy or it is the practice in your setting, make notes in a diary or in a notepad, for example. Make brief notes about things you noticed or felt as soon after the observation as you can and make sure you later write them up fully.

✓ Avoid staring at the child (which is sometimes not easy), as it may make him or her feel uncomfortable.

✓ Avoid making eye contact or facial expressions that may distract the child but do not ignore the child if he or she looks at you or approaches. Try to make yourself as uninteresting to the child as possible.

The factors that might affect the reliability or validity of your observations and why you would document this

There are many factors that might affect the reliability or validity of your observations. One of the most important will be the number of observations you make. Certainly you should never come to a conclusion on the basis of one observation alone; for instance, a baby who is teething may not be smiling and interacting as usual. It is also important to observe children in a variety of situations, for example, during meals and snacks, during care routines, and at arrival and going-home times, as well as indoors and outdoors and during adult interactions with the child. Toddlers are especially liable to changes in moods and unless you observe them for long enough and in different situations, you might not capture their smiles or moments of intense concentration.

Two other important factors that may influence the reliability and validity of your observations are your levels of **self-awareness** and your **objectivity**. Observers need to think hard about their own feelings, knowledge and interest in the child. Those who find it hard to be objective are likely to miss things when observing. For instance, an observer who believes that a particular toddler is 'difficult' may focus on the times when the child is showing frustrated behaviour rather than notice other times when he or she is settled and cooperative. The observer may also fail to pick up the reasons why the toddler has become frustrated.

It is important, therefore, before starting observations, to think about:
- your *feelings* about the child
- your *attitudes* to various types of behaviour (e.g. how do you react when a child has a 'tantrum' or young children are 'play fighting')
- your *expectations* regarding skills or behaviour (e.g. are you realistic about how long a two-year-old can sit still for).

Key terms

Self-awareness is a person's knowledge of his or her own individuality, feelings, attitudes and beliefs.

Objectivity describes an unbiased mental attitude, where a person tries to put aside his or her own beliefs and values, and to examine or think about a situation as honestly and as openly as possible.

 Keys to good practice: Increasing the reliability of your observations

✓ Make sure you are not rushed.

✓ Make notes as soon as possible after the observation if it is not possible to do so during it.

✓ Write notes in, say, a notebook rather than on scraps of paper.

✓ Take care to make your notes legible for others.

✓ Do not allow others to distract you while you are observing.

✓ Take observations seriously; avoid seeing them as a 'chore'.

✓ Always report or record your observation but avoid any temptation to report or record any particular aspect of the child's development that is *not* the main focus of a specific observation.

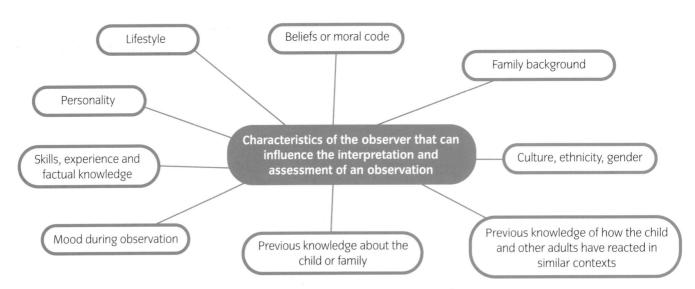

- *Factors that can affect the interpretation and assessment of an observation. If any of these come to the fore, they should be discussed fully with supervisors or mentors or a supportive colleague.*

You may find that you need to do one or more of the following in order to fulfil your professional responsibilities towards a child and perform an unbiased, reliable observation:

- find out more about the child
- find out about a particular culture to ensure that behaviours are not misinterpreted
- reflect on whether you have a tendency to stereotype children who are dressed or who behave in a particular way
- reflect on what equal opportunities actually means
- consider whether you have any tendency to judge first and find out more later.

Case study 2: Being objective

Sara is a key worker to Sam, who is two years old. Sam is showing behaviour that is typical of this age range. He is restless and at times clingy, but he can also be determined to do things for himself. He also has the occasional tantrum when he is tired and frustrated. Sara is finding it hard working with Sam and is beginning to believe that he has behavioural problems. She carries out a hurried observation of Sam and makes notes on a scrap of paper. She records how he pushes another child, grabs a toy and also has a tantrum when another member of staff tries to prevent him from climbing on a chair. She shows the observation to the special needs coordinator in the nursery. The coordinator comes into the room the next day and also carries out an observation. In her observation, she records the way in which Sam smiles at adults and older children, concentrates and is keen to do things for himself. She also witnesses a tantrum, but notes the events that led up to it. She observes that it is near lunchtime and that staff had not tried to distract Sam when he was first starting to become unruly.

1. *Is there evidence that Sara's view of Sam affected her ability to record objectively?*
2. *Why can it be useful for colleagues, parents and others also to observe children?*
3. *Why is it important when looking at negative aspects of behaviour to record the events that lead up to it?*

Baseline information

The idea of baseline information is to provide a starting point for future observations and assessments. When babies and toddlers first come into your care, it is useful to record what skills and interests they have. You may note, for example, that a 7-month-old baby can get into a crawling position, or that an 18-month-old toddler has 30 words. Such baseline information will allow later observations to record progress accurately, for example when the toddler has learnt 10 more words.

Baseline information can be gathered through a range of recording methods, but many practitioners will use checklists or tickcharts. Parents are a good source of baseline information, as they will know their child's strengths, progress and areas of development, and in addition will have seen their child in a different environment.

Future recordings should refer back to the baseline information. Where you have concerns about a baby's or toddler's progress you will need to observe further and also to discuss your thoughts with parents. Where a baby or child's progress seems particularly slow, parents may need to talk to their general practitioner or health visitor.

Check it out

Evaluate the way in which your setting gathers information when children first arrive. Explain the strengths of your current system. Are there any weaknesses? If so, how could these be addressed?

Why it is important to obtain permission from parents before carrying out observations

Most parents are more than happy for early years workers to observe their child, but their permission is still necessary before any formal observations and notes are made. This is because all observations are a form of research – information is being sought about a child to further understanding. What is observed will be questioned and interpreted, and an assessment will be based on the findings, from which a plan of action and/or recommendations will be made (see the first diagram, page 389). All this may affect the care of the child, including activities and interactions, and it is important that parents are involved in this.

It is good practice to talk through with parents your thoughts about what you have observed. Parents can sometimes have a different view or they may have seen their child showing a different interest or skill.

Parents also need to know what will happen to any observations and records that are kept, so that they can give their informed consent. They may, for example, want to know who will have access to photographs.

Active knowledge

Find out how you would obtain permission from parents for observations to be made. How would you help parents to understand the importance of observing their children? Explain how you might reassure parents that information will be properly recorded, stored and kept confidential.

Theories of child development and frameworks of effective practice

Underpinning your understanding of observations is your knowledge and understanding of human development. You need to have a good working knowledge of different theoretical approaches when undertaking observations and assessments because, as Tina Bruce maintains:

Theories help us to predict and to anticipate how children might behave and react. They help us structure what we observe. Theories help us to make sense of what we see… When we analyse play, we find ourselves linking what we have found with what other people (theorists) have found. We may find our observations fit with theories. We may find that they do not. This will help us think deeply… (Bruce, 2001)

Thus, it is helpful to have a good understanding of how children develop and of theories relating to their development. While all areas of development are important in children's early years, it is worth focusing on attachment theory and also theories of how children learn language. These two areas are addressed in detail below, while other theories of how children learn, and of their physical development and behaviour, are considered in Unit 303 (see pages 84–156).

Understanding the structure of language

It is important to have some understanding of the structure of language. All languages have rules that are understood and used by both speaker and listener. The rules are often usually referred to as the grammar. Linguists who study the structure of language use the term 'grammar' to describe the 'package' of a language. This package is formed of three key elements:

- *Phonology.* Languages have a sound system – phonology. When you hear someone speaking, you may recognise the language that they are using, even if you cannot speak it. This recognition may be based on listening to the sounds that are being used. The individual sounds that are used in a language are called 'phones'. Some languages use fewer phones than others. English uses 40 phones. Individual sounds that are combined together are called phonemes.
- *Semantics.* Languages are composed of words or units of meaning. When people learn a language they have to learn what these units are and how they can be changed (e.g. adding 'less' onto the end of some words changes their meaning).
- *Syntax.* Syntax comprises the rules for using words, for example, how their place in a sentence can change the meaning (e.g. 'the cat ate the mouse' has a different meaning to 'the mouse ate the cat', even though the same words have been used).

The sequence of language development

A good starting point when considering language development is to consider how children learn to speak. Table 312.1 outlines the major stages in language development.

The first year of babies' lives is spent trying to 'tune in' to the language that they are hearing, and learning the skills of communication (e.g. making eye contact, and responding to others' facial expressions and words). This first year is often known as the pre-linguistic phase and is now considered to be vital in children's overall language development.

Table 312.1 Stages in language development

Stage	Age	Features	Comments
Pre-linguistic stage			
Cooing	Six weeks	Babies making cooing sounds.	Babies making cooing sounds. Cooing sounds are made to show pleasure. These early sounds are different to sounds made later on, mainly because the mouth is still developing.
Babbling (phonemic expansion)	6–9 months	Babies blend vowels and consonants together to make tuneful sounds such as ba, ma, da.	Babbling has been described as learning the tune before the words. The baby seems to be practising sounds. Babies increase the number of sounds, or phonemes. This is sometimes called phonemic expansion. All babies, even deaf babies, produce a wide range of sounds during this period.
Babbling (phonemic contraction)	9–10 months	Babies babble but the range of sounds is limited.	The range of sounds or phonemes that babies produce becomes more limited and reflects the phonemes used in the language that they are hearing. At this stage, it would in theory be possible to distinguish between babies who are in different language environments. At 10 months babies are understanding 17 or more words.
Linguistic stage			
First words	Around 12 months	Babies repeatedly use one or more sounds which has meaning for them.	The first words are often unclear and so gradually emerge. They are often one sound, but are used regularly in similar situations, for example 'ba' to mean drink and cuddle. Babbling continues.
Holophrases	12–18 months	Toddlers start to use one word in a variety of ways.	Toddlers use holophrases to make their limited vocabulary more useful for them. One word is used in several situations, but the tone of voice and the context helps the adult understand what the toddler means. Most toddlers have 10–15 words by 18 months.
Two-word utterances (telegraphic speech)	18–24 months	Two words are put together to make a mini-sentence.	Toddlers begin to combine words to make sentences. They seem to have grasped which are the key words in a sentence ('dada gone' or 'dada come').

continued on next page

continued from previous page

Language explosion	24–36 months	A large increase in children's vocabulary combined with increasing use of sentences.	This is a period in which children's language evolves rapidly. Children learn words so rapidly that it becomes hard for parents to count them. At the same time the child uses more complicated structures in speech. Plurals and negatives begin to be used (e.g. 'no dogs here').
	3–4 years	Sentences become longer and vocabulary continues to increase.	Children use language in a more complete way. Mistakes in grammar show that they are still absorbing the rules and sometimes misapplying them. Mistakes such as 'I wented' show that they have learnt that 'ed' makes a past tense. These types of mistakes are known 'virtuous errors'.
Fluency	4–5 years	Mastery of the basic skills of the language.	Children have mastered the basic rules of English grammar and are fluent, although will still be making some virtuous errors.

Speech maturity —

Can all children develop language?

While it is generally accepted that humans have an innate ability to learn language, not all children do so. For some children, their cognitive development means that they cannot process and think in symbols. As spoken language is actually based on symbols, this prevents them from mastering it. When the word 'cat' is said, a cat does not necessarily appear. The word stands for the actual animal. Children who find it hard to process symbols are therefore often taught Makaton signs or a picture-based system of communicating. Such communication systems help children because visual symbols or pictures are closely related to the action or object.

● *Makaton signs.*

Children who are learning more than one language

There are many children who speak a different language at home to the one that they use in the early years setting. Children who can speak two languages are referred to as bilingual and those who can speak more than two languages as multilingual. The development of the second and in some cases third language depends on two key factors: the age at which the child is exposed to the language and the amount of time that the child is exposed to it.

Children who learn another language as a baby

Children who are exposed to more than one language at a time as babies or toddlers usually make similar progress to other children, although they may be slightly later in saying their first few words. This slight delay is thought to be caused by the baby needing more time to 'tune in' to two different sound systems. The advice to parents and carers who are hoping that their child will learn more than one language is that the child should learn to associate a language with a person (e.g. the mother always speaks to the child in Greek, the father in English). Speakers jumping from one language to another can be a cause of delayed or confused speech in bi-lingual children.

Children who learn another language in a pre-school setting

Some children come into settings with little or no English. They will require support to help them acquire the new language. The process of learning a new language remains similar to that of a baby learning a first language, although the process is faster. Receptive language (i.e. understanding of spoken words) in particular develops quickly. Once children have some receptive language, they soon learn to speak single words, followed by short sentences. The speed at which children learn the new language does depend on the quality of the adult support and the emotional environment of the setting.

Keys to good practice: Helping children who are learning the language of the setting

✓ Find out about how much language children have before they enter the setting.

✓ Make sure that they are allocated a key person to help them settle in.

✓ Provide plenty of one-to-one support with the key person to help the child to tune in to the sounds of the language and also some key words.

✓ Do not 'force' a child to speak – words will appear when the child is ready.

✓ Repeat key words and use gestures so that the child knows what you are referring to.

✓ Simplify sentences, as you would with a baby or toddler.

✓ Use books with simple pictures of objects and activities to help the child learn some first words.

Yuksel speaks Turkish at home and has very little English. He goes to the Busy Bee Pre-school three times a week. Yuksel's key worker, Becky, has built up a good relationship with him and his parents. Together they agreed that he would need to settle in gradually. When Becky works with Yuksel, she makes sure that he can understand her by using facial gestures and repetition and also by pointing to objects. She tries to stress the key words in any sentence and repeats them. She has also made Yuksel a simple picture book. They look at the book together when the other children are having their story. Yuksel points to the pictures of the sandpit, water tray and other objects that he recognises. Becky repeats the names of the objects. Becky also organises games of picture lotto, which Yuksel and other children play together. In the first few weeks, Yuksel needed to stay close to Becky, but he is now keen to play with the other children and is beginning to point to things and say single words.

1. *Why will young children need to be offered emotional support when joining a setting?*
2. *Give two reasons why Yuksel needs to spend time with his key worker.*
3. *Why are facial expression and gestures important in helping a child to learn a language?*

Is there a critical period for learning language?

The idea of a critical period is an attractive one. It has been suggested that if children are not exposed to language in the first ten years of their lives, they will not be able to learn to speak. There is some evidence for and against this idea.

- Teenagers and adults who have been brain-damaged as a result of an accident find it harder to regain language they have lost, whereas children with similar injuries find it much easier. This would support the idea of a critical period.
- Children who have suffered severe deprivation have still managed to acquire some language. One of the most famous of these children is Genie. Genie was 13 years old when she was rescued in 1957. She had spent her childhood in appalling conditions. She was punished for making any sounds and was strapped down. When she was found she could understand a few words, but essentially had no speech. Although she made progress in learning to speak, she struggled with the rules of language. This case and others would cast doubt on the idea of a 'critical period', because some speech at least was gained.

The role of the adult in language development

There has been some interesting work that has looked specifically at the role of adults in helping children's language development. Adults seem to encourage communication in several ways:
- They interpret a baby's gurgle or babble as an attempt to communicate.
- Objects are used to help the baby (e.g. pointing at cars, dogs and books; this helps put language into context).

- Adults tend to repeat activities and routines with babies, such a pat-a-cake and peek-a-boo. This help gives babies repeated opportunities to respond and teaches them about the social function of language.
- Adults simplify and change the structure of their speech so that babies can understand it. This is known as 'motherese'.
- Babies are encouraged to respond because adults use intonation and leave gaps for babies to fill.
- Adults interpret children's words and repeat them back in an expanded form. For example, a child may say 'Drink all gone', but the adult will respond 'Yes, you've finished your drink now'. Repeating back an expanded form helps children hear the fuller structure.

Formation of early relationships

Attachment

The term *attachment* is widely used by psychologists studying children's early relationships. An attachment can be thought of as a unique emotional tie between a child and another person, usually an adult. Research has repeatedly shown that the quality of these ties or attachments will shape a child's ability to form other relationships later in life. Psychologists have also studied the effects on children when attachments are not made in infancy or when they have been broken (e.g. through separation).

There seems to be a general pattern to the way children develop attachments. Table 312.2 summarises the stages.

Table 312.2. The stages of attachment

Age	Stage	Features
6 weeks to 3 months	–	Babies begin to be attracted to human faces and voices. First smiles begin at around six weeks.
3 months to 7/8 months	Indiscriminate attachments	Babies are learning to distinguish between faces and show obvious pleasure when they recognise familiar faces. They are happy to be handled by strangers, preferring to be in human company rather than left alone (hence the term indiscriminate attachments).
7/8 months	Specific attachments	At around 7 or 8 months, babies begin to miss key people in their lives and show signs of distress, for example crying when they leave the room. Most babies seem to have developed one particularly strong attachment, often to the mother. Babies show a wariness of strangers even when in the presence of their 'key people'. This wariness may quickly develop into fear, if the stranger makes some form of direct contact with the baby, for example by touching them.
From 8 months	Multiple attachments	After making specific attachments, babies then go on to form multiple attachments. This is an important part of their socialisation process.

Bowlby's theory of attachment

The work of John Bowlby has greatly influenced social care policy, child care practices and research into early relationships. Immediately after the Second World War, he was asked to investigate the effects on children's development of being brought up in orphanages or other institutions. He showed that meeting children's physical needs alone was not sufficient: children were being psychologically damaged because of the absence of their mothers. The term 'maternal deprivation' was used to describe this. He reached this conclusion by looking at the life histories of children who had been referred to his clinic: most of these children had suffered early separations from their mothers and families.

- *Monotropy*. Bowlby believed that babies need to form one main attachment and that this relationship would be special and of more importance to the child than any other. He suggested that in most cases this relationship would be formed with the mother, but that it could be formed with the father or another person.
- *Critical period*. Bowlby felt that babies needed to have developed their main attachment by the age of one (the 'critical period') and that during a child's first four years prolonged separation from this person would cause long-term psychological damage.
- *Children need 'parenting'*. Bowlby showed that simply meeting a child's physical needs is not enough for healthy growth and development. Children need to have a main attachment in their early lives that gives them consistent support.
- *Children show distress when separated from their main attachment*. Bowlby outlined a pattern of distress that babies and children show when separated from their carers. This is often referred to as 'separation anxiety' (see page 404). He also showed that adults who had been separated from their mothers in infancy found it hard to form deep and lasting relationships. (Bowlby did not take into consideration the effect of being in poor-quality care, which means that it is hard to be sure that the psychological damage done to the children was only the result of 'maternal deprivation'; later studies have suggested that the good-quality care can help children to adjust to separation.)

Who will babies and children attach to?

Up until the 1950s it was generally thought that babies and children automatically formed the strongest relationships with the people who fed them and met their physical needs. Several pieces of research have shown that this is not necessarily true. For example, babies and children can form equally strong attachments to their fathers as to their mothers, even when the father is not the main carer. There are even some cases which show that children can form a main attachment with another child. These cases are generally in unusual and depressing circumstances and are looked at in more detail below.

One of the major concerns most parents have when leaving babies with nannies or childminders is that the child will attach himself or herself to the professional carer rather than the parents. Although in theory this is possible, it is unlikely, provided the parents spend time responding to and interacting with the baby. This is the idea behind 'quality time', where the quality of the interaction and responsiveness of the parents is more important than the actual time spent with children.

The role of fathers

Recent research has highlighted the importance of a father's role in children's social and emotional development. Fathers seem to offer a different type of contribution, which is nonetheless valued by babies and children.

- Most children aged 7–30 months choose their father to be playmates with in preference to their mother.
- Fathers hold their children in order to play with them, whereas most holding by mothers is linked to caregiving or restricting.
- Fathers play in different ways with their children, giving them more vigorous physical play.
- Strong attachments to both parents rather than just one also seem to help children in unfamiliar situations.

Attachment behaviour

It is important for early years workers to be able to identify when babies and children have made attachments. This generally can be seen in their behaviour. There are four broad indicators that babies and children might show:
- actively seeking to be near that person
- crying or showing visible distress when that person leaves or for babies is no longer visible
- showing joy or relief when that person reappears
- acute awareness of that person's presence (e.g. looking up at him or her from time to time, responding to that voice, following movements).

What happens when babies and children are separated from their main attachments?

Most early years workers will notice that, as children become older, they find it easier to separate from their parents. This is because they have formed attachments to staff and, as children get older, to other children. They have also learnt that although their parents are absent, they will return. Babies and toddlers, however, find it difficult to cope with the absence of their main attachments and will show distress.

Bowlby noted that there seemed to be a pattern to the way children reacted if they were separated from their main attachments. This pattern is often referred to as 'separation anxiety'.

Separation anxiety is clearly seen in babies from around seven months and seems to reach a peak at around 12–15 months. Older children will show separation anxiety if they are separated for long periods.

There seem to be three distinct stages of separation anxiety, as shown in Table 312.3.

Table 312.3. Three stages of separation anxiety

Stage	Features
Protest	Children cry, struggle to escape, kick and show anger.
Despair	Children show calmer behaviour, almost as though they have accepted the separation. They may be withdrawn and sad. Comfort behaviour such as thumb sucking or rocking may be shown.
Detachment	Children may appear to be 'over' the separation and start to join in activities. The child is actually coping by trying to 'forget' the relationship, hence the title detachment. The effects of detachment may be longer lasting as the child may have learnt not to trust people they care for.

Did you know?

Bowlby's work on separation anxiety changed the way in which hospitals worked with young children. Previously, most had had a policy of not allowing contact between parents and children. They found that children were upset after seeing their parents, whereas if there was no contact the children 'recovered' more quickly from the separation. In fact the children were 'detaching' from their parents rather than 'recovering'. As a direct result of Bowlby's work, hospitals began to allow more contact between parents and children and today parents are often able to stay overnight.

 Keys to good practice: Attachment in early years settings

✓ Most early years workers have seen the 'protest' stage while working with young children. It is not always easy to deal with, but it is essential that you are understanding of children who are demonstrating it. One way in which you can help children who are being regularly separated from their main attachment is to provide them with a substitute attachment. This has led to the idea of key workers, to whom babies and children can make a substitute attachment while they are separated from their main attachments.

Frameworks of effective practice

The increasing awareness that what happens in children's first three years can affect their later development has led to the drawing up of frameworks to support effective practice in the home countries of the UK. The first of these frameworks, published in England, is called *Birth to Three Matters*. Local authorities in Wales and Northern Ireland are showing great interest in adopting the *Birth to Three Matters* framework. Scotland has recently produced the document *Birth to Three: Supporting Our Youngest Children*, which advocates the same approach to the care of babies and young children as *Birth to Three Matters*. Unit 309 covers these (see pages 329–333).

Check it out

Explain how you could help children to develop an attachment with a key worker. How could you check that a child has made a special bond with a key worker?

Birth to Three Matters (England)

The *Birth to Three Matters* framework was published by the Department for Education and Skills in 2002 and is for use by all professionals who are involved in the delivery or planning of services for young children in England. The pack comprises an introductory booklet, poster, video, CD-ROM and 16 A4 'component cards' relating to four areas or aspects that have been identified as necessary for the development of all children. These are: a strong child, a skilful communicator, a competent learner and a healthy child. Each of these aspects is then broken down further into four components, as shown in Table 312.4. Each card also offers information and practice examples under eight headings, such as 'Case studies', 'Development matters' and 'Look, listen and note'. The last is intended to support the integral use of observations in day-to-day practice.

Check it out

Look at *Birth to Three Matters*. Pick out an aspect of one of the components. Read through the information and, using this as your baseline, carry out an observation on a child in your setting. In the light of the information on the card and what you have seen, how might you support this child? Look at the other cards that accompany the aspect you have chosen and think further about your observation.

Table 312.4. The four components of each aspect of the curriculum framework *Birth to Three Matters*

Aspect	Component 1	Component 2	Component 3	Component 4
A strong child	Me, myself, I	Being acknowledged and affirmed	Developing self-assurance	A sense of belonging
A skilful communicator	Being together	Finding a voice	Listening and responding	Making meaning
A competent learner	Making connections	Being imaginative	Being creative	Representing
A healthy child	Emotional well-being	Growing and developing	Keeping safe	Healthy choices

Check it out

In 1997, early years development partnerships were set up in each local education authority. In 1998, their remit was extended to include care of children from birth to 14 years and the name also changed to early years development and childcare partnerships. Many partnerships are providing training in support of best use of the *Birth to Three Matters* pack, including how to use the cards and reinforcing knowledge on development. Find out what is being offered in your area.

● *Development is seen not in categories such as physical, emotional, social and intellectual but holistically, at the times when key shifts in development take place, denoted by broad 'descriptors'.*

What is particularly important about *Birth to Three Matters* is the emphasis on seeing each baby as a unique individual and, therefore, development is seen holistically; that is, the authors of the framework have moved away from referring to development in categories such as physical, emotional, social and intellectual. Instead, they have identified the times when key shifts in development take place and have identified these shifts by broad 'descriptors' of the type of development taking place (see diagram on page 406).

Birth to Three: Supporting Our Youngest Children (Scotland)

Birth to Three: Supporting Our Youngest Children looks particularly at the role of the practitioner. The document is organised around three key features of practice that practitioners must show when working with children: relationships, responsive care and respect (see Table 312.5).

Table 312.5. The three key features of practice from *Birth to Three: Supporting Our Youngest Children*

Key feature	Key considerations
Establishing effective relationships	• Providing opportunities for child to establish warm and affectionate bonds with significant people • Providing opportunities for child to interact with others, both adults and children • Maintaining respectful and inclusive partnerships between all those involved with the child • Developing environments that promote security and consistency • Developing environments that promote trust and understanding
Establishing responsive care	• Building a knowledge of the individual child • Building an understanding of the needs and dispositions of each child • Ensuring adults are interested, affectionate and appreciative • Using flexible, personalised and relaxed approaches • Working to enhance sensitivity and respect
Establishing respect	• Valuing diversity, in terms of each child's language, ethnic background, faith and family circumstance • Respecting children's different experiences • Being sensitive to and understanding of differences, to ensure fairness, equality and opportunity

The expected pattern of development for children aged up to three years

In order to observe and evaluate the progress of the babies and young children, it is essential for practitioners to be aware of the markers of progress (these are sometimes referred to as 'milestones' or normative development). In Unit 303, children's development from birth to 16 years is covered in detail. Pages 105–120 look at the development of babies and children under three years, and also provide suggestions for observations.

Organisational policies and procedures for reporting and referring any concerns

Most babies' and toddler's development falls broadly into the pattern and rate of development that is set out in Unit 303. There are, however, always some children whose development in one or more areas does not follow the expected pattern. Some babies become mobile at 6 months, while others do so at 11 or 12 months. Flexibility is therefore need when thinking about rates of progress, although if no progress can be observed in babies and young children then this should be a cause for concern.

Where you do have concerns, it is important both to voice these and to carry out further observations. This has to be done sensitively, as it is important not to alarm parents and not to make inaccurate claims. Most settings should have a procedure in place and it is essential that you follow it. Ideally, good relationships with parents should make it easy for you to report to them the results of each observation and to talk about their child. This prevents situations where parents are suddenly told about a concern in such a way as to cause alarm. When discussing with parents aspects of a child's development, focus on ways in which you may together help the child. This may mean referral to a general practitioner, health visitor or specialist service provider such as a speech therapist. It may also mean planning additional observations and activities. Note that direct referral without gaining a parent's permission is not good practice and should occur only in extreme situations, notably where there is a child protection issue (see page 412).

Why and how to record observations of development accurately and clearly, using accepted language and formats

The reasons for observations

The National Standards for day care (see page 48) set out the following reasons for effective records based on observation:

- They help to identify significant steps in achievement.
- They help to match expectations to what a child can achieve.

Did you know?

You can obtain a copy of the Scottish framework *Birth to Three: Supporting Our Youngest Children* at the website www.ltscotland.org.uk/early years/files/birth2three.pdf. Alternatively, contact Customer Services at Learning and Teaching Scotland (tel: 08700 100 297; fax: 08700 100 298).

Check it out

Compare *Birth To Three Matters* with *Birth to Three: Supporting Our Youngest Children*. What are the differences in the way in which the material is presented? What are the similarities in the way practitioners are being encouraged to work with children?

Check it out

At what ages might children do the following? You may wish to refer to the information provided in Unit 303.

- Begin cooing.
- Show that they want to be picked up by lifting up their arms.
- Begin to have several words.
- Begin to sit up unsupported.
- Show an understanding of object permanence.
- Begin to pretend that a beaker is cup of tea.

- They show what a child knows, understands and can do.
- They provide accurate information for parents, colleagues and other professionals.
- They provide continuity of care by providing a means whereby information can be shared between practitioners and parents as well as other professionals, when and if the need arises (e.g. when further advice and guidance are required to meet a child's specific needs).
- They show how and what the child is learning and the rate of progress.

Did you know?

Verbal language appears to develop once physical mobility has been achieved, that is, from around 14 months (although babies have been *communicating* very well since birth).

Thus, the reasons for observing a child under three years as part of your daily practice are the same as with older children. It is only by observing that you are able to ascertain:

- the particular needs of an individual child (not always as easy as it sounds in the context of group care, for example, pressing adult needs, paperwork, etc.)
- what the *child's* view of his or her world might be
- the child's feelings, attitudes and motivation
- the child's interactions with others
- a 'baseline' for future interaction or assessment
- a good understanding of the child's behaviour.

Within the age range of birth to three years there is no formal assessment. What is necessary is that each child's *needs* are reliably assessed and that accurate records are kept of the child's ongoing achievements. This allows these achievements to be built on and any areas requiring additional support to be identified.

● *Observation in progress.*

Keys to good practice: Effective observations

To carry out good observations you need:

✓ a sound knowledge of development between birth and three years

✓ an ability to recognise when patterns of behaviour seem to occur and to think about why

✓ to confront or challenge accepted opinions if what you have seen provides a contrasting view (for example, a child labelled as 'naughty' could be shown through observation to be expressing distress or boredom or simply trying to establish independence)

✓ an ability to write down information in a clear, readable, jargon-free style and to put on paper only what is considered to be professional and objective

✓ an ability to draw any conclusions only from what you have actually seen – not what you think you might have seen

✓ to think about what you have learned from the observation.

Language and format of observations

The way in which observations are recorded is important. The focus of any observation should be accuracy. This means that language should be concise and free from judgements, especially when recording examples of children's behaviour. Avoid using terms such as 'snatched the toy', for example, that have a negative feeling and so can create a judgemental tone.

The format of the observations will depend on the method that is being used. Tickcharts and checklists are likely to be pre-prepared in type format, while written records, time samples and event samples might be drawn up at the time. If you are drawing up the format, either by hand or on computer, a good tip is to make sure that you allow plenty of space for comments. Where written records are being kept, it is important that the handwriting is legible and that spellings and punctuation are of a high standard. If you know you find this aspect of recording difficult, consider making notes at the time and then writing them up afterwards.

Reflect on your own practice

As you have seen, observations are an essential part of your role. Have a look at the statements below to assess whether you match up to the requirements. The statements all refer to the performance criteria for CCLD 312.1.

Performance criteria statement	Always	Sometimes	Never
Do I clearly identify the purpose and objectives for undertaking observations of individual babies and children, ensuring that organisational policy and procedure are followed?			
Do I always obtain permission to observe babies or children from parents?			
Do I obtain baseline information about the child's development from different sources, including parents, to inform observations?			
Do I evaluate developmental progress based on relevant and significant evidence from observations?			
Do I record the results of observations clearly and legibly, using agreed formats and appropriate language, and including any factors that could affect the reliability, validity or outcome of observations?			
Do I refer any concerns about development to appropriate individuals, professionals or agencies in line with legislation and organisational policy and practice?			

Communication with children under three years to develop positive relationships

What is meant by a warm and respectful approach to babies and young children

Children are people with feelings, likes and dislikes and a particular temperament (e.g. lively and responsive or quieter and taking more time to respond; curious or somewhat anxious). Babies and young children need to form relationships with adults that are warm and responsive, which is why the key worker system is so important (see 'Attachment', above). Being 'warm and respectful' generally means showing genuine affection, interest and concern. For babies and toddlers, physical contact is important: a cuddle when a child is upset or the offer of a hand to a toddler as you walk alongside are ways of showing warmth to a very young child.

Keys to good practice: Warmth and respect

- ✓ Use positive facial expressions and body language.
- ✓ Remember that physical touch reassures babies and toddlers.
- ✓ Use a friendly tone of voice and call children by their preferred names.
- ✓ Observe what children are doing and be sensitive if interrupting them.
- ✓ Tell a baby or young child what you are doing.
- ✓ Notice if the child appears to withdraw and respect this.
- ✓ Allow the child the freedom not to want to play or even to be with you at any one moment.
- ✓ See the child as a *person* in his or her own right, with his or her own style of behaviour and preferences.

Check it out

Some well known research called the 'still face experiment' showed how quickly babies responded to their mother's faces when the mothers were told to suddenly stop smiling and talking and keep a 'still face'. The babies become upset and even though the experiment only lasted a few moments, they took a little while to regain their enjoyment of the interaction.

(Source: Tronick and Cohn, 1989)

It may be difficult at first to imagine a situation where someone would not approach a baby or a very young child in a 'warm and respectful' way but in fact it is not uncommon. For example, have you ever seen a baby or young child 'scooped up' without the adult either looking at or talking to the child? Here are some further examples of not showing respect to babies and young children:

- hurrying a child to make a choice (this can take time for very young children)
- calling a child away from an activity without giving time for the child to adjust or to finish the task
- taking over the child's play

- hurrying a baby or child when feeding, or giving spoon feeds to more than one baby at a time (this is very poor practice)
- not looking at or talking to a baby or young child when giving drink or food or carrying out a care routine, or talking to others instead
- having expectations of behaviour which are too high for the child's developmental stage
- making faces or adverse comments when changing a child's nappy
- showing dislike or disgust if the child 'plays' with food
- lifting, handling and turning babies around without talking to them and soothing
- not allowing babies time to respond to your 'invitations' to play or interact and not allowing them to 'say no' via gesture, head turning, eye closing, for example
- dealing with crying or distress inappropriately (e.g. by rapidly jiggling the baby up and down, waving a toy or, with an older child, making adverse comments like 'Don't be a baby').

The list is long but not exhaustive. The common theme is not seeing children as individuals, with feelings and needs of their own. Respect means acknowledging children for who they are, their humanity and their abilities within their individual as well as 'global' developmental stage.

Check it out

A study by Hart *et al.* (1999) showed how mothers' perceptions – how they felt about the baby's character (fussy, calm, 'good', lively, etc.) – influenced the way they acted towards their babies – and practitioners working with babies and young children must be alert to their *own* attitudes. You may find it useful to make some notes about which children you find the easiest to relate to and which you find difficult. Can you work out why in each case?

Legislation, confidentiality and the sharing of information

Information collected about babies and young children is considered to be confidential. Even if parents may consent to observations being carried out, the information collected still falls under the scope of the Data Protection Act 1998. This is a wide ranging Act that is designed to prevent personal information from being passed on or held on to unnecessarily. The Data Protection Act covers handwritten personal information as well as information stored on computers (see Unit 301, pages 12–14).

Information about babies and children should be shared only with parents or other people who have a direct and legitimate interest in their care and well-being (e.g. other members of staff who share in their care). The passing on of information to others who do not work with the child concerned in your setting needs to be carefully thought through and, generally, parents need to give permission before this is done. The exception to this rule is where there is a medical emergency or where there are serious concerns of a child protection nature; in such extreme cases, local guidelines should be followed.

Engaging the attention and interest of babies

Babies need adults to help them learn how to communicate. Adults have to be responsive to their needs and find ways of gaining their interest and attention.

Babies are helped by the way in which most of adults instinctively speak to them – exaggerating facial expression, mouth movements and pronunciation. This greater emphasis on rhythm, pitch and tone helps babies hear the sounds more clearly and helps them to match sound and lip movements. The way that most people also instinctively put their faces in the mid-line (i.e. directly facing the baby) means that the baby gets maximum impact and equal information to the ears. Babies through these early 'conversations' learn about turn-taking, as the parent pauses, watches for a reaction, then imitates a mouth movement, makes a sound and then talks some more. Babies also learn that words and sounds have endings and beginnings and so they get a sense of time and timing emerges. The production of words requires precise timing and coordination.

What also helps is context. Babies can begin to identify familiar sounds with familiar situations. While dressing a baby, a key worker may talk throughout the procedure and words such as 'sock' may become associated with the feel of the sock on the foot.

It is also important to consider where a baby is on the language journey. The very young baby needs to be held more and will need opportunities to gaze into the eyes of the key worker; for more mobile babies, you may need to go down to their level and to comment about what they are doing. Babies need to hear the sounds of the language they are learning and it will help them if you give a running commentary reflecting what you and they are doing. As babies' babbling becomes more tuneful, it is important to ask them questions and encourage them to 'take turns' in conversations; the adult needs to acknowledge the baby's babbles by smiling and expanding on what has been 'said'.

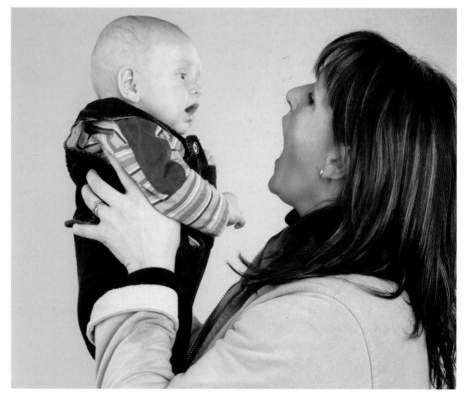

● *Exaggerated facial expressions are a feature of 'conversations' with babies.*

Allowing children to initiate communication and recognising when they do not wish to communicate

Communicating with others is not only about language: it is also about being in contact with others – feeling 'connected'. Babies who are mobile will indicate their interest: they will approach you and will tug at an arm or hand. Pointing is another signal to watch for. Vocalisations and facial expressions are powerful indicators in very young children who are yet to learn words.

Give babies and young children who are engrossed in an activity the freedom to get on with the activity without interruption. Observing their behaviour closely will let you know when they need help, are becoming bored or frustrated and need intervention. When they simply have had enough they are likely to turn to you again.

• *Reaching*

Eye gaze
A powerful indicator of both a wish to communicate and a need to disengage: babies will look away or even close their eyes if their interaction is becoming overwhelming

Body movements and later actions
Raising arms to be picked up, moving away or closer, pulling at an adult's arm, hand or leg

Facial expression
Smiling, frowning, surprise, fear, anger or sadness/dismay (e.g. pouting)

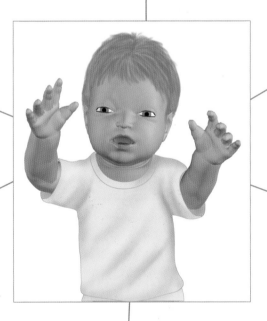

Vocalisations
Babies use crying, cooing or babbling while older children will gradually make attempts to use words

Body language
Waving goodbye or a 'greeting' wave, head shaking, nodding and perhaps shrugging in older children

Imitation
Used by children especially between the ages of 18 and 30 months in their interactions with peers until their confidence in language takes over. Children between the ages of 12 months to 2 years enjoy imitating tasks that adults do (e.g. washing up). This is a form of communication/interaction between child and adult which allows the child to learn more about daily life as well as practising different actions

• *Communication methods of children who have not yet learnt to speak.*

While looking directly at an adult is seen positively in many Western cultures, avoidance of eye contact is seen as polite in some cultures, and indicates respect for the adult. For some children, therefore, the adult demanding 'Look at me when I am speaking to you' may seem confusing and troubling. If you have children from different cultures in your setting, find out about the accepted social norms for children in their interactions with adults to avoid misunderstanding a child's behaviour and potentially interpreting it as a 'problem'.

The range of communication methods

From birth, babies will enjoy social interaction with their carers. Singing to babies, imitating them, showing them books and toys, playing together with simple rattles or 'talking' when holding a soft toy, telling stories, telling them what you are doing, talking while doing care routines – all without any sort of inappropriate 'teaching' – will all support the child's levels of communication.

Check it out

Think about situations where you have felt comforted by someone or known that someone was angry without that person saying anything or understood that you and another are both enjoying a meal – all without words. Then think about how you might transmit your own mood to the children in your care.

Repeating key words

Pointing to objects while speaking (e.g. 'Shall we look at your book? Look, here is the book!')

Using exaggerated facial expressions

Cuddling and gently bouncing a baby while maintaining eye contact

Looking at picture books

Using pictures for toddlers to point to so that they can express their needs (e.g. potty, drink, highchair, cot or bed, nappy)

Playing little games such as 'peek-a-boo' and 'pat-a-cake'

● *Communication methods with babies and young children.*

Case study 4: Language development

Wendy and Pia decided to encourage language development in their setting. They realise that they did not talk enough to the children and did not provide enough situations in which children could talk to each other. This had been prompted because two of the children aged two and a half appeared to have very few words. They decided to change snack time into a more social experience, and sat the children together in groups of two or three; the practitioners commented on what the children were doing at this time. They usually had a drink and some fruit. The children were encouraged to smell as well as taste the fruit; they also helped wash the fruit (and their hands). The practitioners talked about what they were doing when they sliced the fruit in front of the children and encouraged older children to cut the fruit themselves. They modelled sharing, requesting and saying 'thank you'. They also made sure they responded to the children's attempts to communicate in a positive way and to use a minimum amount of instruction.

1. *What other situations could have been used by the practitioners to encourage children to talk to one another?*
2. *How did they promote communication skills?*
3. *How well do you listen to others? How could you find out?*

Recognising communication differences and difficulties

Interestingly, body language, eye contact and physical contact with babies and young children can vary enormously between parents. While babies and young children can adapt to different styles of communication, it is advisable to learn about what a particular child is used to. If you have parents of different cultures or nationalities in your setting or in your neighbourhood, take note of how they interact and communicate with both young babies and toddlers. For example, some mothers may be more physically demonstrative than others and may kiss and hug their children more. Consequently, their children would be used to a much more active style of communication. The use of eye contact and body language also vary across languages and cultures. The gesture for 'no' may be different and so it is essential to learn by watching and taking an interest in the way parents interact with their babies.

Common difficulties in communication

It is important to think about whether babies and children are showing any signs of delayed speech or communication difficulties, as early intervention can make a significant difference.

The cause of communication delay or difficulty need not be one of the physical ones considered below. 'Environmental' causes include:
- lack of understanding by parents/carers and practitioners of the importance of talking and listening to children from birth
- parents/carers or practitioners being 'too busy' to talk to babies and young children

- meal times not being shared with adults
- noisy home environment (e.g. TV or radio always on)
- lack of talking, low interest in reading within the family generally
- child's lack of motivation to communicate because all demands and wishes are pre-empted by carers (sometimes including siblings)
- child being constantly in a pram not facing the 'pusher' or being left alone for long periods when awake.

- *Signs of possible communication difficulties in young children.*

Hearing impairment and sign language

One of the commonest reasons for speech and language delay is hearing impairment. Babies with hearing impairment have problems communicating vocally. Hearing-impaired children babble later than hearing children – for example between 11 and 25 months (although they do babble eventually). This is because they do not have the hearing 'feedback' which allows them to hear the sounds accurately and so the development of their own ability to speak is delayed and has different sound patterns. The signs of hearing loss in young children are presented chronologically in Table 312.6.

Table 312.6. Signs of hearing loss in young children

Age	Signs
Birth–3 months	Child does not startle at sudden loud sounds
3–6 months	Child does not respond to carer's voice
	Child does not enjoy rattles or other noise-making toys
6–12 months	Child does not respond to his or her name
12–18 months	Child cannot imitate simple words or sounds
	Child cannot point to familiar objects when asked
2 years	Child has not started talking
	Child becomes silent and stops babbling

Children with a severe hearing impairment are often taught sign language. The earlier sign language is taught, the more 'natural' and fluent the signing is. There are different sign languages, such as British Sign Language (BSL) and sign-supported English, and different countries have their own

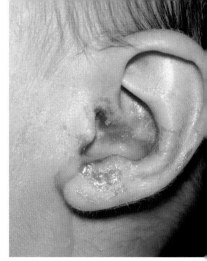

• *Glue ear*

sign languages. In addition, men and women can use different signs and there are also regional variations in signs for the same things.

A signing method known as Makaton is often used instead of BSL with people with learning difficulties. It is an aid to communication, not a language as such. Makaton also uses speech alongside signing. A useful website to learn more about Makaton is www.makaton.org/about/faq.htm.

Causes of communication difficulties other than hearing impairment

An inherited condition or illness or injury can cause a child to have problems with communication. Table 312.7 outlines a range of these.

Table 312.7. Types and causes of communication difficulties in young children

Type of difficulty	Examples/characteristics
Speech and language delay	A child with a speech and language delay develops speech and language following the normal pattern but at a slower rate or later than usual. He or she uses language in the way that a younger child would.
Dyspraxia	This seems to involve a breakdown of the messages between the brain and the muscles used for speech.
Muscle weakness or deformity	Problems with facial and/or tongue movements or facial disability such as a cleft palate.
Emotional problems	Being withdrawn, fearful of adults, possibly as a result of abuse or neglect.
Frequent ear infections	For example glue ear.
Phonological difficulties	Child finds it problematic to select and use the correct sounds necessary for speech.
Expressive difficulties	Child finds it hard to convey thoughts in words. For example, a child might use the word 'chair' instead of ' table' while fully understanding the difference between the two.
Pragmatic difficulties	A child may have difficulty understanding other people's language and behaviour, and may have problems using appropriate language for the setting.
Receptive difficulties	A child has problems in understanding spoken language.
Stuttering	Most children go through a perfectly normal phase of not being able to pronounce words in the accepted way, repeating words and not being fluent. If a proper stutter does develop, it will usually be between the ages of two and five years. Children who stutter have difficulty in coordinating the airflow into their mouths and the muscles around their mouths. Stressful situations (e.g. talking in front of a group) can make it worse. It is important to allow the child time to speak and not to finish a sentence for the child. Help with props and provide lots of reassurance. Referral to a specialist (e.g. speech therapist, for highly skilled advice and support) may be required.

Keys to good practice: Children with communication difficulties

✓ Children with communication difficulties do not necessarily have any learning impairment. Do not *assume* that a child's ability to understand, listen and learn is diminished because he or she has difficulties in communication.

✓ Make sure that a child with communication difficulties – for whatever reason – is not bullied or teased by other children. Your example will provide the role model for behaviour towards the child.

Visual impairment

Whether or not young children can see is not always thought about in relation to speech and language problems. It is, however, one reason why some babies' and children's communication is delayed. Adults often point things out to babies and toddlers and so a child who cannot see will not be able to make the connection between the word and the object.

Speech dysfluency

It is common for children from around two years to stutter or stammer as they speak. This is usually thought to be a result of a mismatch between what they want to say and their ability literally to get the words out. For most young children this is a temporary difficulty, but for some it can become a habit. It is essential that children who are showing signs of speech dysfluency are given plenty of calm time, when they can communicate with just one adult. Children can be helped by looking for relaxed situations when they can talk and by slowing down your own speech slightly. It is also important not to try to finish off sentences or interrupt a child.

Did you know?

People almost never stutter when singing, whispering, speaking along with other people or when they cannot hear their own voice.

Supporting children with communication difficulties

The importance of encouraging good communication skills in children from birth simply by talking, listening and playing with them cannot be over-emphasised. The Royal College of Speech and Language Therapists (1999) issued a report which states that 'A high proportion of children (41–75%) with identified speech and language difficulties in their pre-school years go on to have difficulties with reading skills during their school years'.

If you have concerns about a child's ability to communicate, positive relationships with the parents are vital in order that the degree of difficulty can be established. Help and advice can also be sought from your local early years advisory teams, special education needs coordinators, educational psychologists, health visitors and, of course, speech therapists. It is good practice to observe the child over time and during various activities, as infants and young children may communicate differently with different adults and in different situations.

How to manage children's emotional and behavioural responses to differences in communication

Babies and young children are all unique individuals. Their responses to their particular difficulties in communication will depend on a number of factors, including the following:

- what abilities the child has (always consider first what the child can do)
- the degree and type of difficulty
- the cause of the 'problem'
- the support and responsiveness of carers
- the chronological age and developmental stage of the child (remember that these are not necessarily the same and that aspects of development can vary in the same child, who may, for example, be very mobile but have difficulty with fine motor activities)
- the personality and temperament of the child
- cultural differences in expression and behavioural expectations.

The way in which children behave as a result of experiencing difficulties in communication will vary. In toddlers tantrums are common, for example, as are biting, hitting and throwing toys. Withdrawal is also possible and so carrying out an observation to check the frequency with which a baby or child attempts to communicate can be helpful.

Keys to good practice: Supporting children who have difficulties in communication

✓ Be patient.

✓ Allow children time and space in which to speak, gesture or otherwise indicate what they want.

✓ Provide and show prompts to aid their communication.

✓ Be accepting of a child's frustration while providing firm behavioural boundaries at the same time.

✓ Do not talk *over* the child.

✓ Do not speak for the child.

✓ Do not interrupt or say the words that you think the child might be trying to say (you could be wrong).

✓ Do not necessarily talk more slowly or speak in an exaggerated voice but ensure your own communication is clear, concise and matched to the child's developmental level.

✓ Do provide ample opportunity for pretend play to encourage communication.

✓ Talk to the child often.

✓ Consider using pictures so that children can point or give you a picture to help them to communicate their needs.

For many young children, comprehension exceeds their ability to vocalise, so frustration is common. You will not always be able to understand what a child is trying to communicate and in these circumstances ensure that you take responsibility for this. Pictures can work very well in helping toddlers to communicate; also, encourage children to take you over to what they have seen or what they want to do.

Check it out

Do you know what support or help is available in your area for children who have communication difficulties? Find out how and where you would go for help if you had concerns. What are the policies and procedures in your own setting?

Reflect on your own practice

As you have seen, using communication to develop positive relationships is an essential part of your role. Have a look at the statements below to assess whether you match up to the requirements. The statements all refer to the performance criteria for CCLD 309.2.

Performance criteria statement	Always	Sometimes	Never
Do I use a warm and respectful approach when initiating relationships with babies and children?			
Do I allow babies and young children to initiate and engage in communication at their own pace, making eye contact only when baby or child is comfortable with communication initiatives?			
Do I engage the interest and attention of babies and young children, using methods appropriate to age and developmental level?			
Do I explore the baby or child's range of interests, sharing activities and using these as a topic of communication in order to develop relationships?			
Do I recognise when babies and young children do not wish to communicate, or wish to disengage from communication, and respect their wishes?			
Do I use a range of communication methods, including singing, talking, stories, sounds, rhymes, games and language activities?			
Do I encourage babies and young children to communicate respectfully with adults and with each other?			

Plan and implement activities to enhance development

Activities to support different areas of learning and development

What adults do with babies and young children forms the mainstay of their development, and you can plan activities to support specific areas of development.

Very young babies

Many practitioners are worried about how to support the development of very young babies in their care. First and foremost, very young babies are interested in faces. If you are caring for babies under three months of age, the most important 'task' for them is the regulation of their bodily processes – for example regulation of body temperature, adapting to night and day patterns and learning how bodily needs such as hunger and cold are met by carers.

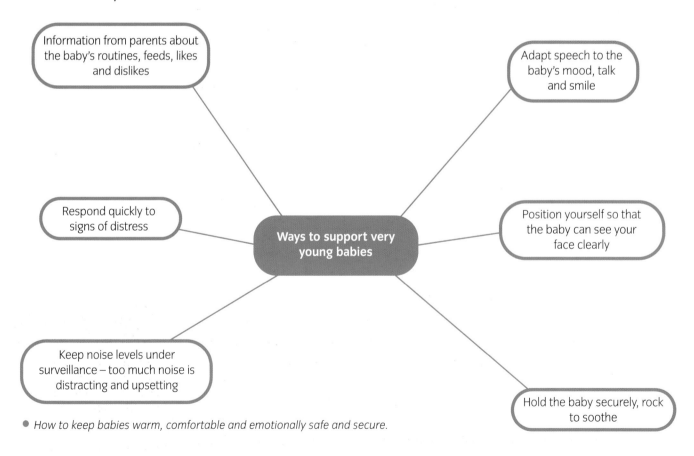

● *How to keep babies warm, comfortable and emotionally safe and secure.*

Simple activities such as stroking fingers, lifting arms and legs while talking and smiling, allowing the baby to kick freely during nappy changing, giving soft toys and presenting the baby with brightly coloured toys and mobiles will help overall development. Again, at this stage and later, position yourself in the mid-line (directly in front of the baby) when talking, to help them focus and enjoy your conversation. Allow the baby time to respond and imitate the child's mouth movements. Full smiles usually occur around four to six weeks, bringing even greater joy to the interactions.

Observation

Observe a baby's mood when he or she wakens. Some babies wake up alert, others take time and others are grumpy – just like adults. Think about how this would influence how you treat each baby on wakening.

Most of the babies in your care will probably be over the age of three months and will usually have established a broad pattern of feeding, sleeping and active times. For example, frequency of crying may now be reduced. They will enjoy rattles, play centres, your singing and telling rhymes, soft toys that produce sounds when patted or rolled and, of course, you, the early years worker, will be their most important 'toy'. They will also explore objects by mouthing and touching (see also Unit 303, pages 105–108). Between the ages of three and seven months some amazing development takes place – babies' physical systems are settling down, vision is more acute and babies are becoming more active agents in their own environment as their physical skills develop. Weaning is often taking place and babies learn the amazing new skill of being able to coordinate their lips and tongue to suck food off a spoon rather than the action they already know of sucking at nipple or teat. At around six months babies are very interested in playing with toys and objects and once they can sit steadily will spend time exploring such things as a 'treasure basket' with great concentration and enjoyment.

Treasure basket and heuristic play

Treasure basket play and **heuristic play** are popular with babies and toddlers. The aim is to provide a collection of safe but interesting objects for them to explore by themselves. Treasure basket play is often used with babies and consists of objects made from natural materials (e.g. coconuts, bristle brushes, leather purses, metal spoons). Heuristic play is used for toddlers and will include manmade materials such as plastic bottles or bracelets, but will be objects from the adult world. Toys are not included, as the idea is that by playing with a selection of objects and materials, babies and toddlers can discover for themselves what they can do.

Key terms

Heuristic play is a type of play that encourages children to explore the possibilities of ordinary objects.

Benefits of this type of play

Treasure basket play and heuristic play are designed to promote babies' and toddlers' concentration, exploration and independence skills. They stimulate their curiosity and teach them naturally about the properties of materials. Fine motor control and hand–eye coordination are also developed as babies and toddlers handle the items.

Sensory activities

Babies and toddlers enjoy learning by using their senses, particularly taste, touch and vision. Below are three examples of sensory activities that children enjoy.

'Gloop'

This is cornflour mixed with water. It is suitable for babies and toddlers as both groups enjoy its texture. Toddlers are also likely to enjoy mark-making with this mixture if it is spread thinly on a plastic tray.

Cooked pasta

Babies and toddlers enjoy touching, playing with and eating cold cooked pasta. This is suitable for older babies and toddlers, although it is important to check that children do not have a wheat allergy.

Water

While water play may take the form of bath time for babies, toddlers will also enjoy playing with washing-up bowls or in paddling pools. It is of course essential that, where water is used, adults supervise constantly and then remove the water when it is not in use.

Benefits of sensory activities

Through using sensory materials, babies and toddlers learn about textures, cause and effect, and being independent. Sensory activities also promote coordination and fine motor development, and help babies and toddlers to concentrate as well as to express themselves.

Toys and equipment to promote development

In addition to activities, there is also a range of toys and equipment that will support the development of babies and toddlers (see Table 312.8). While toys and equipment are valuable, it is always important to remember that the support and interaction of an adult alongside the child enhances the value of any play materials.

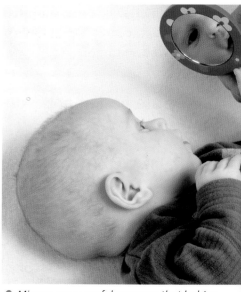

● *Mirrors are a useful resource that babies will enjoy.*

Table 312.8. Toys and equipment that will support the development of babies and toddlers

Toys and equipment	Suitable for	Role of adult	Skills developed
Mobiles	All babies and toddlers	Make sure that they are out of reach.	Builds an awareness of colour, shape and stimulates vision.
Baby gym	Babies who are not mobile	Play with the baby and make the object move.	Stimulates physical movements. Helps teach babies about cause and effect.
Rattles, shakers and musical instruments	From around four months	Show how they make sounds. Encourage the child to explore.	Encourages an awareness of sounds and auditory discrimination. Helps emotional expression. Develops fine motor movements and hand–eye coordination.
Stacking beakers	From around four months	Stack beakers up and encourage babies to knock them down. Use beakers to support early role play with toddlers.	Encourages learning about shape, size and also cause and effect. Develops fine motor movements and hand–eye coordination. Encourages self-expression.
Books	From around four months	Share books while cuddling or encouraging child to snuggle in. Choose some books that show familiar objects.	Develops fine motor development and hand–eye coordination. Promotes language and communication development. Encourages understanding of symbols.
Pop-up toys	From around six months	Show how the toy works. Encourage the child to work it. Find more complex wind-up and pop-up toys for toddlers.	Encourages learning about shape, size and also cause and effect. Develops fine motor development and hand–eye coordination. Promotes language and communication development.
Posting toys	From three months	Show babies by putting objects inside. Encourage toddlers to do it for themselves.	Encourages learning about shape, size and also cause and effect. Develops fine motor development and hand–eye coordination. Promotes language and communication development.
Bath time and water toys	From six months	Use bath time as well as washing-up bowls. Make sure that play is supervised.	Encourages learning about shape, size and also cause and effect. Develops fine motor development and hand–eye coordination. Promotes language and communication development. Helps emotional expression.

continued on next page

Toys and equipment	Suitable for	Role of adult	Skills developed
Balls	From six months	Choose a ball that is appropriate to the age of the child. Roll balls to babies. Encourage toddlers to throw.	Encourages visual skills and hand–eye coordination. Promotes gross motor movements in mobile children. Encourages turn taking as well as learning about cause and effect.
Push-and-pull toys	Babies who are sitting or children who are mobile	Show the child how to make the toy move. Note that toddlers might swing toys while walking and this can be dangerous for other children.	Encourages physical movements and coordination. Helps children to feel in control. Encourages learning about speed, space and distance.
Large wheeled toys (e.g. brick trolley, sit-and-ride, tricycles)	For mobile children	Observe children carefully to ensure the most appropriate equipment is provided.	Develops gross motor movements. Helps children learn about speed, space and distance. Encourages self-reliance.
Toy telephone	From nine months	To demonstrate use and join in when invited.	Encourages imagination and language skills.
Small-world toys (e.g. wooden animals)	From 18 months	Make sure that the toys are suitable for the age of the child (e.g. very small toys can be a choking hazard). Sit on floor and play with toddler (e.g. take the Noah's ark animals up the ramp, put play people in and out of cars or house).	Develops fine motor skills and hand–eye coordination. Promote language development. Encourage imagination and creative skills.
Mark-making, painting	From 12 months	Provide large marking pens, paintbrushes, large crayons. Model painting and drawing.	Develops fine motor skills and hand–eye coordination. Promotes language development. Helps children learn about using symbols. Helps children to express themselves.

Changes to routines and activities

The benefits of routines

A good routine is often at the heart of helping babies and young children to feel settled. It also is central in helping children to learn. An unhurried nappy change by a baby's key worker should be a moment when communication, interaction and emotional reinforcement take place. Similarly, snack time for a toddler might also be about learning to pour drinks and about social interaction, as well as eating and drinking.

Check it out

Choose one child or one group of children of the same age in your setting. Check out the toys and equipment you use with this age group. Are the activities suitable? Are there any improvements that you would recommend?

Babies in particular benefit from a good routine where physical care is also seen as a learning opportunity. Counting spoonfuls as an eight-month-old eats and saying 'all gone' develops a very early sense of mathematics and language. This is the approach taken in the *Birth to Three Matters* and other frameworks that the home countries are developing.

Table 312.9 sets out a 'timetable' for a baby room (for children in the first year) provided by a nursery in London. The day starts at 8–8.30, which is 'arrival time'. Music plays an important part in this day care setting. You will notice that while there is a basic daily routine, there is plenty of room for individual attention by key workers to their specific babies.

Table 312.9. A 'timetable' for a baby room

Time	Flexibly scheduled activities
8–8.30	Arrive to classical music – breakfast and then play until around 9.30.
9.30	Tidy up from breakfast and play.
9.45	Large-group time, when everyone is welcomed, and then singing and playing instruments. This is where an activity is chosen that may be of interest to all the babies in the room (e.g. lots of balls all over the floor or towers of bricks to be knocked down around the room). This is not the same as for toddlers, who may sit with their key workers in a circle for a short song or to play music.
10.00	Light snack.
10.30	Discovery time and individual activities.
11.15	Tidy up (to music) and outside time.
12.00	Lunch.
12.30	Discovery time for some, rest for others.
1.30	Discovery time and afternoon children arrive.
2.30	Discovery time and individualised activities.
3.00	Drink time and quiet time.
3.30	Tidy up and outside time.
4.00	Teatime.
4.45	General care of children and then play until home time (latest 6.30).

Individual patterns of sleep and feeds which fall outside these times are obviously accommodated and timing is never rigid.

Keys to good practice: Routines for babies and young children

✓ Ensure consistency and familiarity.

✓ Give pattern and rhythm to the day, which children can recognise and become familiar with.

✓ Keep the main furniture and equipment in the same place to encourage independence and confidence.

✓ Have a slow, relaxed and unhurried pace, especially during care routines.

✓ Work with parents to ensure that routines meet their child's needs.

✓ Observe individual children to check that the routine provides sufficient time for stimulation, interaction, rest and sleep and feeding.

✓ Adapt the routine in line with a child's changing needs.

✓ Ensure meal preparation and times are flexible, to meet individual needs.

✓ Ensure staff support each other so that the key workers are usually free to change, feed and settle their key children.

✓ Incorporate any routines from home as far as possible.

Changes to routines, resources and activities

There are times when a change is imposed to the routines or activities for either a group of children or an individual child. For instance, a room might need to be decorated or a member of staff might be on holiday. Changes to a routine sometimes distress young children and so need to be handled carefully. The way in which children cope will depend on the nature of the upheaval and also the age of the child, although all children tend to react badly to changes in staffing. This is because a familiar adult provides huge amounts of security for children and babies and children form attachments to their carers. If there is a planned absence (e.g. a holiday or a training day), it is important for babies and young children to be familiar with the person who will be looking after them instead.

Babies tend to be more affected by changes to their physical care routine. For example, the clock going forward by an hour in the spring can be very disruptive as they can miss out on an hour's sleep. Babies' physical care routines need to be as constant as possible as it is easy for them to become overtired and distressed.

While the physical care routine remains important for toddlers, they are more likely to be affected by changes to their environment. These, however, can be cushioned if they remain with a familiar adult and the changes are explained to them. It can also be helpful if the toddler can be involved in the changes. A toddler who is transferring to a bed from a cot may want to put their teddy in the new bed, for instance.

Check it out

How many different adults change, feed, support and settle the children in your care? Do the key workers mainly carry out these important care routines? How consistent is the care of children in your setting?

Adapting routines

Sometimes routines need to be adapted because they are no longer age appropriate, the children seem anxious or unhappy, or individual children need activities that are more (or sometimes less) stimulating. Recognising that a routine is not working for children is one reason why observations are essential.

Routines may also need to be adapted to meet the wishes of parents, for example for cultural or religious reasons. If you are changing an aspect of a routine because of the needs of a particular family, it is also important that you ensure the child is not singled out for comment and that the situation is explained carefully to other parents, who may question the decision of the practitioner team.

Change must always be handled sensitively, especially for the child, as any change brings with it the loss of the familiar.

Keys to good practice: Changing routines

✓ Help children by ensuring that they are with familiar adults during changes.

✓ Give extra physical reassurance and comfort to babies and toddlers.

✓ Allow toddlers to use a comforter to help them adapt to changes.

✓ Explain to toddlers simply the reasons for changes.

✓ Look for ways of helping toddlers to gain a little control of the changes.

✓ Talk to parents about changes to routines.

✓ Use observations to assess whether routines are working for individual children.

How to encourage children to communicate through play and learning activities

Babies can show that they want to interact with an adult by pointing to things; gradually, older, mobile children begin to bring over teacups, teddies and other small toys to show adults. This is a clear signal that they would like the adult to engage in their play and acknowledge what they are doing. You may, for example, pretend to drink a cup of tea or give teddy a cuddle. To support children's communication, it is important that you use language to support the play ('Thank you for my lovely cup of tea' or 'Teddy is feeling a bit tired'). The key when children are playing is therefore to follow their agenda for talk and language. Toy telephones are popular.

Case study 5: Observing Ben

Leanna is observing Ben, who is sitting between the legs of another practitioner, Leroy. Ben is 11 months old. Leroy has placed an activity centre in front of Ben and has shown Ben the different sounds and movements. Ben seems particularly attracted by a large red button, which when pushed makes a whirring sound and another section rotates. Leroy pushes the button several times so that Ben can understand how to make it work. He then leans back as Ben sits forward and pats the button. Ben works very hard with an expression of great concentration as he works to coordinate his arm and hand movements to reach the button and to push it. During this time, Leroy gives a running commentary on what Ben is doing ('Go on Ben, you can do it'). Eventually Ben succeeds in patting it hard enough to make it work and grins delightedly. Leroy laughs and claps. Ben laughs and then immediately sets about making it work again.

In this example, Leroy has shown Ben the different actions on the activity centre, has noted Ben's particular interest, has demonstrated the required action and then has waited patiently while Ben tries to repeat the action. He also has commented on it to maintain contact and support language development in an appropriate way and has then joined in with Ben's pleasure at his achievement. He understands that Ben will need to repeat this action, as this is part of his learning to coordinate muscle, hand and eye movements.

1. *How might Ben's learning be different if Leroy had taken Ben's hand and pushed the button for him?*
2. *How might Ben's running commentary have helped Ben?*
3. *Explain why Ben immediately tries to repeat the movements.*
4. *Consider what points Leanna might have noted down about Ben's development.*

Keys to good practice: Language and social skills

✓ To encourage children to communicate with others, be responsive to them.

✓ Imitate very young children's sounds and facial expressions.

✓ Notice the child – see the child as an individual.

✓ React to very young children as well as initiating contact.

✓ Respect their efforts.

✓ Encourage them to indicate what they want. For example, follow the direction of their gaze to find out what might have caught their interest, or when they are old enough to begin to point (at around eight months), look and comment. The child in this case has initiated the contact and you follow their lead.

Play is the most appropriate and useful way of supporting children's learning and language development. Table 312.10 sets out some examples of how this might be done.

● *Tickle games encourage communicati*

● *Pat-a-cake with an older child.*

● *Asking children about their artwork is a good way of encouraging communication.*

Table 312.10. Play to encourage language in young children of different ages

Age range	Types of activities
6–12 months	• Use lots of different sounds to interest a child. • Draw a child's attention to sounds in his or her environment, talk to the child during care routines such as nappy changing and feeding. • Take turns in a conversation – pause and allow the baby to 'reply', then imitate what the baby does. • Sing nursery rhymes, play finger and tickle games. Children usually become ticklish by about 6 months. Peek-a-boo and 'round and round the garden' are good games to play. • Find out about traditional lullabies, singing games and so on from other cultures. There are some beautiful lullabies for example from Celtic culture. Parents who may come from many parts of the world may be willing to share songs and rhymes from their country.
12–18 months	• Continue singing nursery rhymes and playing games like pat-a-cake and peek-a-boo. • Toys and objects that make a noise, as well as noisy books and tapes, encourage children's attention and listening skills but do not rely on these – they are simply fun additions to the adult talking. • Talk to the child about what you are doing. When shopping for example, show cans to the child, point out the bread on the shelves, pick up an apple, smell it and talk about how it feels and smells. Let the child feel the apple – but don't let them eat it until after the checkout! • If you see the child pointing at something, tell the child what it is. If the child tries to say the word, say it back. If the child pronounces a word incorrectly, simply repeat the word correctly to them. • Name the objects the child sees.

continued on next page

continued from previous page

Age range	Types of activities
18 months–2 years	• Keep talking about everyday activities like putting things away and let them help if possible.
	• Help the child understand your instructions and questions by using gestures or objects.
	• Give *simple* choices such as 'Do you want juice or milk?' or 'Do you want the puzzle or teddy?'
	• Use books to look at pictures and talk about them and let the child to feel the book.
	• Help the child string more words together, for example by saying 'Oh, your drink has all gone' while showing the empty cup.
	• Give the child prompts such as props or show a cup if you think he or she wants a drink.
	• Provide materials which allow the child to experiment safely with textures and colours and so on (e.g. paints, dough). Talk about their 'pictures' – ask the child to 'tell me about your picture' without first giving your own interpretation of what you think it might be.
2–3 years	• Expanding a child's sentences can show how words fit.
	• Children enjoy helping and imitating (e.g. tidying up) – talk about what you and they are doing.
	• Use puppets, pictures of characters in a story as well as pictures in a book to help a child listen to and enjoy stories. Repetition is particularly important.
	• Stories and action rhymes such as 'Going on a bear hunt' help children make up their own stories about themselves, families, pets or fantasy characters. Tape these or write them down so that they can be shared with parents.
	• Pretend-play will help expand the child's vocabulary – talking on a pretend telephone, being another 'character', acting out scenes from home or from television will all encourage a wider range of communication, in both word and gesture. Simple props such as hats, bags, cardboard boxes and blankets are more adaptable to different play situations than specific outfits or equipment (e.g. plastic microwave cooker or fire-fighter's outfit).

Observation

Carry out two observations each on two small groups of children (no more than three per group). Try to have a reasonably wide age gap between your groups. Observe them in an adult-led activity and during free play. Pay particular attention to the language that the children use in each of these situations.

● Is there a difference in the language used by each group of children in the adult-led activity and in the free play?
● What is the difference in the language used between the two ages?
● Do all the children show the same level of language within their groups?
● How will you use this information to help you in supporting the children's communication in general?
● Have you identified any specific needs in particular children?

You may find it very useful to tape or video the children while you are observing (make sure you have appropriate permissions – check with your setting).

Patterns of communication development

Early years workers need to understand the way in which children's communication and language develop (see pages 414–416). The skill of communication begins at birth, when babies first learn to use sounds and facial expressions to attract adults' attention. From this early start, babies quickly learn the sounds of particular carers (e.g. they can recognise their parents' voices). At the same time, babies start noticing the responses of others and in this way begin to learn how to use facial expression, signs such as waving and body language. Adults must think about their own responsiveness to babies and toddlers.

Early interest in reading

Although of course babies are unable to read, they are generally interested in books from an early age. It is never too early to start showing and sharing books with them (babies as young as four months have been seen to turn pages in books). Books designed for babies often reflect their interests and things that they are likely to see in their environment (e.g. picture books may have a photo of a beaker and a highchair). Books also promote language development, as they draw babies' and toddlers' attention to pictures and simple books allow them quickly to recognise images. Sharing books with babies and toddlers also supports emotional well-being, as the adult should be 'snuggled' up to the child (the toddler may sit on a lap or close by the adult). Interestingly, as toddlers develop favourite books, they begin increasingly to point to words and pictures. This is an important pre-reading skill.

Keys to good practice: Encouraging an early interest in books

- ✓ Make sure that babies and toddlers have opportunities to share books with adults.
- ✓ Introduce a range of books as early as possible (e.g. fabric, picture, pop-up, card books).
- ✓ Draw babies' and toddlers' attention to pictures and things of interest in the book.
- ✓ Observe which books appear to be of interest to individual children and make sure that these are often offered.
- ✓ Be ready to share the same book over and over again.
- ✓ Encourage babies and toddlers to handle books (e.g. turn pages).

Early interest in writing and mark-making

Mark-making begins very early on. Babies, for example, often enjoy the sensation of smearing their food or drawing circles in a spilt drink. A useful activity is to put some 'gloop' (see above) in a highchair tray and encourage the baby to enjoy the texture and use fingers to make marks.

From this type of activity, you can move to providing large markers and large sheets of paper for toddlers of around 15 months. Many of the marks made will be rotational and from this early starting point you are likely also to see the emergence of meaningful drawings. It is also useful if adults model mark-making. This does not mean teaching the child, but simply sitting down and drawing or writing so that children become interested. Mark-making and early writing can also be an outdoor activity. Many young children enjoy 'painting' a wall with water using large paintbrushes.

Keys to good practice: Encouraging early mark-making

✓ Remember that interest in mark-making begins early on with sensory activities such as playing with gloop on a plastic surface.

✓ Provide large-scale mark-making and painting opportunities (e.g. painting walls).

✓ Use outdoor walls for children to draw, paint and 'wash'.

✓ Model drawing and marking so that children become interested.

✓ Avoid the temptation to 'teach' letter formation.

Policies and practices regarding risk assessment

While the environment in which children are cared for must be stimulating, it also needs to be safe. Toddlers and babies have little or no sense of danger and so require adults around them to supervise them and to think about necessary measures to keep them safe. It is therefore important for you to understand the health and safety procedures in the environment in which you work (see also Unit 306, pages 230–238). If you are working in a group care or education setting, it will have a written policy and also a member of staff is likely to be designated as being responsible for health and safety. If you are working as a childminder or nanny, you can gain information directly from organisations such as the Child Accident Prevention Trust (CAPT) or the Royal Society for the Prevention of Accidents (RoSPA). Childminders may also gain support from childminding networks.

Risk assessment is an important part of health and safety procedures. The idea is to evaluate possible risks during activities and in the environment and then to consider how best to minimise these (see also Unit 302, pages 64–65).

Where there are policies and procedures in place it is essential that these are followed, as you have not only a moral duty to keep children safe but also a legal one. This requires, for example, the use of safety equipment such as stair gates and harnesses, and keeping equipment clean.

Challenging activities for babies and children and the importance of risk assessment

During the first three years of life, development does not 'just happen': for development to occur, the baby and toddler must be presented with a stimulating environment and activities, as well as adult support and interaction. Making sure that activities are challenging enough prevents children from becoming bored and also stimulates their development.

Using observations as a starting point, you should look at ways of challenging babies and children. You may, for example, put a stack of beakers very slightly out of the reach of an eight-month-old baby who is on the verge of crawling. If the baby is ready, this may just be the stimulus that is needed to promote mobility. Similarly, instead of carrying a toddler down a flight of steps, you might hold a hand and slowly help the child to walk down them one by one. Sometimes, babies and toddlers find their own challenges; for instance, a toddler might try put on shoes on or a baby might try to crawl up some steps. In such situations, adults need to work out whether the activity poses any serious risk and wherever possible to step back and allow the child to meet the challenge. This might mean that the baby is allowed to go up the steps but the adult is close at hand, while the toddler who is trying to put on shoes is praised and gently helped to fasten them up.

Some types of challenging activities, such as providing a sit-and-ride toy for a toddler, are not without risk. While keeping children safe is a priority, it is important nevertheless to find a balance so that you do not prevent children from learning new skills, otherwise the toddler will never learn to balance and steer, for example. To gain the balance of providing challenging activities and to avoid the danger of a sterile and boring environment, it is important to carry out risk assessments. To do this well means being aware of the dangers that particularly affect this age group. These are:

- suffocating, choking and swallowing
- falls
- drowning
- burns and scalds
- poisoning.

Once you are aware of the possible dangers, the next step is to work out how to minimise them. Close supervision is one of the best ways of allowing toddlers to explore, climb and learn about their environment, while for babies being aware of small items on which they might choke will be necessary. Table 312.11 lists some of the safety equipment that is commonly used with very young children.

Table 312.11. Common safety equipment

Type of equipment	Reason for use	How to use
Harnesses and reins	To prevent children from falling out of pushchairs or highchairs. To prevent children from running into the road or straying.	Should be a snug fit. Make sure that you can release babies and toddlers easily when they are being fed in case they choke.
Playpens	To keep mobile babies in a safe environment for a short period.	Do not use for long periods. Playpens are not a substitute for adult supervision. They must be suitable for the age and stage of the baby.
Socket covers	To prevent children from poking electric sockets.	They must be consistently used.
Corner covers	To prevent toddlers from catching their heads or eyes on furniture.	It is always better to remove unsuitable furniture.
Drawer and cupboard catches; window catches	To prevent children from opening drawers, cupboards and windows.	It is always better to make sure that children are not allowed in areas where there are dangerous items such as chemicals. Some catches can weaken over time and so are not completely childproof.
Safety gates	To prevent toddlers and young children from falling down stairs or having access to certain areas (e.g. kitchen).	Adults must use them consistently. Regular checks are needed that they are securely in position.

Taking action if the surroundings or equipment are unsafe

A risk assessment may lead you to become aware of a danger in the environment that you cannot safely manage. In such situations, you may need either to remove the child from the danger or to remove the piece of equipment or danger itself. A bowl of glass beads, for example, cannot be made safe for a baby to play with. As well as preventing an immediate accident, it is essential to report the danger to other people you work with. If you have removed equipment that is faulty or broken, such reporting will ensure that other people do not unwittingly put it back into circulation.

As you have seen, planning and implementing positive environments for very young children are an essential part of your role. Have a look at the statements below to assess whether you match up to the requirements. The statements all refer to the performance criteria for CCLD 312.3.

Performance criteria statement	Always	Sometimes	Never
Do I identify specific activities for individual babies and children that meet their interests and developmental capabilities?			
Do I provide a range of play activities for individual babies and children under three years that are challenging but achievable and appropriate to the child's level of development?			
Do I provide activities that encourage babies and young children to extend their range and level of skills and understanding?			
Do I adequately assess risk, in line with legislation and organisational policy, without limiting opportunities to extend and challenge the skills and knowledge of babies and children under three years?			

Exchange information and respond to parents' needs and preferences

The importance of sharing information with parents

To work well with parents, it is important to share information effectively with them. While older children can tell their parents if they have had a good day or tell early years workers that they have already had some breakfast, a very young child is likely to find this difficult. Where good relationships and systems of exchanging information are in place, children's needs and interests can be responded to more easily. Good communication should prevent situations where toddlers are given the same dinner twice or are put down for a nap even though they have already slept in the car.

Parents will want day-to-day information about their child. With babies and very young children it is much more likely that this can be passed on directly to the parents when the child is collected or brought to the setting. However, parents will still want to know about their child's developmental progress and whether their child is contented and settled. Written records and observations will be applicable here, just as with older children. A home–setting diary or notebook is useful; comments can be put in for parents and parents can put in snippets of information for staff. Photographs are a useful way of recording key moments for parents.

Examples of day-to-day information to share with parents include:
- the child's interests during the day
- information about the physical care of the child (e.g. amount of sleep, food and drink, nappy changes)
- changes in the child's behaviour, health or routine
- developmental information gained from observing the child.

Parents are likely to want to know (and should understand) the procedures and policies of the setting. Most settings provide copies of these, as parents can then refer to it. Examples of information about the setting to share with parents include:
- the policies and procedures within the setting, including those covering fire drills, health and safety, and child protection
- the name and training of staff who are first-aiders
- the name and training of staff who will administer any medication that the child must have, how this is recorded and where such information is kept
- the procedures if the child is ill or has an accident
- how and when observations are carried out.

Check it out

In order for you to tell parents about policies and procedures, you need to be familiar with them yourself. Make sure that you and your colleagues know where telephone numbers are kept and that these are easily located in an emergency.

● *Personally greeting parents by name helps establish an effective relationship with them.*

Keys to good practice: Sharing information

✓ Make the entrance to the setting look as inviting as possible. Greet parents with a smile and by name.

✓ Allow time for parents to talk.

✓ Invite parents to ask questions, look around the setting, visit or attend for a morning or afternoon.

✓ Provide clear information about the principles and practice within the setting.

✓ Show parents how their child's development is being monitored and assessed (this will also support consistency in expectations of the child).

✓ Show parents where and how information about their child is kept and their rights of access to it.

✓ Always be approachable and willing to help or answer questions. Answer questions honestly and clearly.

✓ Provide positive feedback about the child, as this will support the child, encourage the relationship between the parent and the child, and demonstrate individual interest in each child's achievements.

✓ Encourage parent helpers in the setting.

✓ If English is not the family's first language, discuss with staff how best to pass on information.

Parents' preferences concerning care routines

Care routines need to be talked through in detail with parents. Every child is different, as is every parent. Some parents, for example, are keen for their children to be fed on demand, while others may want a more structured approach; some parents are keen to use skin products such as barrier creams after a nappy change, while others are not. To avoid misunderstandings, it is important that time is spent when a baby or toddler is about to join a setting carefully talking through the physical care routines. One parent may assume, for example, that all food is organic or that nappies are provided, while another parent may assume that comforters are not allowed.

Checking out that care routines match the needs of the child is especially important where a child has an allergy, medical routine or a need relating to religion or culture. It can also be useful to ask parents to show you how they do tasks such as nappy changing or feeding, so that if there are significant differences with how these are done in the setting these can be discussed. By working closely with parents in this way, you can help babies and toddlers to settle in, and you can also avoid misunderstandings.

Reaching agreement where parents' preferences do not meet the requirements of good practice

Most practitioners working with babies and toddlers find that there are occasions when parents' views about their child's care routines do not concur with good professional practice. Parents may, for example, want a child to be potty training before he or she is ready, or may ask you to stop their child from having a nap in the afternoon, even though the child desperately needs to sleep. If you have good relationships with parents, you should be able to explain the boundaries of what you are able to do as a professional practitioner. You may need to explain that childminders, nurseries and pre-schools are all regulated and that you have to operate to the standards of care that are laid down.

It is also important that you talk to parents about the reasons for their wishes. It may be, for example, that they are keen to get their child out of nappies before going on holiday or before the birth of a sibling.

While it is necessary to give due consideration to parents' views, you must remember, as an early years worker, that your duty is always to ensure that the child's needs and welfare come first.

Case study 6: Disagreement about routines and practices

Fran's mother has asked to see Fran's key worker, Jenny. Fran is two years old and her mother finds that getting her to sleep in the evening is becoming increasingly difficult. She wants Fran's key worker to prevent her from falling asleep in the afternoon. She thinks that if Fran comes home tired she will go to sleep more easily. Jenny has seen that on the days when Fran has not had a nap in the afternoon she gets overtired and often has tantrums or simply cries. She has also seen Fran fall asleep over her teatime snack.

Jenny sits down with Fran's mother for a proper discussion. She listens carefully as Fran's mother talks and notes how frustrated and tired she seems. She learns that Fran does go to bed, but then often plays around and gets up several times. She also refuses to go to sleep unless Fran's mother is sitting on the bed. Jenny reassures Fran's mother that this type of behaviour is quite common in children of this age and that there are two issues here: sleep and attention seeking. She explains that it is virtually impossible to keep a very tired child awake in the afternoon and that, as a professional practitioner, she must first of all think about Fran's needs. Jenny suggests that they compromise about the nap in the afternoon. She suggests that Fran gets an earlier but shorter nap in the afternoon so that she does not fall asleep when it is very late in the day. She also suggests that, when Fran gets home, she is given some 'special time' before going to bed so that the attention seeking can be solved. Jenny also suggests some sources of information for Fan's mother about helping young children sleep. They agree to try this regime out for the next few weeks to see if the situation improves.

1. *Why is it important to listen to parents' wishes and needs?*
2. *Why is it helpful to explain to parents the duties that professional carers have towards the child?*
3. *Explain why Jenny and Fran's mother need to keep talking about Fran's sleep and nap patterns.*

Sources of advice available to families

Raising a baby or young child is often stressful. A crying baby or a toddler having a tantrum can cause parents to feel desperate. Fortunately, there are a number of sources of advice both locally and nationally that will help parents. Table 312.12 lists some of these.

National SureStart programmes often include a range of professionals to support families. In addition, families should have contact with their local health visitor, who will be able to offer invaluable advice regarding child development, carry out routine developmental checks and advise on referral if necessary. In some areas, health visitors also work closely with day care settings.

In addition, educational psychologists, speech therapists, and play and occupational therapists often are part of local teams that will be available for more specialist help. Support is also available from voluntary organisations such as Parentline Plus, an organisation that provides telephone support for parents. More specific help is offered by organisations such as Cry-sis, which helps parents whose babies cry excessively.

Check it out

Find out about your local SureStart programme. Are there any other initiatives based on interventions for children under three? Are you confident about the role of different professionals, such as educational psychologists? If not, find out!

Finally, the internet can provide a wide range of help for parents. Social services and the citizens' advice bureaux are also good sources of help and advice for parents and staff on a range of issues.

Table 312.12. National sources of advice and support for parents in the UK

Organisation	Description	Website	Telephone
Parentline Plus	Parentline Plus is a UK registered charity which offers support to anyone parenting a child	www.parentlineplus.org.uk	0808 800 2222
Parentscentre	Parents Online has been created by the Department for Education and Skills (DfES) to promote home–school links by helping parents understand the English education system	www.parentscentre.gov.uk	–
Cry-sis	Cry-sis offers support for families with excessively crying, sleepless and demanding babies	www.cry-sis.org.uk/contact.html	08451 228 669
Home-Start	Freephone national information line offering support, friendship and practical help to parents with young children in local communities throughout the UK	www.homestart.org.uk	08000 683 368
Disabled Parents Network (DPN)	National organisation of and for disabled people who are parents or who hope to become parents, and their families, friends and supporters	www.disabledparentsnetwork.org.uk	08702 410 450
Positive Parenting	National registered charity specialising in the support of parents and those who work with them	www.parenting.org.uk	023 9252 8787
The Twins and Multiple Births Association (TAMBA)	Nationwide UK charity providing information and mutual support networks for families of twins, triplets and more. TAMBA operates a Freephone helpline, Twinline, a national, confidential, support, listening and information service for all parents of twins, triplets and more, and the professionals involved in their care. Information is provided in several languages	www.tamba.org.uk	0870 770 3305

continued on next page

continued from previous page

Organisation	Description	Website	Telephone
What About The Children (WATCh)	National charity that promotes parental responsibility with particular emphasis on the emotional needs of children during their crucial first three years	www.whataboutthechildren.org.uk/	01892 863 245
I-CAN	National charity that helps children with speech and language difficulties. It provides a combination of specialist therapy and education for children, information for parents, and training and advice for teachers and other professionals	www.ican.org.uk	0845 225 4071

Reflect on your own practice

Have a look at the statements below to assess whether you match up to the requirements of working with children under three years of age. The statements all refer to the performance criteria for CCLD 312.4.

Performance criteria statement	Always	Sometimes	Never
Do I encourage the parents of young children to share information that may affect the care and well-being of their children?			
Do I discuss preferred care routines for young children with their parents and obtain information to ensure routines are followed?			
Do I regularly exchange information on progress and achievements with parents and discuss any changes to routines and the reasons for these?			
Do I monitor, adapt and change routines to ensure they continue to meet the child's needs?			

End-of-unit knowledge check

1. What type of professional might you contact if you were concerned about the speech and language development of a child in your care?
2. Where would you seek general advice on an initiative such as *Birth to Three Matters*?
3. What action would you take if parents complained that they had no idea what went on in the nursery and, as they were working, they could not visit during the day?
4. What advice would you give to a new member of staff about the importance of interactions with babies?
5. What are the key features you would need to consider in order to ensure individualised care for a group of children aged between one and two years?
6. What factors may influence a child's ability to learn?
7. What measures might be taken to ensure a safe and healthy environment for this age range?
8. What might be the impact on babies and toddlers if practitioners 'change rooms' every six months?

References

Abbott, L. and Nutbrown, C. (eds) *Experiencing Reggio Emilia. Implications for Pre-school Provision.* Open University Press (2001).

Barnes, P. (ed.) *Personal, Social and Emotional Development of Children.* Open University Press (1995).

Bee, H. *The Developing Child.* Harper Collins (2000).

Bruce, T. *Learning Through Play – Babies, Toddlers and the Foundation Stage.* Hodder & Stoughton (2001).

Goldschmied, E. and Jackson, S. *People Under Three.* Routledge (1994).

Gopnik, A., Melzoff, A. and Kuhl, P. *How Babies Think: The Science of Childhood.* Weidenfeld and Nicolson (1999).

Hart S., Field, T. and Roitfarb M. Depressed mothers' assessments of their neonates' behaviours. *Infant Mental Health Journal*, vol. 20, pp. 200–210 (1999).

Locke, J. L. *The Child's Path to Spoken Language.* Harvard University Press (1995).

Manning-Morton, J. and Thorp, M. *Key Times: A Framework for Developing High Quality Provision for Children Under Three Years Old.* Print Emporium Ltd/Camden Early Years Under Threes Development Group (2001).

Oates, J. (ed.) *The Foundations of Child Development.* Open University Press (1994).

Piaget, J. *The Language and Thought of the Child*. Routledge Classics (2002 edition).

Robinson, M. *From Birth to One – The Year of Opportunity*. Open University Press (2003).

Royal College of Speech and Language Therapists *Early Communication Audit Manual*. Royal College of Speech and Language Therapy (1999).

Svenberg, P. O. G. Attachment, resilience and prevention. *Journal of Mental Health*, vol. 7, pp. 543–578 (1998).

Tronick, E. Z. and Cohn, J. F. Infant–mother face-to-face interaction. *Child Development*, vol. 59, pp. 85–92 (1989).

Create environments that promote positive behaviour

Children in the past had no rights and were expected by adults simply to be submissive and obedient. Today, it is recognised that children have rights and are entitled to be valued. This view is now reflected in professional practice, and especially in attitudes towards how children should be helped to show positive behaviour.

What you must know and understand

- The different approaches to the management of behaviour (K3D691)
- The possible effects of communication difficulties and attention deficits (K3C457)
- Possible reasons for children's challenging behaviour... (K3D700)
- How adults' expectations affect children's behaviour and can reinforce challenging behaviour (K3D701)
- Policies and procedures that enable a structured approach to the management of behaviour (K3D692)
- Why it is important to agree behaviour management programmes with families and colleagues (K3D693)
- Situations in which such programmes might be necessary (K3D694)
- How you would monitor the effects of such programmes on individual children (K3D695)
- Under what circumstance behaviour management programmes might be modified (K3D696)
- What is meant by a firm and respectful approach (K3D697)
- What is meant by unambiguous directions, limited choices and defined boundaries for children; why these are important in managing behaviour (K3D698)
- The links between behaviour, self-esteem and relationships with others (K3D699)

Implement behaviour policies and procedures

The different approaches to the management of behaviour

Traditional methods of managing children's behaviour looked at control. These methods, though, are not as effective as a more child-centred approach. A child-centred approach does not mean that children can do exactly they want, but it does mean that adults are aware of their needs. This move away from the authoritarian and dictatorial approach can be difficult for some practitioners, especially if as children they were frequently instructed to 'Do as you are told'. The approach that is recommended today is not about managing children's behaviour, as this suggests controlling children, but rather about promoting positive behaviour, by adopting a firm yet respectful approach.

Defining appropriate behaviour is not easy

The term 'appropriate behaviour' is often used, but it is extremely vague. Behaviour that is appropriate for some people is not for others. Also, attitudes towards some types of behaviour change over time. A few decades ago it would have been frowned upon for people to eat in the street, for example; and many children now call adults by their first names, which would have been seen as rude. Appropriate behaviour also varies according to situations and circumstances. Shouting is not a problem if you are alone on a beach, but is not appropriate on a bus.

Behaviour also has cultural variations, which is why you need to work alongside parents to understand their perspectives and to discover common ground.

Finally, it is necessary to accept different types of behaviour from children of different ages or stages of development. Most people do not get cross if a baby tries to pull their hair but they would do if a 15-year-old tried it.

Respect should be the focus

At the heart of most codes of conduct is the concept of respect. Children need to learn that their actions can have an effect on other people, and so appropriate behaviour is usually about respecting other people as well

● *This behaviour would be unacceptable from an older child.*

as the environment and themselves. This means that as soon as children are able, they should be encouraged to wait their turn rather than push others out of the way, and should use a space in such a way that they do not hurt anyone else or themselves. A focus on respect often helps children to understand why they cannot follow their impulses. It also prevents situations in which adults simply say 'Do this because I tell you to'. The behaviour policy in settings should reflect the concept that appropriate behaviour is usually about respect rather than consisting of rules that exist purely for their own sake.

Check it out

Think about three rules in your setting. Are they fundamentally about children needing to respect others, themselves and the environment?

● *Unwelcome behaviour can be seen as a lack of respect – for the environment as well.*

Child-centred approaches to behaviour

Traditionally, children who did not obey adults or who showed unwelcome behaviour were considered to be a problem. Little thought was given to why they were exhibiting unwelcome behaviour. Child-centred approaches consider that most children's unwelcome behaviour is linked to underlying issues. For example, a child who is not accepted by other children may try to sabotage their games. While this is not acceptable behaviour, the underlying reason is the child's social skills. Similarly, attention-seeking behaviour in older children might be linked to their need to be accepted by their peers.

Child-centred approaches to behaviour focus on the underlying causes to prevent unwelcome behaviours. Taking a child-centred approach is not a soft option. It can, however, be remarkably effective, whereas simply managing or containing children's behaviour may not result in overall improvement in the longer term.

Inclusive approaches to behaviour

Some ways of managing behaviour can isolate children from their peers or prevent them from having the same opportunities as other children. A child who, as a punishment, is not able to go outside to play might be missing out on opportunities to develop physical skills or build friendships with other children. A child who is told to leave the story time for fidgeting may be missing out on an opportunity for language development. The recent focus on inclusion and helping children with special needs, including behavioural needs, means that you must think carefully about the strategies that you use with children.

Language and behaviour

There is a significant link between children's language and their ability to control their behaviour. Children who are good at talking can often explain what they are feeling and use language to object to what others are doing. Good language skills also help children to plan and organise their thinking. This is one reason why children under the age of three years find it much harder to wait and control their impulses. Many children whose language has not developed show aggressive and frustrated types of behaviour (e.g. a two-year-old may have a tantrum or a four-year-old may bite another child). While such unwelcome behaviours are unacceptable, it is important to work on children's communication skills in order to make lasting progress.

Case study 1: Hitting

Liam is six years old. He often hits other children when he is outdoors playing. Staff have tried many different tactics, including telling him that he cannot go outdoors to play. While this approach does stop other children being hurt, staff find that, when he does go outside again, the behaviour is repeated. A member of staff has been on a behaviour training day and has decided to observe Liam carefully. She notices that while he is involved in structured activities with an adult present, he can cope, but he has difficulty playing with other children when there is no adult to organise the activity. She wonders whether he has not yet acquired the play and joining skills that he needs to go over to a group of children and be accepted. She observes further and discovers that he does not really have any particular friendship group. A decision is made to work on these skills with Liam.

1. Why was keeping Liam inside excluding him?
2. Explain why it is important to observe children's behaviour carefully.
3. Why might Liam's behaviour improve now?

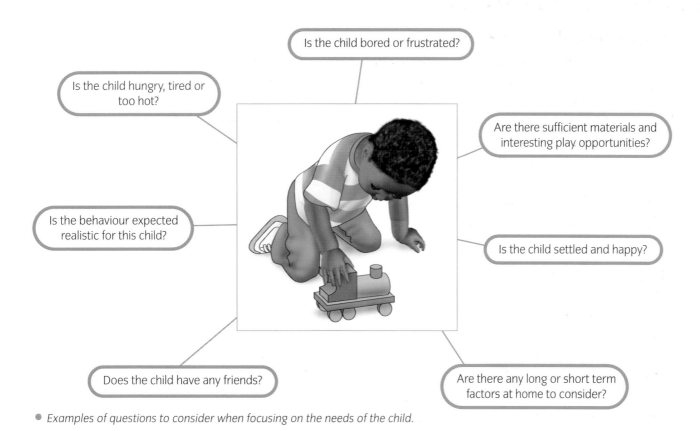

Is the child bored or frustrated?

Is the child hungry, tired or too hot?

Are there sufficient materials and interesting play opportunities?

Is the behaviour expected realistic for this child?

Is the child settled and happy?

Does the child have any friends?

Are there any long or short term factors at home to consider?

● *Examples of questions to consider when focusing on the needs of the child.*

Theories of how children learn behaviour

Many aspects of children's unwelcome behaviour are well understood. You can use the same behavioural processes to help them learn more appropriate types of behaviour. The theories themselves are covered in some detail in Unit 303 (see pages 130–134); here, the focus is on how they can be used to promote positive behaviour.

Social learning theory

Social learning theory suggests that children learn appropriate as well as unwelcome behaviour by imitating others, especially those who are significant in their lives. Social learning theory suggests that, alongside parents and family members, children will be influenced by the other adults with whom they spend time. You therefore need to consider your own actions and reactions carefully, as children are likely to 'model' them.

Using the social learning theory with children

The social learning theory relates to **role modelling**. It suggests that anyone working with children will need to be a good role model, which includes being polite, showing consideration for others and waiting with patience. The theory also suggests that adults need to evaluate television and computer programmes likely to be viewed by children.

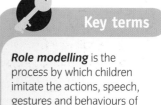

Key terms

Role modelling is the process by which children imitate the actions, speech, gestures and behaviours of adults and others.

Behaviourist theory

Behaviourist theory forms the basis of some specific behavioural management programmes. The theory suggests that certain types of behaviour are repeated if they are rewarded in some way. For example, a child who says 'Thank you' and is praised for doing so will be more likely to show this behaviour again. Rewards are referred to as positive reinforcements. Types of behaviour that are not rewarded or that are punished in some way are less likely to be repeated. People are more influenced by positive reinforcements than by punishments. Where rewards are used, good behaviour is seen over the long term, even when no more rewards are given. Where punishments are used, good behaviour may be shown, but once the threat of punishments has been lifted the behaviour is more likely to return.

Positive reinforcers are anything that acts as a reward. Common ones used by adults with young children are praise, stickers, extra attention, cuddles and sometimes food.

The timing of positive reinforcers is extremely important – where a reward happens quickly after the behaviour, there is a chance of the behaviour being repeated. Surprisingly, if children are rewarded only occasionally, or the positive reinforcement is not automatic but occasional, the behaviour is more likely to persist than if the reward is consistently given. It is almost as if they come to an understanding that sometimes they will get a reward and sometimes not, although it is always worth trying just in case a reward follows. Thus children do not need to be praised or positively reinforced for every single action in order that they continue doing it.

Unfortunately, there is a downside to this, because children who are intermittently reinforced can show persistent unwelcome behaviour. The following example demonstrates this:

Monday:	Jane screams for an ice-cream and is given one.
Tuesday:	Jane screams for an ice-cream but is not given one.
Wednesday:	Jane screams for an ice-cream but is not given one.
Thursday:	Jane screams for an ice-cream and is eventually handed one.
Friday:	Jane screams for an ice-cream but is not given one.

Jane has learnt that it is worth screaming – you might sometimes get what you want. Her unwelcome behaviour is harder to break because she has been intermittently reinforced.

Did you know?

The evidence of the social learning theory can be seen in many different areas. Newborn babies, for example, will stick out their tongue in imitation of an adult doing the same, while children playing in the home corner will often faithfully imitate the way an adult has taken the register in the morning. Some research has also considered whether TV and computer games influence children. It is thought that some children can be influenced by aggressive scenes, especially those that accurately reflect real life, in contrast to traditional cartoons, which children are able to see are imaginary.

Why some children repeatedly show unwelcome behaviour

The behaviourist theory can explain why children show unwelcome behaviour. In many cases, children who show unwelcome behaviour receive some type of adult attention, even though it will usually be disapproving. For some children the adult attention acts as a positive reinforcer, even though the adult had not intended it to. The example below illustrates this:

> Mary is throwing sand. The supervisor tells her not to throw sand and then moves away to talk to another group of children. Mary continues to play for a minute or so. Mary looks across at the supervisor and throws the sand again. The supervisor leaves the group of children to reprimand her.

In this example, Mary has learnt that by throwing sand she can attract an adult's attention: she has been positively reinforced for throwing sand. The supervisor will not have intended this to happen. Sometimes you need to be careful that children do not learn to behave inappropriately in order to gain your attention. The example below shows how the supervisor might have handled this situation differently:

> Mary is throwing sand. The supervisor tells her not to throw sand and then moves away to talk to another group of children. Mary continues to play for a minute or so. The supervisor smiles at Mary and tells her how pleased she is that she is now playing so well.

Keys to good practice: Positive reinforcement and praise

✓ Give positive reinforcement when children show desired behaviour (e.g. praise when they are sharing equipment).

✓ Praise or give some other form of positive reinforcement while the children are showing the behaviour, or immediately afterwards, so that they associate a reward with their behaviour.

✓ Make sure children understand why they are being rewarded (e.g. 'Here is a special sticker because I saw how kind you were being to James').

✓ Do not be reticent with praise – frequent praise simply helps children to keep on showing wanted behaviour.

✓ Choose rewards carefully so that children do not simply show behaviour to gain a large reward (it would be inappropriate to give a child a whole chocolate bar because he or she said 'Thank you').

How adults' expectations can influence children's behaviour

Adults can influence how children behave. The self-fulfilling prophecy is often the theory used to explain this. The charts on pages 432 –435 look at the types of behaviour and goals that adults might have for children at different ages.

Self-fulfilling prophecy

This theory suggests that the expectations adults have about children, and their attitudes towards them, will influence their behaviour. For example, where an adult believes that a child is 'difficult', the child is more likely to behave in this way, whereas an adult who is positive about a child will probably find that the child shows appropriate behaviour. It seems that children can sense the level of behaviour expected from them and will meet these expectations.

Using self-fulfilling prophecy with children

The implication of this theory is that if you feel positive about the children you are working with, they will present fewer challenging behaviours. You must show children that you have positive expectations of their behaviour, not negative ones. For example, 'I hope you won't be silly again this afternoon' is a negative comment because it suggests that you are half expecting the child to show unwelcome behaviour.

Avoid labelling children

The self-fulfilling prophecy also implies that you must pass on information about children carefully to others, so that they do not have negative expectations of those children even before they work with them. For example, 'He's a bit of a handful' or 'You need to keep an eye on him' are remarks that can label a child and make the adults less positive in their approach.

Possible reasons for children's challenging behaviour

It is important to consider whether there are any background difficulties that might be at the heart of a child's behaviour. Understanding the needs of children and thinking about what might be influencing their behaviour is at the heart of helping to promote positive behaviour. While some factors such as feeling unwell might be short-lived, others such as the formation of a new family unit might be longer term. It is also important to think about whether any changes of behaviour might be linked to the child being the subject of abuse (see unit 305 Protect and promote children's rights).

Cause	Possible effects on behaviour
Hungry	Irritable, unreasonable, temper tantrums, poor concentration
Feeling poorly	Withdrawn, irritable, poor concentration
Overheated, hot	Irritable, quarrelsome, poor concentration
Moving home	Clingy, unreasonable, poor concentration
Change to family unit, e.g. separation of parents, arrival of step-parent	Clingy, irritable, jealous, temper tantrums, aggression, withdrawn, attention-seeking
Long term medical condition	Poor concentration, irritable, clingy, tired, withdrawn, anxious, attention-seeking
Birth of sibling	Clingy, attention-seeking, aggressive, demanding
Parents struggling with boundary setting	Clingy, attention-seeking, aggressive, demanding
Moving setting	Clingy, withdrawn, attention-seeking

The possible effects of communication difficulties and attention deficits

On page 448 we looked at the way in which children's behaviour is linked to their language acquisition. Children who have difficulties in expressing their needs or who are not using a language fluently often find it harder to manage their behaviour. This means that we may observe behaviours that are linked to frustration, especially tantrums, anger outbursts and aggressive acts such as biting. By looking at ways of improving communication, or by being good at predicting the child's needs, we can help children's behaviour. This might mean introducing pictures or systems such as Makaton to support communication. Advice can usually be gained from your local speech and language team on which methods to use with individual children.

Attention deficit

Some children have naturally low levels of arousal. This means that they have difficulties in concentrating as, in order to concentrate, you need to have sustained arousal levels. Where children have low levels of arousal or 'attention deficit', they are likely to show erratic and restless behaviours. These behaviours are easily misinterpreted as the child being uncooperative or disruptive, especially during quiet activities such as story time. While working with children who have attention deficit is challenging, it is important to find ways of keeping and retaining their interest. Sadly, children's learning is affected by attention deficit, as they are often not settled enough to learn. The following tips can be useful when working with these children:

- Provide plenty of sensory activities.
- Keep to strong routines and structures.
- Avoid situations in which the child is kept waiting.
- Make sure that activities are open-ended so that the child can leave them if their concentration wanes.
- Provide frequent feedback to the child, including incentives such as stickers.
- Use visual cues and props rather than 'telling' the child.

Policies and procedures

The importance of behavioural policies

Imagine driving a car and not knowing the rules of the road. Working them out would not necessarily be easy, and while doing so you would be likely to get into trouble. Imagine also that every time you got into the car, the rules had changed. For young children, learning about behaviour is also about understanding boundaries and what is expected of them. They need to know that boundary setting is not arbitrary and prone to random change.

Most settings have developed a policy on behaviour that fits their aims and needs. A good policy will help new staff understand how to promote children's positive behaviour and will also provide procedures to follow in situations in which a child is showing unwelcome or non-cooperative behaviour. Behaviour policies need to be consistent with the care standards for the home country in which you work. They also need to be regularly reviewed in order to make sure that they remain effective. Everyone who works in the setting must understand the policy and agree to apply the procedures consistently. This helps children to feel secure, and most children tend to conform once they understand what is and is not acceptable behaviour.

Key terms

Boundary setting is the placing of limits on children's behaviour, which can be negotiated with them.

MAPLEHURST NURSERY

BEHAVIOUR POLICY

Maplehurst Nursery's policy is based on the National Children's Homes principles. As a staff body we are trying to create an environment where children, parents and staff all value, respect and care for each other. We believe the principles listed below will help build a happy and relaxed atmosphere.

1. Always reject the behaviour, not the child. Never label children as bad or naughty either to them or to someone else in their hearing – they will live up to it!

2. Give direction and correction to children in a positive way, e.g. – 'keep the sand in the sand tray' not 'don't drop the sand on the floor.'

3. Give praise as often as possible – notice behaviour you like and remark on it.

4. Set limits. Children need to be secure in knowing you will not let either their behaviour or their feelings get out of control. You will neither let them hurt nor be hurt.

5. Be consistent. The same reaction to the same situation each time gives children a feeling of security. You give them the power to predict the future and an ability to avoid unhappy situations.

6. Do what you have said.
   Do not threaten what you can't do.
   Build up trust.

7. When talking to children about their behaviour be close, calm and at their level.

8. Never force children to say 'sorry': you may just be teaching them to lie.

9. Make children sensitive to their own feelings and other people's. Feed back how they are feeling, e.g. 'You look angry to me'. Give them different options of how to express or deal with feelings. Get them to be aware that other people have feelings. Point out physical signs – tears, smiles – and ask them to remember how they felt when they did these.

10. Sometimes there isn't time for reasoning. Children need to recognise an adult's authority and respond to 'No'.

● *Example of a behaviour policy.*

Drawing up a programme

The starting point should be to consider what exactly needs to be achieved. If there are several issues that need tackling, it is likely to be necessary to prioritise them, rather than attempt to tackle them all at once. It is essential at this point that expectations are in line with the child's ability to meet them. It is also important that ways of reducing the effect of the underlying issues are also examined. Many children who show unwelcome behaviour, for example, do not use language to help them express themselves or to reflect on their actions. For these children, the behaviour management programme must also link to language activities so that the underlying difficulty with language can be addressed.

Setting targets

Behaviour management programmes work well when they are written clearly and goals or targets are identified. These have to be both realistic and focused. It is also important to set out a timescale and a date to review progress; this might be a week or a fortnight ahead at first. Once parents and practitioners begin to take an agreed approach, progress can sometimes be quite swift. It is also important for everyone to stay in close contact so that any difficulties, relapses and, of course, successes can be shared.

Why it is important to agree behaviour management programmes with families and colleagues

Parents and other people who care for children need also to understand the aims of the setting and the ways in which the setting promotes positive behaviour. Some settings make this part of the admissions procedure to ensure that parents are aware and broadly in agreement. Other settings find it helpful to run an information session so that parents can understand and also ask questions about issues that commonly arise.

When parents and settings work together in this way, children find it easier to adapt from one environment to another. Discussing behavioural goals and strategies to encourage parents can be particularly helpful where children are showing unwelcome behaviour either in the home or in the setting. By working together with families, as well as colleagues, you can often work out the needs of the child and so work more effectively. Case study 2 is a good illustration of how a child can be helped by early years workers and parents working together.

Case study 2: Working together

Aaron is three years old. His mother has recently had a baby, and at home and at nursery Aaron is showing that he is unsettled. He has been clingy with both his key worker and his mother, but is also showing some attention-seeking behaviour. His mother feels that she is constantly saying 'no' to him at home because of his behaviour, and staff at the nursery are also finding him demanding. The key worker and Aaron's mother decide to take a joint approach. They agree that Aaron does need more attention, but that it should be given only when he is showing wanted behaviours. They agree not to focus on his inappropriate behaviours, but to praise and spend time with Aaron when he is showing positive behaviours. As Aaron is keen on animals, they have decided to use a small finger puppet as a little incentive and also a distraction. The plan is for the finger puppet to come out when Aaron is showing more cooperative behaviours and also to distract him in situations in which he is likely to be less compliant. Aaron loves the finger puppet and is delighted with the extra attention.

1. *Why is it important for staff and parents to think about the causes of unwanted behaviour?*
2. *Why is it important for staff and parents to talk together about methods of guiding children's behaviour?*
3. *How does Aaron benefit from the staff and his mother working together?*

Involving children

It is good practice to involve children as soon as they are old enough. With older children, this can be quite revealing, as they sometimes explain how they are feeling. Working with older children to draw up a contract of behaviour can be very successful. It allows children to recognise and take responsibility for their behaviour. With younger children, you may simply explain what the new boundaries and consequences are for their behaviour. They should also know that when they show positive behaviour they will gain attention, praise and perhaps small tokens or rewards, if appropriate.

Situations in which such behaviour programmes may be necessary

A quiet word, negotiation or praise is sufficient to help most children show positive behaviour. For the minority of children, this is not quite enough; these you need to provide with structured support that will help them show positive behaviour. Some may have a learning difficulty such as autism and others may simply be going through a period in their lives when they are keen to explore the boundaries. For these children, a structured approach with clear behavioural boundaries will help provide them with security, and they will know exactly what is expected of them.

Gaining information about the child's needs

Most unwelcome behaviour that children show is symptomatic of other issues. Before drawing up a behaviour management programme, it is vital to have some understanding of why the child shows unwelcome behaviour. You must involve the child's parents so that you can pool information. It is also important to observe and record a child's behaviour so that you can understand more; if you monitor the child through a series of observations you will be able to determine whether a particular strategy is working. In some cases, simply observing children carefully will reveal what is triggering the unwelcome behaviour.

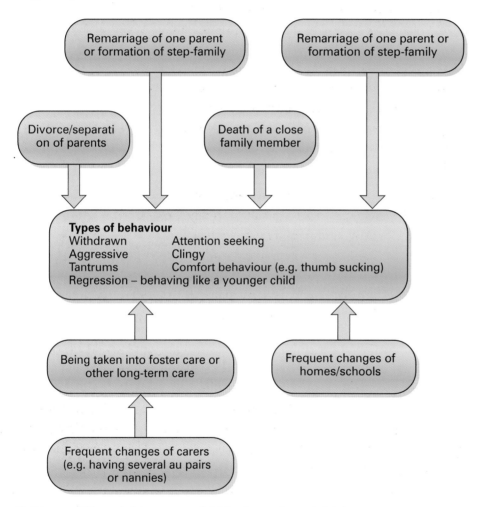

● *Some possible underlying causes of children's unwelcome behaviour.*

Monitoring programmes

It is essential to monitor a behaviour management programme. You need to see how the child is coping, as do other colleagues and parents. It is important to be observant, so that small changes and breakthroughs will be seen, as there is always a danger of noticing unwelcome behaviour much more readily than positive behaviour.

One observation technique that lends itself well to observing and evaluating progress is the event or frequency sample. This will allow you to see over a period of days or weeks whether there has been a reduction in the number of incidents of unwelcome behaviour or, conversely, more incidents of positive behaviour. (For details about how to use the method see Unit 303, page 92.)

Making changes to programmes

While some children quickly show progress in their behaviour, others take longer, especially older children. It is also quite common for children to have a few 'good' sessions and then disappoint everyone by reverting to their previous types of behaviour. This has to be expected, as children are often also trying out a new identity. If they have seen themselves as being 'naughty', it can take a few weeks before they can readjust their self-concept to seeing themselves as children who are capable of showing positive behaviour. It is therefore essential to see changing children's behaviour as a process. A child may make good progress but should still be given time. Therefore, before considering making changes to any behaviour programme, it is worth waiting and being patient.

If changes are to be made, it is worth making slight alterations and then again reviewing how the child is doing. If, however, a child is no longer responding to a certain reward, or parents or colleagues are finding the new approach difficult to manage, it will be important to review the programme; otherwise it may simply become redundant and any gains will have been lost. This can in turn cause further problems for a child, especially if inconsistency in dealing with unwelcome behaviour has been part of the underlying cause.

Case study 3: Changing a behaviour programme

Mark, aged four, is showing unwelcome behaviour both at home and in the nursery. His parents and the staff feel that this is probably in response to the birth of his brother. He has had several violent tantrums in which he has thrown objects. His parents and the key worker have met to talk about ways in which they can help Mark, as they realise that a consistent approach would be helpful. Mark's parents have found that they are often giving in to his demands rather than risking a tantrum, but this is not helping, as Mark is becoming increasingly difficult to manage. The key worker explains how the nursery normally handles tantrums in which other children could be hurt. Together they agree on a programme: Mark is to be praised and have plenty of adult attention; they will try a tactic of giving no eye contact and attention when he is having a tantrum; and they will praise him once he is behaving more appropriately. They have also decided to keep in close contact about Mark's behaviour and have agreed to meet again in a few days' time to review the programme.

1. *Why will this joint approach be helpful for Mark?*
2. *Why is it important for the parents and the setting to remain in contact?*
3. *Why is it important that the programme be reviewed?*

Reflect on your own practice

As you have seen, implementing behaviour policies and procedures is an essential part of your role. Have a look at the statements below to assess whether you match up to the requirements. The statements all refer to the performance criteria for CCLD 337.1.

Performance criteria statement	Always	Sometimes	Never
Do I identify appropriate policies and procedures for the management of behaviour in the setting?			
Do I liaise with professionals, families and children to plan the implementation of evidence-based behaviour programmes?			
Do I implement the agreed approach in partnership with colleagues and families?			

Promote positive aspects of behaviour

A firm and respectful approach

Strategies to deal with unwelcome behaviour

As an early years worker, you should be aiming to use preventive strategies to avoid unwelcome behaviour rather than having to deal with it. This means anticipating potential sources of conflict or danger and making sure that children are well supervised and have interesting activities. However, there will be times when unwelcome behaviour occurs and needs to be managed.

It is important that unwelcome behaviour is dealt with sensitively. Intervention needs to be prompt, calm and controlled. There are several ways in which you can intervene, depending on the situation.

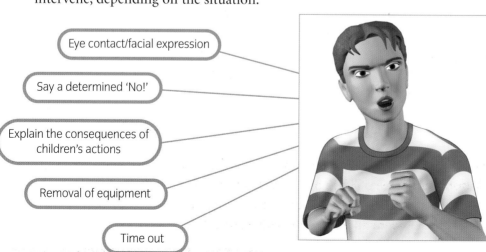

Eye contact/facial expression

Say a determined 'No!'

Explain the consequences of children's actions

Removal of equipment

Time out

● Strategies to deal with unwelcome behaviour.

Through eye contact/facial expression

Sometimes a simple look will warn children that they are stepping over the boundary and this will be enough to help them remember that their behaviour is not appropriate. Eye contact may need to be held with a child, accompanied by an expression of disapproval. Once the child starts to show appropriate behaviour, you should make sure that immediate praise is given. This strategy is particularly useful if you are working with a group and you do not want to disrupt the activity.

Say a determined 'No!'

Most children respond to this expression and understand its meaning. For this to work, it is important that you use it sparingly. It is also important that children understand that 'no means no', and that you do not allow children to continue with inappropriate behaviour. This strategy is particularly effective if combined with facial expression and is useful in situations in which children need to be prevented from doing something potentially dangerous.

Explain the consequences of children's actions

It is good practice to make children aware of the consequences of their actions. They may not realise that throwing sand may lead to pain for a child who gets it in the eye. It is also worth explaining to older children what will happen if they continue to show unwelcome behaviour – this sets clear boundaries for them (e.g. 'If you carry on kicking the ball towards the road, I will have to take it away in case it hits a car'). Once you have suggested that there will be a sanction, it is essential that you are prepared to carry it out. Do not threaten sanctions that you cannot justify or carry out, otherwise children will not believe you another time.

Removal of equipment

Taking away equipment should be a final measure, but may be necessary if children have either been threatened with this sanction or are putting themselves or others in danger, for example by tying a rope around a child's neck to play horses. This type of activity may be so exciting that even if you warn children about the dangers, they will still be tempted to carry on. If you remove equipment, it is a good idea to give children something else to do so that they do not go from one inappropriate situation into another.

Time out

The idea of time out is not to punish children, but simply to allow them to calm down and step back from the problem. Time out should not be used with very young children as they can simply feel rejected and will not have the skills to reflect and calm down. Older children particularly benefit from time out, especially if a sympathetic adult can talk about why they are needing to calm down. Children should not be made to feel that they are being rejected, but rather that you are helping them to avoid conflict or temptation. Used properly, time out should be a supportive strategy for children. Long periods of time out for a child are tantamount to exclusion and should not be used.

Physical punishment and restraint

At one time it was considered acceptable to use physical punishment as a way of controlling and disciplining children. This is no longer the case, and children's rights are protected by legislation such as the Children Act 1989. The message is very clear to those who care for children: physical punishment is not an option; it is an offence.

Physical restraint of children

There are very few occasions when it is acceptable to use physical restraint on children. The prime reasons would be if:
- children are in danger of harming themselves
- children are in danger of harming others.

If restraint is needed, it must be kept to the minimum and must not be used as a way of disciplining or controlling children. You should also protect yourself from allegations of abusing children by recording the incident and, if possible, ensuring that another adult is present. Physical restraints such as reins and harnesses should be used only to keep young children safe (e.g. when walking by busy roads), and in no circumstances should children be punished by being harnessed.

Unambiguous directions, limited choices and defined boundaries

It is important when working with children that your communication with them is clear and appropriate to their level of language development. Young children sometimes do not understand what adults are saying or wanting. This can lead to them appearing either not to have listened or to be deliberately uncooperative. An adult who says to a child 'Shall we tidy up?' is giving the impression to the child that a choice is involved, but what the adult really means 'It's time to tidy up'. Similarly, sarcastic comments should be avoided for all age ranges, not only because they are demeaning but also because they can cause confusion. It is helpful, too, to think through what you want children to do and to avoid leaving children unsure (e.g. 'You can put it somewhere over there or, actually, it might be better here').

It is also helpful to make sure that you have children's full attention before communicating with them. A child who is immersed in playing with dough may completely forget to go to wash their hands even though an adult has called out from across the room. It is also important to remember that some children have a hearing impairment or may be unable to focus on words if there are distracting sounds.

Finally, it is worth thinking about the timing of instructions and directions. Young children who are active may forget about something that has been said to them 15 minutes before.

Keys to good practice: Communicating with children

✓ Make sure that your messages convey exactly what you mean.

✓ Avoid giving children the impression of choice if there is none.

✓ Make sure that you have children's full attention before giving instructions.

✓ Adapt your style of communication to suit children's language development.

The link between stages of development and defining boundaries

It is essential that adults working with children have realistic expectations of those children's behaviour. This can help us in defining boundaries. Learning appropriate behaviour is a gradual process and depends on other areas of a child's development. For example, a child whose language development is impaired will find it hard to express his or her needs and frustrations and so is likely to be more aggressive than other children of the same age. Some skills, such as being able to share, are linked to a child's social and cognitive development, and this means that children under three years find it difficult to play alongside other children. Table 337.1 looks at the stages of development and possible goals for behaviour. The table is only a guide: there are many factors that influence the development of children's behaviour.

Table 337.1. Realistic expectations of behaviour by stage of development

Age	Stage of development	Goals for behaviour	Role of adult
1–2 years	Actively explores environment	To play alongside other children (parallel play)	**Good supervision**, as children of this age do not understand the dangers around them.
	Imitates adults in simple tasks	To carry out simple instructions such as 'Please find your coat'	**Distraction**, to stop unwanted behaviour, as children often forget what they were doing. For example, if a child wants another child's toy, offer him or her a different toy instead.

continued on next page

Age	Stage of development	Goals for behaviour	Role of adult
	Repeats actions that gain attention		**Praise**, so that children understand how to get an adult's attention in positive ways and to help develop self-esteem.
	Alternates between clinging and independence		**Calm and patience**, as children of this age are often persistent and may, for example, keep going back to something that is potentially dangerous.
	Has understanding that toys and other objects may belong to others		**A good role model**, as children are learning behaviour by imitating those around them.
2–3 years	Wants to be independent but does not always have the skills	To wait for needs to be met, for example at meal times	**Good supervision and anticipation** – the keys to working with this age range. Children are trying to be independent, but lack some of the physical and cognitive skills they need. This can make them frustrated and angry. Adults need to anticipate possible sources of frustration and support children, either by offering help or by distracting them. For example, a child who is trying to put on a coat may need an adult to make a game of it so that the child does not become frustrated. Where possible, adults should try to provide as many opportunities as possible for children to be independent.
	Becomes frustrated easily and has tantrums	To share toy or food with one other child, with adult help	**Calm and patience**, as children who are frustrated can trigger negative feelings in adults. This has the potential to inflame a situation. It is a good idea to allow plenty of time for children to complete day-to-day tasks. Children of this age often forget and need reminding about boundaries and goals.
	Is jealous of attention shown to other children	To play alongside other children	**Praise and encouragement**, to enable children to learn what behaviour adults are expecting of them. Some unwanted behaviour that is not dangerous should be ignored so that children do not repeat it in the hope of gaining adult attention. Adults should also provide plenty of love and attention if children have had a tantrum as some children can be frightened by the force of their own emotions.

continued on next page

continued from previous page

Age	Stage of development	Goals for behaviour	Role of adult
	Has no understanding of the need to wait	To sit and share a story for five minutes	**Consistency**, as children are trying to work out the limits on their behaviour.
	Finds sharing difficult	To say 'please' and 'thank you' if reminded	**A good role model**, as children model their behaviour on others. This is especially important at this age as they act out their experiences through play.
	Is active and restless	To follow simple instructions, with help, such as 'Wash your hands'	
3–4 years	Follows simple rules by imitating other children; for example, collects apron before painting	To follow rules in games (e.g. lotto) when helped by adult	**Praise and encouragement**, to build children's confidence and make them more likely to show desirable behaviour.
	Is able to communicate wishes	To say 'please' and 'thank you', often without reminder	**Explanation** of rules as children are now more likely to remember and understand them.
	Enjoys activities such as painting	To take turns and share equipment	**Patience**, as children will still need reminders about the boundaries and goals for behaviour.
	Enjoys being with other children	To follow instructions of adults (e.g. 'Let Simon have a turn') most of the time	**Good supervision**, as although children are able to do many things for themselves, they are still unaware of the dangers around them. Most of the time children will be able to play well together, but squabbles will break out.
	Can play cooperatively	To help tidy away	**A good role model**, to help children learn the social skills they will need to resolve arguments and express their feelings.
	Enjoys helping adults		
4–5 years	Plays with other children without help from adults	To consider other people's feelings	**Providing activities and tasks** that are stimulating and allow children to develop confidence. Children of this age are keen to help adults and enjoy being busy. Tasks such as setting the table or fetching things allow children to feel independent.
	Is able to communicate feelings and wishes	To comfort playmates in distress	**Praise and encouragement**, so that children feel good about themselves. This is important because children are often

continued on next page

continued from previous page

Age	Stage of development	Goals for behaviour	Role of adult
			starting school at this time. They need to feel that they are able to be 'good'.
	Understands the needs for rules	To say 'please' and 'thank you' without reminder	**Explanation**, to help children to remember and understand the need for rules or decisions.
	Can wait for needs to be met	To ask playmates for permission to use their toys	**A good role model** to help children to learn social skills, as they are copying what they see.
		To tidy up after activities	
5–8 years	Is developing strong friendships	To apologise to others	**Praise and encouragement**, as children become more aware of others and compare themselves critically. Praise also prevents children from looking for other ways of gaining attention.
	Will argue and question decisions	To listen to others	**Explanation** so that children can understand the reasons for rules and decisions. Children should also be made to consider the effects of their actions on others.
	Copies behaviour of older children (e.g. swearing and spitting)	To follow instructions	**Set and enforce clear boundaries**, to counter children's tendency to argue back as they become older.
	Understands the needs for rules and plays games that have rules	From 6 years onwards:	**Being a good role model** is still important as children are trying to understand more about the adults they are with. Speech and actions are modelled increasingly on adults whom children admire.
	Understands the difference between right and wrong	To work independently and quietly in school settings	**Encourage children to take responsibility for their actions** by asking them what the boundaries or limits on their behaviour should be.
	Has many self-help skills such as getting dressed, wiping up spills	To be helpful and thoughtful	**Provide activities and responsibilities** to help children to 'mature' as they learn more about their capabilities. Small responsibilities help children to become independent and give them confidence (e.g. they may be asked to tidy areas of a setting or pour out drinks for other children).
		To take responsibility for actions	

Making boundaries effective

Most people accept the need for children to have boundaries and goals to help them show appropriate behaviour. The spider diagram shows the factors that will make a framework for behaviour effective.

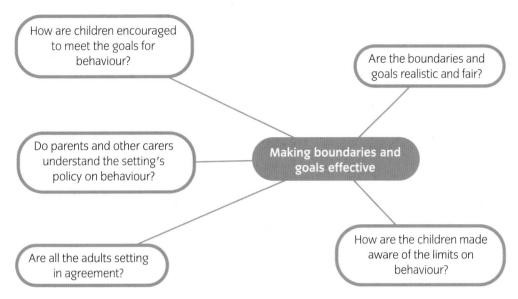

How are children encouraged to meet the goals for behaviour?

Are the boundaries and goals realistic and fair?

Do parents and other carers understand the setting's policy on behaviour?

Making boundaries and goals effective

Are all the adults setting in agreement?

How are the children made aware of the limits on behaviour?

● *Factors that influence the success of a behaviour policy.*

The importance of having realistic expectations

Expectations that are too high may cause children to feel that they are always in trouble. This can cause problems because there seems to be a strong link between self-esteem and behaviour (see below). Children who come to believe that they are 'naughty' are likely to give up trying to be good. On the other hand, where expectations are too low, children's social development will be hindered. For example, a child who has not been encouraged to share and take turns will find it difficult to make friends.

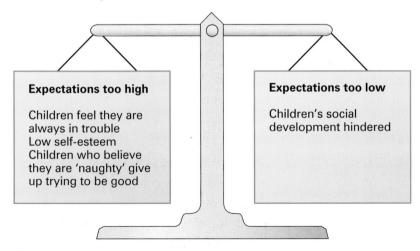

Expectations too high

Children feel they are always in trouble
Low self-esteem
Children who believe they are 'naughty' give up trying to be good

Expectations too low

Children's social development hindered

● *It is important to get the balance of expectations right.*

Using supervision as a tool to prevent unwelcome behaviour

Most accidents and serious incidents of unwanted behaviour happen when children are unsupervised or are bored. Wanted behaviour can be encouraged simply by providing interesting activities, supervising children carefully and being responsive to signs that they are becoming bored or angry. If you see that children are losing interest in an activity, you should act quickly to provide another activity or give children additional equipment to make the current activity more interesting.

Signs that adult intervention is required include:
- raised voices
- children beginning to use equipment inappropriately, for example throwing a musical instrument
- children looking around rather than concentrating on an activity
- squeals of laughter
- silence
- offensive comments.

These signs often show that children are starting to become bored or that they have found something inappropriate to do. By acting immediately, you may be able to prevent children from learning unwanted behaviour. You should explain to children why you are intervening. If they understand what is and is not appropriate behaviour, they are more likely to remember in future and feel positive about the intervention.

Behaviour, self-esteem and relationships with others

When children are young they are developing a picture of themselves or 'self-concept' (see Unit 308, page 303). This in turn will be an essential part of their self-esteem. Children should see themselves as being capable of showing positive behaviour. This is why strategies to deal with unwelcome behaviour in young children often appear to take a 'softy softly' approach. Making children feel bad about themselves on a regular basis is likely to give children the idea that they are 'bad'. They may also learn how to annoy and irritate adults. Ironically, as children move into their teenage years, their self-esteem can be quite high as they may gain approval from their peers for appalling behaviour. This is one important reason why it is essential that early years workers endeavour to help young children enjoy being cooperative and see that they can gain approval and praise from behaving positively.

Keys to good practice: Using language that avoids damaging children's self-esteem

✓ When intervening in children's unwelcome behaviour, do not create any future problems by damaging their self-confidence.

✓ Explain to children why you have intervened.

✓ Make sure that they understand you are unhappy with the behaviour, not the children.

✓ Make them feel that you believe in their ability to show appropriate behaviour.

✓ Do not remind children about their previous misdemeanours (e.g. by saying 'You were naughty last week. I hope you have learnt to behave'). This will only make them feel miserable and less likely to be positive about their behaviour.

Consolidation:

- 'You were naughty to push Simon over like that. I will be looking this afternoon to see that you don't do that again.'
- 'Pushing Simon over was a silly thing to do. He might have hurt his head. This afternoon, you can show me how well you can really play together.'

Which approach is more likely to make the child feel that he or she can show appropriate behaviour?

Why will it be important to praise the child as soon as he or she is playing appropriately?

Developing children's self-esteem and independence through positive behaviour

As an early years worker, you can help children show appropriate behaviour by making sure that children believe in themselves. Children who feel confident and have high self-esteem are more likely to show appropriate behaviour. A child who feels that he or she is 'only good at being bad' will give up trying to show wanted behaviour. Self-esteem can be raised in children by giving them plenty of praise and also by making sure that they feel that those around them believe in them. In practical terms, this means making sure that tasks and activities are not so demanding that children will fail, while still encouraging children to be as independent as they can.

Children's self-esteem may also be enhanced by making sure that their parents are told of their achievements ('Harvey was so good today: he helped Sarah to find her cuddly rabbit'). On the other hand, if you need to share information with parents that is not positive, you must make sure that children are not around, as this may lower their self-esteem.

The importance of relationships and behaviour

Relationships count for a lot. People behave differently according to whom they are with. Children are no different. Interestingly, they often respond very well to people with whom they know the boundaries, but also trust and feel valued by. Some children who show unwelcome behaviour are simply trying to attract attention. They may not feel as secure as they should and so learn how to get time with adults. Interestingly, these same children can be 'angels' when they are being given attention. This is because their underlying needs are being met. With children who are being uncooperative, it is essential that you remember that building a better relationship with them might be the key, even though they are likely to be wearing and irritating. It is necessary to get to know these children as individuals, instead of seeing them as 'problems'. This often involves noticing children's strong points, as this in turn can affect their behaviour in a positive way.

Case study 4: New relationship for Sandie

Sandie is five years old. She has a 'track record' in the setting already. Everyone knows her name. A new adult came into the setting and was determined to help Sandie. She spent time getting to know her and made sure that she gave her plenty of attention. She looked for opportunities to praise Sandie and gave her chances to play alongside other children, although this at first was often in a supervised and structured way. When Sandie flooded the toilets, the adult did not respond in the way she expected. Nothing was said, but Sandie was passed a mop and a cloth and the adult started to clear up. Sandie was unsure but joined in. Together with Sandie's grandmother, who cared for her, a strategy was developed to ensure that the number of positive comments and acknowledgements aimed at Sandie was increased. Over a period of a few weeks, Sandie's behaviour improved and gradually stabilised.

1. *Why is it important to make sure that children hear more positive than negative comments?*
2. *Why was it important to work with Sandie's grandmother?*
3. *Explain why it can be useful not to react to an incident of unwelcome behaviour in a way that a child is expecting.*

Observation

With the permission of your supervisor and parents, where appropriate, focus on a child in your setting who regularly shows unwelcome behaviour. Carry out an event sample to check how often and in what circumstances the unwelcome behaviour is shown. Consider the child's wider needs and then produce recommendations about how this child might be helped to show more appropriate behaviour.

Reflect on your own practice

As you have seen, promoting positive aspects of behaviour is an essential part of your role. Have a look at the statements below to assess whether you match up to the requirements. The statements all refer to the performance criteria for CCLD 337.2.

Performance criteria statement	Always	Sometimes	Never
Do I adopt a firm and respectful approach when managing the behaviour of children?			
Do I give children unambiguous directions and limited choices within clearly defined boundaries?			
Do I implement agreed procedures when children are non-compliant?			
Do I encourage cooperation and problem-solving between children?			
Do I positively reward compliance in ways that demonstrate that the child is valued as an individual?			

End-of-unit knowledge check

1. Describe some factors that might affect children's behaviour.
2. Give three examples of rewards that could be used with children to reinforce wanted behaviour.
3. Explain why children may show more cooperative behaviour if they see good role models.
4. By what age can most children share and play cooperatively?
5. Why is it important for settings to have a behaviour policy?
6. What is meant by the term 'boundary setting'?
7. Why is it important to talk to parents about children's behaviour?
8. Explain the importance of supervision in preventing unwanted behaviour.
9. Why is it important to report changes in children's behaviour?
10. Explain the link between self-esteem and children's behaviour.

Glossary of key terms

Access	– opportunities for participation.
Agency	– control over your life. It is about being able to do things for yourself and setting your own challenges.
Induction period	– a time during which new staff and volunteers learn about the policies and procedures in a setting.
Anti-discriminatory practice	– taking action to counter discrimination; this will involve identifying and challenging discrimination and being positive in your practice about people's differences.
Appropriate behaviour	– behaviour that is not abusive or derogatory to the child, physically, emotionally or sexually and demonstrates that the child is respected and valued.
Approved codes of practice	– examples and advice as to how the law should be complied with. They also have special legal status and employers can be prosecuted for a breach of health and safety law, if it can be shown that they have not followed the provisions of the relevant Code of Practice
Balanced diet	– one that includes a large variety of foods, so adequate intakes of all the nutrients are achieved.
Best practice benchmarks	– standards that are widely agreed as providing the most advanced, up-to-date thinking and practice against which you can measure what you are doing – not minimum standards. Benchmarks can be statutory/regulatory or based on other requirements or research.
Boundary setting	– the placing of limits on children's behaviour, which can be negotiated with them.
Child abuse	– where a child is suffering or likely to suffer significant harm from physical, emotional or sexual abuse, neglect and failure to thrive not based on illness, or bullying and harassment.

Child protection	– the safeguarding of the basic right of children to be protected from abuse.
Children	– the age groups 0–3, 4–7, 8–12, 13–16 years, including boys, girls, disabled children and those with special educational needs.
Communication	– verbal and non-verbal methods of exchanging information, which include speaking, listening, reading and writing.
Confidential information	– that which should be shared only with people who have a right to have it, for example your lead practitioner, supervisor or manager.
Continuing professional development	– ongoing training and professional updating.
Curriculum plan	– an arrangement of activities and experiences.
Development	– children's gaining of skills and competence.
Disability	– physical or mental impairment which has a substantial and long-term adverse effect on the child's ability to carry out normal day-to-activities.
Disclosure of abuse	– when a child tells you he or she has been abused.
Emergencies	– for example, injuries, fires or other threats to the safety of children and colleagues in the environment. Missing children.
Environment	– the provision that is made for children to play, learn and relax, both indoor and outdoor. It encompasses both the physical aspects, such as the layout, furniture and equipment, and the atmosphere that is created for children.
Fine motor skills	– the ability to perform small, accurate movements, for example with the fingers to draw or sew.
Formative assessment	– ongoing assessment that does not draw overall conclusions.
Gross motor skills	– the ability to move the whole body well, for example running and jumping.

Guidance	– advice that is given to help those responsible for health and safety to comply with the law. Guidance is not compulsory.
Hand–eye coordination	– the ability to direct hand movements (generally unconsciously) in relation to an object (often moving), for example hitting a ball with a bat.
Hazard	– something that is likely to cause harm.
Inclusion	– the process of identifying, understanding, and breaking down barriers to participation and belonging.
Individuality	– someone being different from others, for example because of their appearance, attitudes or behaviour.
Key Stage 1	– the part of the National Curriculum that applies to children aged 5–7 years.
Objectivity	– an unbiased mental attitude where a person tries to put aside his or her own beliefs and values, and to examine or think about a situation as honestly and as openly as possible
Ofsted	– the Office for Standards in Education. It is the government department that is responsible for the inspection of child care and pre-school providers, schools and local education authorities in England.
Pattern of development	– the rate and sequence of development.
Policies	– what your organisation has agreed its staff should or should not do in certain situations.
Planning cycle	– a constant cycle of planning, implementing and reviewing/evaluating.
Provision	– can be a physical setting or a peripatetic service based in the community, or other service.
Rate of development	– the time frame in which development occurs.
Reflective practice	– the process of thinking about and critically analysing your actions with the goal of changing and improving occupational practice.

Registered person – is the term Ofsted uses to describe the person or organisation legally responsible for providing the child care.

Regressing/regression – when children under stress revert to a younger way of behaving.

Regulations – mandatory guidelines approved by Parliament. They are usually made under the provisions of the Health and Safety at Work Act 1974. They are legally binding.

Resilience – the ability to withstand normal, everyday disappointments, hurts and assaults on one's confidence, without it affecting self-esteem.

Risk – the seriousness of a hazard and its likelihood actually to cause harm.

Risk assessments – must be carried out in order to identify hazards and find out the safest way to carry out certain tasks and procedures.

Role modelling – the process by which children imitate the actions, speech, gestures and behaviours of adults and others.

Self-awareness – a person's knowledge of his or her own individuality, feelings, attitudes and beliefs.

Sequence of development – the order in which development occurs.

Sociograms – method used to chart the social relationships or friendship groups within a particular setting. They are useful for identifying whether a child is being 'left out' in a class. Children can be asked who is the person they most like or like to spend time with, who is the second and third. A chart is then made up of the results.

Special educational needs – needs displayed by children who learn differently from most children of the same age. They may require extra or different help.

Standard Assessment Tasks (SATs) – tasks set externally that are intended to assess a child's educational level at stages throughout their education. Key Stage 1 SATs take place towards the end of year 2 in primary school.

Summative assessment	–	draws findings together and may have an overall conclusion.
Unconditional acceptance	–	letting children know children that they are valued not for what they do but simply because they are there. It allows them to feel safe and nurtured.
Well-being	–	children's physical and mental health, as well as their confidence and ability to cope in a variety of situations. In some ways it could be dubbed 'inner strength and confidence'.

Index

A

access to services, lack of 191, 192-6
   reducing barriers 195-6
accidents 46, 49, 58, 66
   by age group 50-5
   1–3 years 53-5
   5–11 years 55
   11 years upwards 55
   reporting 65–6, 234–5
   types of 49–55
active listening 29–30
activities 424
   adapting or changing 269
   age appropriate 150
   challenging 316-17, 435-6
   encouraging participation 273-6
   encouraging physical skills 266-8
   and exploration 153
   extending skills 271-6
   layout of 240
   plans 353-6
   providing range of 243-5
   reflection on 163
   rest and recovery 277-8
   safety 60
adolescence 120, 129
adult relationships 38-42
adult-dominated learning 342
affection and warmth 303
agency 316
allergies 13
anti-discriminatory practice 14–15, 203
   monitoring 207
appropriate behaviour of adults 23-4
approval 20
Area Child Protection Committees 217
assessment of needs, disability 203–7
assessments
  confidentiality and data protection 381
  formative and summative 383
  multilingual settings 372
  objective 380
  people involved 380
  requirements 373-5
  safeguards 379-80
  stage of development 373
  to improve provision 384

uses of 371
asthma 77-8, 297
Athey, Chris 343
attachment 18, 402-5
   Bowlby on 403
   good practice 405
   role of fathers 404
   staffing implications 250
   stages of 138, 402
attention deficit 453-4
attention, focused 323-4
attention span 359-60

B

babies 105-10, 357
   at one month 106
   at three months 107
   at six months 108
   at nine months 109
   at one year 110
   building relationships with 17–18
   common accidents 50-1
   communication with 413-14
   newborn 105, 127
   supporting development 422-8
   timetable for baby room 427
balance 125
balanced diet 281-2
Bandura, Albert 133-4
baseline information 395-6
behaviour
   and adult expectations 452
   approaches to management of 446-8
   and attention deficit 453-4
   challenging 451, 452-3
   child-centred approaches 447-9
   and communication 34-5
   and communication difficulties 453
   and conditioning 131
   consistent responses to 151
   cultural variations 446
   dealing with negative 34–5, 460–2
   defining appropriate 446
   eye contact 461
   focus on respect 446-7
   inclusive approaches 448
   intervention strategies 460-2
   and language 448
   policies and procedures 446-59

reasons for negative 458
   and relationships 470
behaviour management programmes 456-9
   adult intervention 468
   boundaries 462-7
   and colleagues and parents 456
   explaining consequences 461
   eye contact 461
   gathering information 458
   involving children 457
   and language 456, 469
   making changes 459-60
   monitoring 458-9
   punishment and restraint 462
   removal of equipment 461
   saying no 461
   and self-esteem 467, 468, 469
   setting targets 456
   supervision as tool 468
   time out 461-2
   when necessary 457
behaviourist learning theory 450–1
belonging, sense of 310
best practice benchmarks 159
bilingual children 399-400
Birth to Three Matters 330, 374, 405-7
   curriculum framework 406
Birth to Three (Scotland) 405, 407
bleeding 72-3
Bobo doll experiment 134
body language 16, 18, 19, 414
books 433
boundaries 151, 462-7
   and development stages 463–6
   effective 467
   setting 310-11, 454
Bowlby, John 403, 405
Bruce, Tina 396-7
Bruner, Jerome 136-7
buildings and maintenance safety 57
bullying and harassment 213-14
   emotional 213

C

carers, change of 250-1
CE mark 47
challenging activities 316-17
checklists and tickcharts 87, 90–1, 390
chest compression 70-1

child abuse
  avoiding allegations 254
  avoiding premature judgements 219
  indicators of 210-14
  NSPCC survey 208-9
  policies and procedures 218
  protecting children 253
  recognition of 215
  reducing vulnerability 221-3
  reporting 217-18
  responding to disclosure 224
  risk factors 215-16
  services available 224-5
  support and referral 216
  supporting parents 221
  working practices 219-20
Child at the Centre 375
child care: barriers to access 192-6
Children Act (1989) 210, 462
Children Bill (2004) 209
children's rights 183-226
Children's Rights Director 200
choices, making 24-5
cleanliness of environment 57
cognitive development 122
  behaviourist approaches 130-3
  Bruner's theory 136-7
  constructivist approaches 134-7
  learning theories 130-4
  Piaget's theory 134-6, 342-3
  and play 102
  theories of 129-37
  Vygotsky's theory 136, 137
colleagues 10
  interaction as role model 311
  reflection on work with 164-5
  communication with adults
    38-43
  difficulties 40
  good practice 40
  using 'I' statements 39-40
communication and children 28-38, 103,
  420-1
  babies 413-15
  and behaviour 34-5
  components of 28, 30
  developing positive relationships 411-21
  development of 122
  different ways of 147-8
  difficulties 416-19
  encouraging 151, 153, 155
  encouraging through play 429–32
  good practice 463
  hearing loss 417-18
  individual needs 31
  patterns of development 433-4
  reasons for difficulties 418-19
  thinking of others 31-2
comparison with others 303
conditioning 130-3
  classical 130
  extinction 130
  operant 131-3
confidence
  and adult conflict 41-2
  and control 306
  developing 144, 153, 274
  and experimentation 272-3
confidential information 12-13
confidentiality 14
  and assessments 381

breaching 13
  and legislation 11-12
  and observations 85
conflict
  adult intervention in 36-7
  adult to adult 41-2
  dealing 35, 252
consistency 151, 302
consistent relationships 310
continuing professional development 169-82
control, giving children 305-7
COSHH Regulations 45, 47, 63, 231-2
crawling babies, common accidents 51-2
creams and lotions 63
creative play 351
creativity 338, 362
cross-infection 293-4
culture 14, 364, 415, 446
  as barrier to child care 194-5
  respecting 252
curriculum frameworks 330-2
  alternative 334-5
  assess children's progress 370-85
  assessment requirements 373-8
  children's views on 366
  different requirements 329-30
  Foundation Stage 330-1, 334, 374-5, 377
  involving parents 366, 367
  Key Stage 1 330, 331, 332, 334, 375, 377
  monitoring 366-9
  plan and implement 328-65
  SATs 331, 332, 375
  support for planning 336
curriculum planning
  based on play 349-57
  equipment and activities 337-40
  implementation 337-65
  and learning styles 362-4
  play resources 337-40
  providing learning experiences 343-4
  reflecting on practice 366

D

data protection 381
Data Protection Act (1998) 10, 12, 412
decision-making, encouraging 24-5
develop and maintain a healthy, safe and
  secure environment 44–83
development of children 97-103
  activities to enhance 267-8, 422-34
  babies 105-10
  by age 106-20
  2 years 112
  2 and a half years 113
  up to 3years 408
  3 years 114
  4 years 115
  5-6 years 116
  7-8 years 117
  9-11 years 118
  11-13 years 119
  13-16 years 120
  causes for concern 121
  and diet 102
  discrimination 100
  effect of illness 297-8
  family circumstances 100
  as holistic 123

influence of adults 99
  influences after birth 98-9
  influences before and at birth 98
  influences on 97-102
  key principles 146, 149, 152, 154
  and learning 373
  moral development 140-3
  observing and assessing progress 388-96
  patterns of 103-20
  personality 143-4
  physical 124-9
  and play 101, 102-3
  promoting 84-156
  rate of 103
  sequence 103, 126
  and stimulation 101
  supporting development by ages 146-55
  theories of 129-37
  toddlers 111
  variations 103-4
  see also physical development
developmental milestones 390
diabetes 78
disability 201
  and abuse 215-16
  assessment of needs 203-7
  discrimination 100-1
  legislation 185, 187, 202-3
  medical model 204
  social model 203-4
Disability Discrimination Act (1995) 201-2,
  238, 261
discrimination 188, 205
  basis of 188-9
  challenging 191
  consequences of 190-1
  and development 100-1
diseases 234
diversity of children 266

E

Education Act (1996) 201-2
Education Act (2002) 330-1
emergencies 62, 81-2
emotional abuse 212, 213
emotional needs 301, 309-11
emotionally safe environment 309-11
emotions 33, 148-9
empathy 325
encouragement 153, 155
English as additional language 365, 372
environment
  dividing into areas 244-5
  emotionally safe 309-11
  plan and organise 227-63
  provision of safe 146, 149–50, 153
Environmental Protection Act (1990) 282
epilepsy 78
equal opportunities 48, 340
Equal Opportunities
  Co-ordinators 196
equality of access 185-96
equipment 48, 424-6
  adaptation for special needs 206-7
  buying 339
  for curriculum stages 337-40
  and failure 320
  safety of 57, 271

Erikson, Erik 144
evacuation procedures 81
event sample 87, 92-3
Every Child Matters 209
expectations of children 303
    and development stages 463-6
      realistic 467
experimentation and confidence 272-3
eye contact 28, 415
    and unwelcome behaviour 461

F

failure, managing 320-2
families 311
    sources of advice for 440-2
    supporting new 249
feedback to parents 249
feelings, acknowledging and expressing 312-16
    activities to help 314-16
    imaginative play 314
    learning about others' 33
    mark-making and drawing 315-16
    music and dance 316
    of practitioner 325-6
    puppets and toys 315
    role of language 313
    sensory materials 315
    small world play 314
fine motor skills 125, 266
fire precautions 235-6
Fire Precautions (Workplace) Regulations (1997) 235
fire procedures 81-2
first aid 46, 67-79
    assessing casualty 67, 75
    by age group 70-2
    by emergency 73-4
    kit 66-7, 236
    opening airway 69
First Aid Regulations 236
food and drink 48
    appropriate and inappropriate 283
    babies 283-4
    dietary requirements 287-90, 292
    encouraging healthy eating 290-1, 292
    food groups and nutrients 280-1
    government guidelines 279-80, 292
    handling and storage 260
    lack of appetite 291
    meeting nutritional needs 279–92
    planning 265
    pre-school 284-5
    preparation safety checks 57
    schoolchildren 285
food hygiene 285-6
foot-eye coordination 125
formative assessment 85, 383
frameworks of effective practice 405-10
free description 87, 89-90, 390
free play 24, 347, 348
Freud, Sigmund 143-4
friendship, development of 140

G

Gessell, Arnold 126
greeting children 22-3, 248
gross motor skills 125, 266, 267, 268

H

hair care 258-9
hand washing 256-7, 293-4
hand-eye coordination 125, 266, 267, 268
hazardous substances 231-4
hazards 49
head lice 258-9
health 295-6
    checks 295-7
    child's awareness of 295
health and safety 58
    and employers 231-2
    legislation 45-9, 230-6
    and practitioners 231
    risk assessment 434-7
Health and Safety at Work Act (1974) 46, 81, 230-1
hearing loss 31, 417-18
heuristic play 423, 424
Highscope 335
Human Rights Act (1998) 11
hygiene 233-4, 293-4
    children's 256

I

ICT and curriculum 338, 340-1
ideal self 304-5
illnesses 79-81, 297-8
imaginative play 314, 351
immunisation 296
inappropriate behaviour 23-4
    avoiding allegations of 254
inclusion 14-15, 147, 150
    good practice 203
    implementing guidelines 201-3
    resources for 197-200
independence 144, 153, 155
    encouraging 246
individual education plan 85
individuality, respecting 26
induction period 254
inequalities in society 191-6
information
    confidential 12-13
    practitioner's personal 23-4
    sharing 10, 412
    sharing with parents 437-8
    storing 13
inhalers 259
inspectorates, requirements of 376-8
interaction, encouraging 28

K

Keepsafe Code 222, 223
Kitemark (BSI) 46-7
Kohlberg, Lawrence 141-2

L

labelling 37, 95, 189, 379, 380, 452
Laming report 209
language 338
    assessment issues 372
    as barrier to child care 194
    behaviour management programmes 456
    being a partner 21
    recasting and expanding 30
    structure 397
language development 122, 360-1, 397-402
    bilingual and multilingual 399
    and books 433
    critical period 401
    linguistic stage 398-9
    and play 103
    pre-linguistic stage 398
    receptive language 400
    role of adult 401-2
learned helplessness 306
learning
    activities 151
    effect of self-esteem 345, 381
    equipment to support 343
    formal as inappropriate 344
    models of 341-2
    needs 364
    observational 34
    spiral of 348-9
    and stage of development 342-3
    styles 362-4
    supporting 155
    through play 337-9, 344-7
learning difficulties and behaviour 457
learning theories 130-4
    behaviourist 450-1
    social learning 133-4, 449
legislation 10-12, 185-8
    access and provision 238
    and confidentiality 11-12
    disability 202-3
    health and safety 45-9
    and information sharing 412
life chances 192
lifting and carrying children 49
listening 20, 302
    and adult conflict 42
    and responding 29-30

M

Makaton 31, 399, 418
manipulative play 351
manual handling regulations 49
mark-making 338, 426, 433-4
mathematics 338, 361
meal and snack times 248
medical crises 75-9
medicines 63, 259, 260
memory 360
meningitis 75-7
missing children 82
monitoring provision 366-7
Montessori, Maria 335
moral development 140-3
Moyles, Janet 348

multi-disciplinary approach 368
multilingual children 399-400
music and dance 316

N

nappy changing 248
National Curriculum 331-2, 334
National Standards 45, 47-8, 202, 228-9, 408
needs 152, 154, 155
    considering individual 364
    emotional 309-11
    individual and group 27, 150
    of parents 437-9
neglect 212-13
negotiation skills 25-6, 32
non-judgemental, being 324-5
non-participant observation 88-9, 393
Northern Ireland 45, 230
    assessment requirements 376, 378
    early years curriculum 332, 333
nutritional needs 279-92

O

observation cycle 388-9
observational learning 34
observations 84-96
    areas of focus with very young 391-2
    avoiding premature conclusions 95
    babies and under 3 years 388-96
    baseline information 395-6
    carrying out 89-94
    confidentiality 85
    effective practice frameworks 405-10
    factors affecting interpretation 393-4
    good practice 392, 409
    involving parents 95-6
    language and formats 409-10
    methods 87, 88-4
    objectivity 95, 393-5, 410
    open and closed recording 87
    parental permission 396
    planning 86-9
    practicalities with babies 393
    reasons for 408-9
    recording methods 86-7
    reliability and validity 393-5
    and self-awareness 393-4
    types of observation 390
    types of observer 88-9
    underpinning theories 396-405
Ofsted 202, 330, 331, 332, 377
    inspectorate 45, 47-8
    work of 334
oral hygiene 293
organisation of space and resources 239-45
outdoor activities 274-5
    benefits and risks 271-2
    safety checks 57, 58, 59, 271
    supervising 242-3, 271
outdoor areas 242-3
outings 61-2, 64, 65

P

parents 10
    asking permission 381, 396
    communicating with 40
    and confidential information 13
    and curriculum planning 336
    partnerships with 210
    preferences 439
    reflection on work with 165
    relationships with 10
    sharing information with 383, 437-8
participant observation 89, 393
participation in activities 273-6
partnerships with parents and
    families 210, 366-7
Pavlov, Ivan 130
personal care 255-63
personal development plan 169–74
personal effectiveness evaluation 158
personal, social and emotional development
123
personality 143-4
physical abuse 211-12
physical activities, planning and
    implementing 265-79
physical bullying 214
physical care 293-8
physical contact
    babies 17
    inappropriate 147
    1-3 years 19
physical development 122, 124–9
    by age 127-9
    1-3 years 127-8
    4 years 128
    13-16 years 129
    changes in body shape 125-6
    coordination 125
    key principles of 126
    links to central nervous system 127
    links to overall development 124
    motor skills 125
    and play 102
    types of physical skills 124-5
Piaget, Jean 134-6, 141, 342-3
planning
    flexible 351-2
    good practice 350, 352
    long, medium and short term 352-7
    play based curriculum 349-57
planning cycle 350
    assessments as part of 382
play 20, 148, 151
    at 2 years 112, 346
    being a partner 21
    benefits of 24
    by age 346-7
    categories of 347-8
    and cognitive development 102
    curriculum based on 349-57
    and development 101, 102-3
    equipment and activities 337-40
    exploring 148
    extending opportunities 359
    five areas of 350-1
    heuristic 423, 424
    imaginative 314, 351
    and language development 430–2
    and physical development 102
    skill development 351

treasure basket 423, 424
    types of 351
play therapists 269
positive behaviour 251
    acknowledging 34
    create environments for 445-71
positive environments for babies and under
    3 years 386-444
positive relationships 15, 31
    adult to adult 38-42
    develop and promote 8-43
    effect of role models 37
poverty 191, 192
    and life chances 192
    and SureStart 198
praising children 153, 155
prejudice 189, 190
    personal 16
preparing for sessions 241
privacy 11, 250
    and toileting 261
product marking 46-7
profiles 85
protecting children 48, 208-25, 253
    during care routines 253-4
    legislation 209-10
puberty 119, 120, 129
punishment 450, 462
qualifications, obtaining 176-9
questions, answering 154
quiet periods 250, 277-8

R

Race Relations (Amendment) Act (2000) 185
racist bullying 214
reassurance 20
recovery position 68-9
referrals 408
reflective practice 158-68
    benefits of 159
    challenging existing practice 165–6
    cluster groups 167
    on effectiveness of sessions 164
    gaining feedback 168
    keeping open mind 160
    learning from others 167, 168
    as a mirror 161-5
    on play opportunities 163
    reflective analysis 160
    on responding to behaviour 162
    training courses 167
    uncomfortable results 167
    on work with colleagues 164-5
    on work with parents 165
reflexes 105
registered person 334
reinforcement 131-3, 450, 451
relating to others 323-6
relationships
    with babies 17-18
    and behaviour 470
    child to child 32-3
    with children 16-27, 147, 150
    formation of early 138-40, 402-5
    integrating anti-bias practice
    15-16
    with 1-3 year olds 18-20
    with 3-6 years 20-1

with 7-11 years 21-2
with 11 years upwards 22
reporting accidents and injuries 234-5
reporting concerns 408
Reporting of Injuries, Diseases and
  Dangerous Occurrences Regulations 234
rescue breaths 69
resilience 301
  balancing care and restriction 307–8
  not judging children 324-5
  pressures affecting 302-3
  and supportive environment 305-7
resources, planning use of 339-40
respect 411-12, 446-7
responsiveness
  and babies 18
  1-3 year olds 19
rest periods 277-8
restraint 462
rights of child 10-11
risk assessment 64-5, 308
  activities 64
  by children 150-1, 153, 155
  and challenging activities 435-6
  outdoor activities 271-2
  policies and practices 434-5
risk taking 155
  and resilience 306-9
role model 37, 150, 465, 466
  and expressing feelings 313
  and learning theory 449
  and managing failure 322
  and team relationships 311
role play 103, 314
room layout 239-42
routines 147
  and babies 18
  benefits of 426-7
  changes to 428-9
  and child development 246-8
  examples of 248
  flexibility of 357-8
  good practice 428
  and individual needs 27
  as part of curriculum 357-8

S

safety checks of environment 56–60
safety equipment 237-8, 436
safety of equipment regulations 236–7
school meals 282
science 338, 361-2
Scotland 201
  assessment requirements 375, 378
  Birth to Three 405, 407
  early years curriculum 332, 333

National Standards 45, 230
security arrangements 61
self-concept 303-5, 468
self-esteem 304-5, 324
  and abuse 221
  and behaviour management 467, 468, 469
  enhancing 382, 469
  and learning 345, 381
self-fulfilling prophecy 452
self-reliance 144, 145
sensory activities 424
sensory development 361
separation anxiety 403, 404-5
services for children 199-200,
  224-5
settling in 139-40
sexual abuse 213
sexual bullying 214
sickle cell disease 78, 297
sign language 417-18
  skin care 256, 257
in sun 257-8
Skinner, B.F. 131
small world play 314, 426
social constructivist learning 342
social and emotional development 138-45
  and play 103
social learning theory 133-4, 449
social model of disability 203-4
social play 351
social services departments 198-9
sound recordings as observation 390
spaces, child's ownership of 22
special educational needs 121, 186, 201-2
  discrimination 100-1
Special Educational Needs and
  Disability Act (2001) 185, 202-3
special needs 48, 200, 241-2
  adapting equipment 206-7
speech dysfluency 419
spiral of learning 348-9
spontaneous play 347, 348
staff meetings 166
Steiner, Rudolf 335
stereotyping 189
structured play 347, 348
success and failure, managing 317–22
  good practice 322
suitable person 48
summative assessment 85, 383
supervision of children 308
SureStart 195-6, 197-8, 440

T

tantrums 144, 149, 363, 448, 453, 464
target child observation 87, 94

teamwork, encouraging 33
teeth, care of 259, 293
time sample 87, 92
toilet training 128, 260-1
  good practice 261
toileting 248
Toy (Safety) Regulations (1995) 236-7
toys 60, 148, 424-6
  and expressing feelings 315
training opportunities 175-81
  integrating new information 182
transitions 139, 154
transmission model of learning 342
treasure basket play 423, 424

U

UN Convention on the Rights of the Child
10-11, 185, 186-8, 238
  Article 19 215
unconditional acceptance 311

V

value system 16
valuing children 22-3
vegetarian diets 287-9
visual impairment 419
Vygotsky, Lev 136, 137, 347

W

Wales 45, 230
  assessment requirements 375-6, 378
  early years curriculum 332, 333
warmth and respect 411-12
waste disposal 282, 294
well-being and resilience 301-27
working relationships 10
writing 433-4

Z

zone of proximal development 136